Microsoft

Exam Ref 70-532
Developing Microsoft
Azure Solutions
2nd Edition

Zoiner Tejada
Michele Leroux Bustamante
Ike Ellis

D1377882

Exam Ref 70-532 Developing Microsoft Azure Solutions, 2nd Edition

Published with the authorization of Microsoft Corporation by:
Pearson Education, Inc.

Copyright © 2018 by Pearson Education

ISBN-13: 978-1-5093-0459-2
ISBN-10: 1-5093-0459-2

Library of Congress Control Number: 2017953300
1 18

Trademarks

Microsoft and the trademarks listed at *https://www.microsoft.com* on the "Trademarks" webpage are trademarks of the Microsoft group of companies. All other marks are property of their respective owners.

Warning and Disclaimer

Special Sales

For information about buying this title in bulk quantities, or for special sales opportunities (which may include electronic versions; custom cover designs; and content particular to your business, training goals, marketing focus, or branding interests), please contact our corporate sales department at corpsales@pearsoned.com or (800) 382-3419.

For government sales inquiries, please contact governmentsales@pearsoned.com.

For questions about sales outside the U.S., please contact intlcs@pearson.com.

Editor-in-Chief	Greg Wiegand
Acquisitions Editor	Laura Norman
Development Editor	Troy Mott
Managing Editor	Sandra Schroeder
Senior Project Editor	Tracey Croom
Editorial Production	Backstop Media
Copy Editor	Liv Bainbridge
Indexer	Julie Grady
Proofreader	Christina Rudloff
Technical Editor	Jason Haley
Cover Designer	Twist Creative, Seattle

Contents at a glance

Contents

What do you think of this book? We want to hear from you!

Microsoft is interested in hearing your feedback so we can continually improve our
books and learning resources for you. To participate in a brief online survey, please visit:

https://aka.ms/tellpress

Chapter 4 **Design and implement Azure PaaS compute
and web and mobile services**   **281**

What do you think of this book? We want to hear from you!

Microsoft is interested in hearing your feedback so we can continually improve our
books and learning resources for you. To participate in a brief online survey, please visit:

https://aka.ms/tellpress

Introduction

The 70-532 exam focuses the skills necessary to develop software on the Microsoft Azure Cloud. It covers Infrastructure-as-a-Service (IaaS) offerings like Azure VMs and Platform-as-a-Service (PaaS) offerings like Azure Storage, Azure CosmosDB, Azure Active Directory, Azure Service Bus, Azure Event Hub, Azure App Services, Azure Service Fabric, Azure Functions and other relevant marketplace applications. This book will help get started with these and other features of Azure so that you can begin developing and deploying Azure applications.

This book is geared toward cloud application developers who focus on Azure as the target host environment. It covers choosing from Azure compute options for IaaS and Paas, incorporating storage and data platforms. It will help you choose when to use features such as Web Apps, API Apps, API Management, Logic Apps and Mobile Apps. It will explain your data storage options between Azure CosmosDB, Azure Redis Cache, Azure Search, and Azure SQL Database. It also covers how to secure applications with Azure Active Directory using B2C and B2B features for single sign-on based on OpenID Connect, OAuth2 and SAML-P protocols, and how to use Azure Vault to protect secrets.

This book covers every major topic area found on the exam, but it does not cover every exam question. Only the Microsoft exam team has access to the exam questions, and Microsoft regularly adds new questions to the exam, making it impossible to cover specific questions. You should consider this book a supplement to your relevant real-world experience and other study materials. If you encounter a topic in this book that you do not feel completely comfortable with, use the "Need more review?" links you'll find in the text to find more information and take the time to research and study the topic. Great information is available on MSDN, TechNet, and in blogs and forums.

Organization of this book

This book is organized by the "Skills measured" list published for the exam. The "Skills measured" list is available for each exam on the Microsoft Learning website: *https://aka.ms/examlist*. Each chapter in this book corresponds to a major topic area in the list, and the technical tasks in each topic area determine a chapter's organization. If an exam covers six major topic areas, for example, the book will contain six chapters.

Microsoft certifications

Microsoft certifications distinguish you by proving your command of a broad set of skills and experience with current Microsoft products and technologies. The exams and corresponding certifications are developed to validate your mastery of critical competencies as you design and develop, or implement and support, solutions with Microsoft products and technologies both on-premises and in the cloud. Certification brings a variety of benefits to the individual and to employers and organizations.

> **MORE INFO**   **ALL MICROSOFT CERTIFICATIONS**
>
> For information about Microsoft certifications, including a full list of available certifications, go to *https://www.microsoft.com/learning*.

Acknowledgments

Zoiner Tejada A book of this scope takes a village, and I'm honored to have received the support of one in making this second edition happen. My deepest thanks to the team at Solliance who helped make this possible: my co-authors Michele Leroux Bustamante and Ike Ellis and the hidden heroes, and Joel Hulen and Kyle Bunting helped us with research and coverage on critical topics as the scope of the book grew with the fast pace of Azure. Laura Norman, our editor, thank you for helping us navigate the path to completion with structure and compassion. To my wife Ashley Tejada, my eternal thanks for supporting me in this effort, the little things count and they don't go unnoticed.

Michele Leroux Bustamante I want to thank Joel Hulen, Virgilio Esteves and Khaled Hikmat – who have been part of key Solliance projects in Azure, including this book – and this work and experience reflects in the guidance shared in the book. Thank you for being part of this journey! Thank you also to, Laura Norman, our editor – who was very supporting during challenging deadlines. A level head keeps us all sane. To my husband and son – thank you for tolerating the writing schedule – again. I owe you - again. Much love.

Ike Ellis First and foremost, I'd like to thank my wife, Margo Sloan, for her support in taking care of all the necessities of life while I wrote. Our editor, Laura Norman, had her hands full in wrangling three busy co-authors, and I'm very grateful for her diligence. I'm very grateful to my co-authors, Zoiner and Michele. It's a joy to work with them on all of our combined projects.

Microsoft Virtual Academy

Build your knowledge of Microsoft technologies with free expert-led online training from Microsoft Virtual Academy (MVA). MVA offers a comprehensive library of videos, live events, and more to help you learn the latest technologies and prepare for certification exams. You'll find what you need here:

https://www.microsoftvirtualacademy.com

Quick access to online references

Throughout this book are addresses to webpages that the author has recommended you visit for more information. Some of these addresses (also known as URLs) can be painstaking to type into a web browser, so we've compiled all of them into a single list that readers of the print edition can refer to while they read.

Download the list at *https://aka.ms/examref5322E/downloads*.

The URLs are organized by chapter and heading. Every time you come across a URL in the book, find the hyperlink in the list to go directly to the webpage.

Errata, updates, & book support

We've made every effort to ensure the accuracy of this book and its companion content. You can access updates to this book—in the form of a list of submitted errata and their related corrections—at:

https://aka.ms/examref5322E/errata

If you discover an error that is not already listed, please submit it to us at the same page.

If you need additional support, email Microsoft Press Book Support at *mspinput@microsoft.com*.

Please note that product support for Microsoft software and hardware is not offered through the previous addresses. For help with Microsoft software or hardware, go to *https://support.microsoft.com*.

We want to hear from you

At Microsoft Press, your satisfaction is our top priority, and your feedback our most valuable asset. Please tell us what you think of this book at:

https://aka.ms/tellpress

We know you're busy, so we've kept it short with just a few questions. Your answers go directly to the editors at Microsoft Press. (No personal information will be requested.) Thanks in advance for your input!

Stay in touch

Let's keep the conversation going! We're on Twitter: *http://twitter.com/MicrosoftPress*.

Preparing for the exam

Microsoft certification exams are a great way to build your resume and let the world know about your level of expertise. Certification exams validate your on-the-job experience and product knowledge. Although there is no substitute for on-the-job experience, preparation through study and hands-on practice can help you prepare for the exam. We recommend that you augment your exam preparation plan by using a combination of available study materials and courses. For example, you might use the Exam ref and another study guide for your "at home" preparation, and take a Microsoft Official Curriculum course for the classroom experience. Choose the combination that you think works best for you.

Note that this Exam Ref is based on publicly available information about the exam and the author's experience. To safeguard the integrity of the exam, authors do not have access to the live exam.

## CHAPTER 1

Create and manage virtual machines

Virtual machines (VMs) are part of the Microsoft Azure Infrastructure-as-a-Service (IaaS) offering. With VMs, you can deploy Windows Server and Linux-based workloads and have greater control over the infrastructure, your deployment topology, and configuration as compared to Platform-as-a-Service (PaaS) offerings such as Web Apps and API Apps. That means you can more easily migrate existing applications and VMs without modifying code or configuration settings, but still benefit from Azure features such as management through a centralized web-based portal, monitoring, and scaling.

> **IMPORTANT**
>
> ***Have you read page xvii***
>
> It contains valuable information regarding the skills you need to pass the exam.

Skills in this chapter:

- Skill 1.1: Deploy workloads on Azure ARM virtual machines
- Skill 1.2: Perform configuration management
- Skill 1.3: Scale ARM VMs
- Skill 1.4: Design and implement ARM VM storage
- Skill 1.5: Monitor ARM VMs
- Skill 1.6: Manage ARM VM availability
- Skill 1.7: Design and implement DevTest Labs

Skill 1.1: Deploy workloads on Azure ARM virtual machines

Microsoft Azure ARM VMs can run more than just Windows and .NET applications. They provide support for running many forms of applications using various operating systems. This section describes where and how to analyze what is supported and how to deploy three different forms of VMs.

Identify supported workloads

A workload describes the nature of a solution, including consideration such as: whether it is an application that runs on a single machine or it requires a complex topology that prescribes the operating system used, the additional software installed, the performance requirements, and the networking environment. Azure enables you to deploy a wide variety of VM workloads, including:

- "Bare bones" VM workloads that run various versions of Windows Client, Windows Server and Linux (such as Debian, Red Hat, SUSE and Ubuntu)
- Web servers (such as Apache Tomcat and Jetty)
- Data science, database and big-data workloads (such as Microsoft SQL Server, Data Science Virtual Machine, IBM DB2, Teradata, Couchbase, Cloudera, and Hortonworks Data Platform)
- Complete application infrastructures (for example, those requiring server farms or clusters like DC/OS, SharePoint, SQL Server AlwaysOn, and SAP)
- Workloads that provide security and protection (such as antivirus, intrusion detection systems, firewalls, data encryption, and key management)
- Workloads that support developer productivity (such as the Windows 10 client operating system, Visual Studio, or the Java Development Kit)

There are two approaches to identifying supported Azure workloads. The first is to determine whether the workload is already explicitly supported and offered through the Azure Marketplace, which provides a large collection of free and for-pay solutions from Microsoft and third parties that deploy to VMs. The Marketplace also offers access to the VM Depot, which provides a large collection of community provided and maintained VMs. The VM configuration and all of the required software it contains on the disk (or disks) is called a VM image. The topology that deploys the VM and any supporting infrastructure is described in an Azure Resource Manager (ARM) template that is used by the Marketplace to provision and configure the required resources.

The second approach is to compare the requirements of the workload you want to deploy directly to the published capabilities of Azure VMs or, in some cases, to perform proof of concept deployments to measure whether the requirements can be met. The following is a representative, though not exhaustive, list of the requirements you typically need to take into consideration:

- CPU and RAM memory requirements
- Disk storage capacity requirements, in gigabytes (GBs)
- Disk performance requirements, usually in terms of input/output operations per second (IOPS) and data throughput (typically in megabytes per second)
- Operating system compatibility
- Networking requirements
- Availability requirements
- Security and compliance requirements

This section covers what is required to deploy the "bare bones" VM (that is, one that has the operating system and minimal features installed) that can serve as the basis for your more complex workloads, and describes the options for deploying a pre-built workload from the Marketplace.

Create a Windows Server VM

Fundamentally, there are two approaches to creating a new VM. You can upload a VM that you have built on-premises, or you can instantiate one from the pre-built images available in the Marketplace. This section focuses on the latter and defers coverage of the upload scenario until the next section.

To create a bare bones Windows Server VM in the portal, complete the following steps:

1. Navigate to the portal accessed via *https://portal.azure.com*.
2. Select New on the command bar.
3. Within the Marketplace list, select the Compute option.
4. On the Compute blade, select the image for the version of Windows Server you want for your VM (such as Windows Server 2016 VM).
5. On the Basics blade, provide a name for your VM, the Disk Type, a User Name and Password, and choose the Subscription, Resource Group and Location into which you want to deploy (Figure 1-1).

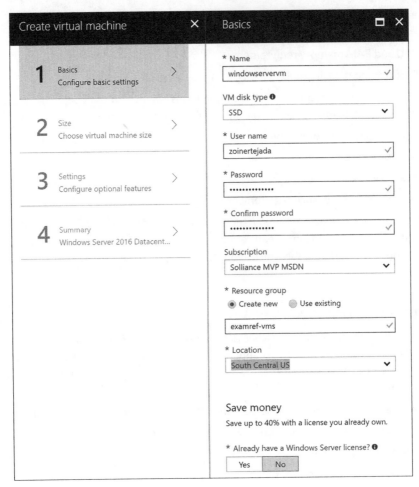

FIGURE 1-1 The Basics blade

6. Select OK.

7. On the Choose A Size Blade, select the desired tier and size for your VM (Figure 1-2).

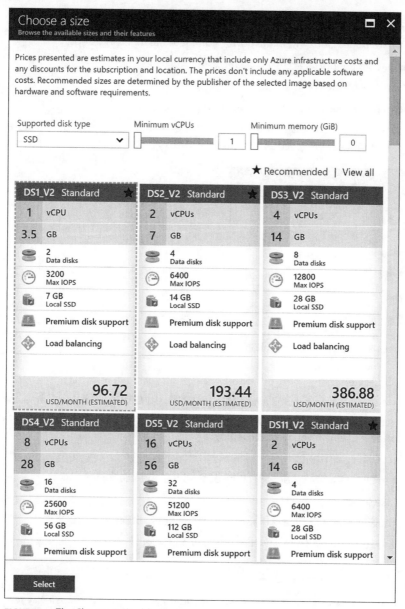

FIGURE 1-2 The Choose A Size blade

8. Choose Select.

9. On the Settings blade, leave the settings at their defaults and select OK.

10. On the Purchase blade, review the summary and select Purchase to deploy the VM.

Create a Linux VM

To create a bare bones Linux VM in the portal, complete the following steps:

1. Navigate to the portal accessed via *https://portal.azure.com*.

2. Select New on the command bar.

3. Within the Marketplace list, select the Compute option.

4. On the Compute blade, select the image for the version of Ubuntu Server (Figure 1-3) you want for your VM (such as Ubuntu Server 16.04 LTS).

FIGURE 1-3 The Ubuntu Server option

5. Select Create.

6. On the Basics blade, provide a name for your VM, the Disk Type, a User Name and Password (or SSH public key if preferred), and choose the Subscription, Resource Group and Location into which you want to deploy.

7. Select OK.

8. On the Choose a size blade, select the desired tier and size for your VM.

9. Choose select.

10. On the Settings blade, leave the settings at their defaults and select OK.

11. On the Purchase blade, review the summary and select Purchase to deploy the VM.

> ***MORE INFO*** **SSH KEY GENERATION**
>
> To create the SSH public key that you need to provision your Linux VM, run **ssh-keygen** on a Mac OSX or Linux terminal, or, if you are running Windows, use PuTTYgen. A good reference, if you are not familiar with using SSH from Windows, is available at: *https://docs. microsoft.com/azure/virtual-machines/linux/ssh-from-windows*.

Create a SQL Server VM

The steps for creating a VM that has SQL Server installed on top of Windows Server are identical to those described earlier for provisioning a Windows Server VM using the portal. The primary differences surface in the fourth step: instead of selecting a Windows Server from the Marketplace list, select a SQL Server option (such as SQL Server 2016 SP1 Enterprise) and follow the prompts to complete the configuration (such as the storage configuration, patching schedule and enablement of features like SQL Authentication and R Services) of the VM with SQL Server and to deploy the VM.

Skill 1.2: Perform configuration management

A number of configuration management tools are available for provisioning, configuring, and managing your VMs. In this section, you learn how to use Windows PowerShell Desired State Configuration (DSC) and the VM Agent (via custom script extensions) to perform configuration management tasks, including automating the process of provisioning VMs, deploying applications to those VMs, and automating configuration of those applications based on the environment, such as development, test, or production.

> **This skill covers how to:**
> - Automate configuration management by using PowerShell Desired State Configuration (DSC) and the VM Agent (using custom script extensions)
> - Configure VMs with Custom Script Extension
> - Use PowerShell DSC
> - Configure VMs with DSC
> - Enable remote debugging

Automate configuration management by using PowerShell Desired State Configuration (DSC) and the VM Agent (using custom script extensions)

Before describing the details of using PowerShell DSC and the Custom Script Extension, this section provides some background on the relationship between these tools and the relevance of the Azure Virtual Machine Agent (VM Agent) and Azure virtual machine extensions (VM extensions).

When you create a new VM in the portal, the VM Agent is installed by default. The VM Agent is a lightweight process used for bootstrapping additional tools on the VM by way of installing, configuring, and managing VM extensions. VM extensions can be added through the portal, but they are also commonly installed with Windows PowerShell cmdlets or through the Azure Cross Platform Command Line Interface (Azure CLI).

With the VM Agent installed, you can add VM extensions. Popular VM extensions include the following:

- PowerShell Desired State Configuration (for Windows VMs)
- Custom Script Extension (for Windows or Linux)
- Team Services Agent (for Windows or Linux VMs)
- Microsoft Antimalware Agent (for Windows VMs)
- Network Watcher Agent (for Windows or Linux VMs)
- Octopus Deploy Tentacle Agent (for Windows VMs)
- Docker extension (for Linux VMs)
- Puppet Agent (for Windows VMs)
- Chef extension (for Windows or Linux)

You can add VM extensions as you create the VM through the portal, as well as run them using the Azure CLI, PowerShell and Azure Resource Manager templates.

Configure VMs with Custom Script Extension

Custom Script Extension makes it possible to automatically download files from Azure Storage and run Windows PowerShell (on Windows VMs) or Shell scripts (on Linux VMs) to copy files and otherwise configure the VM. This can be done when the VM is being created or when it is already running. You can do this from the portal or from a Windows PowerShell command line interface, the Azure CLI, or by using ARM templates.

Configuring a new VM with Custom Script Extension

Create a Windows Server VM following the steps presented in the earlier section, "Creating a Windows Server VM." After creating the VM, complete the following steps to set up the Custom Script Extension:

1. Navigate to the blade for your VM in the portal accessed via *https://portal.azure.com*.
2. From the menu, scroll down to the Settings section, and select Extensions (Figure 1-4).

FIGURE 1-4 The Extensions option

3. On the Extensions blade, select Add on the command bar.

4. From the New Resource blade, select Custom Script Extension (Figure 1-5).

FIGURE 1-5 The New Resource blade

5. On the Custom Script blade, select Create.

6. On the Install Extension blade (Figure 1-6), select the Folder button and choose the .ps1 file containing the script you want to run when the VM starts. Optionally, provide arguments. The Version of DSC is required, for example 2.21.

FIGURE 1-6 The Install Extenson blade

7. Select OK.

> **MORE INFO** **CONFIGURING THE CUSTOM SCRIPT EXTENSION**
>
> You can also configure the Custom Script Extension using the Set-AzureRmVMCustom-ScriptExtension Windows PowerShell cmdlet (see *https://docs.microsoft.com/en-us/azure/virtual-machines/windows/extensions-customscript#powershell-deployment*) or via the "az vm extension set" Azure CLI command (*see https://docs.microsoft.com/en-us/azure/virtual-machines/linux/extensions-customscript#azure-cli*).

Use PowerShell DSC

PowerShell Desired State Configuration (DSC) is a management platform introduced with Windows PowerShell 4.0, available as a Windows feature on Windows Server 2012 R2. PowerShell DSC is implemented using Windows PowerShell. You can use it to configure a set of servers (or nodes) declaratively, providing a description of the desired state for each node in the system topology. You can describe which application resources to add, remove, or update based on the current state of a server node. The easy, declarative syntax simplifies configuration management tasks.

With PowerShell DSC, you can instruct a VM to self-provision to a desired state on first deployment and then have it automatically update if there is "configuration drift." Configuration drift happens when the desired state of the node no longer matches what is described by DSC.

DSC resources

Resources are core building blocks for DSC. A script can describe the target state of one or more resources, such as a Windows feature, the Registry, the file system, and other services. For example, a DSC script can describe the following intentions:

- Manage server roles and Windows features
- Manage registry keys
- Copy files and folders
- Deploy software
- Run Windows PowerShell scripts

> **MORE INFO** **DSC BUILT-IN RESOURCES**
>
> For a more extensive list of DSC resources for both Windows and Linux, see: *https://msdn. microsoft.com/en-us/powershell/dsc/resources*.

Configuration keyword

DSC extends Windows PowerShell 4.0 with a Configuration keyword used to express the desired state of one or more target nodes. For example, the following configuration indicates that a server should have IIS enabled during provisioning:

```
Configuration EnableIIS
{
    Node WebServer
    {
        WindowsFeature IIS {
                Ensure = "Present",
                Name = "Web-Server"
        }
    }
}
```

The Configuration keyword can wrap one or more Node elements, each describing the desired configuration state of one or more resources on the node. In the preceding example, the server node is named WebServer, the contents of which indicate that the Windows Feature "IIS" should be configured, and that the Web-Server component of IIS should be confirmed present or installed if absent.

EXAM TIP

After the DSC runs, a Managed Object Format (MOF) file is created, which is a standard endorsed by the Distributed Management Task Force (DTMF). See: *http://www.dmtf.org/education/mof.*

Custom resources

Many resources are predefined and exposed to DSC; however, you may also require extended capabilities that warrant creating a custom resource for DSC configuration. You can implement custom resources by creating a Windows PowerShell module. The module includes a MOF schema, a script module, and a module manifest.

> **MORE INFO   CUSTOM DSC RESOURCES**
>
> For more information on building custom DSC resources, see *https://msdn.microsoft.com/en-us/powershell/dsc/authoringResource.*

> **MORE INFO   DSC RESOURCES IN THE POWERSHELL GALLERY**
>
> The Windows PowerShell team released a number of DSC resources to simplify working with Active Directory, SQL Server, and IIS. See the PowerShell Gallery at *http://www.powershell-gallery.com/items* and search for items in the DSC Resource category.

Local Configuration Manager

Local Configuration Manager is the engine of DSC, which runs on all target nodes and enables the following scenarios for DSC:

- Pushing configurations to bootstrap a target node
- Pulling configuration from a specified location to bootstrap or update a target node
- Applying the configuration defined in the MOF file to the target node, either during the bootstrapping stage or to repair configuration drift

Local Configuration Manager runs invoke the configuration specified by your DSC configuration file. You can optionally configure Local Configuration Manager to apply new configurations only, to report differences resulting from configuration drift, or to automatically correct configuration drift.

Configure VMs with DSC

To configure a VM using DSC, first create a Windows PowerShell script that describes the desired configuration state. As discussed earlier, this involves selecting resources to configure and providing the appropriate settings. When you have a configuration script, you can use one of a number of methods to initialize a VM to run the script on startup.

Creating a configuration script

Use any text editor to create a Windows PowerShell file. Include a collection of resources to configure, for one or more nodes, in the file. If you are copying files as part of the node configuration, they should be available in the specified source path, and a target path should also be specified. For example, the following script ensures IIS is enabled and copies a single file to the default website:

```
configuration DeployWebPage
{
    node ("localhost")
    {
        WindowsFeature IIS
        {
            Ensure = "Present"
            Name = "Web-Server"
        }

        File WebPage
        {
            Ensure          = "Present"
            DestinationPath = "C:\inetpub\wwwroot\index.html"
            Force           = $true
            Type            = "File"
            Contents        = '<html><body><h1>Hello Web Page!</h1></body></html>'

        }
    }
}
```

Deploying a DSC configuration package

After creating your configuration script and allocating any resources it requires, you need to produce a compressed zip file containing the configuration script in the root, along with any resources needed by the script. You create the zip and copy it up to Azure Storage in one command using Publish-AzureRMVmDscConfiguration using Windows PowerShell and then apply the configuration with SetAzureRmVmDscExtension.

Assume you have the following configuration script in the file iisInstall.ps1 on your local machine:

```
configuration IISInstall
{
    node "localhost"
    {
        WindowsFeature IIS
        {
            Ensure = "Present"
            Name = "Web-Server"
        }
    }
}
```

You would then run the following PowerShell cmdlets to upload and apply the configuration:

```
#Load the Azure PowerShell cmdlets
Import-Module Azure
#Login to your Azure Account and select your subscription (if your account has multiple
  subscriptions)
Login-AzureRmAccount
Set-AzureRmContext -SubscriptionId <YourSubscriptionId>
$resourceGroup = "dscdemogroup"
$vmName = "myVM"
$storageName = "demostorage"
#Publish the configuration script into Azure storage
Publish-AzureRmVMDscConfiguration -ConfigurationPath .\iisInstall.ps1
    -ResourceGroupName $resourceGroup -StorageAccountName $storageName -force
#Configure the VM to run the DSC configuration
Set-AzureRmVmDscExtension -Version 2.21
    -ResourceGroupName $resourceGroup -VMName $vmName
    -ArchiveStorageAccountName $storageName
    -ArchiveBlobName iisInstall.ps1.zip -AutoUpdate:$true -ConfigurationName
"IISInstall"
```

Configuring an existing VM using the Azure Portal

Before configuring an existing VM using the Azure Portal, you will need to create a ZIP package around your PowerShell script. To do so, run the Publish-AzureVMDscConfiguration cmdlet providing the path to your PowerShell script and the name of that destination zip file to create, for example:

```
Publish-AzureVMDscConfiguration .\iisInstall.ps1 -ConfigurationArchivePath .\iisInstall.
ps1.zip
```

Then you can proceed in the Azure Portal. To configure an existing VM in the portal, complete the following steps:

1. Navigate to the blade for your VM in the portal accessed via *https://portal.azure.com*.
2. From the menu, scroll down to the Settings section, and select Extensions.
3. On the Extensions blade, select Add on the command bar.
4. From the New Resource blade, select PowerShell Desired State Configuration.

5. On the PowerShell Desired State Configuration blade, select Create.

6. On the Install Extension blade, select the folder button and choose the zip file containing the DSC configuration.

7. Provide the module-qualified name of the configuration in your .ps1 that you want to apply. This value is constructed from the name of your .ps1 file including the extension, a slash (\) and the name of the configuration as it appears within the .ps1 file. For example, if your file is iisInstall.ps1 and you have a configuration named IISInstall, you would set this to "iisInstall.ps1\IISInstall".

8. Optionally provide any Data PSD1 file and configuration arguments required by your script.

9. Specify the version of the DSC extension (Figure 1-7) you want to install (e.g., 2.21).

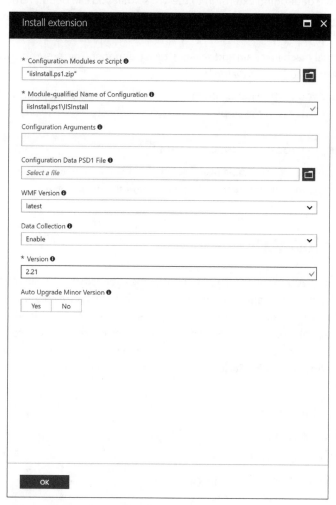

FIGURE 1-7 Using the Install Extension

10. Select OK.

Enable remote debugging

You can use remote debugging to debug applications running on your Windows VMs. Server Explorer in Visual Studio shows your VMs in a list, and from there you can enable remote debugging and attach to a process following these steps:

1. In Visual Studio, open Cloud Explorer.

2. Expand the node of the subscription containing your VM, and then expand the Virtual Machines node.

3. Right-click the VM you want to debug and select Enable Debugging. Click Yes in the dialog box to confirm.

4. This installs a remote debugging extension to the VM so that you can debug remotely. The progress will be shown in the Microsoft Azure Activity Log. After the debugging extension is installed, you can continue.

5. Right-click the virtual machine again and select Attach Debugger. This presents a list of processes in the Attach To Process dialog box.

6. Select the processes you want to debug on the VM and click Attach. To debug a web application, select w3wp.exe, for example.

MORE INFO **DEBUGGING PROCESSES IN VISUAL STUDIO**

For additional information about debugging processes in Visual Studio, see this reference: *https://docs.microsoft.com/en-us/visualstudio/debugger/debug-multiple-processes*.

Skill 1.3: Scale ARM VMs

Similar to Azure Web Apps, Azure Virtual Machines provides the capability to scale in terms of both instance size and instance count and supports auto-scale on the instance count. However, unlike Websites that can automatically provision new instances as a part of scale out, Virtual Machines on their own must be pre-provisioned in order for auto-scale to turn instances on or off during a scaling operation. To achieve scale-out without having to perform any pre-provisioning of VM resources, Virtual Machine Scale Sets should be deployed.

This skill covers how to:

- Scale up and scale down VM sizes
- Deploy ARM VM Scale Sets (VMSS)
- Configure auto-scale on ARM VM Scale Sets

Scale up and scale down VM sizes

Using the portal or Windows PowerShell, you can scale VM sizes up or down to alter the capacity of the VM, which collectively adjusts:

- The number of data disks that can be attached and the total IOPS capacity
- The size of the local temp disk
- The number of CPU cores
- The amount of RAM memory available
- The network performance
- The quantity of network interface cards (NICs) supported

> **MORE INFO**   **LIMITS BY VM SIZE**
>
> To view the detailed listing of limits by VM size, see *https://docs.microsoft.com/azure/virtual-machines/windows/sizes*.

Scaling up and scaling down VM size using the Portal

To scale a VM up or down in the portal, complete these steps:

1. Navigate to the blade of your VM in the portal accessed via *https://portal.azure.com*.
2. From the menu, select Size.
3. On the Choose a size blade, select the new size you would like for the VM.
4. Choose Select to apply the new size.

Scaling up and scaling down VM size using Windows PowerShell

The instance size can also be adjusted using the following Windows PowerShell script:

```
$ResourceGroupName = "examref"
$VMName = "vmname"
$NewVMSize = "Standard_A5"
$vm = Get-AzureRmVM -ResourceGroupName $ResourceGroupName -Name $VMName
$vm.HardwareProfile.vmSize = $NewVMSize
Update-AzureRmVM -ResourceGroupName $ResourceGroupName -VM $vm
```

In the previous script, you specify the name of the Resource Group containing your VM, the name of the VM you want to scale, and the label of the size (for example, "Standard_A5") to which you want to scale it.

You can get the list of VM sizes available in each Azure region by running the following PowerShell (supplying the Location value desired):

```
Get-AzureRmVmSize -Location "East US" | Sort-Object Name |
ft Name, NumberOfCores, MemoryInMB, MaxDataDiskCount -AutoSize
```

Deploy ARM VM Scale Sets (VMSS)

Virtual Machine Scale Sets enable you to automate the scaling process. During a scale-out event, a VM Scale Set deploys additional, identical copies of ARM VMs. During a scale-in it simply removes deployed instances. No VM in the Scale Set is allowed to have any unique configuration, and can contain only one size and tier of VM, in other words each VM in the Scale Set will also have the same size and tier as all the others in the Scale Set.

VM Scale Sets support VMs running either Windows or Linux. A great way to understand Scale Sets is to compare them to the features of standalone Virtual Machines:

- In a Scale Set, each Virtual Machine must be identical to the other, as opposed to stand alone Virtual Machines where you can customize each VM individually.

- You adjust the capacity of Scale Set simply by adjusting the capacity property, and this in turn deploys more VMs in parallel. In contrast, scaling out stand alone VMs would mean writing a script to orchestrate the deployment of many individual VMs.

- Scale Sets support overprovisioning during a scale out event, meaning that the Scale Set will actually deploy more VMs than you asked for, and then when the requested number of VMs are successfully provisioned the extra VMs are deleted (you are not charged for the extra VMs and they do not count against your quota limits). This approach improves the provisioning success rate and reduces deployment time. For standalone VMs, this adds extra requirements and complexity to any script orchestrating the deployment. Moreover, you would be charged for the extra standalone VM's and they would count against your quota limits.

- Scale Set can roll out upgrades using an upgrade policy across the VMs in your Scale Set. With standalone VMs you would have to orchestrate this update process yourself.

- Azure Autoscale can be used to automatically scale a Scale Set, but cannot be used against standalone VMs.

- The Networking of Scale Sets is similar to standalone VMs deployed in a Virtual Network. Scale Sets deploy the VMs they manage into a single subnet of a Virtual Network. To access any particular Scale Set VM you either use an Azure Load Balancer with NAT rules (e.g. where each external port can map to a Scale Set instance VM) or you deploy a publicly accessible "jumpbox" VM in the same Virtual Network subnet as the Scale Set VMs, and access the Scale Set VMs via the jumpbox (to which you are either RDP or SSH connected).

The maximum number of VMs to which a VM Scale Set can scale, referred to as the capacity, depends on three factors:

- Support for multiple placement groups
- The use of managed disks
- If the VM's use an image from the Marketplace or are created from a user supplied image

Placement groups are a Scale Set specific concept that is similar to Availability Sets, where a Placement group is implicitly an Availability Set with five fault domains and five update domains, and supports up to 100 VM's. When you deploy a Scale Set you can restrict to only allow a single placement group, which will effectively limit your Scale Set capacity to 100 VM's. However, if you allow multiple placement groups during deployment, then your Scale Set may support up to 1,000 VM's, depending on the other two factors (managed disks and image source).

During Scale Set deployment, you can also choose whether to use unmanaged (for example, the traditional disks in an Azure Storage Account you control) or managed disks (where the disk itself is the resource you manage, and the Storage Account is no longer a concern of yours). If you choose unmanaged storage, you will also need to be limited to using a single placement group, and therefore the capacity of your Scale Set limited to 100 VMs. However, if you opt to use managed disks then your Scale Set may support up to 1,000 VMs subject only to our last factor (the image source).

The final factor affecting your Scale Set's maximum capacity is the source of the image used when the Scale Set provisions the VMs it manages. If the image source is a Marketplace image (like any of the baseline images for Windows Server or Linux) then your Scale Set supports up to 1,000 VMs. However, if your VMs will be based off of a custom image you supply then your Scale Set will have a capacity of 100 VMs.

Deploy ARM VM Scale Sets using the Portal

To deploy a Scale Set using the Azure Portal, you deploy a Scale Set and as a part of that process select the Marketplace image to use for the VMs it will manage. You cannot select a VM Marketplace image and then choose to include it in a Scale Set (as you might when selecting a Resource Group). To deploy a Scale Set in the portal, complete these steps (Figure 1-8):

1. Navigate to the portal accessed via https://portal.azure.com.
2. Select + New and in the Search the Marketplace box, enter "scale sets" and select the "Virtual machine scale set" item that appears.
3. On the Virtual machine scale set blade, select Create.
4. In the Basics property group, provide a name for the scale set.
5. Select the OS type (Window or Linux).
6. Choose your Subscription, Resource group and Location. Note that the Resource group you select for the Scale Set must either be empty or be created new with Scale Set.
7. Enter a user name and password (for Windows), an SSH user name and password (for Linux) or an SSH public key (for Linux).

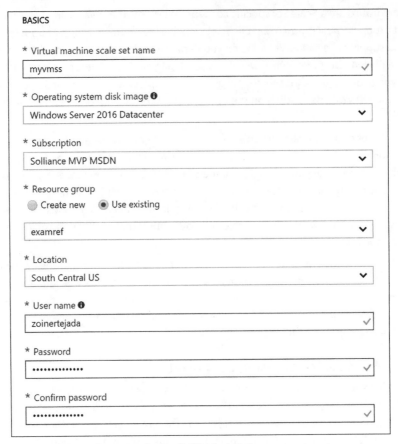

FIGURE 1-8 The Basics properties for the VM Scale Set

8. In the Instances and Load Balancer property group, set the instance count to the desired number of instances to deploy initially.

9. Select the virtual machine instance size for all machines in the Scale Set.

10. Choose whether to limit to a single placement group or not by selecting the option to Enable scaling beyond 100 instances. A selection of "No" will limit your deployment to a single placement group.

11. Select to use managed or unmanaged disks. If you chose to sue multiple placement groups, then managed disks are the only option and will be automatically selected for you.

12. If you chose to use a single placement group, configure the public IP address name you can use to access VMs via a Load Balancer. If you allowed multiple placement groups, then this option is unavailable.

13. Similarly, if you chose to use a single placement group, configure the public IP allocation mode (which can be Dynamic or Static) and provide a label for your domain name. If you allowed multiple placement groups, then this option is unavailable (Figure 1-9).

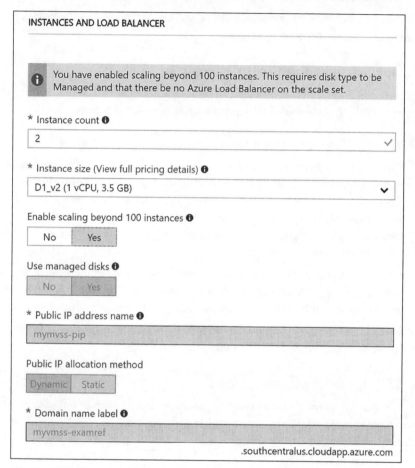

FIGURE 1-9 The Instances And Load Balancer properties for a VM Scale Set

14. In the Autoscale property group, leave Autoscale set to Disabled.

15. Select Create.

MORE INFO **DEPLOYING A SCALE SET USING POWERSHELL OR AZURE CLI**

You can also deploy a Scale Set using PowerShell or the Azure CLI. For the detailed step by step instructions, see *https://docs.microsoft.com/azure/virtual-machine-scale-sets/virtual-machine-scale-sets-create*.

Deploying a Scale Set using a Custom Image

To deploy a Scale Set where the VMs are created from custom or user-supplied image you must perform the following:

1. Generalize and capture an unmanaged VM disk from a standalone VM. The disk is saved in an Azure Storage Account you provide.

> **MORE INFO** **CREATING A GENERALIZED VM DISK**
>
> To generalize and capture a VM from a VM you have already deployed in Azure, see *https:// docs.microsoft.com/azure/virtual-machines/windows/sa-copy-generalized*.

2. Create an ARM Template that at minimum:

   A. Creates a managed image based on the generalized unmanaged disk available in Azure Storage. Your template needs to define a resource of type "Microsoft. Compute/images" that references the VHD image by its URI. Alternately, you can pre-create the managed image (which allows you to specify the VHDs for the OS Disk and any Data Disks), for example by creating an image using the Portal, and omit this section in your template.

   B. Configures the Scale Set to use the managed image. Your template needs to defines a resource of type "Microsoft.Compute/virtualMachineScaleSets" that, in its "storageProfile" contains a reference to the image you defined previously.

3. Deploy the ARM template. Deploy the ARM template using the approach of your choice (for example, Portal, PowerShell or by using the Azure CLI).

> **MORE INFO** **DEPLOYING ARM TEMPLATES**
>
> For instructions on deploying an ARM template, see *https://docs.microsoft.com/azure/ azure-resource-manager/resource-group-template-deploy-portal#deploy-resources-from-custom-template*.

The following code snippet shows an example of a complete ARM template for deploying a VM Scale Set that uses Linux VMs, where the authentication for the VM's is username and password based, and the VHD source is a generalized, unmanaged VHD disk stored in an Azure Storage Account. When the template is deployed, the user needs to specify the admin username and password to establish on all VMs in the Scale Set, as well as the URI to the source VHD in Azure Storage blobs.

```
{
  "$schema": "http://schema.management.azure.com/schemas/
2015-01-01/deploymentTemplate.json",
  "contentVersion": "1.0.0.0",
  "parameters": {
    "adminUsername": {
      "type": "string"
    },
```

```
      "adminPassword": {
        "type": "securestring"
      },
      "sourceImageVhdUri": {
        "type": "string",
        "metadata": {
          "description": "The source of the generalized blob containing the custom image"
        }
      }
    },
    "variables": {},
    "resources": [
      {
        "type": "Microsoft.Compute/images",
        "apiVersion": "2016-04-30-preview",
        "name": "myCustomImage",
        "location": "[resourceGroup().location]",
        "properties": {
          "storageProfile": {
            "osDisk": {
              "osType": "Linux",
              "osState": "Generalized",
              "blobUri": "[parameters('sourceImageVhdUri')]",
              "storageAccountType": "Standard_LRS"
            }
          }
        }
      },
      {
        "type": "Microsoft.Network/virtualNetworks",
        "name": "myVnet",
        "location": "[resourceGroup().location]",
        "apiVersion": "2016-12-01",
        "properties": {
          "addressSpace": {
            "addressPrefixes": [
              "10.0.0.0/16"
            ]
          },
          "subnets": [
            {
              "name": "mySubnet",
              "properties": {
                "addressPrefix": "10.0.0.0/16"
              }
            }
          ]
        }
      },
      {
        "type": "Microsoft.Compute/virtualMachineScaleSets",
        "name": "myScaleSet",
        "location": "[resourceGroup().location]",
        "apiVersion": "2016-04-30-preview",
        "dependsOn": [
```

```
        "Microsoft.Network/virtualNetworks/myVnet",
        "Microsoft.Compute/images/myCustomImage"
    ],
    "sku": {
      "name": "Standard_A1",
      "capacity": 2
    },
    "properties": {
      "upgradePolicy": {
        "mode": "Manual"
      },
      "virtualMachineProfile": {
        "storageProfile": {
          "imageReference": {
            "id": "[resourceId('Microsoft.Compute/images', 'myCustomImage')]"
          }
        },
        "osProfile": {
          "computerNamePrefix": "vm",
          "adminUsername": "[parameters('adminUsername')]",
          "adminPassword": "[parameters('adminPassword')]"
        },
        "networkProfile": {
          "networkInterfaceConfigurations": [
            {
              "name": "myNic",
              "properties": {
                "primary": "true",
                "ipConfigurations": [
                  {
                    "name": "myIpConfig",
                    "properties": {
                      "subnet": {
                        "id": "[concat(resourceId('Microsoft.Network/virtualNetworks',
                          'myVnet'), '/subnets/mySubnet')]"
                      }
                    }
                  }
                ]
              }
            }
          ]
        }
      }
    }
  }
]
}
```

> **MORE INFO** **TEMPLATE SOURCE**
>
> You can download the ARM template shown from: *https://github.com/gatneil/mvss/blob/custom-image/azuredeploy.json.*

Configure Autoscale

Autoscale is a feature of the Azure Monitor service in Microsoft Azure that enables you to automatically scale resources based on rules evaluated against metrics provided by those resources. Autoscale can be used with Virtual Machine Scale Sets to adjust the capacity according to metrics like CPU utilization, network utilization and memory utilization across the VMs in the Scale Set. Additionally, Autoscale can be configured to adjust the capacity of the Scale Set according to metrics from other services, such as the number of messages in an Azure Queue or Service Bus queue.

Configuring Autoscale when provisioning VM Scale Set using the Portal

You can configure a Scale Set to autoscale when provisioning a new Scale Set in the Azure Portal. When configuring it during provisioning, the only metric you can scale against is CPU utilization. To provision a Scale Set with CPU based autoscale, complete the following steps:

1. Navigate to the portal accessed via *https://portal.azure.com*.

2. Select + New and in the Search the Marketplace box, enter "scale sets" and select the "Virtual machine scale set" item that appears.

3. On the Virtual machine scale set blade, select Create.

4. In the Basics property group, provide a name for the scale set.

5. Select the OS type (Window or Linux).

6. Choose your Subscription, Resource group and Location. Note that the Resource group you select for the Scale Set must either be empty or be created new with Scale Set.

7. Enter a user name and password (for Windows), an SSH user name and password (for Linux) or an SSH public key (for Linux).

8. In the Instances and Load Balancer property group, set the instance count to the desired number of instances to deploy initially.

9. Select the virtual machine instance size for all machines in the Scale Set.

10. Choose whether to limit to a single placement group or not by selecting the option to Enable scaling beyond 100 instances. A selection of "No" will limit your deployment to a single placement group.

11. Select to use managed or unmanaged disks. If you chose to sue multiple placement groups, then managed disks are the only option and will be automatically selected for you.

12. If you chose to use a single placement group, configure the public IP address name you can use to access VMs via a Load Balancer. If you allowed multiple placement groups, then this option is unavailable.

13. Similarly, if you chose to use a single placement group, configure the public IP allocation mode (which can be Dynamic or Static) and provide a label for your domain name. If you allowed multiple placement groups, then this option is unavailable.

14. In the Autoscale property group, chose to enable autoscale. If you enable autoscale, provide the desired VM instance count ranges, the scale out or scale in CPU thresholds and instance counts to scale out or scale in by (Figure 1-10).

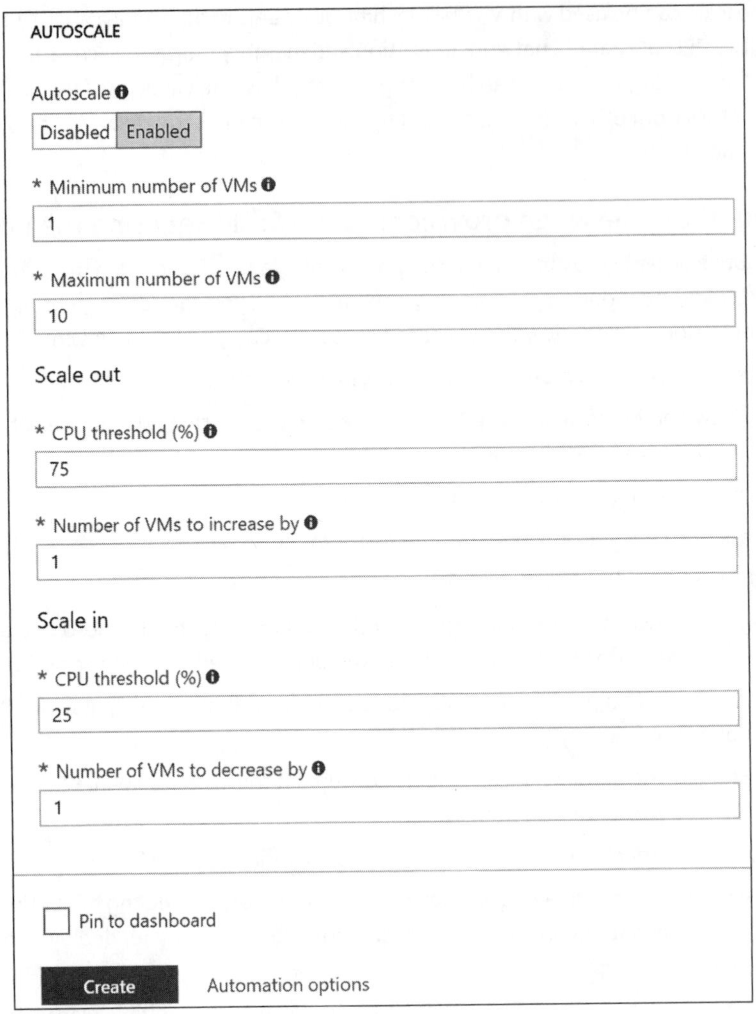

AUTOSCALE

Autoscale ❶

| Disabled | Enabled |

* Minimum number of VMs ❶

| 1 |

* Maximum number of VMs ❶

| 10 |

Scale out

* CPU threshold (%) ❶

| 75 |

* Number of VMs to increase by ❶

| 1 |

Scale in

* CPU threshold (%) ❶

| 25 |

* Number of VMs to decrease by ❶

| 1 |

☐ Pin to dashboard

| **Create** | Automation options |

FIGURE 1-10 The Autoscale settings for a VM Scale Set

15. Select Create.

Configuring Autoscale on an existing VM Scale Set using the Portal

You can configure a Scale Set to Autoscale after it is deployed using the Portal. When configuring this way, you can scale according to any of the available metrics. To further configure Autoscale on an existing Scale Set with Autoscale already enabled, complete the following steps:

1. Navigate to the portal accessed via *https://portal.azure.com*.

2. Navigate to your Virtual machine scale set in the Portal.

3. From the menu, under Settings, select Scaling.

4. Select Add Default Scale Condition or Add A Scale Condition. The default scale condition (Figure 1-11) will run when none of the other scale conditions match.

5. For the scale condition, choose the scale mode. You can scale based on a metric or scale to a specific instance count.

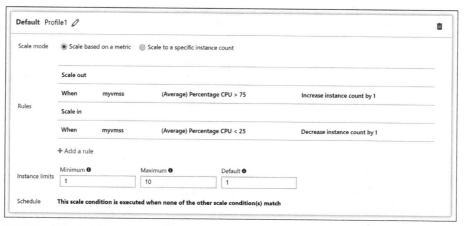

FIGURE 1-11 The Default scale condition

6. When choosing to scale based on a metric (Figure 1-12):

   ■ Select Add rule to define the metric source (e.g., the Scale Set itself or another Azure resource), the Criteria (e.g., the metric name, time grain and value range), and the Action (e.g., to scale out or scale in).

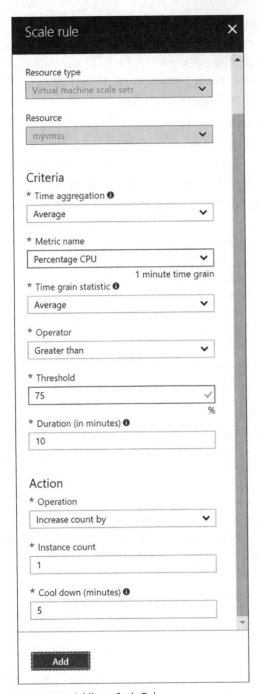

FIGURE 1-12 Adding a Scale Rule

7. When choosing to scale to a specific instance count:

- For the default scale condition, you can only specify the target instance count to which the Scale Set capacity will reset.
- For non-default scale conditions, you specify the desired instance count and a time based schedule during which that instance count will apply. Specify the time by using a start and end dates or according to a recurring schedule that repeats during a time range on selected days of the week (Figure 1-13).

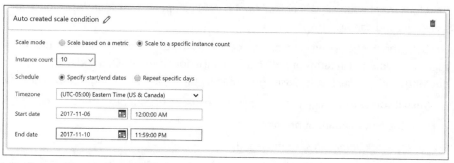

FIGURE 1-13 Adding a Scale Condition

8. Select Save in the command bar to apply your Autoscale settings.

> **MORE INFO** **VM SCALE SET AND AUTOSCALE DEPLOYMENT WITH POWERSHELL**
>
> For an end-to-end example walking thru of the steps to create a VM Scale Set configured with Autoscale showing how to deploy with PowerShell, see: *https://docs.microsoft.com/azure/virtual-machine-scale-sets/virtual-machine-scale-sets-windows-autoscale.*

Skill 1.4: Design and implement ARM VM storage

There is more to managing your VM storage than attaching data disks. In this skill, you explore multiple considerations that are critical to your VM storage strategy.

This skill covers how to:
- Plan for storage capacity
- Configure storage pools
- Configure disk caching
- Configure geo-replication
- Configure shared storage using Azure File storage
- Implement ARM VMs with Standard and Premium Storage
- Implement Azure Disk Encryption for Windows and Linux ARM VMs

Plan for storage capacity

VMs leverage a local disk provided by the host machine for the temp drive (D: on Windows and /dev/sdb1 on Linux) and Azure Storage for the operating system and data disks (collectively referred to as virtual machine disks), wherein each disk is a VHD stored as a blob in Blob storage. The temp drive, however, uses a local disk provided by the host machine. The physical disk underlying this temp drive may be shared among all the VMs running on the host and, therefore, may be subject to a noisy neighbor that competes with your VM instance for read/write IOPS and bandwidth.

For the operating system and data disks, use of Azure Storage blobs means that the storage capacity of your VM in terms of both performance (for example, IOPS and read/write throughput MB/s) and size (such as in GBs) is governed by the capacity of a single blob in Blob storage.

When it comes to storage performance and capacity of your disks there are two big factors:

1. Is the disk standard or premium?

2. Is the disk unmanaged or managed?

When you provision a VM (either in the portal or via PowerShell or the Azure CLI), it will ask for the disk type, which is either HDD (backed by magnetic disks with physical spindles) or SSD (backed by solid state drives). Standard disks are stored in a standard Azure Storage Account backed by the HDD disk type. Premium disks are stored in a premium Azure Storage Account backed by the SSD disk type.

When provisioning a VM, you will also need to choose between using unmanaged disks or managed disks. Unmanaged disks require the creation of an Azure Storage Account in your subscription that will be used to store all of the disks required by the VM. Managed disks simplify the disk management because they manage the associated Storage Account for you, and you are only responsible for managing the disk resource. In other words, you only need to specify the size and type of disk and Azure takes care of the rest for you. The primary benefit to using managed disks over unmanaged disks is that you are no longer limited by Storage Account limits. In particular, the limit of 20,000 IOPS per Storage Account means that you would need to carefully manage the creation of unmanaged disks in Azure Storage, limiting the number of disks typically to 20-40 disks per Storage Account. When you need more disks, you need to create additional Storage Accounts to support the next batch of 20-40 disks.

The following summarizes the differences between standard and premium disks in both unmanaged and managed scenarios, shown in Table 1.1.

TABLE 1-1 Comparing Standard and Premium disks

Feature	Standard (unmanaged)	STANDARD (MANAGED)	Premium (UN-MANGED)	PREMIUM (MANAGED)
Max IOPS for storage account	20k IOPS	N/A	60k -127.5k IOPS	N/A
Max bandwidth for storage account	N/A	N/A	50 Gbps	N/A
Max storage capacity per storage account	500 TB	N/A	35 TB	N/A
Max IOPS per VM	Depends on VM Size	Depends on VM Size	Depends on VM Size	Depends on VM Size
Max throughput per VM	Depends on VM Size	Depends on VM Size	Depends on VM Size	Depends on VM Size
Max disk size	4TB	32GB - 4TB	32GB - 4TB	32GB - 4TB
Max 8 KB IOPS per disk	300 - 500 IOPS	500 IOPS	500 - 7,500 IOPS	120 - 7,500 IOPS
Max throughput per disk	60 MB/s	60 MB/s	100 MB/s - 250 MB/s	25 MB/s - 250 MB/s

> **MORE INFO   IOPS**
>
> An IOPS is a unit of measure counting the number of input/output operations per second and serves as a useful measure for the number of read, write, or read/write operations that can be completed in a period of time for data sets of a certain size (usually 8 KB). To learn more, you can read about IOPS at *http://en.wikipedia.org/wiki/IOPS*.

Given the scalability targets, how can you configure a VM that has an IOPS capacity greater than 500 IOPS or 60 MB/s throughput, or provides more than one terabyte of storage? One approach is to use multiple blobs, which means using multiple disks striped into a single volume (in Windows Server 2012 and later VMs, the approach is to use Storage Spaces and create a storage pool across all of the disks). Another option is to use premium disks at the P20 size or higher.

> **MORE INFO   STORAGE SCALABILITY TARGETS**
>
> For a detailed breakdown of the capabilities by storage type, disk type and size, see: *https://docs.microsoft.com/azure/storage/storage-scalability-targets*.

For Azure VMs, the general rule governing the number of disks you can attach is twice the number of CPU cores. For example, an A4-sized VM instance has 8 cores and can mount 16 disks. Currently, there are only a few exceptions to this rule such as the A9 instances, which map on one times the number of cores (so an A9 has 16 cores and can mount 16 disks). Expect such exceptions to change over time as the VM configurations evolve. Also, the maximum number of disks that can currently be mounted to a VM is 64 and the maximum IOPS is 80,000 IOPS (when using a Standard GS5).

> **MORE INFO** **HOW MANY DISKS CAN YOU MOUNT?**
>
> As the list of VM sizes grows and changes over time, you should review the following web page that details the number of disks you can mount by VM size and tier: *http://msdn.micro-soft.com/library/azure/dn197896.aspx*.

Configure storage pools

Storage Spaces enables you to group together a set of disks and then create a volume from the available aggregate capacity. Assuming you have created your VM and attached all of the empty disks you want to it, the following steps explain how to create a storage pool from those disks. You next create a storage space in that pool, and from that storage space, mount a volume you can access with a drive letter.

1. Launch Remote Desktop and connect to the VM on which you want to configure the storage space.
2. If Server Manager (Figure 1-14) does not appear by default, run it from the Start screen.
3. Click the File And Storage Services tile near the middle of the window.

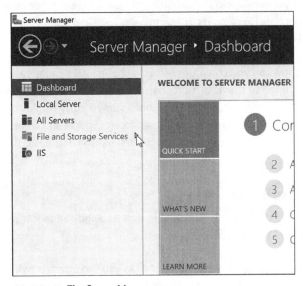

FIGURE 1-14 The Server Manager

4. In the navigation pane, click Storage Pools (Figure 1-15).

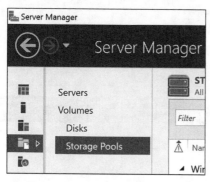

FIGURE 1-15 Storage Pools in the Server Manager

5. In the Storage Pools area, click the Tasks drop-down list and select New Storage Pool (Figure 1-16).

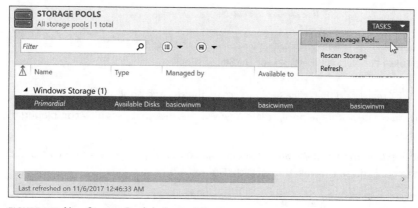

FIGURE 1-16 New Storage Pools in Server Manager

6. In the New Storage Pool Wizard, click Next on the first page.

7. Provide a name for the new storage pool, and click Next.

8. Select all the disks you want to include in your storage pool, and click Next (Figure 1-17).

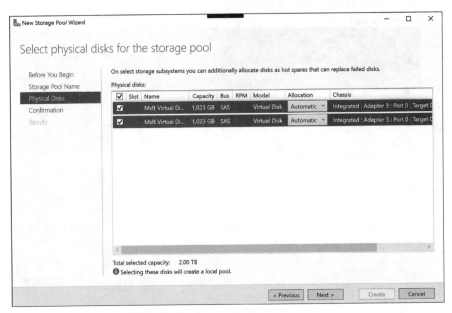

FIGURE 1-17 Select Physical Disks For The Storage Pool

9. Click Create, and then click Close to create the storage pool.

After you create a storage pool, create a new virtual disk that uses it by completing the following steps:

1. In Server Manager, in the Storage Pools dialog box, right-click your newly created storage pool and select New Virtual Disk (Figure 1-18).

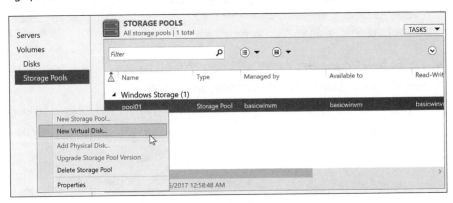

FIGURE 1-18 Create a New Virtual Disk in Storage Pools

2. Select your storage pool, and select OK (Figure 1-19).

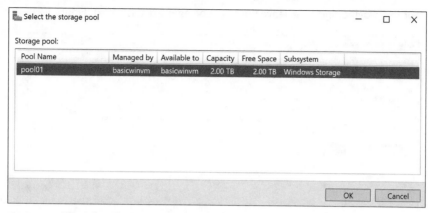

FIGURE 1-19 The Select The Storage Pool dialog

3. Click Next on the first page of the wizard.

4. Provide a name for the new virtual disk, and click Next.

5. On the Specify enclosure resiliency page, click Next.

6. Select the simple storage layout (because your VHDs are already triple replicated by Azure Storage, you do not need additional redundancy), and click Next (Figure 1-20).

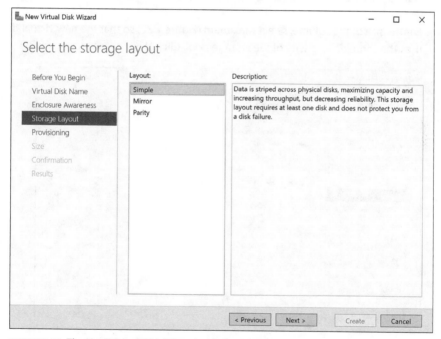

FIGURE 1-20 The New Virtual Disk Wizard with the Select The Storage Layout page

7. For the provisioning type, leave the selection as Fixed. Click Next (Figure 1-21).

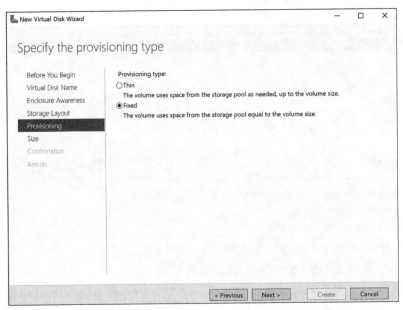

FIGURE 1-21 Specify The Provisioning Type page in the New Virtual Disk Wizard

8. For the size of the volume, select Maximum (Figure 1-22) so that the new virtual disk uses the complete capacity of the storage pool. Click Next.

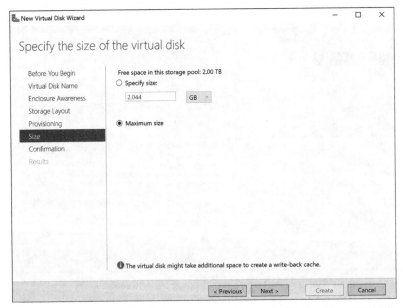

FIGURE 1-22 The Specify The Size Of The Virtual Disk page in the New Virtual Disk Wizard

9. On the Summary page, click Create.

10. Click Close when the process completes.

When the New Virtual Disk Wizard closes, the New Volume Wizard appears. Follow these steps to create a volume:

1. Click Next to skip past the first page of the wizard.

2. On the Server And Disk Selection page, select the disk you just created (Figure 1-23). Click Next.

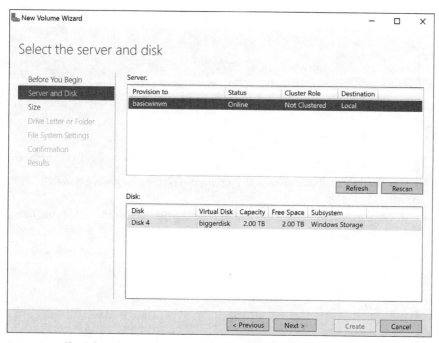

FIGURE 1-23 The Select The Server And Disk page in the New Volume Wizard

3. Leave the volume size set to the maximum value and click Next (Figure 1-24).

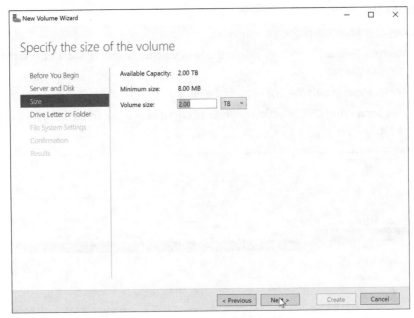

FIGURE 1-24 The Specify The Size Of The Volume page in the New Volume Wizard

4. Leave Assign A Drive Letter selected and select a drive letter to use for your new drive. Click Next (Figure 1-25).

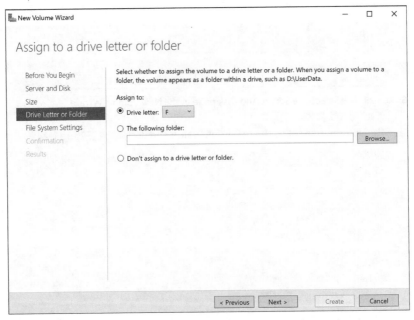

FIGURE 1-25 The Assign To A Drive Letter Or Folder in the New Volume Wizard

5. Provide a name for the new volume, and click Next (Figure 1-26).

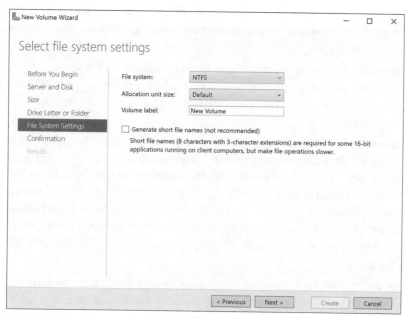

FIGURE 1-26 The Select File System Settings in the New Volume Wizard

6. Click Create.

7. When the process completes, click Close.

8. Open Windows Explorer to see your new drive listed.

Applications running within your VM can use the new drive and benefit from the increased IOPS and total storage capacity that results from having multiple blobs backing your multiple VHDs grouping in a storage pool.

> **MORE INFO   CONFIGURING STRIPED LOGICAL VOLUMES IN LINUX VMS**
>
> Linux Virtual Machines can use the Logical Volume Manager (LVM) to create volumes that span multiple attached data disks, for step by step instructions on doing this for Linux VMs in Azure, see: *https://docs.microsoft.com/en-us/azure/virtual-machines/linux/configure-lvm*.

Configure disk caching

Each disk you attach to a VM has a host cache preference setting for managing a local cache used for read or read/write operations that can improve performance (and even reduce storage transaction costs) in certain situations by averting a read or write to Azure Storage. This local cache does not live within your VM instance; it is external to the VM and resides on the machine hosting your VM. The local cache uses a combination of memory and disk on the host (outside of your control). There are three cache options:

- **None**   No caching is performed.
- **Read Only**   Assuming an empty cache or the desired data is not found in the local cache, reads read from Azure Storage and are then cached in local cache. Writes go directly to Azure Storage.
- **Read/Write**   Assuming an empty cache or the desired data is not found in the local cache, reads read from Azure Storage and are then cached in local cache. Writes go to the local cache and at some later point (determined by algorithms of the local cache) to Azure Storage.

When you create a new VM, the default is set to Read/Write for operating system disks and Read-only for data disks. Operating system disks are limited to read only or read/write, data disks can disable caching using the None option. The reasoning for this is that Azure Storage can provide a higher rate of random I/Os than the local disk used for caching. For predominantly random I/O workloads, therefore, it is best to set the cache to None and let Azure Storage handle the load directly. Because most applications will have predominantly random I/O workloads, the host cache preference is set to None by default for the data disks that would be supporting the applications.

For sequential I/O workloads, however, the local cache will provide some performance improvement and also minimize transaction costs (because the request to storage is averted). Operating system startup sequences are great examples of highly sequential I/O workloads and why the host cache preference is enabled for the operating system disks.

You can configure the host cache preference when you create and attach an empty disk to a VM or change it after the fact.

Configuring disk caching

To configure disk caching using the portal, complete the following steps:

1. Navigate to the blade for your VM in the portal accessed via *https://portal.azure.com.*
2. From the menu, select Disks (Figure 1-27).

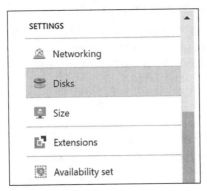

FIGURE 1-27 The Disks option from the VM menu

3. On the Disks blade, select Edit from the command bar.

4. Select the Host Caching drop down for the row representing the disk whose setting you want to alter and select the new value (Figure 1-28).

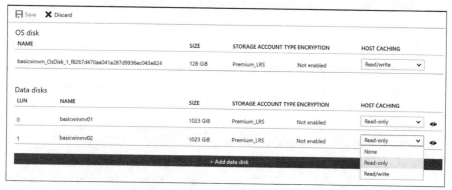

FIGURE 1-28 Data disk dropdown

5. Select Save in the command bar to apply your changes.

Configure geo-replication

With Azure Storage, you can leverage geo-replication for blobs to maintain replicated copies of your VHD blobs in multiple regions around the world in addition to three copies that are maintained within the datacenter. Note that geo-replication is not synchronized across blob files and, therefore, VHD disks. This means writes for a file that is spread across multiple disks, as happens when you use storage pools in Windows VMs or striped logical volumes in Linux VMs, could be replicated out of order. As a result, if you mount the replicated copies to a VM, the disks will almost certainly be corrupt. To avoid this problem, configure the disks to use locally redundant replication, which does not add any additional availability and reduces costs (since geo-replicated storage is more expensive).

Configure shared storage using Azure File storage

If you have ever used a local network on-premises to access files on a remote machine through a Universal Naming Convention (UNC) path like \\server\share, or if you have mapped a drive letter to a network share, you will find Azure File storage familiar.

Azure File storage enables your VMs to access files using a share located within the same region as your VMs. It does not matter if your VMs' data disks are located in a different storage account or even if your share uses a storage account that is within a different Azure subscription than your VMs. As long as your shares are created within the same region as your VMs, those VMs will have access.

Azure File storage provides support for most of the Server Message Block (SMB) 2.1 and 3.0 protocols, which means it supports the common scenarios you might encounter accessing files across the network:

- Supporting applications that rely on file shares for access to data
- Providing access to shared application settings
- Centralizing storage of logs, metrics, and crash dumps
- Storing common tools and utilities needed for development, administration, or setup

Azure File storage is built upon the same underlying infrastructure as Azure Storage, inheriting the same availability, durability, and scalability characteristics.

> **MORE INFO UNSUPPORTED SMB FEATURES**
>
> Azure File storage supports a subset of SMB. Depending on your application needs, some features may preclude your usage of Azure File storage. Notable unsupported features include named pipes and short file names (in the legacy 8.3 alias format, like myfilen~1.txt).
>
> For the complete list of features not supported by Azure File storage, see: *http://msdn. microsoft.com/en-us/library/azure/dn744326.aspx.*

Azure File storage requires an Azure Storage account. Access is controlled with the storage account name and key; therefore, as long as your VMs are in the same region, they can access the share using your storage credentials. Also, while Azure Storage provides support for read-only secondary access to your blobs, this does not enable you to access your shares from the secondary region.

> **MORE INFO NAMING REQUIREMENTS**
>
> Interestingly, while Blob storage is case sensitive, share, directory, and file names are case insensitive but will preserve the case you use. For more information, see: *http://msdn.micro-soft.com/en-us/library/azure/dn167011.aspx.*

Within each Azure Storage account, you can define one or more shares. Each share is an SMB file share. All directories and files must be created within this share, and it can contain an unlimited number of files and directories (limited in depth by the length of the path name and a maximum depth of 250 subdirectories). Note that you cannot create a share below another share. Within the share or any directory below it, each file can be up to one terabyte (the maximum size of a single file in Blob storage), and the maximum capacity of a share is five terabytes. In terms of performance, a share has a maximum of 1,000 IOPS (when measured using 8-KB operations and a throughput of 60 MB/s).

A unique feature of Azure File storage is that you can manage shares, such as to create or delete shares, list shares, get share ETag and LastModified properties, get or set user-defined share metadata key and value pairs. You can get share content, for example list directories and files, create directories and files, get a file, delete a file, get file properties, get or set user-defined metadata, and get or set ranges of bytes within a file. This is accomplished using REST APIs available through endpoints named *https://<accountName>.file.core.windows.net/<shareName>* and through the SMB protocol. In contrast to Azure Storage, Azure File storage only allows you to use a REST API to manage the files. This can prove beneficial to certain application scenarios. For example, it can be helpful if you have a web application (perhaps running in an Azure website) receiving uploads from the browser. Your web application can upload the files through the REST API to the share, but your back-end applications running on a VM can process those files by accessing them using a network share. In situations like this, the REST API will respect any file locks placed on files by clients using the SMB protocol.

> **MORE INFO**   **FILE LOCK INTERACTION BETWEEN SMB AND REST**
>
> If you are curious about how file locking is managed between SMB and REST endpoints for clients interacting with the same file at the same time, the following is a good resource for more information: *https://docs.microsoft.com/en-us/rest/api/storageservices/Managing-File-Locks*.

Creating a file share

The following cmdlet first creates an Azure Storage context, which encapsulates your Storage account name and key, and then uses that context to create the share with the name of your choosing:

```
$ctx = New-AzureStorageContext <Storage-AccountName> <Storage-AccountKey>
New-AzureStorageShare <ShareName> -Context $ctx
```

With a share in place, you can access it from any VM that is in the same region as your share.

Mounting the share

To access the share within a VM, you mount it to your VM. You can mount a share to a VM so that it will remain available indefinitely to the VM, regardless of restarts. The following steps show you how to accomplish this, assuming you are using a Windows Server guest operating system within your VM.

1. Launch Remote Desktop to connect to the VM where you want to mount the share.

2. Open a Windows PowerShell prompt or the command prompt within the VM.

3. So they are available across restarts, add your Azure Storage account credentials to the Windows Credentials Manager using the following command:

   ```
   cmdkey /add:<Storage-AccountName>.file.core.windows.net /user:<Storage-AccountName> /pass:<Storage-AccountKey>
   ```

4. Mount the file share using the stored credentials by using the following command (which you can issue from the Windows PowerShell prompt or a command prompt). Note that you can use any available drive letter (drive Z is typically used).

   ```
   net use z: \\<Storage-AccountName>.file.core.windows.net\<ShareName>
   ```

5. The previous command mounts the share to drive Z, but if the VM is restarted, this share may disappear if net use was not configured for persistent connections (it is enabled for persistent connection by default, but that can be changed). To ensure a persistent share that will survive a restart, use the following command that adds the persistent switch with a value of yes.

```
net use z: \\<Storage-AccountName>.file.core.windows.net\<ShareName>
/Persistent: YES
```

6. To verify that your network share was added (or continues to exist) at any time, run the following command:

```
net use
```

After you mount the share, you can work with its contents as you would work with the contents of any other network drive. Drive Z will show a five-terabyte drive mounted in Windows Explorer.

Accessing files within the share

With a share mounted within a VM, you may next consider how to get your files and folders into that share. There are multiple approaches to this, and you should choose the approach that makes the most sense in your scenario.

- **Remote Desktop (RDP)** If you are running a Windows guest operating system, you can remote desktop into a VM that has access to the share. As a part of configuring your RDP session, you can mount the drives from your local machine so that they are visible using Windows Explorer in the remote session. Then you can copy and paste files between the drives using Windows Explorer in the remote desktop session. Alternately, you can copy files using Windows Explorer on your local machine and then paste them into the share within Windows Explorer running in the RDP session.

- **AZCopy** Using AZCopy, you can recursively upload directories and files to a share from your local machine to the remote share, as well as download from the share to your local machine. For examples of how to do this, see: *http://blogs.msdn.com/b/windowsazurestorage/archive/2014/05/12/introducing-microsoft-azure-file-service.aspx*.

- **Azure PowerShell** You can use the Azure PowerShell cmdlets to upload or download a single file at a time. You use Set-AzureStorageFileContent (*https://docs.microsoft.com/powershell/module/azure.storage/set-azurestoragefilecontent*) and Get-AzureStorageFileContent (*https://docs.microsoft.com/powershell/module/azure.storage/get-azurestoragefilecontent*) to upload and download, respectively.

- **Storage Client Library** If you are writing an application in .NET, you can use the Azure Storage Client Library, which provides a convenience layer atop the REST APIs. You will find all the classes you need below the Microsoft.WindowsAzure.Storage.File namespace, primarily using the CloudFileDirectory and CloudFile classes to access directories and file content within the share. For an example of using these classes see *https://docs.microsoft.com/azure/storage/storage-dotnet-how-to-use-files*.

- **REST APIs** If you prefer to communicate directly using any client that can perform REST style requests, you can use REST API. The reference documentation for REST APIs is available at *https://docs.microsoft.com/en-us/rest/api/storageservices/File-Service-REST-API*.

Implement ARM VMs with Standard and Premium Storage

As previously introduced, you can create ARM VMs that use either Standard or Premium Storage.

Implement ARM VMs with Standard and Premium Storage using the Portal

The following steps describe how to create a Windows Server based Virtual Machine using the Portal and configure it to use either Standard or Premium disks (the steps are similar for a Linux based VM):

1. Navigate to the portal accessed via *https://portal.azure.com*.
2. Select New on the command bar.
3. Within the Marketplace list, select the Compute option.
4. On the Compute blade, select the image for the version of Windows Server you want for your VM (such as Windows Server 2016).
5. On the Basics blade, provide a name for your VM.
6. Select the VM disk type- a VM disk type of SSD will use Premium Storage and a type of HDD will use Standard Storage.
7. Provide a user name and password, and choose the subscription, resource group and location into which you want to deploy.
8. Select OK.
9. On the Choose a size blade, select the desired tier and size for your VM.
10. Choose select.
11. On the Settings blade, leave the settings at their defaults and select OK.
12. On the Purchase blade, review the summary and select Purchase to deploy the VM.

Implement Azure Disk Encryption for Windows and Linux ARM VMs

Azure supports two different kinds of encryption that can be applied to the disks attached to a Windows or Linux VM. The first kind of encryption is Azure Storage Service Encryption (SSE) which transparently encrypts data on write to Azure Storage, and decrypts data on read from Azure Storage. The storage service itself performs the encryption/decryption using keys that are managed by Microsoft. The second kind of encryption is Azure Disk Encryption (ADE). With ADE, Windows drives are encrypted with using BitLocker and Linux drives are encrypted with DM-Crypt. The primary benefit of ADE is that the keys used for encryption are under your control, and managed by an instance of Azure Key Vault that only you have access to.

Implement Azure Disk Encryption for Windows and Linux ARM VMs using PowerShell

Currently, the only way to enable Azure Disk Encryption is by using PowerShell and targeting your deployed VM. To enable ADE on your Windows or Linux ARM VM, follow these steps:

1. Deploy an instance of Azure Key Vault, if you do not have one already. Key Vault must be deployed in the same region as the VMs you will encrypt. For instructions on deploying and configuring your Key Vault, see: *https://docs.microsoft.com/azure/key-vault/key-vault-get-started*.

2. Create an Azure Active Directory application that has permissions to write secrets to the Key Vault, and acquire the Client ID and Client Secret for that application. For detailed instructions on this, see: *https://docs.microsoft.com/en-us/azure/key-vault/key-vault-get-started#register*.

3. With your VM deployed, Key Vault deployed and Client ID and Secret in hand, you are ready to encrypt your VM by running the following PowerShell.

```
# Login to your subscription
Login-AzureRmAccount

# Select the subscription to work within
Select-AzureRmSubscription -SubscriptionName "<subscription name>"

# Identify the VM you want to encrypt by name and resource group name
$rgName = '<resourceGroupName>';
$vmName = '<vmname>';

# Provide the Client ID and Client Secret
$aadClientID = <aad-client-id>;
$aadClientSecret = <aad-client-secret>;

# Get a reference to your Key Vault and capture its URL and Resource ID
$KeyVaultName = '<keyVaultName>';
$KeyVault = Get-AzureRmKeyVault -VaultName $KeyVaultName -ResourceGroupName
  $rgname;
$diskEncryptionKeyVaultUrl = $KeyVault.VaultUri;
$KeyVaultResourceId = $KeyVault.ResourceId;
```

```
# Enable Azure to access the secrets in your Key Vault to boot the encrypted VM.
Set-AzureRmKeyVaultAccessPolicy -VaultName $KeyVaultName -ResourceGroupName
$rgname -
EnabledForDiskEncryption

# Encrypt the VM
Set-AzureRmVMDiskEncryptionExtension -ResourceGroupName $rgname -VMName $vmName -
AadClientID $aadClientID -AadClientSecret $aadClientSecret -
DiskEncryptionKeyVaultUrl
$diskEncryptionKeyVaultUrl -DiskEncryptionKeyVaultId $KeyVaultResourceId;
```

You can later verify the encryption status by running:

```
Get-AzureRmVmDiskEncryptionStatus  -ResourceGroupName $rgname -VMName $vmName
```

The output "OsVolumeEncrypted: True" means the OS disk was encrypted and "DataVolumesEncrypted: True" means the data disks were encrypted.

> **MORE INFO** **ENABLING ENCRYPTION WITH THE AZURE CLI**
>
> For a step by step guide on enabling encryption using the Azure CLI *https://docs.microsoft.com/azure/security/azure-security-disk-encryption#disk-encryption-deployment-scenarios-and-user-experiences.*

Skill 1.5: Monitor VMs

Monitoring an Azure VM involves collecting and analyzing metrics as well as collecting log data from system log files and from applications running within the VM. You can configure an email alert to an administrator that's triggered when certain criteria involving these metrics is met. With monitoring, you gain insight into the status of your VMs, their resource utilization, their operational health, and diagnostic details that can help you troubleshoot problems.

> **This skill covers how to:**
> - Configure monitoring and diagnostics for a new VM
> - Configure monitoring and diagnostics for an existing VM
> - Configure alerts
> - Monitor metrics

When you provision a VM, by default you install the Azure Virtual Machine Agent, which installs and manages extensions running within your VM. Both Windows and Linux VMs collect the following metrics at the host level. In other words, no extension needs to be installed to collect them out of the box:

- Disk read, disk write (in terms of KB/s or MB/s)
- CPU percentage
- Network in, network out (in terms of KB/s or MB/s)

Another set of metrics is collected from within the guest operating system by an Azure Diagnostics extension. On Windows guest operating system VMs, the Azure Virtual Machine Agent installs the IaaSDiagnostics extension for collecting monitoring and diagnostic data. On Linux VMs, the Microsoft.Insights.VMDiagnosticsSettings extension provides the same capabilities.

You can enable diagnostics, and when you do, the appropriate diagnostic extension is installed and used to collect additional metrics.

The metrics collected differs for Windows and Linux VMS. For Linux VMs, the metrics data collection includes data from the following groups of performance counter data:

- CPU
- Disk
- Memory
- Network
- Packets
- Page
- Swap

For Windows VMs, the metrics data collection includes data from the following groups of performance counter data:

- CPU
- Disk
- Memory
- Network
- ASP.NET
- SQL Server

The metrics are stored in Azure Storage Tables, which you can view using the Azure Storage tool of your choice, or visualize the data in chart form using the Azure Portal. By default, all of the above metrics are collected every minute as a new row in the table.

For Windows VMs, metric data is written to the WADPerformanceCountersTable, with aggregates of these performance counter metrics aggregated to the minute or to the hour written to tables that start with the name WADMetricsPT1M for by minute and WADMetricsPT1H for by hour.

In addition to metrics, system logs are also collected. For Linux VM's, the Syslog is collected into the LinuxsyslogVer2v0 table. For Windows VMs, all event log entries for the three event logs (application, security and system logs) are written to the WADWindowsEventLogsTable, where the log is indicated by the Channels column in the table, which will have the value System, Security, or Application to indicate the log source.

Windows VMs can collect other types of logs. Diagnostic infrastructure logs (events generated by the Azure Diagnostic Agent, such as issues collecting metrics) are written to the WADDiagnosticInfrastructureLogsTable, and application logs (the trace output from your .NET application running in the VM) are stored in the WADLogsTable. Windows VMs can also collect Event Tracing for Windows Events. These events are collected into the WADETWEventTable.

The Table 1-2 summarizes the Azure Storage tables used for Linux and Windows VMs.

TABLE 1-2 Storage Tables used for VM logs and diagnostics.

Linux	Windows
LinuxCpuVer2v0	WADMetricsPT1M*
LinuxDiskVer2v0	WADMetricsPT1H*
LinuxMemoryVer2v0	WADPerformanceCountersTable
LinuxsyslogVer2v0	WADWindowsEventLogsTable
	WADDiagnosticInfrastructureLogsTable
	WADLogsTable
	WADETWEventTable

*If IIS is installed within the VM, IIS logs can also be collected. The IIS logs (requests and failed request traces) are different from the others in that they are written as blobs to Azure Storage under the wad-iis-logfiles container.

*Windows VMs can be enabled to collect minidumps or full crash dumps for a configured process. The dump file is stored in an Azure Storage container whose name you specify.

One final form of diagnostics that is supported by both Windows and Linux VMs is boot diagnostics. Boot diagnostics captures the serial console output (for Linux VMs) and screenshots (for both Windows and Linux VMs) of the machine running on a host to help diagnose startup issues. The log file and bitmap (*.bmp) screenshots for a VM with the name vmname are stored in Azure Storage container named with the prefix bootdiagnostics-vmname.

Configure monitoring and diagnostics for a new VM

You can enable monitoring and diagnostics when deploying a VM. To configure monitoring diagnostics using the portal, complete the following steps:

1. Navigate to the portal accessed via *https://portal.azure.com*.

2. Select New on the command bar.

3. Within the Marketplace list, select the Compute option.

4. On the Compute blade, select the image for the version of Windows Server or Linux you want for your VM

5. On the Basics blade, provide a name for your VM.

6. Select the VM disk type, which is either a VM disk type of SSD that will use Premium Storage or a type of HDD that will use Standard Storage.

7. Provide a user name and password (or SSH public key), and choose the subscription, resource group, and location into which you want to deploy.

8. Select OK.

9. On the Choose a size blade, select the desired tier and size for your VM.

10. Choose select.

11. On the Settings blade, under the Monitoring header, enable Boot diagnostics by setting the toggle to Enabled.

12. Similarly, enable diagnostics by setting the Guest OS diagnostics toggle to Enabled.

13. Optionally, configure the name of the new Storage Account to use to store the diagnostics or choose an existing Storage Account (Figure 1-29).

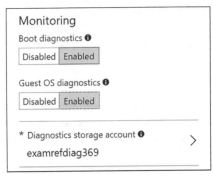

FIGURE 1-29 Monitoring are of the Settings blade

14. Select OK.

15. On the Purchase blade, review the summary and select Purchase to deploy the VM.

Configure monitoring and diagnostics for an existing VM

To enable and configure monitoring and diagnostics for an existing VM, complete the following steps:

1. Navigate to the blade for your VM in the Azure Portal.

2. From the menu, scroll down to the Monitoring section (Figure 1-30) and select Diagnostic settings.

FIGURE 1-30 The Monitoring section

3. For Linux VMs, enable diagnostics by setting the Status toggle to On and selecting Save in the command bar (Figure 1-31).

FIGURE 1-31 Linux VM toggling enable diagnostics

4. For Windows VMs, you have more granular options:

   A. On the Overview tab, select Enable guest-level monitoring (Figure 1-32).

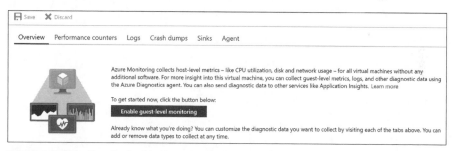

FIGURE 1-32 Selecting the Enable Guest-Level Monitoring button

   B. To adjust the Performance Counters collected, select the Performance Counters tab, then select either Basic (to view a summarized list of counters) or Custom (to view the complete list of available counters). When using the Custom view, you can also set the sample rate, which defaults to every minute. Select the desired counters by checking the box next to each (Figure 1-33).

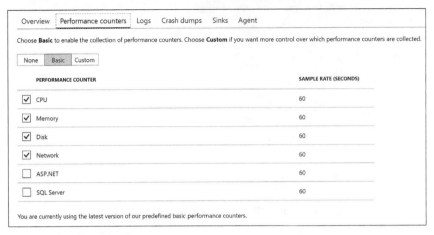

FIGURE 1-33 Performance Counters

C. To adjust the collected Event Logs, IIS Logs, and Application Logs, select the Logs tab. For Event Logs, select the Basic toggle to collect the default set of Event Logs or select Custom to specify specific event logs and levels to collect. For IIS Logs, select the desired logs and specify the path the Azure Storage container name in which to store them. For Application Logs, select the Enabled toggle and then select the desired Log level. For Event Tracing for Windows events, set the toggle to Enabled and configure the desired event sources by entering a provider class and log level. Configure the event manifests by entering the manifest GUID and log level (Figure 1-34).

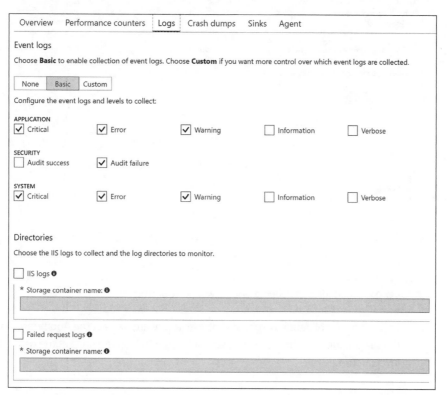

FIGURE 1-34 Configuring Logs for VM

D. To enable a collection of crash dumps, select the Crash Dumps tab and then set the toggle to Enabled. Enter the name of the process to monitor and select Add. Enter the name of the Azure Storage container to use in storing the dump, and select whether to capture a full dump or a minidump (Figure 1-35).

FIGURE 1-35 Configuring crash dumps for the w3wp.exe process

E. To enable the collection diagnostic infrastructure logs, select the Agent tab. Under the Diagnostic infrastructure logs, set the toggle to Enabled and set the desired log level (Figure 1-36).

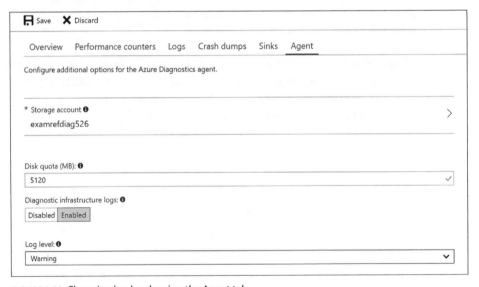

FIGURE 1-36 Changing log levels using the Agent tab

5. Select Save in the command bar to apply the new settings.

Configure alerts

After your VM is configured to collect metrics, you can configure alert rules that can send an email, invoke a Webhook, run an Azure Automation runbook, or run a Logic App when certain conditions relative to a metric are met. Additionally, you can configure alert rules on logs that can trigger an email, an SMS message, or a Webhook when a particular log event is encountered.

Configuring alerts

To configure alerts using the portal, complete the following steps:

1. Navigate to the blade for your VM in the Azure Portal.

2. In the Menu, scroll down to the Monitoring group and select Alert rules.

3. On the Alert Rules blade, select Add metric alert to specify an alert rule that triggers based upon a metric. Provide a name for the rule, select the metric source, specify the condition, and then select the desired action to take when the condition is met.

4. Select Add Activity Log Alert to specify an alert rule that triggers based upon an event appearing in the activity log. Provide a name for the rule, specify the criteria that described the desired event, provide an action group name and short name, and then select the desired action to take when the event is matched.

5. Click OK to create the new rule.

Monitor metrics

You can assess the status and health of your VM by viewing its metrics in the portal, by querying table storage for diagnostic logs, or by downloading IIS logs from Azure Storage.

Monitoring metrics

Using the portal you can drill into charts and change the metrics displayed in detail by completing the following steps:

1. Navigate to the blade for your VM in the Portal.

2. From the menu, scroll down to the Monitoring group and select Metrics.

3. Select from the desired metrics from the list of available host and guest OS metrics.

4. The charts will update to display the desired metrics (Figure 1-37).

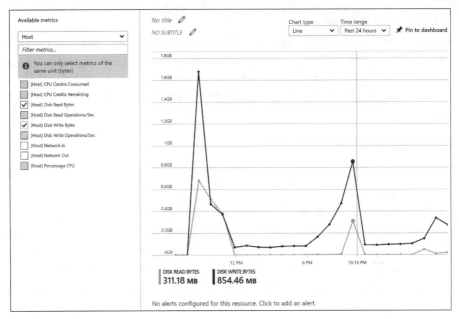

FIGURE 1-37 Selecting Disk Read Bytes and Disk Write Bytes metrics

5. Use the Chart type drop down to change the visualization used and the Time range drop down to adjust the time period over which the metric is displayed (Figure 1-38).

FIGURE 1-38 The Line Chart Type

Viewing event logs, diagnostic infrastructure logs, and application logs

You can view Windows event logs, the diagnostic infrastructure logs, and application logs by querying their respective tables (WADWindowsEventLogsTable, WADDiagnosticInfrastructure-LogsTable, WADLogsTable) in Table storage using the tool of your choice. The following steps demonstrate how to do this using Visual Studio.

1. Launch Visual Studio.

2. On the View menu, click Server Explorer.

3. Expand the node labeled Azure. If prompted to do so, log in with your organizational account or the Microsoft account that is associated with the website you want to manage.

4. Expand Storage.

5. Expand the storage account containing the logs.

6. Expand Tables.

7. Right-click the table you want to query and select View Table to display its contents.

Viewing IIS logs

IIS logs can be retrieved from Blob storage using the tool of your choice. The following steps show how to do this using Visual Studio.

1. Launch Visual Studio.

2. On the View menu, click Server Explorer.

3. Expand the node labeled Azure. If prompted to do so, log in with your organizational account or the Microsoft account that is associated with the website you want to manage.

4. Expand Storage.

5. Expand Blobs.

6. Right-click wad-iis-logs and select View Blob Container to display its contents. Each log is listed, so double-click a log to download and open it.

Viewing boot diagnostics

The collected boot diagnostic logs or screenshot can be viewed using the Azure Portal.

1. Navigate to the blade for your VM in the Azure Portal.

2. From the menu, scroll down to then Support + Troubleshooting section and select Boot diagnostics.

3. For Linux VM's the log will be displayed by default. From the command bar, use the Log button to download the log file or the Screenshot button to download the latest screenshot bitmap. For Windows VM's, the latest screenshot will be displayed. Use the Screenshot button in the command bar to download a copy of the screenshot.

Skill 1.6: Manage ARM VM Availability

For an application running in Azure to remain highly available, it should run across multiple identical Virtual Machines so that the overall availability of the application is not affected when a small subset of the Virtual Machines are unavailable due to events like updates, networking failures and power failures. The actual approach to achieving this requires the proper configuration of availability sets and may require the use of the Azure Load Balancer.

> **This skill covers how to:**
> - Configure availability sets
> - Combine the Load Balancer with availability sets

Configure availability sets

Availability sets enable you to improve the availability of VMs deployed to your cloud service by identifying to Azure a group of VMs that should never be brought down simultaneously during updates and that should be physically separated (that is, connected to a separate power source and network switch) so that the failure of a host does not cause all of the VMs in that group to fail. In other words, an availability set does what it says, it describes a set of VMs that Azure will respect to ensure that the service provided by the VMs remains available because at no point in time should all VMs in the set be offline.

By defining an availability set, you constrain how Azure locates your VM in update and fault domains.

Update domains

An update domain constrains how Azure performs updates to the underlying host machine that is running your VM. VMs located in separate update domains will never experience an update (or a restart of the host machine) at the same time. Azure uses five update domains by default in which it places your VMs in a round-robin process. When you add VMs to an availability set, Azure places the first five VMs in separate update domains, then continues to distribute additional VMs across update domains in a round-robin fashion, assigning the sixth VM to the first update domain, the seventh VM to the second update domain, and so on until all VMs have been assigned to one of the five update domains. The constraint on update domains is that Azure will never bring down more than one update domain at a time, effectively ensuring that when Azure updates the host machines, never more than 50 percent of your VMs will be affected (assuming you have two VMs) or, if you are filling all update domains, 20 percent (assuming you have five or more VMs).

Fault domains

Whereas update domains apply to the roll out of host machine updates, fault domains consider isolation in terms of power and network. When two VMs are placed in separate fault domains, they will never be located such that they share the power source or network switch, which basically means that they will not be on the same host machine or even on the same server rack as one another. When you add VMs to an availability set, they are distributed between by default between two fault domains in round-robin fashion.

In short, the strategic placement of your VMs across update and fault domains is controlled simply by their membership in an availability set.

Availability sets and application tiers

For multi-tier applications (such as those having separate front-end, middle, and back-end tiers), it is a best practice to place all the VMs belonging to a single tier in a single availability set and to have separate availability sets for each application tier. This helps ensure that at no point are all instances for a particular tier in the solution down and, therefore, that the complete solution across all tiers is available.

Configuring availability sets

There are multiples ways to define an availability set and to configure the VMs that belong to it. When you are creating a new VM, you can create a new availability set and add the VM to it, or you can specify an existing availability set and add the new VM to it. The same options exist if you have an existing VM.

Configuring an availability set for a new ARM VM

To create a new VM and associate it with an availability group, complete the following steps:

1. Navigate to the portal accessed via *https://portal.azure.com*.

2. Select New on the command bar.

3. Within the Marketplace list, select the Compute option.

4. On the Compute blade, select the image for the version of Windows Server or Linux you want for your VM.

5. On the Basics blade, provide a name for your VM.

6. Select the VM disk type: a VM disk type of SSD will use Premium Storage and a type of HDD will use Standard Storage.

7. Provide a user name and password (or SSH public key), and choose the subscription, resource group and location into which you want to deploy.

8. Select OK.

9. On the Choose a size blade, select the desired tier and size for your VM.

10. Choose select.

11. On the Settings blade, under the High availability header, select Availability set (Figure 1-39).

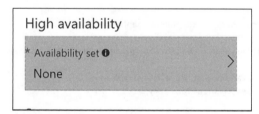

FIGURE 1-39 High Availability Set

12. Choose an existing Availability Set (Figure 1-40), or select the Create new option to define a new availability set. When defining a new availability set, provide a name for the availability set, the desired number of fault domains (between 1 and 3), the number of update domains (between 1 and 20).

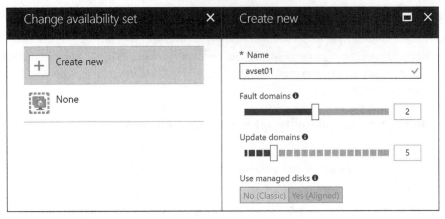

FIGURE 1-40 Create New option

13. Select OK.

14. Select OK once more.

15. On the Purchase blade, review the summary and select Purchase to deploy the VM.

Configuring an availability set for an existing ARM VM

Once a VM has been deployed, you cannot alter the availability set to which it belongs. The availability set can only be configured when creating a virtual machine. You must recreate the virtual machine to move it in or out of an availability set.

Configuring an availability set using Windows PowerShell

An availability set can be created using Windows PowerShell only during the process of creating a new VM:

```
New-AzureRmAvailabilitySet -ResourceGroupName "<ResourceGroupName>"
    -Name "<AvailabilitySetName>" -Location "<Location>"
$AvailabilitySet = Get-AzureRmAvailabilitySet -ResourceGroupName "<ResourceGroupName>"
    -Name "<AvailabilitySetName>"
$VirtualMachine = New-AzureRmVMConfig -VMName "<VirtualMachineName>"
    -VMSize "<VM_Size>" -AvailabilitySetID $AvailabilitySet.Id
```

After the preceding command, use the following cmdlet to provision and start the VM:

```
Start-AzureRmVM -ResourceGroupName "<ResourceGroupName>"
    -Name "<VirtualMachineName>"
```

Combine the Load Balancer with availability sets

The Azure Load Balancer enables you to distribute traffic entering from either a public IP address or from an internal IP to the collection of VMs in an availability set in a round robin manner. It can also automatically remove non-responsive VMs from rotation so that they are not routed traffic when they are unavailable.

Configuring a Load Balancer for VMs in an Availability Set

Once you have deployed your VMs in an availability set, you can perform load balancing between them by performing the following steps:

1. In the Azure Portal, select New and search for Load Balancer and select the Load Balancer entry.

2. On the Load Balancer select Create.

3. On the Create a Load Balancer, provide a name for the new load balancer.

4. If you want to load balance traffic from the public Internet:

5. For the type, select Public.

6. Select Public IP address and select an existing Public IP or create a new one. If you create a new Public IP, provide a name for the Public IP and select if it should have a dynamically assigned IP or a statically assigned IP by setting the Assignment toggle to Dynamic or Static respectively (Figure 1-41).

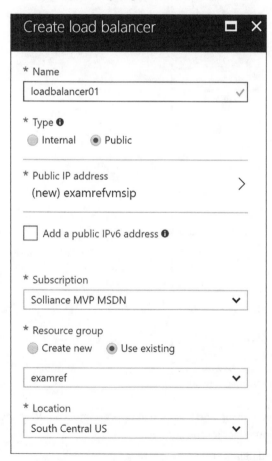

FIGURE 1-41 Create Load Balancer

7. If you want to load balance traffic only within your Virtual Network:

8. For the type, select Internal.

9. Select Virtual network and choose an existing Virtual Network.

10. Select Subnet and choose a subnet within the Virtual Network.

11. Select if the Load Balancer (Figure 1-42) should have a dynamically assigned IP or a statically assigned IP by setting the IP address assignment toggle to Dynamic or Static respectively.

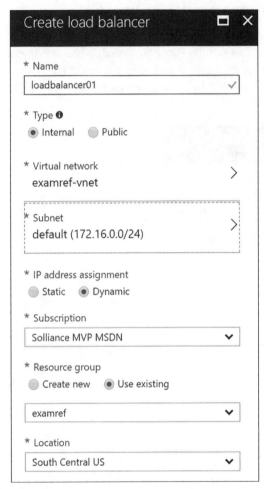

FIGURE 1-42 Load Balancer within a Virtual Network

12. Select the Subscription, Resource Group and Location as appropriate. Your VMs should exist in the same Location as you select for the Load Balancer.

13. Select create to deploy the Load Balancer.

14. When your Load Balancer is deployed, navigate to it in the Azure Portal.

15. From the menu, under the Settings header, select Backend Pools (Figure 1-43).

16. Select +Add.

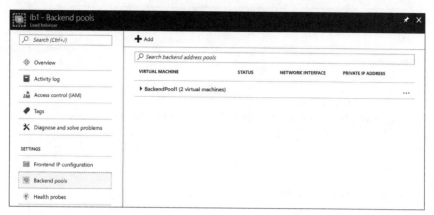

FIGURE 1-43 Backend Pools

17. On the Add backend pool blade, provide a name for the new Backend pool, and in the Associated to dropdown list, select Availability Set.

18. In the dropdown that appears, select the Availability Set that contains your VMs to load balance.

19. For each VM that you want to add to backend pool, perform the following:

20. Select +Add target network IP configuration.

21. Select the VM from the Target virtual machine dropdown.

22. Select the IP configuration for the VM from the Network IP configuration dropdown.

23. Select OK (Figure 1-44).

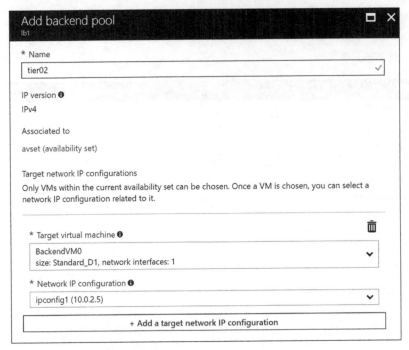

FIGURE 1-44 Add Backend Pool

24. From the menu, under the Setting header, select Health probes.

25. Select +Add.

26. Provide a name for the health probe (Figure 1-45).

27. Choose protocol (either HTTP or TCP).

28. Provide the Port that the probe will use in testing the VMs availability.

29. If you chose the HTTP protocol, also specify the path on the HTTP endpoint to use when probing the VMs availability.

30. Specify an interval in seconds between probe attempts in the Interval field.

31. In the Unhealthy threshold, specify the number of consecutive probe failures that must occur before the VM is considered unhealthy.

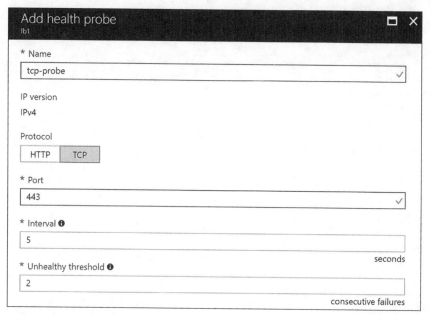

FIGURE 1-45 Add Health Probe

32. Select OK.

33. From the menu, under the Setting header, select Load balancing rules.

34. Select +Add.

35. On the Add load balancing rule, provide a name.

36. Set the protocol to TCP or UDP as desired.

37. Specify the Port for incoming traffic.

38. Specify the Backend port used when communicating with the VMs.

39. From the Backend pool dropdown, select the pool your previously created.

40. From the Health probe dropdown, select the health probe you previously created (Figure 1-46).

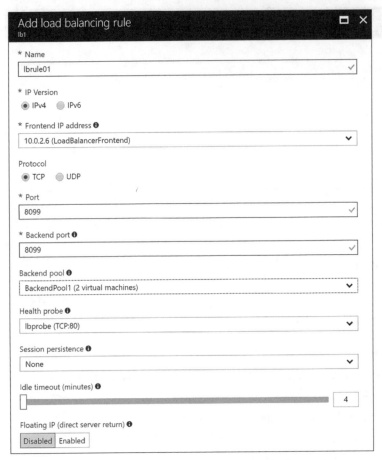

FIGURE 1-46 Add Load Balancing Rule

41. Select OK to apply load balancing rule.

> **MORE INFO** **CONFIGURING A LOAD BALANCED DEPLOYMENT WITH POWERSHELL**
>
> For a step by step guide on performing the previous steps using PowerShell, see: *https://docs.microsoft.com/en-us/azure/virtual-machines/windows/tutorial-load-balancer.*

Skill 1.7: Design and implement DevTest Labs

Azure DevTest Labs is a service designed to help developers and testers quickly spin up virtual machines (VMs) or complete environments in Azure, enabling rapid deployment and testing of applications. This allows you to easily spin up and tear down development and test resources, minimizing waste and providing better control cost. You can test the latest version of your application by quickly provisioning environments using reusable templates and artifacts, integrate it with your deployment pipeline, or create pre-provisioned environments for training and demos.

This skill covers how to:

- Create and manage custom images and formulas
- Configure a lab to include policies and procedures
- Configure cost management
- Secure access to labs
- Use environments in a lab

Create a lab

To get started, complete the following steps to create a lab:

1. Navigate to the Azure portal, accessed via *https://portal.azure.com*.

2. From the main menu on the left side, select More services (at the bottom of the list), and then select DevTest Labs (Figure 1-47) from the list of available services.

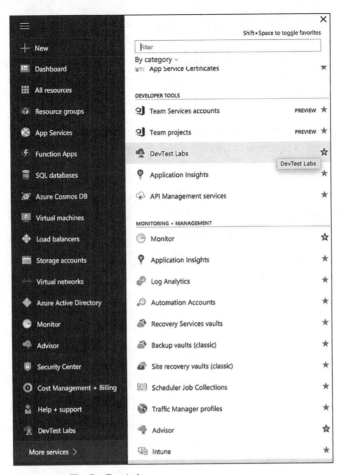

FIGURE 1-47 The DevTest Labs

3. In the DevTest Labs blade, select +Add (Figure 1-48).

FIGURE 1-48 Add a new DevTest Labs

4. On the Create a DevTest Lab blade:

   A. Enter a Lab Name for the new lab.

   B. Select the Subscription to associate with the lab.

   C. Select a Location in which to store the lab.

   D. Select Auto-shutdown to specify if you want to enable, and define parameters for, the automatic shutting down of all of the lab's VMs. The auto-shutdown feature is mainly a cost-saving feature whereby you can specify when you want the VMs to automatically be shut down. You can change auto-shutdown settings after creating the lab by following the steps outlined in the Auto-shutdown section below.

   E. Enter NAME and VALUE information for Tags if you want to create custom tagging that is added to every resource you will create in the lab. Tags are useful to help you manage and organize lab resources by category.

   F. Select Create (Figure 1-49).

FIGURE 1-49 The Create A DevTest Lab blade

The deployment of a DevTest lab creates a new resource group. Within that resource group, you will find the following resources:

- The DevTest Lab instance
- A Key vault instance
- A Storage account
- A Virtual network

Add a VM to a lab

Upon initially accessing your DevTest Lab, you will want to create your first VM. This can be accomplished using a custom image or formula, or by using a pre-loaded base Marketplace image. This section focuses on the latter, and defers coverage of using custom images and formulas to the Create and manage custom images and formulas section.

1. Navigate to the blade for your DevTest Lab in the Azure portal.

2. On the lab's Overview blade, select +Add (Figure 1-50).

FIGURE 1-50 A New VM to DevTest Lab

3. On the Choose a base blade, select a base image for the VM.

4. On the Virtual Machine blade:

    A. Enter a name for the new VM in the Virtual Machine Name text box.

    B. Enter a User Name that is granted administrator privileges on the VM.

    C. Enter a password in the text field labeled Type a value. We will cover the Use a saved secret check box in the Secure access to your lab section below.

    D. The Virtual machine disk type determines which storage disk type is allowed for the VMs in the lab. Select Hard Drive Disks (HDD) or Solid-State Drives (SSD).

    E. Select Virtual machine size, and select one of the predefined items that specify the processor cores, RAM size, and the hard drive size of the VM to create.

    F. Select Artifacts and, from the list of artifacts, select and configure the artifacts that you want to add to the base image.

    G. Select Advanced settings to configure the VM's Network options, expiration policy, and Claim options. Set Make this machine claimable to Yes if you want the machine to be claimable by lab users.

    H. Select Create to add the new VM to the lab (Figure 1-51).

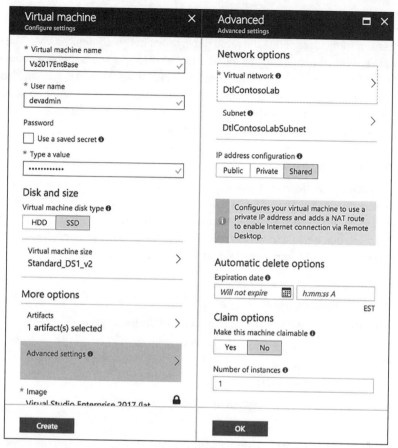

FIGURE 1-51 Virtual Maching and Advanced settings

When a VM is created, ownership is assigned to either you (the creator), or it can be made claimable. Claimable VMs are unassigned, and can be claimed by lab user. To make a VM claimable you can select Yes under Make this machine claimable on the Advanced settings blade during the VM creation process. It is also possible to make a VM you own claimable, by selecting Unclaim from the VM's overview blade (Figure 1-52).

FIGURE 1-52 Unclaiming a VM

Unclaiming a VM will result in it being moved from your My Virtual Machines section to the Claimable Virtual Machines section on the lab's blade.

Create and manage custom images and formulas

Custom images and formulas facilitate the rapid deployment of pre-configured VMs. The key difference between custom images and formulas is that a custom image is simply an image based on a VHD, while a formula is an image based on a VHD in addition to preconfigured settings, such as VM size, virtual network, subnet, and artifacts. These preconfigured settings are set up with default values that can be overridden at the time of VM creation. Both custom images and formulas can be used as bases for creating new VMs.

Creating custom images

Custom images provide a static, immutable way to create VMs from a desired configuration. They allow you to pre-install all the software that you need in a Virtual Hard Disk (VHD) file, and then use that VHD file to create a VM. Because the software is already installed, the VM creation time is much quicker. In addition, custom images can be used to clone VMs by creating a custom image from a VM, and then creating VMs based on that custom image.

> **Pros of using custom images:**
>
> - VM provisioning is fast as nothing changes after the VM is spun up from the image.
> - VMs created from a single custom image are identical.
>
> **Cons of using custom images:**
>
> - If you need to update any aspect of the custom image, the image must be recreated.

There are several ways to create a custom image in Azure DevTest Labs. You can create an image from an existing VM, or create on from a VHD, using either the Azure portal or PowerShell. Before creating a custom image from a VHD, the VHD needs to be uploaded to the storage account associated with the lab in which you are creating the custom image.

Create a custom image from a provisioned virtual machine

To create a custom image from a provisioned VM, following these steps:

1. Navigate to the blade of your DevTest Labs instance.
2. On your lab's blade, select All virtual machines (Figure 1-53).

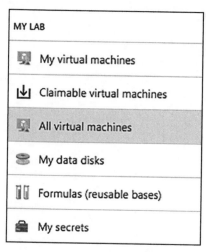

FIGURE 1-53 List of VMs in the Lab

3. On the All virtual machines blade, select the VM from which you want to create the custom image.

4. On the VM's blade, select Create custom image (Figure 1-54).

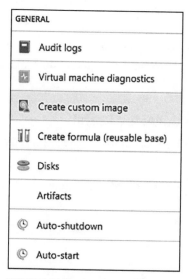

FIGURE 1-54 Custom image from a VM

5. On the Custom image blade (Figure 1-55), enter a name and description for your custom image. This information is displayed in the list of bases when you create a VM.

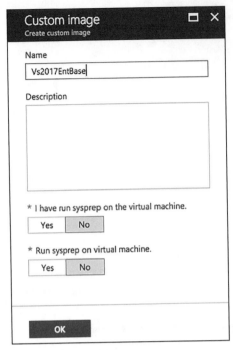

FIGURE 1-55 Custom Image

6. Select whether sysprep was run on the VM. If the sysprep was not run on the VM, specify whether you want sysprep run when a VM is created from this custom image.

7. Select OK when finished to create the custom image.

Create a custom image from a VHD using the Azure Portal

To create a custom image from a VHD using the Azure portal, complete the following steps:

1. Navigate to the blade of your DevTest Labs instance.

2. From your lab's Configuration and policies blade, select Custom images (Figure 1-56).

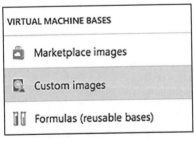

FIGURE 1-56 Custom images in the Lab

3. On the Custom images blade, select +Add (Figure 1-57).

FIGURE 1-57 New Custom image

4. Enter the name of the custom image. This will be displayed in the list of base images when creating a VM.

5. Enter a description for the custom image. This will be displayed in the list base images.

6. Select an OS Type – Windows or Linux.

7. If Windows is selected as the OS Type, select whether sysprep has been run on the VHD image.

8. Select a VHD image.

9. Select OK to create the custom image (Figure 1-58).

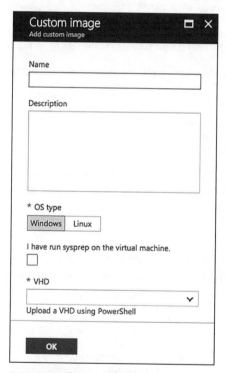

FIGURE 1-58 Custom VHD image

Create a custom image from a VHD using PowerShell

To create a custom image from a VHD using PowerShell, complete these steps:

1. At a PowerShell prompt, log into your Azure account with the following call to the Login-AzureRmAccount cmdlet.

   ```
   Login-AzureRmAccount
   ```

2. Select the desired Azure subscription by calling the Select-AzureRmSubscription cmdlet. Replace the placeholder for $subscriptionId variable with a valid Azure subscription ID.

   ```
   $subscriptionId = '<Specify your subscription ID here>'
   Select-AzureRmSubscription -SubscriptionId $subscriptionId
   ```

3. Get the lab object by calling the Get-AzureRmResource cmdlet. Replace the following placeholders for the $labRg and $labName variables with the appropriate values for your environment.

   ```
   $labRg = '<Specify your lab resource group name here>'
   $labName = '<Specify your lab name here>'
   $lab = Get-AzureRmResource -ResourceId ('/subscriptions/' + $subscriptionId +
   '/resourceGroups/' + $labRg + '/providers/Microsoft.DevTestLab/labs/' + $labName)
   ```

4. Get the lab storage account and lab storage account key values from the lab object.

   ```
   $labStorageAccount = Get-AzureRmResource -ResourceId
   $lab.Properties.defaultStorageAccount
   $labStorageAccountKey = (Get-AzureRmStorageAccountKey -ResourceGroupName
   $labStorageAccount.ResourceGroupName -Name
   $labStorageAccount.ResourceName)[0].Value
   ```

5. Replace the following placeholder for the $vhdUri variable with the URI to your up-loaded VHD file. You can get the VHD file's URI from the storage account's blob blade in the Azure portal.

   ```
   $vhdUri = '<Specify the VHD URI here>'
   ```

6. Create the custom image using the New-AzureRmResourceGroupDeployment cmdlet. Replace the following placeholders for the $customImageName and $customImageDe-scription variables to meaningful names for your environment.

   ```
   $customImageName = '<Specify the custom image name>'
   $customImageDescription = '<Specify the custom image description>'

   $parameters = @{existingLabName="$($lab.Name)"; existingVhdUri=$vhdUri;
   imageOsType='windows'; isVhdSysPrepped=$false; imageName=$customImageName;
   imageDescription=$customImageDescription}

   New-AzureRmResourceGroupDeployment -ResourceGroupName $lab.ResourceGroupName
   -Name CreateCustomImage -TemplateUri 'https://raw.githubusercontent.com/
   Azure/azure-devtestlab/master/Samples/201-dtl-create-customimage-from
   -vhd/azuredeploy.json' -TemplateParameterObject $parameters
   ```

Delete a custom image

You may find that there are times when an image is no longer needed, and should be removed from your lab. To delete a custom image, complete the following steps:

1. Navigate to the blade of your DevTest Labs instance.
2. On the lab's Overview blade, select Custom images.
3. On the Custom images blade, select the ellipsis to the right of the custom image you wish to delete, then select Delete on the context menu (Figure 1-59).

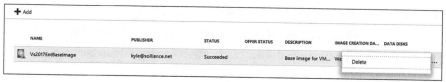

FIGURE 1-59 Deleting an image

4. Select Yes to the deletion confirmation dialog.

Creating formulas

Formulas are lists of default property values, providing a dynamic way to create VMs from a desired configuration. When creating a VM from a formula, the default values can be used as-is, or modified. Like custom and Marketplace images, formulas provide a mechanism for fast VM provisioning. Like custom images, they enable you to create a base image from a VHD file. The base image can then be used to provision a new VM.

> **Pros of using formulas**
>
> - Changes in the environment can be captured on the fly via artifacts. For example, if you want a VM installed with the latest bits from your release pipeline, you can specify an artifact that deploys the latest bits or enlists the latest code in the formula together with a target base image. Whenever this formula is used to create VMs, the latest bits/code are deployed/enlisted to the VM.
> - Formulas can define default settings that custom images cannot provide.
> - The settings saved in a formula are default values, and can be modified when the VM is created.
>
> **Cons of using formulas**
>
> - Creating a VM from a formula can take more time than creating a VM from a custom image

Anyone in the DevTest Labs User role can create VMs using a formula as a base. There are two ways to create formulas:

- From a base (custom image, Marketplace image, or another formula)—Use when you want to define all the characteristics of the formula.

- From an existing lab VM—Use when you want to create a formula based on the settings of an existing VM.

Create a formula from a base

The following steps outline the process of creating a formula for a custom image, Marketplace image, or another formula.

1. Navigate to the blade of your DevTest Labs instance.

2. From your lab's blade, select Configuration and policies (Figure 1-60).

3. On the Configuration and policies blade, select Formulas (reusable bases).

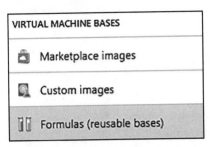

FIGURE 1-60 Navigating to formulas

4. Select +Add on the Configuration and policies – Formulas (reusable bases) blade (Figure 1-61).

FIGURE 1-61 Add new formula

5. On the Choose a base blade, select an image to use for the formula.

6. On the Create formula blade:

   A. Enter a name for the formula into the Formula name text box. This value is displayed in the list of base images when you create a VM.

   B. Enter a description for the formula. This value is available from the formula's context menu when you create a VM.

   C. Enter a User name, which will have administrative privileges on the VM.

   D. Enter a password.

   E. Specify either HDD (hard-disk drive) or SSD (solid-state drive) to indicate which storage disk type is allowed for the virtual machines provisioned using this base image.

   F. Select one of the predefined items that specify the processor cores, RAM size, and the hard drive size of the VM to create.

G. Select to open the Add artifacts blade, in which you select and configure the artifacts that you want to add to the base image.

H. Select to open the Advanced blade where you configure the following settings:

- Virtual network - Specify the desired virtual network.

- Subnet - Specify the desired subnet.

- IP address configuration - Specify if you want the Public, Private, or Shared IP addresses. For more information about shared IP addresses, see Understand shared IP addresses in Azure DevTest Labs.

- Make this machine claimable - Making a machine "claimable" means that it will not be assigned ownership at the time of creation. Instead lab users will be able to take ownership ("claim") the machine in the lab's blade.

I. Select Create to create the formula (Figure 1-62).

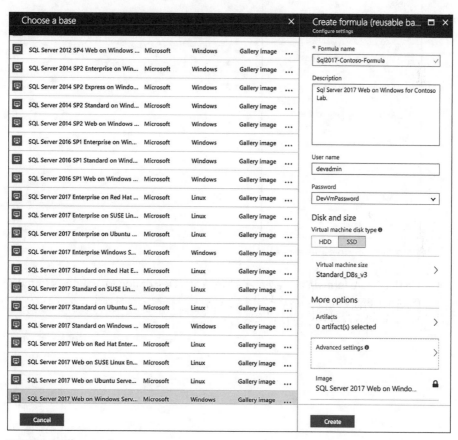

FIGURE 1-62 Choose a base

Create a formula from a VM

To create a formula based on an existing VM, complete the following steps:

1. Navigate to the blade of your DevTest Labs instance.

2. From your lab's Overview blade, select the VM from which you wish to create the formula (Figure 1-63).

Claimable virtual machines				
NAME	STATUS	AUTO-START	AUTO-SHUTDOWN	BASE
Vs2017EntBase	⊘ Available	● No	● No	Visual Studio Enterprise 2017 (latest release) on Windows Server 2016 (x64)

FIGURE 1-63 Claimable Virtual Machines

3. On the VM's blade (Figure 1-64), select Create formula (reusable base).

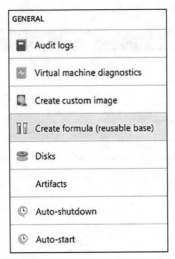

FIGURE 1-64 Custom image for a VM

4. On the Create formula blade, enter a Name and Description for your new formula (Figure 1-65).

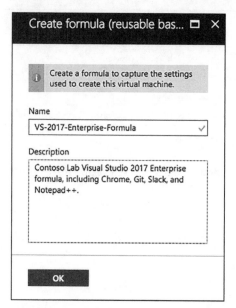

FIGURE 1-65 Create a new formula (reusable base)

5. Select OK to create the formula.

Modify a formula

After creating a formula, it is possible to modify the properties of that formula. To modify an existing formula, follow these steps:

1. Navigate to the blade of your DevTest Labs instance.

2. On your lab's Overview blade (Figure 1-66), select Formulas (reusable bases).

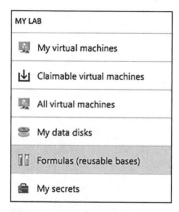

FIGURE 1-66 Navigating Formulas

3. On the Lab formulas blade, select the formula you wish to modify (Figure 1-67).

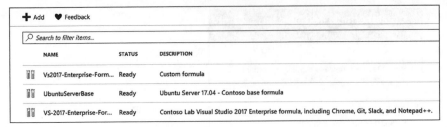

NAME	STATUS	DESCRIPTION
Vs2017-Enterprise-Form...	Ready	Custom formula
UbuntuServerBase	Ready	Ubuntu Server 17.04 - Contoso base formula
VS-2017-Enterprise-For...	Ready	Contoso Lab Visual Studio 2017 Enterprise formula, including Chrome, Git, Slack, and Notepad++.

FIGURE 1-67 Modify the list of available formulas in Lab

4. On the Update formula blade, make the desired edits, and select Update (Figure 1-68).

FIGURE 1-68 Update Formula

Delete a formula

To delete a formula, complete the steps below:

1. Navigate to the blade of your DevTest Labs instance.

2. On your lab's Overview blade, select Formulas (reusable bases).

3. On the Lab formulas blade, select the ellipsis to the right of the formula you wish to delete, then select Delete on the context menu (Figure 1-69).

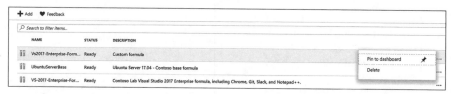

FIGURE 1-69 Deleting from the context menu

4. Select Yes to the deletion confirmation dialog.

Configure a lab to include policies and procedures

In Azure DevTest Labs, a lab is defined as the infrastructure that encompasses a group of resources, such as VMs. Labs enable you to better manage those resources by specifying limits and quotas. For each lab you create, you can control cost and minimize waste by managing policies (settings).

Configure allowed virtual machine sizes policy

The policy for setting the allowed VM sizes helps to minimize lab waste by enabling you to specify which VM sizes are allowed in the lab. If this policy is activated, only VM sizes from this list can be used to create VMs, allowing you to be very specific about what size VMs can be deployed into your lab environment. To configure the virtual machine sizes allowed in your lab, complete the following steps:

1. Navigate to the blade of your DevTest Labs instance.

2. On your lab's Overview blade, select Configuration and policies, under Settings (Figure 1-70).

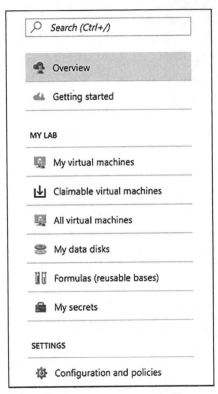

FIGURE 1-70 The Configuration and Policies blade

3. Select Allowed virtual machine sizes under Settings, on the Configuration and policies blade (Figure 1-71).

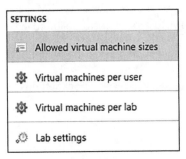

FIGURE 1-71 Allowed Virtual Machine Sizes

4. Select On to enable this policy, and Off to disable it (Figure 1-72).

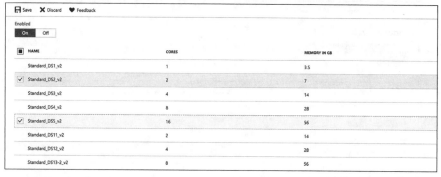

FIGURE 1-72 The allowed VM sizes policy

5. If enabled, select one or more VM sizes that you want to be allowed the creation of in your lab.

6. Select Save.

Configure virtual machines per user policy

The Virtual machines per user policy allows you to specify the maximum number of VMs that can be created or claimed by an individual user. You can also specify limits on the number of VMs using premium OS disks. Should a user attempt to create or claim a VM when their user limit has been met, an error message indicating that the VM cannot be created/claimed will be displayed. To manage the virtual machines per user policy, follow the steps below:

1. Navigate to the blade of your DevTest Labs instance.

2. On your lab's blade, select Configuration and policies.

3. On the Configuration and policies blade, select Virtual machines per user (Figure 1-73).

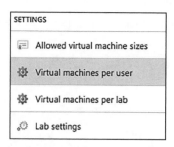

FIGURE 1-73 Virtual Machines Per User

4. Select Yes to enable limiting the number of virtual machines per user, and No to disable limits.

5. If yes is selected, enter a numeric value indicating the maximum number of VMs that can be created or claimed by a user (Figure 1-74).

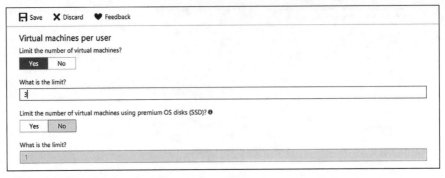

FIGURE 1-74 The VMs per user policy

6. Select Yes to enable limiting the number of VMs using premium OS disks (SSD), and No to remove limits on premium disk utilization.

7. If Yes is selected, enter a numeric value to specify the limit of VMs that can be created using SSDs.

8. Select Save to save your policy settings.

Configure virtual machines per lab policy

The policy for Virtual machines per lab allows you to specify the maximum number of VMs that can be created for the current lab, setting a limitation on the overall lab itself. Like the Virtual machines per user policy, you can also set limitations on the use of premium OS disks. If any user attempts to create a VM when the lab limit has been met, an error message indicates that the VM cannot be created. The virtual machines per lab policy can be configured by completing the following steps:

1. Navigate to the blade of your DevTest Labs instance.

2. On the lab's blade, select Configuration and policies.

3. On the Configuration and policies menu, select Virtual machines per user (Figure 1-75).

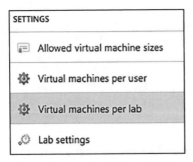

FIGURE 1-75 Virtual Machines per lab

4. Select Yes to enable limiting the number of virtual machines per user, and No to disable limits.

5. If Yes is selected, enter a numeric value indicating the maximum number of VMs that can be created in the lab (Figure 1-76).

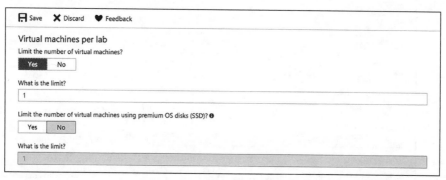

FIGURE 1-76 The VMs per user policy

6. Select Yes to enable limiting the number of virtual machines using premium OD disks (SSD), and No to disable limits on premium disk utilization.

7. If Yes is selected, enter a numeric value to specify the limit.

8. Select Save to save your policy settings.

Configure auto-shutdown policy

The auto-shutdown policy in Azure DevTest Labs is one of the most important policies for helping you to minimize lab waste and control cost, allowing you to specify a time that the lab's VMs will automatically shut down. This helps to prevent incurring costs when the VMs are not in use, and ensures VMs are shut down, even when you forget to do it at the end of a work day. To configure the auto-shutdown policy, follow the below steps:

1. Navigate to the blade of your DevTest Labs instance.

2. On the lab's Configuration and policies blade, select Auto-shutdown (Figure 1-77).

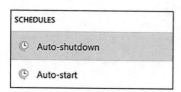

FIGURE 1-77 Auto-Shutdown policies

3. Select On to enable this policy, and Off to disable it (Figure 1-78).

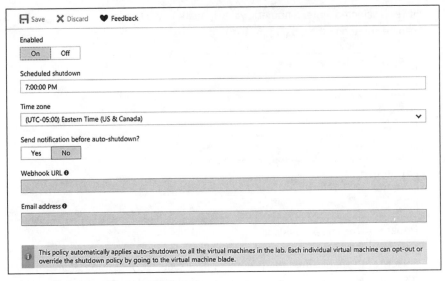

FIGURE 1-78 The Auto-Shutdown Policy

4. If you enable this policy, specify the time and time zone to shut down all VMs in the current lab.

5. Specify Yes or No for the option to send a notification before auto-shutdown. Notifications will be sent 15 minutes prior to the specified auto-shutdown time. If you specified Yes, enter either a Webhook URL endpoint or an email address to receive the notifications.

6. Select Save.

By default, once enabled, the auto-shutdown policy applies to all VMs in the current lab. This policy can be overridden on each individual VM in the lab, enabling more fine-tuned management of the policy. To alter this setting for a specific VM, complete the steps below:

1. Open the target VM's blade.

2. Select the Auto-shutdown tile on the VM's blade (Figure 1-79).

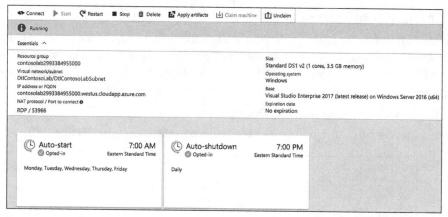

FIGURE 1-79 Auto-Shutdown Tile

3. On the Auto-shutdown blade, select On to enable the policy, or Off to disable it. If On is selected, enter a scheduled shutdown time, and time zone, and specify if notifications should be sent before auto-shutdown. If notifications are to be sent, provide a Webhook URL or email address to send notifications (Figure 1-80).

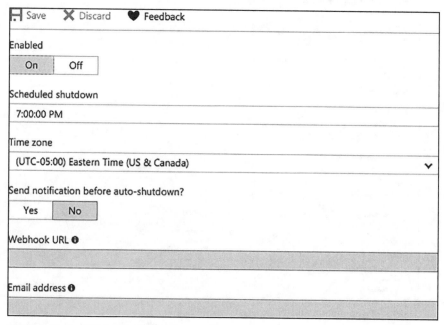

FIGURE 1-80 Configuring Aut0-Shutdown policy

Configure auto-start policy

Azure DevTest Labs' auto-start policy lets you specify when the VMs in the current lab should be automatically started, allowing all VMs to be started at a specific day and time. For example, if you want all your VMs to start at 7:00 AM each weekday, you can set up the policy to accommodate that configuration. Complete the following steps to configure the auto-start policy:

1. Navigate to the blade of your DevTest Labs instance.

2. On your lab's Configuration and policies blade, select Auto-start (Figure 1-81).

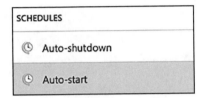

FIGURE 1-81 Auto-Start Policy settings

3. Select On to enable this policy, and Off to disable it (Figure 1-82).

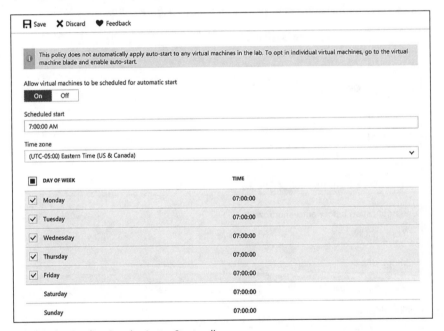

FIGURE 1-82 Configuring the Autto-Start policy

4. If you enable this policy, specify the scheduled start time, time zone, and the days of the week for which the time applies.

5. Select Save.

Like the auto-shutdown policy, the auto-start policy applies to all VMs in the current lab, once enabled. The steps to modify this policy for an individual VM are similar to those for the auto-shutdown policy, but you will select the Auto-start tile on the VM's blade, and modify the policy from there.

Set expiration date policy

Another option for managing the life of a VM is the ability to set an expiration date for the VM. This option is available when creating a new VM, and could be used if you want to ensure the VM is automatically deleted at a specified date and time. To set the expiration date for a VM:

1. During the VM creation process, select Advanced settings on the Virtual machine blade.

2. Choose the calendar icon to specify a date and time on which the VM will be automatically deleted. By default, VMs never expire.

3. Select OK on the Advanced settings blade (Figure 1-83).

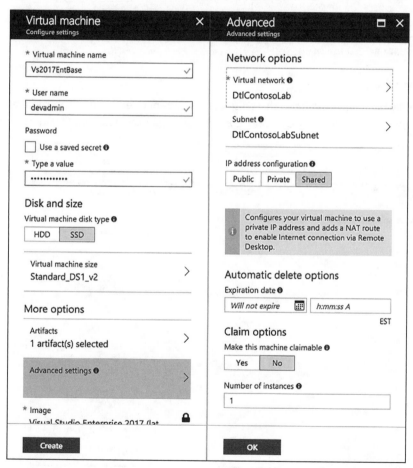

FIGURE 1-83 Auto-Delete options

Configure cost management

Azure DevTest Labs was designed to help development teams more effectively manage costs and resources. One of the key features of this is Cost Management, which allows you to track the cost associated with operating your lab. You can also view trends, set cost targets and thresholds, and configure alerts to keep you informed about your monthly costs. Cost threshold targets allow you to monitor usage throughout the month, and potentially alter behavior accordingly if you see spending happening faster than anticipated during a specified time period.

To view your Cost trend chart, navigate to the blade for your DevTest Labs instance, and select Cost trend from the Configuration and policies blade of your lab (Figure 1-84).

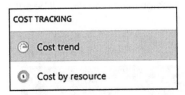

FIGURE 1-84 Cost Trend

Cost trend

The Monthly Estimated Cost Trend chart displays the current calendar month's estimated cost-to-date, and the projected end-of-month cost for the current calendar month (Figure 1-85).

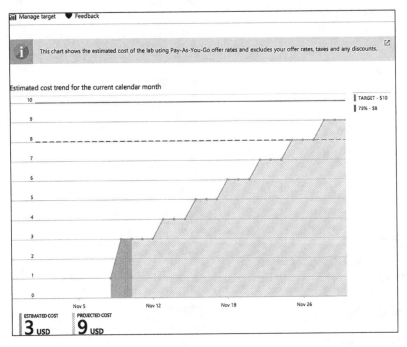

FIGURE 1-85 Cost trend chart

Azure DevTest Labs allows you to modify the time span displayed on the chart, specify target costs, and set up notifications. You can configure these options by completing the following steps:

1. From the Cost trend blade, select Manage target (Figure 1-86).

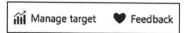

FIGURE 1-86 Manage Target

2. On the Manage target blade:

   A. Select the time period you would like displayed on the chart. Monthly is the default, and will display the current month. Selecting Fixed allows you to specify a set time period to display on the chart (Figure 1-87).

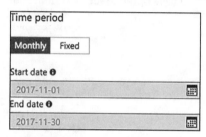

FIGURE 1-87 Target Time Period

   B. Specify a numeric value (in USD) for your target monthly cost (Figure 1-88).

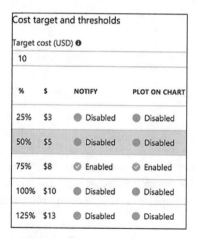

FIGURE 1-88 Target cost value

   C. Select any desired cost thresholds, and on the Cost threshold blade, specify whether to send notifications, and if you would like the threshold displayed on the trend chart, then select OK (Figure 1-89).

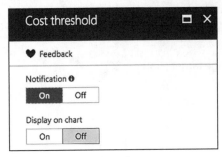

FIGURE 1-89 Target thresholds

D. If you chose to enable notifications, click to add an integration of a Webhook under Cost integrations. The lab will post a notification to the specified endpoint if lab spending reaches a threshold for which you have opted to receive notification (Figure 1-90).

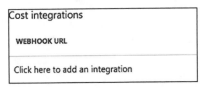

Figure 1-90 Add Webhook integration

E. On the Configure notification blade, enter a Webhook URL, and Select OK (Figure 1-91).

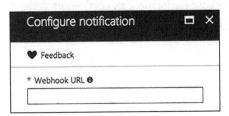

FIGURE 1-91 Webhook URL

F. Select OK to save the trend chart targets.

The estimated cost value is the current calendar month's estimated cost-to-date. The projected cost is the estimated cost for the entire calendar month, calculated using the lab cost for the previous five days. These cost numbers are rounded up the nearest whole number, and do not reflect actual costs.

> *MORE INFO* **WEBHOOKS**
>
> Webhooks are user defined HTTP/HTTPS endpoints that are usually triggered by an event. You must create a Webhook prior to entering it here. For more details on creating Webhooks, see: *https://docs.microsoft.com/azure/azure-functions/functions-create-github-webhook-triggered-function.*

Cost by resource

To provide you with more insight into cost of operating each individual resource in your lab, you can also view a breakdown of cost by resource. To view this breakdown, follow these steps:

1. Navigate to the blade of your DevTest Labs instance.

2. On the Configuration and policies blade for your lab, select Cost by resource (Figure 1-92).

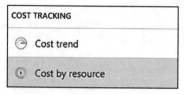

FIGURE 1-92 Cost By Resource

3. View the list of individual resources, and how much money (in USD) is being spent per resource (Figure 1-93).

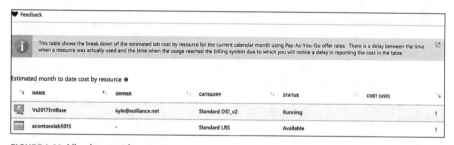

FIGURE 1-93 Viewing cost by resource

4. The list can be sorted to easier view those resources which have the most associated cost.

Secure access to labs

Security access in DevTest Labs is determined by Azure Role-Based Access Control (RBAC). To understand how access works, it helps to understand the differences between a permission, a role, and a scope as defined by RBAC.

- Permission Defined access to a specific action (e.g. read-access to all virtual machines).

- Role A set of permissions that can be grouped and assigned to a user. For example, the subscription owner role has access to all resources within a subscription.

- Scope A level within the hierarchy of an Azure resource, such as a resource group, a single lab, or the entire subscription.

Using RBAC, you can segregate duties within your team into roles where you grant only the amount of access necessary to users to perform their jobs. The three RBAC roles most relevant to Azure DevTest Labs are Owner, DevTest Labs User, and Contributor.

The Table 1-3 provides a breakdown of the actions that can be performed by users in each of these roles.

TABLE 1-3 Actions that can be performed by users in specified roles.

Actions users in this role can perform	DevTest Labs User	Owner	Contributor
LAB TASKS			
Add users to a lab	No	Yes	No
Update cost settings	No	Yes	Yes
VM BASE TASKS			
Add and remove custom images	No	Yes	Yes
Add, update, and delete formulas	Yes	Yes	Yes
Whitelist Azure Marketplace images	No	Yes	Yes
VM TASKS			
Create VMs	Yes	Yes	Yes
Start, stop, and delete VMs	Only VMs created by the user	Yes	Yes
Update VM policies	No	Yes	Yes
Add/remove data disks to/from VMs	Only VMs created by the user	Yes	Yes
ARTIFACT TASKS			
Add and remove artifact repositories	No	Yes	Yes
Apply artifacts	Yes	Yes	Yes

Add an owner or user at the lab level

Owners and users can be added at the lab level via the Azure portal. This includes external users with a valid Microsoft account (MSA). The following steps guide you through the process of adding an owner or user to a lab in Azure DevTest Labs:

1. Navigate to the blade of your DevTest Labs instance.

2. On your lab's blade, select Configuration and policies.

3. On the Configuration and policies blade (Figure 1-94), select Access control (IAM).

FIGURE 1-94 Access Control (IAM)

4. Select +Add

5. On the Add permission blade, select a role, Owner or DevTest Labs User (Figure 1-95).

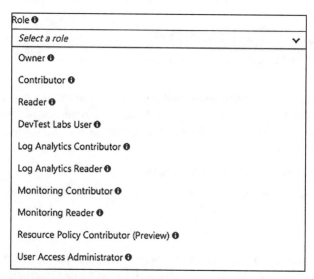

FIGURE 1-95 New lab owner role

6. On the Add permissions blade, enter a name or an email address, and select the user (Figure 1-96).

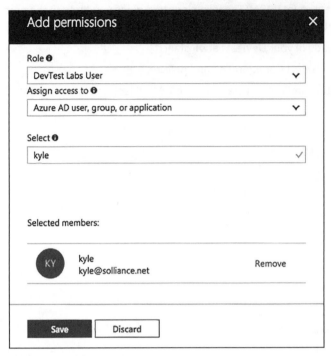

FIGURE 1-96 Add permissions to users

7. Click Save.

Add an external user to a lab using PowerShell

In addition to adding users in the Azure portal, you can add an external user to your lab using a PowerShell script.

The PowerShell script below assumes that the specified user has been added as a guest to the Active Directory, and will fail if that is not the case. To add a user not in the Active Directory to a lab, use the Azure portal to assign the user to a role as illustrated in the section, Add an owner or user at the lab level, above.

To add an external user to a lab, complete the following steps:

1. At a PowerShell prompt, log into your Azure account with the following call to the Login-AzureRmAccount cmdlet.

```
Login-AzureRmAccount
```

2. Select the desired Azure subscription by calling the Select-AzureRmSubscription cmdlet. Replace the placeholder for $subscriptionId variable with a valid Azure subscription ID.

```
$subscriptionId = '<Specify your subscription ID here>'
```

```
Select-AzureRmSubscription -SubscriptionId $subscriptionId
```

3. Retrieve the user object with the Get-AzureRmAdUser cmdlet. Replace the $userDis-playName placeholder with the appropriate value.

```
$userDisplayName = "<Specify the User's Display Name here>"
$adObject = Get-AzureRmADUser -SearchString $userDisplayName
```

4. Get the lab object by calling the Get-AzureRmResource cmdlet. Replace the following placeholders for the $labRg and $labName variables with the appropriate values for your environment.

```
$labRg = '<Specify your lab resource group name here>'
$labName = '<Specify your lab name here>'
$lab = Get-AzureRmResource -ResourceId ('/subscriptions/' + $subscriptionId +
'/resourceGroups/' + $labRg + '/providers/Microsoft.DevTestLab/labs/' + $labName)
```

5. Create the role assignment, using the New-AzureRmRoleAssignment cmdlet.

```
New-AzureRmRoleAssignment -ObjectId $adObject.Id -RoleDefinitionName 'DevTest
Labs User' -Scope $labId
```

Use lab settings to set access rights to the environment

Lab settings allow you to modify the access rights of your lab users to the resource group containing your lab resources. By giving your lab users Contributor access rights, you enable them to edit resources, such as SQL Server or Cosmos DB, in the resource group that contains your lab environment. By default, lab users have Reader access rights, and cannot change the resources in the resource group.

1. Navigate to the blade of your DevTest Labs instance.

2. On the DevTest Lab's Overview blade, select Configuration and policies.

3. On the lab's Configuration and policies menu, select Lab settings (Figure 1-97).

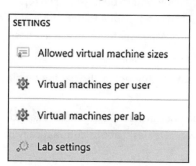

FIGURE 1-97 Lab Settings blade

4. Specify whether lab users should have Contributor or Reader access rights on the environment resource group (Figure 1-98).

FIGURE 1-98 Access rights for lab users

5. Select Save.

Use environments in a lab

The Azure portal enables you to easily create and add VMs to your lab one at a time. Sometimes, however, there is a requirement to deploy an environment containing multiple VMs, such as a multi-tier web app or a SharePoint farm. For this scenario, you can use Azure Resource Manager (ARM) templates to spin up a complete environment in DevTest labs, allowing your infrastructure to be as complicated as it needs to be for your environment.

> **MORE INFO   ARM TEMPLATES**
>
> For more information on the benefits of using ARM templates to deploy, update, or delete all your lab resources in a single operation, see: *https://docs.microsoft.com/azure/azure-resource-manager/resource-group-overview#the-benefits-of-using-resource-manager*.

Following infrastructure-as-code and configuration-as-code best practices, environment templates are managed in source control. Azure DevTest Labs loads all ARM templates directly from your GitHub or VSTS Git repositories. As a result, Resource Manager templates can be used across the entire release cycle, from the test environment to the production environment.

Configure an ARM template repository

To provide the greatest flexibility, Azure DevTest Labs allow you to build your own repositories, which can contain multiple environment templates, each in a separate folder. There are a couple of rules to follow for organizing your Azure Resource Manager templates in a repository:

1. The master template file must be named azuredeploy.json.

2. If you want to use parameter values defined in a parameter file, the parameter file must be named azuredeploy.parameters.json.

3. You can use the parameters _artifactsLocation and _artifactsLocationSasToken to construct the parametersLink URI value, allowing DevTest Labs to automatically manage nested templates.

4. Metadata can be defined to specify the template display name and description. This metadata must be in a file named metadata.json. The following example metadata file illustrated how to specify the display name and description:

```
{
"itemDisplayName": "<your template name>",
"description": "<description of the template>"
}
```

With your ARM template added to the repo, you are now ready to add the repository to your lab. To add a repository to your lab using the Azure portal, follow the steps below:

1. Navigate to the blade of your DevTest Labs instance.

2. On your lab's blade, select Configuration and policies.

3. From the Configuration and policies blade, select Repositories. The Repositories blade (Figure 1-99) lists the repositories that have been added to the lab. A repository named Public Repo is automatically generated for all labs, and connects to the DevTest Labs GitHub repo that contains several VM artifacts for your use.

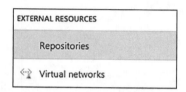

FIGURE 1-99 Repositories blade

4. Select +Add to add your Azure Resource Manager template repository.

5. When the second Repositories blade opens, enter the necessary information as follows:

    A. Enter a name for the repository.

    B. Enter the GIT HTTPS clone URL from GitHub or Visual Studio Team Services account.

    C. Enter the branch name to access your Azure Resource Manager template definitions.

    D. The personal access token is used to securely access your repository. To get your token from Visual Studio Team Services, select <YourName> > My profile > Security > Public access token. To get your token from GitHub, select your avatar followed by selecting Settings > Public access token.

    E. Using one of the two input fields, enter a folder path that starts with a forward slash - / - and is relative to your Git clone URI to either your artifact definitions (first input field) or your Azure Resource Manager template definitions (Figure 1-100).

FIGURE 1-100 Repositories configuration

6. Select Save (Figure 1-101).

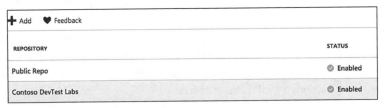

FIGURE 1-101 Available repositories

Create an environment from an ARM template

Once an ARM template repository has been configured in the lab, your lab users can create an environment using the Azure portal by following the steps below:

1. Navigate to the blade of your DevTest Labs instance.

2. On your lab's Overview blade, select +Add.

3. On the Choose a base blade, you will see resources with a Type of ARM template listed first. Select the desired ARM Template.

4. On the Add blade, enter an Environment name value. This is what will be displayed to your users in the lab. The remaining input fields come from the parameters defined in the ARM template. If default values are defined in the template or the azuredeploy. parameters.json file is present, default values are displayed in those input fields. For parameter types of secure string, you can use the secrets store in the lab's personal secret store (Figure 1-102).

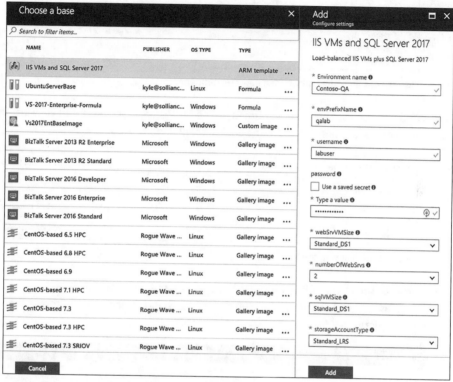

FIGURE 1-102 New environment from ARM template

5. Select Add to create the environment. The environment starts provisioning immediately with the status displaying in the My Virtual Machines list. A new resource group is automatically created by the lab to provision all the resources defined in the ARM template (Figure 1-103).

My virtual machines					
	NAME	STATUS	AUTO-START	AUTO-SHUTDOWN	BASE
	Vs2017EntBase	⊘ Running	⊘ Yes	⊘ Yes	Visual Studio Enterprise 2017
▸	ContosoQA	⊘ Creating			IIS VMs and SQL Server 2017

FIGURE 1-103 My Virtual Machines blade

6. Once the deployment of the environment completes, select the environment in the My Virtual Machines list to open the resource group blade, and browse all the resources provisioned in the environment (Figure 1-104).

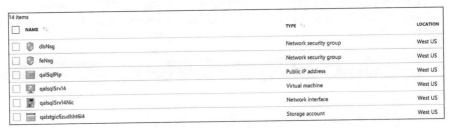

FIGURE 1-104 Resource group for a new environment

7. You can also expand the environment in the My Virtual Machines list to view just the list of VMs that are provisioned in the environment (Figure 1-105).

FIGURE 1-105 Viewing the VMs

8. You can select any of the resources in the environment to view the available actions, such as applying artifacts, attaching data disks, changing the auto-shutdown time, and more (Figure 1-106).

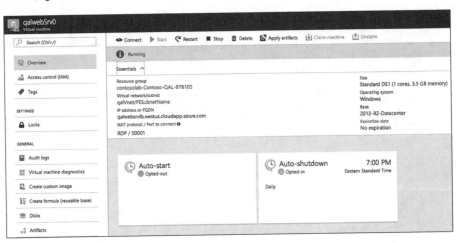

FIGURE 1-106 Available actions

Thought experiment

In this thought experiment, apply what you've learned about this skill. You can find answers to these questions in the "Answers" section at the end of this chapter.

Your solution architecture has two tiers: a front-end web tier that you want to configure the so that is available and scales out during the busiest times, which are weekdays, and a diagnostics VM that enables you to analyze any issues with the web tier VM instances.

1. How would you place the VMs within Scale Sets and what constraints would you need to ensure you meet them?

2. How would you configure scaling?

Thought experiment answer

This section contains the answers to the thought experiment.

1. You should ensure that you create a Virtual machine scale set for the web tier VM's The diagnostic VM, since it does not have any scaling needs, should not be placed in a Virtual machine scale set, but it should be deployed in the same Virtual Network as used by the Scale Set so that it can reach the VM instances across the network.

2. You should configure Autoscale on the Scale Set with a condition that increases the VMs count to the desired capacity on weekdays and a default condition that sets the VM count that is in effect at all other times

Chapter summary

- There are two approaches to identifying supported workloads in Azure: looking for explicit support by a listing in the Marketplace and performing a manual comparison of the workload requirements against the capacities of VMs.

- New VMs can be created by uploading a VM you have already created on-premises or by instantiating one from a selection of pre-built images that are available in the Marketplace.

- Azure supports the creation of "bare-bones" VMs that provide just Windows or Linux operating system from pre-built images available in the Marketplace.

- The Marketplace provides the ability to provision single VMs with pre-configured applications. The example shown in this chapter provisions SQL Server in a VM.

- The Marketplace use ARM templates to deploy and configure a complex topology consisting of multiple VMs, such as a SQL Server AlwaysOn or a SharePoint farm, the network resources and any supporting resources required.

- The VM Agent is a very lightweight process. When installed on a VM, it makes it possible to bootstrap additional VM extensions such as DSC.

- The Custom Script Extension makes it possible to download files from Azure Storage, run Windows PowerShell of Linux Shell scripts, and automate copying files and configuring a VM.

- DSC helps you avoid configuration drift by specifying the desired state for VM provisioning and subsequent updates.

- Azure VM sizes control the capacity of the resources available to a VM instance. The size can be scaled up and scaled down using the portal or Windows PowerShell.

- Virtual machine scale sets enable you to easily manage the scale up and scale down of the number of instances of a particular virtual machine image.

- Autoscale can be used with Virtual Machine Scale Sets to adjust the capacity based on resource metrics or according to a schedule.

- Storage capacity for VMs is dictated by the scalability limits (IOPS, throughput, and maximum file size) of Azure Storage as well as per-VM limits that adjust with the VM size (the number of VHD disks that can be attached).

- Azure VMs support Standard Storage and Premium storage in both unmanaged and managed variants.

- Disk caching provides a cache on the machine hosting your VM that can avert the need to read from or write to Blob storage. The options are None, Read Only, and Read/Write.

- Geo-replication should not be used for Azure Storage accounts that store VHDs because the added redundancy does not provide additional protection against corrupting the data and may in fact result in data loss if you attempt to restore from a geo-replication.

- Azure File storage enables you to use network shares to provide distributed access to files from your VMs.

- A VM can be configured to collect diagnostics data (that is, logs) as well as performance counter metrics (CPU percentage, memory utilization, and so on).

- Endpoint monitoring can be configured on a VM to provide outside-in monitoring of HTTP or HTTPS endpoints provided by your VM.

- You can monitor various metrics using the management portal, and you can configure alerts on these metrics to send out emails when a metric threshold is exceeded.

- Diagnostic logs can be retrieved from Azure Storage (Table or Blob storage, depending on the specific type of log).

- An availability set defines both the update domains and fault domains to which VMs are assigned.

- VMs in the same update domain will not all be updated at the same time.

- VMs in the same fault domain share either the same power supply, network switch or both.

- An Azure Load Balancer can be used to load balance traffic between VMs in an availability set.

- It is a best practice to deploy VMs that represent the same application tier in the same availability set.

- Azure DevTest Labs allows you to quickly spin up virtual machines (VMs) or complete environments in Azure.

- Custom images and formulas facilitate the rapid deployment of pre-configured VMs in DevTest Labs.

- Custom images provide a static, immutable way to create VMs from a desired configuration, and can be created from a provisioned VM, or from a VDH, using either PowerShell or the Azure portal.

- Formulas are modifiable lists of default property values, providing a dynamic way to create VMs from a desired configuration, and can be created from a base image or an existing VM.

- DevTest Labs enable you to better manage resources by specifying limits and quotas, allowing you to better control cost and minimize waste by managing policies.

- Security access in DevTest Labs is determined by Azure Role-Based Access Control (RBAC), mainly using the owner, DevTest Labs user, and contributor roles.

- Azure Resource Manager (ARM) templates can be used to spin up complete environments in DevTest labs, allowing your infrastructure to be as complicated as it needs to be for your environment.

## CHAPTER 2

Design and implement a storage and data strategy

In this section, we'll look at most of the various methods of handling data and state in Microsoft Azure. All of the different data options can be somewhat overwhelming. For the last several decades, application state was primarily stored in a relational database system, like Microsoft SQL Server. Microsoft Azure has non-relational storage products, like Azure Storage Tables, Azure CosmosDB, and Azure Redis Cache. You might ask yourself which data product do you choose? What are the differences between each one? How do I get started if I have little or no experience with one? This chapter will explain the differences between relational data stores, file storage, and JSON document storage. It will also help you get started with the various Azure data products.

Skills in this chapter:

- Skill 2.1: Implement Azure Storage blobs and Azure files
- Skill 2.2: Implement Azure Storage tables and queues
- Skill 2.3. Manage access and monitor storage
- Skill 2.4: Implement Azure SQL Databases
- Skill 2.5: Implement Azure Cosmos DB
- Skill 2.6: Implement Redis caching
- Skill 2.7: Implement Azure Search

Skill 2.1: Implement Azure Storage blobs and Azure files

File storage is incredibly useful in a wide variety of solutions for your organization. Whether storing sensor data from refrigeration trucks that check in every few minutes, storing resumes as PDFs for your company website, or storing SQL Server backup files to comply with a retention policy. Microsoft Azure provides several methods of storing files, including Azure Storage blobs and Azure Files. We will look at the differences between these products and teach you how to begin using each one.

This skill covers how to:

- Create a blob storage account
- Read data and change data
- Set metadata on a container
- Store data using block and page blobss
- Stream data using blobs
- Access blobs securely
- Implement async blob copy
- Configure Content Delivery Network (CDN)
- Design blob hierarchies
- Configure custom domains
- Scale blob storage
- Implement blob leasing
- Create connections to files from on-premises or cloud-based Windows or Linux machines
- Shard large datasets

Azure Storage blobs

Azure Storage blobs are the perfect product to use when you have files that you're storing using a custom application. Other developers might also write applications that store files in Azure Storage blobs, which is the storage location for many Microsoft Azure products, like Azure HDInsight, Azure VMs, and Azure Data Lake Analytics. Azure Storage blobs should not be used as a file location for users directly, like a corporate shared drive. Azure Storage blobs provide client libraries and a REST interface that allows unstructured data to be stored and accessed at a massive scale in block blobs.

Create a blob storage account

1. Sign in to the Azure portal.
2. Click the green plus symbol on the left side.
3. On the Hub menu, select New > Storage > Storage account–blob, file, table, queue.
4. Click Create.
5. Enter a name for your storage account.
6. For most of the options, you can choose the defaults.

7. Specify the Resource Manager deployment model. You should choose an Azure Resource Manager deployment. This is the newest deployment API. Classic deployment will eventually be retired.

8. Your application is typically made up of many components, for instance a website and a database. These components are not separate entities, but one application. You want to deploy and monitor them as a group, called a resource group. Azure Resource Manager enables you to work with the resources in your solution as a group.

9. Select the General Purpose type of storage account.

   There are two types of storage accounts: General purpose or Blob storage. General purpose storage type allows you to store tables, queues, and blobs all-in-one storage. Blob storage is just for blobs. The difference is that Blob storage has hot and cold tiers for performance and pricing and a few other features just for Blob storage. We'll choose General Purpose so we can use table storage later.

10. Under performance, specify the standard storage method. Standard storage uses magnetic disks that are lower performing than Premium storage. Premium storage uses solid-state drives.

11. Storage service encryption will encrypt your data at rest. This might slow data access, but will satisfy security audit requirements.

12. Secure transfer required will force the client application to use SSL in their data transfers.

13. You can choose several types of replication options. Select the replication option for the storage account.

14. The data in your Microsoft Azure storage account is always replicated to ensure durability and high availability. Replication copies your data, either within the same data center, or to a second data center, depending on which replication option you choose. For replication, choose carefully, as this will affect pricing. The most affordable option is Locally Redundant Storage (LRS).

15. Select the subscription in which you want to create the new storage account.

16. Specify a new resource group or select an existing resource group. Resource groups allow you to keep components of an application in the same area for performance and management. It is highly recommended that you use a resource group. All service placed in a resource group will be logically organized together in the portal. In addition, all of the services in that resource group can be deleted as a unit.

17. Select the geographic location for your storage account. Try to choose one that is geographically close to you to reduce latency and improve performance.

18. Click Create to create the storage account.

Once created, you will have two components that allow you to interact with your Azure Storage account via an SDK. SDKs exist for several languages, including C#, JavaScript, and Python. In this module, we'll focus on using the SDK in C#. Those two components are the URI and the access key. The URI will look like this: *http://{your storage account name from step 4}.blob.core.windows.net*.

Your access key will look like this: KEsm421/uwSie13dipSGGL124K0124SxoHAXq3jk124vuCjw35124f-
HRIk142WIbxbTmQrzIQdM4K5Zyf9ZvUg==

Read and change data

First, let's use the Azure SDK for .NET to load data into your storage account.

1. Create a console application.

2. Use Nuget Package Manager to install WindowsAzure.Storage.

3. In the Using section, add a using to Microsoft.WindowsAzure.Storage and Microsoft.WindowsAzure.Storage.Blob.

4. Create a storage account in your application like this:

```
CloudStorageAccount storageAccount;
storageAccount =
 CloudStorageAccount.Parse("DefaultEndpointsProtocol=https;AccountName={your
 storage account name};AccountKey={your storage key}");
```

Azure Storage blobs are organized with containers. Each storage account can have an unlimited amount of containers. Think of containers like folders, but they are very flat with no sub-containers. In order to load blobs into an Azure Storage account, you must first choose the container.

5. Create a container using the following code:

```
CloudBlobClient blobClient = storageAccount.CreateCloudBlobClient();

CloudBlobContainer container = blobClient.GetContainerReference("democontainerblo
ckblob");
try
{
    await container.CreateIfNotExistsAsync();
}
catch (StorageException ex)
{

    Console.WriteLine(ex.Message);
    Console.ReadLine();
    throw;
}
```

6. In the following code, you need to set the path of the file you want to upload using the ImageToUpload variable.

```
const string ImageToUpload = @"C:\temp\HelloWorld.png";
CloudBlockBlob blockBlob = container.GetBlockBlobReference("HelloWorld.png");
// Create or overwrite the "myblob" blob with contents from a local file.
using (var fileStream = System.IO.File.OpenRead(ImageToUpload))
{
    blockBlob.UploadFromStream(fileStream);
}
```

7. Every blob has an individual URI. By default, you can gain access to that blob as long as you have the storage account name and the access key. We can change the default by changing the Access Policy of the Azure Storage blob container. By default, containers are set to private. They can be changed to either blob or container. When set to Public Container, no credentials are required to access the container and its blobs. When set to Public Blob, only blobs can be accessed without credentials if the full URL is known. We can read that blob using the following code:

```
foreach (IListBlobItem blob in container.ListBlobs())
{
    Console.WriteLine("- {0} (type: {1})", blob.Uri, blob.GetType());
}
```

Note how we use the container to list the blobs to get the URI. We also have all of the information necessary to download the blob in the future.

Set metadata on a container

Metadata is useful in Azure Storage blobs. It can be used to set content types for web artifacts or it can be used to determine when files have been updated. There are two different types of metadata in Azure Storage Blobs: System Properties and User-defined Metadata. System properties give you information about access, file types, and more. Some of them are read-only. User-defined metadata is a key-value pair that you specify for your application. Maybe you need to make a note of the source, or the time the file was processed. Data like that is perfect for user-defined metadata.

Blobs and containers have metadata attached to them. There are two forms of metadata:

- System properties metadata
- User-defined metadata

System properties can influence how the blob behaves, while user-defined metadata is your own set of name/value pairs that your applications can use. A container has only read-only system properties, while blobs have both read-only and read-write properties.

Setting user-defined metadata

To set user-defined metadata for a container, get the container reference using GetContainerReference(), and then use the Metadata member to set values. After setting all the desired values, call SetMetadata() to persist the values, as in the following example:

```
CloudBlobClient blobClient = storageAccount.CreateCloudBlobClient();
CloudBlobContainer container =
blobClient.GetContainerReference("democontainerblockblob");
container.Metadata.Add("counter", "100");container.SetMetadata();
```

Reading user-defined metadata

To read user-defined metadata for a container, get the container reference using GetContainerReference(), and then use the Metadata member to retrieve a dictionary of values and access them by key, as in the following example:

```
container.FetchAttributes();

foreach (var metadataItem in container.Metadata)
{
    Console.WriteLine("\tKey: {0}", metadataItem.Key);
    Console.WriteLine("\tValue: {0}", metadataItem.Value);
}
```

EXAM TIP

If the metadata key doesn't exist, an exception is thrown.

Reading system properties

To read a container's system properties, first get a reference to the container using GetContainerReference(), and then use the Properties member to retrieve values. The following code illustrates accessing container system properties:

```
container = blobClient.GetContainerReference("democontainerblockblob");
container.FetchAttributes();
Console.WriteLine("LastModifiedUTC: " + container.Properties.LastModified);
Console.WriteLine("ETag: " + container.Properties.ETag);
```

Store data using block and page blobs

There are three types of blobs used in Azure Storage Blobs: Block, Append, and Page. Block blobs are used to upload large files. They are comprised of blocks, each with its own block ID. Because the blob is divided up in blocks, it allows for easy updating or resending when transferring large files. You can insert, replace, or delete an existing block in any order. Once a block is updated, added, or removed, the list of blocks needs to be committed for the file to actually record the update.

Page blobs are comprised of 512-byte pages that are optimized for random read and write operations. Writes happen in place and are immediately committed. Page blobs are good for VHDs in Azure VMs and other files that have frequent, random access.

Append blobs are optimized for append operations. Append blobs are good for logging and streaming data. When you modify an append blob, blocks are added to the end of the blob.

In most cases, block blobs will be the type you will use. Block blobs are perfect for text files, images, and videos.

A previous section demonstrated how to interact with a block blob. Here's how to write a page blob:

```
string pageBlobName = "random";
CloudPageBlob pageBlob = container.GetPageBlobReference(pageBlobName);
await pageBlob.CreateAsync(512 * 2 /*size*/); // size needs to be multiple of 512 bytes

byte[] samplePagedata = new byte[512];
Random random = new Random();
random.NextBytes(samplePagedata);
await pageBlob.UploadFromByteArrayAsync(samplePagedata, 0, samplePagedata.Length);
```

To read a page blob, use the following code:

```
int bytesRead = await pageBlob.DownloadRangeToByteArrayAsync(samplePagedata,
 0, 0, samplePagedata.Count());
```

Stream data using blobs

You can stream blobs by downloading to a stream using the DownloadToStream() API method. The advantage of this is that it avoids loading the entire blob into memory, for example before saving it to a file or returning it to a web request.

Access blobs securely

Secure access to blob storage implies a secure connection for data transfer and controlled access through authentication and authorization.

Azure Storage supports both HTTP and secure HTTPS requests. For data transfer security, you should always use HTTPS connections. To authorize access to content, you can authenticate in three different ways to your storage account and content:

- **Shared Key**   Constructed from a set of fields related to the request. Computed with a SHA-256 algorithm and encoded in Base64.
- **Shared Key Lite**   Similar to Shared Key, but compatible with previous versions of Azure Storage. This provides backwards compatibility with code that was written against versions prior to 19 September 2009. This allows for migration to newer versions with minimal changes.
- **Shared Access Signature**   Grants restricted access rights to containers and blobs. You can provide a shared access signature to users you don't trust with your storage account key. You can give them a shared access signature that will grant them specific permissions to the resource for a specified amount of time. This is discussed in a later section.

To interact with blob storage content authenticated with the account key, you can use the Storage Client Library as illustrated in earlier sections. When you create an instance of the CloudStorageAccount using the account name and key, each call to interact with blob storage will be secured, as shown in the following code:

```
string accountName = "ACCOUNTNAME";
string accountKey = "ACCOUNTKEY";
CloudStorageAccount storageAccount = new CloudStorageAccount(new
StorageCredentials(accountName, accountKey), true);
```

Implement Async blob copy

It is possible to copy blobs between storage accounts. You may want to do this to create a point-in-time backup of your blobs before a dangerous update or operation. You may also want to do this if you're migrating files from one account to another one. You cannot change blob types during an async copy operation. Block blobs will stay block blobs. Any files with the same name on the destination account will be overwritten.

Blob copy operations are truly asynchronous. When you call the API and get a success message, this means the copy operation has been successfully scheduled. The success message will be returned after checking the permissions on the source and destination accounts.

You can perform a copy in conjunction with the Shared Access Signature method of gaining permissions to the account. We'll cover that security method in a later topic.

Configure a Content Delivery Network with Azure Blob Storage

A Content Delivery Network (CDN) is used to cache static files to different parts of the world. For instance, let's say you were developing an online catalog for a retail organization with a global audience. Your main website was hosted in western United States. Users of the application in Florida complain of slowness while users in Washington state compliment you for how fast it is. A CDN would be a perfect solution for serving files close to the users, without the added latency of going across country. Once files are hosted in an Azure Storage Account, a configured CDN will store and replicate those files for you without any added management.

The CDN cache is perfect for style sheets, documents, images, JavaScript files, packages, and HTML pages.

After creating an Azure Storage Account like you did earlier, you must configure it for use with the Azure CDN service. Once that is done, you can call the files from the CDN inside the application.

To enable the CDN for the storage account, follow these steps:

1. In the Storage Account navigation pane, find Azure CDN towards the bottom. Click on it.

2. Create a new CDN endpoint by filling out the form that popped up.

   A. Azure CDN is hosted by two different CDN networks. These are partner companies that actually host and replicate the data. Choosing a correct network will affect the features available to you and the price you pay. No matter which tier you use, you will only be billed through the Microsoft Azure Portal, not through the third-party. There are three pricing tiers:

      - **Premium Verizon** The most expensive tier. This tier offers advanced real-time analytics so you can know what users are hitting what content and when.
      - **Standard Verizon** The standard CDN offering on Verizon's network.
      - **Standard Akamai** The standard CDN offering on Akamai's network.

   B. Specify a Profile and an endpoint name. After the CDN endpoint is created, it will appear on the list above.

3. Once this is done, you can configure the CDN if needed. For instance, you can use a custom domain name is it looks like your content is coming from your website.

4. Once the CDN endpoint is created, you can reference your files using a path similar to the following:

   ```
   Error! Hyperlink reference not valid.>
   ```

If a file needs to be replaced or removed, you can delete it from the Azure Storage blob container. Remember that the file is being cached in the CDN. It will be removed or updated when the Time-to-Live (TTL) expires. If no cache expiry period is specified, it will be cached in the CDN for seven days. You set the TTL is the web application by using the clientCache element in the web.config file. Remember when you place that in the web.config file it affects all folders and subfolders for that application.

Design blob hierarchies

Azure Storage blobs are stored in containers, which are very flat. This means that you cannot have child containers contained inside a parent container. This can lead to organizational confusion for users who rely on folders and subfolders to organize files.

A hierarchy can be replicated by naming the files something that's similar to a folder structure. For instance, you can have a storage account named "sally." Your container could be named "pictures." Your file could be named "product1\mainFrontPanel.jpg." The URI to your file would look like this: *http://sally.blob.core.windows.net/pictures/product1/mainFrontPanel.jpg*

In this manner, a folder/subfolder relationship can be maintained. This might prove useful in migrating legacy applications over to Azure.

Configure custom domains

The default endpoint for Azure Storage blobs is: (Storage Account Name).blob.core.windows. net. Using the default can negatively affect SEO. You might also not want to make it obvious that you are hosting your files in Azure. To obfuscate this, you can configure Azure Storage to respond to a custom domain. To do this, follow these steps:

1. Navigate to your storage account in the Azure portal.

2. On the navigation pane, find BLOB SERVICE. Click Custom Domain.

3. Check the Use Indirect CNAME Validation check box. We use this method because it does not incur any downtime for your application or website.

4. Log on to your DNS provider. Add a CName record with the subdomain alias that includes the Asverify subdomain. For example, if you are holding pictures in your blob storage account and you want to note that in the URL, then the CName would be Asverify.pictures (your custom domain including the .com or .edu, etc.) Then provide the hostname for the CNAME alias, which would also include Asverify. If we follow the earlier example of pictures, the hostname URL would be sverify.pictures.blob.core.win-dows.net. The hostname to use appears in #2 of the Custom domain blade in the Azure portal from the previous step.

5. In the text box on the Custom domain blade, enter the name of your custom domain, but without the Asverify. In our example, it would be pictures.(your custom domain including the .com or .edu, etc.) .

6. Select Save.

7. Now return to your DNS provider's website and create another CNAME record that maps your subdomain to your blob service endpoint. In our example, we can make pictures.(your custom domain) point to pictures.blob.core.windows.net.

8. Now you can delete the azverify CName now that it has been verified by Azure.

Why did we go through the azverify steps? We were allowing Azure to recognize that you own that custom domain before doing the redirection. This allows the CNAME to work with no downtime.

In the previous example, we referenced a file like this: *http://sally.blob.core.windows.net/ pictures/product1/mainFrontPanel.jpg*.

With the custom domain, it would now look like this: *http://pictures.(your custom domain)/pic-tures/product1/mainFrontPanel.jpg*.

Scale blob storage

We can scale blob storage both in terms of storage capacity and performance. Each Azure subscription can have 200 storage accounts, with 500TB of capacity each. That means that each Azure subscription can have 100 petabytes of data in it without creating another subscription.

An individual block blob can have 50,000 100MB blocks with a total size of 4.75TB. An append blob has a max size of 195GB. A page blob has a max size of 8TB.

In order to scale performance, we have several features available to us. We can implement an Azure CDN to enable geo-caching to keep blobs close to the users. We can implement read access geo-redundant storage and offload some of the reads to another geographic location (thus creating a mini-CDN that will be slower, but cheaper).

Azure Storage blobs (and tables, queues, and files, too) have an amazing feature. By far, the most expensive services for most cloud vendors is compute time. You pay for how many and how fast the processors are in the service you are using. Azure Storage doesn't charge for compute. It only charges for disk space used and network bandwidth (which is a fairly nominal charge). Azure Storage blobs are partitioned by storage account name + container name + blob name. This means that each blob is retrieved by one and only one server. Many small files will perform better in Azure Storage than one large file. Blobs use containers for logical grouping, but each blob can be retrieved by different compute resources, even if they are in the same container.

Azure files

Azure file storage provides a way for applications to share storage accessible via SMB 2.1 protocol. It is particularly useful for VMs and cloud services as a mounted share, and applications can use the File Storage API to access file storage.

> **MORE INFO** **FILE STORAGE DOCUMENTATION**
>
> For additional information on file storage, see the guide at: *http://azure.microsoft.com/en-us/documentation/articles/storage-dotnet-how-to-use-files/*.

Implement blob leasing

You can create a lock on a blob for write and delete operations. The lock can be between 15 and 60 seconds or it can be infinite. To write to a blob with an active lease, the client must include the active lease ID with the request.

When a client requests a lease, a lease ID is returned. The client may then use this lease ID to renew, change, or release the lease. When the lease is active, the lease ID must be included to write to the blob, set any meta data, add to the blob (through append), copy the blob, or delete the blob. You may still read a blob that has an active lease ID to another client and without using the lease ID.

The code to acquire a lease looks like the following example (assuming the blockBlob variable was instantiated earlier):

```
TimeSpan? leaseTime = TimeSpan.FromSeconds(60);
string leaseID = blockBlob.AcquireLease(leaseTime, null);
```

Create connections to files from on-premises or cloudbased Windows or, Linux machines

Azure Files can be used to replace on-premise file servers or NAS devices. You can connect to Azure Files using Windows, Linux, or MacOS.

You can mount an Azure File share using Windows File Explorer, PowerShell, or the Command Prompt. To use File Explorer, follow these steps:

1. Open File Explorer

2. Under the computer menu, click Map Network Drive (see Figure 2-1).

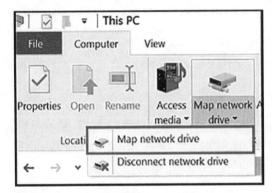

FIGURE 2-1 Map network Drive

3. Copy the UNC path from the Connect pane in the Azure portal, as shown in Figure 2-2.

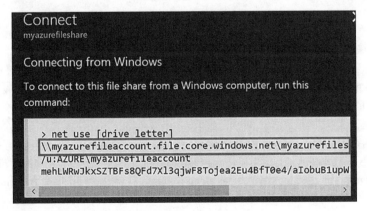

FIGURE 2-2 Azure portal UNC path

4. Select the drive letter and enter the UNC path.

5. Use the storage account name prepended with Azure\ as the username and the Storage Account Key as the password (see Figure 2-3).

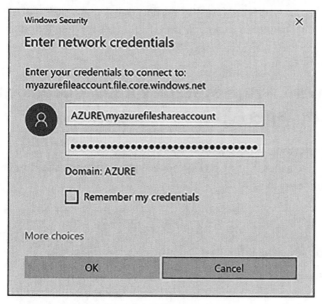

FIGURE 2-3 Login credentials for Azure Files

The PowerShell code to map a drive to Azure Files looks like this:

```
$acctKey = ConvertTo-SecureString -String "<storage-account-key>" -AsPlainText
-Force
$credential = New-Object System.Management.Automation.PSCredential -ArgumentList
  "Azure\<storage-account-name>", $acctKey
New-PSDrive -Name <desired-drive-letter> -PSProvider FileSystem -Root
"\\<storage-account-name>.file.core.windows.net\<share-name>" -Credential $credential
```

To map a drive using a command prompt, use a command that looks like this:

```
net use <desired-drive-letter>: \\<storage-account-name>.file.core.windows.net
\<share-name> <storage-account-key> /user:Azure\<storage-account-name>
```

To use Azure Files on a Linux machine, first install the cifs-utils package. Then create a folder for a mount point using mkdir. Afterwards, use the mount command with code similar to the following:

```
sudo mount -t cifs //<storage-account-name>.file.core.windows.net/<share-name>
  ./mymountpoint -o vers=2.1,username=<storage-account-name>,password=<storage-
account-key>,dir_mode=0777,file_mode=0777,serverino
```

Shard large datasets

Each blob is held in a container in Azure Storage. You can use containers to group related blobs that have the same security requirements. The partition key of a blob is account name + container name + blob name. Each blob can have its own partition if load on the blob demands it. A single blob can only be served by a single server. If sharding is needed, you need to create multiple blobs.

Skill 2.2: Implement Azure Storage tables, queues, and Azure Cosmos DB Table API

Azure Tables are used to store simple tabular data at petabyte scale on Microsoft Azure. Azure Queue storage is used to provide messaging between application components so they can be de-coupled and scale under heavy load.

This skill covers how to:

- Implement CRUD with and without transactions;
- Design and manage partitions;
- Query using OData;
- Designing, managing, and scaling tablepartitions;
- Add and process queue messages;
- Retrieve a batch of messages;
- Scale queues
- Choose between Azure Storage Tables and Azure Cosmos DB Table API

Azure Table Storage

Azure Tables are simple tables filled with rows and columns. They are a key-value database solution, which references how the data is stored and retrieved, not how complex the table can be. Tables store data as a collection of entities. Each entity has a property. Azure Tables can have 255 properties (or columns to hijack the relational vocabulary). The total entity size (or row size) cannot exceed 1MB. That might seem small initially, but 1MB can store a lot of tabular data per entity. Azure Tables are similar to Azure Storage blobs, in that you are not charged for compute time for inserting, updating, or retrieving your data. You are only charged for the total storage of your data.

Azure Tables are stored in the same storage account as Azure Storage blobs discussed earlier. Where blobs organize data based on container, Azure Tables organize data based on table name. Entities that are functionally the same should be stored in the same table. For example, all customers should be stored in the Customers table, while their orders should be stored in the Orders table.

Azure Tables store entities based on a partition key and a row key. Partition keys are the partition boundary. All entities stored with the same PartitionKey property are grouped into the same partition and are served by the same partition server. Choosing the correct partition key is a key responsibility of the Azure developer. Having a few partitions will improve scalability, as it will increase the number of partition servers handling your requests. Having too many partitions, however, will affect how you do batch operations like batch updates or large data retrieval. We will discuss this further at the end of this section.

Later in this chapter, we will discuss Azure SQL Database. Azure SQL Database also allows you to store tabular data. Why would you use Azure Tables vs Azure SQL Database? Why have two products that have similar functions? Well, actually they are very different.

Azure Tables service does not enforce any schema for tables. It simply stores the properties of your entity based on the partition key and the row key. If the data in the entity matches the data in your object model, your object is populated with the right values when the data is retrieved. Developers need to enforce the schema on the client side. All business logic for your application should be inside the application and not expected to be enforced in Azure Tables. Azure SQL Database also has an incredible amount of features that Azure Tables do not have including: stored procedures, triggers, indexes, constraints, functions, default values, row and column level security, SQL injection detection, and much, much more.

If Azure Tables are missing all of these features, why is the service so popular among developers? As we said earlier, you are not charged for compute resources when using Azure Tables, and you are charged in Azure SQL DB. This makes Azure Tables extremely affordable for large datasets. If we effectively use table partitioning, Azure Tables will also scale very well without sacrificing performance.

Now that you have a good overview of Azure Tables, let's dive right in and look at using it. If you've been following along through Azure Storage blobs, some of this code will be familiar to you.

Using basic CRUD operations

In this section, you learn how to access table storage programmatically.

Creating a table

1. Create a C# console application.

2. In your app.config file, add an entry under the Configuration element, replacing the account name and key with your own storage account details:

```
<configuration>
  <appSettings>
    <add key="StorageConnectionString" value="DefaultEndpointsProtocol=
https;AccountName=<your account name>;AccountKey=<your account key>" />
  </appSettings>
</configuration>
```

Use NuGet to obtain the Microsoft.WindowsAzure.Storage.dll. An easy way to do this is by using the following command in the NuGet console:

1. Install-package windowsazure.storage

2. Add the following using statements to the top of your Program.cs file:

```
using Microsoft.WindowsAzure.Storage;
using Microsoft.WindowsAzure.Storage.Auth;
using Microsoft.WindowsAzure.Storage.Table;
using Microsoft.WindowsAzure;
using System.Configuration;
```

3. Add a reference to System.Configuration.

4. Type the following command to retrieve your connection string in the Main function of Program.cs:

```
var storageAccount =CloudStorageAccount.Parse
( ConfigurationManager.AppSettings["StorageConnectionString"]);
```

5. Use the following command to create a table if one doesn't already exist:

```
CloudTableClient tableClient = storageAccount.CreateCloudTableClient();
CloudTable table = tableClient.GetTableReference("orders");
table.CreateIfNotExists();
```

Inserting records

To add entries to a table, you create objects based on the TableEntity base class and serialize them into the table using the Storage Client Library. The following properties are provided for you in this base class:

- **Partition Key**   Used to partition data across storage infrastructure
- **Row Key**   Unique identifier in a partition
- **Timestamp**   Time of last update maintained by Azure Storage
- **ETag**   Used internally to provide optimistic concurrency

The combination of partition key and row key must be unique within the table. This combination is used for load balancing and scaling, as well as for querying and sorting entities.

Follow these steps to add code that inserts records:

1. Add a class to your project, and then add the following code to it:

```
using System;
using Microsoft.WindowsAzure.Storage.Table;
public class OrderEntity : TableEntity
{
 public OrderEntity(string customerName, string orderDate)
 {
  this.PartitionKey = customerName;
  this.RowKey = orderDate;
 }
 public OrderEntity() { }
```

```
    public string OrderNumber { get; set; }
    public DateTime RequiredDate { get; set; }
    public DateTime ShippedDate { get; set; }
    public string Status { get; set; }
}
```

2. Add the following code to the console program to insert a record:

```
CloudTableClient tableClient = storageAccount.CreateCloudTableClient();

CloudTable table = tableClient.GetTableReference("orders");

OrderEntity newOrder = new OrderEntity("Archer", "20141216");

newOrder.OrderNumber = "101";

newOrder.ShippedDate = Convert.ToDateTime("12/18/2017");

newOrder.RequiredDate = Convert.ToDateTime("12/14/2017");

newOrder.Status = "shipped";

TableOperation insertOperation = TableOperation.Insert(newOrder);

table.Execute(insertOperation);
```

Inserting multiple records in a transaction

You can group inserts and other operations into a single batch transaction. All operations in the batch must take place on the same partition. You can have up to 100 entities in a batch. The total batch payload size cannot be greater than four MBs.

The following code illustrates how to insert several records as part of a single transaction. This is done after creating a storage account object and table.:

```
TableBatchOperation batchOperation = new TableBatchOperation();

OrderEntity newOrder1 = new OrderEntity("Lana", "20141217");
newOrder1.OrderNumber = "102";
newOrder1.ShippedDate = Convert.ToDateTime("1/1/1900");
newOrder1.RequiredDate = Convert.ToDateTime("1/1/1900");
newOrder1.Status = "pending";
OrderEntity newOrder2 = new OrderEntity("Lana", "20141218");
newOrder2.OrderNumber = "103";
newOrder2.ShippedDate = Convert.ToDateTime("1/1/1900");
newOrder2.RequiredDate = Convert.ToDateTime("12/25/2014");
newOrder2.Status = "open";
OrderEntity newOrder3 = new OrderEntity("Lana", "20141219");
newOrder3.OrderNumber = "103";
newOrder3.ShippedDate = Convert.ToDateTime("12/17/2014");
newOrder3.RequiredDate = Convert.ToDateTime("12/17/2014");
newOrder3.Status = "shipped";
```

```
batchOperation.Insert(newOrder1);
batchOperation.Insert(newOrder2);
batchOperation.Insert(newOrder3);
table.ExecuteBatch(batchOperation);
```

> **MORE INFO**   **ENTITY GROUP TRANSACTIONS**
>
> You can batch transactions that belong to the same table and partition group for insert, update, merge, delete, and related actions programmatically or by using the Storage API. For more information, see the reference at *http://msdn.microsoft.com/en-us/library/dd894038.aspx*.

Getting records in a partition

You can select all of the entities in a partition or a range of entities by partition and row key. Wherever possible, you should try to query with the partition key and row key. Querying entities by other properties does not work well because it launches a scan of the entire table.

Within a table, entities are ordered within the partition key. Within a partition, entities are ordered by the row key. RowKey is a string property, so sorting is handled as a string sort. If you are using a date value for your RowKey property use the following order: year, month, day. For instance, use 20140108 for January 8, 2014.

The following code requests all records within a partition using the PartitionKey property to query:

```
TableQuery<OrderEntity> query = new TableQuery<OrderEntity>().Where(
TableQuery.GenerateFilterCondition("PartitionKey", QueryComparisons.Equal, "Lana"));

foreach (OrderEntity entity in table.ExecuteQuery(query))
{
 Console.WriteLine("{0}, {1}\t{2}\t{3}", entity.PartitionKey, entity.RowKey,
 entity.Status, entity.RequiredDate);
}
Console.ReadKey();
```

Updating records

One technique you can use to update a record is to use InsertOrReplace(). This creates the record if one does not already exist or updates an existing record, based on the partition key and the row key. In this example, we retrieve a record we inserted during the batch insert example, change the status and shippedDate property and then execute an InsertOrReplace operation:

```
TableOperation retrieveOperation = TableOperation.Retrieve<OrderEntity>("Lana",
"20141217");
TableResult retrievedResult = table.Execute(retrieveOperation);
OrderEntity updateEntity = (OrderEntity)retrievedResult.Result;
if (updateEntity != null)
{
```

```
    updateEntity.Status = "shipped";
    updateEntity.ShippedDate = Convert.ToDateTime("12/20/2014");
    TableOperation insertOrReplaceOperation = TableOperation.
InsertOrReplace(updateEntity);
    table.Execute(insertOrReplaceOperation);
}
```

Deleting a record

To delete a record, first retrieve the record as shown in earlier examples, and then delete it with code, such as assuming deleteEntity is declared and populated similar to how we created one earlier:

```
TableOperation deleteOperation = TableOperation.Delete(deleteEntity);
table.Execute(deleteOperation);
Console.WriteLine("Entity deleted.");
```

Querying using ODATA

The Storage API for tables supports OData, which exposes a simple query interface for interacting with table data. Table storage does not support anonymous access, so you must supply credentials using the account key or a Shared Access Signature (SAS) (discussed in "Manage Access") before you can perform requests using OData.

To query what tables you have created, provide credentials, and issue a GET request as follows:

```
https://myaccount.table.core.windows.net/Tables
```

To query the entities in a specific table, provide credentials, and issue a GET request formatted as follows:

```
    https://<your account name>.table.core.windows.net/<your table
name>(PartitionKey='<partition-key>',RowKey='<row-key>')?$select=
<comma separated
property names>
```

> **NOTE   QUERY LIMITATIONS**
>
> The result is limited to 1,000 entities per request, and the query will run for a maximum of five seconds.

> **MORE INFO   ODATA**
>
> For more information on OData, see the reference at *http://msdn.microsoft.com/en-us/library/azure/dn535600.aspx*.

Designing, managing, and scaling table partitions

The Azure Table service can scale to handle massive amounts of structured data and billions of records. To handle that amount, tables are partitioned. The partition key is the unit of scale for storage tables. The table service will spread your table to multiple servers and key all rows with the same partition key co-located. Thus, the partition key is an important grouping, not only for querying but also for scalability.

There are three types of partition keys to choose from:

- **Single value**   There is one partition key for the entire table. This favors a small number of entities. It also makes batch transactions easier since batch transactions need to share a partition key to run without error. It does not scale well for large tables since all rows will be on the same partition server.

- **Multiple values**   This might place each partition on its own partition server. If the partition size is smaller, it's easier for Azure to load balance the partitions. Partitions might get slower as the number of entities increases. This might make further partitioning necessary at some point.

- **Unique values**   This is many small partitions. This is highly scalable, but batch transactions are not possible.

For query performance, you should use the partition key and row key together when possible. This leads to an exact row match. The next best thing is to have an exact partition match with a row range. It is best to avoid scanning the entire table.

Azure Storage Queues

The Azure Storage Queue service provides a mechanism for reliable inter-application messaging to support asynchronous distributed application workflows. This section covers a few fundamental features of the Queue service for adding messages to a queue, processing those messages individually or in a batch, and scaling the service.

> **MORE INFO**   **QUEUE SERVICE**
>
> For a general overview of working with the Queue service, see the reference at *http://azure. microsoft.com/en-us/documentation/articles/storage-dotnet-how-to-use-queues/.*

Adding messages to a queue

You can access your storage queues and add messages to a queue using many storage browsing tools; however, it is more likely you will add messages programmatically as part of your application workflow.

The following code demonstrates how to add messages to a queue. In order to use it, you will need a using statement for Microsoft.WindowsAzure.Storage.Queue. You can also create a queue in the portal called, "queue:"

```
CloudQueueClient queueClient = storageAccount.CreateCloudQueueClient();

//This code assumes you have a queue called "queue" already.  If you don't have one, you
should call queue.CreateIfNotExists();

CloudQueue queue = queueClient.GetQueueReference("queue");
queue.AddMessage(new CloudQueueMessage("Queued message 1"));
queue.AddMessage(new CloudQueueMessage("Queued message 2"));
queue.AddMessage(new CloudQueueMessage("Queued message 3"));
```

In the Azure Portal, you can browse to your storage account, browse to Queues, click the queue in the list and see the above messages.

> **NOTE   MESSAGE IDENTIFIERS**
>
> The Queue service assigns a message identifier to each message when it is added to the queue. This is opaque to the client, but it is used by the Storage Client Library to identify a message uniquely when retrieving, processing, and deleting messages.

> **MORE INFO   LARGE MESSAGES**
>
> There is a limit of 64 KB per message stored in a queue. It is considered best practice to keep the message small and to store any required data for processing in a durable store, such as SQL Azure, storage tables, or storage blobs. This also increases system reliability since each queued message can expire after seven days if not processed. For more information, see the reference at *https://docs.microsoft.com/en-us/azure/service-bus-messaging/service-bus-azure-and-service-bus-queues-compared-contrasted.*

Processing messages

Messages are typically published by a separate application in the system from the application that listens to the queue and processes messages. As shown in the previous section, you can create a CloudQueue reference and then proceed to call GetMessage() to de-queue the next available message from the queue as follows:

```
CloudQueueMessage message = queue.GetMessage(new TimeSpan(0, 5, 0));
if (message != null)
{
 string theMessage = message.AsString;
 // your processing code goes here
}
```

Retrieving a batch of messages

A queue listener can be implemented as single-threaded (processing one message at a time) or multi-threaded (processing messages in a batch on separate threads). You can retrieve up to 32 messages from a queue using the GetMessages() method to process multiple messages in parallel. As discussed in the previous sections, create a CloudQueue reference, and then proceed to call GetMessages(). Specify the number of items to de-queue up to 32 (this number can exceed the number of items in the queue) as follows:

```
IEnumerable<CloudQueueMessage> batch = queue.GetMessages(10, new TimeSpan(0, 5, 0));
foreach (CloudQueueMessage batchMessage in batch)
{
 Console.WriteLine(batchMessage.AsString);
}
```

Scaling queues

When working with Azure Storage queues, you need to consider a few scalability issues, including the messaging throughput of the queue itself and the design topology for processing messages and scaling out as needed.

Each individual queue has a target of approximately 20,000 messages per second (assuming a message is within 1 KB). You can partition your application to use multiple queues to increase this throughput value.

As for processing messages, it is more cost effective and efficient to pull multiple messages from the queue for processing in parallel on a single compute node; however, this depends on the type of processing and resources required. Scaling out compute nodes to increase processing throughput is usually also required.

You can configure VMs or cloud services to auto-scale by queue. You can specify the average number of messages to be processed per instance, and the auto-scale algorithm will queue to run scale actions to increase or decrease available instances accordingly.

> *MORE INFO* **BACK OFF POLLING**
>
> To control storage costs, you should implement a back off polling algorithm for queue message processing. This and other scale considerations are discussed in the reference at *https://docs.microsoft.com/en-us/azure/storage/common/storage-performance-checklist.*

Choose between Azure Storage Tables and Azure Cosmos DB Table API

Azure Cosmos DB is a cloud-hosted, NoSQL database that allows different data models to be implemented. NoSQL databases can be key/value stores, table stores, and graph stores (along with several others). Azure Cosmos DB has different engines that accommodate these different models. Azure Cosmos DB Table API is a key value store that is very similar to Azure Storage Tables.

The main differences between these products are:

- Azure Cosmos DB is much faster, with latency lower than 10ms on reads and 15ms on writes at any scale.

- Azure Table Storage only supports a single region with one optional readable secondary for high availability. Azure Cosmos DB supports over 30 regions.

- Azure Table Storage only indexes the partition key and the row key. Azure Cosmos DB automatically indexes all properties.

- Azure Table Storage only supports strong or eventual consistency. Consistency refers to how up to date the data is that you read and weather you see the latest writes from other users. Stronger consistency means less overall throughput and concurrent performance while having more up to date data. Eventual consistency allows for high concurrent throughput but you might see older data. Azure Cosmos DB supports five different consistency models and allows those models to be specified at the session level. This means that one user or feature might have a different consistency level than a different user or feature.

- Azure Table Storage only charges you for the storage fees, not for compute fees. This makes Azure Table Storage very affordable. Azure Cosmos DB charges for a Request Unit (RU) which really is a way for a PAAS product to charge for compute fees. If you need more RUs, you can scale them up. This makes Cosmos DB significantly more expensive than Azure Storage Tables.

Skill 2.3: Manage access and monitor storage

We have already learned how Azure Storage allows access through access keys, but what happens if we want to gain access to specific resources without giving keys to the entire storage account? In this topic, we'll introduce security issues that may arise and how to solve them.

Azure Storage has a built-in analytics feature called Azure Storage Analytics used for collecting metrics and logging storage request activity. You enable Storage Analytics Metrics to collect aggregate transaction and capacity data, and you enable Storage Analytics Logging to capture successful and failed request attempts to your storage account. This section covers how to enable monitoring and logging, control logging levels, set retention policies, and analyze the logs.

> **This skill covers how to:**
> - Generate shared access signatures, including client renewal and data validation
> - Create stored access policies
> - Regenerate storage account keys
> - Configure and use Cross-Origin Resource Sharing (CORS)
> - Set retention policies and logging levels
> - Analyze logs

Generate shared access signatures

By default, storage resources are protected at the service level. Only authenticated callers can access tables and queues. Blob containers and blobs can optionally be exposed for anonymous access, but you would typically allow anonymous access only to individual blobs. To authenticate to any storage service, a primary or secondary key is used, but this grants the caller access to all actions on the storage account.

An SAS is used to delegate access to specific storage account resources without enabling access to the entire account. An SAS token lets you control the lifetime by setting the start and expiration time of the signature, the resources you are granting access to, and the permissions being granted.

The following is a list of operations supported by SAS:

- Reading or writing blobs, blob properties, and blob metadata
- Leasing or creating a snapshot of a blob
- Listing blobs in a container
- Deleting a blob
- Adding, updating, or deleting table entities
- Querying tables

- Processing queue messages (read and delete)
- Adding and updating queue messages
- Retrieving queue metadata

This section covers creating an SAS token to access storage services using the Storage Client Library.

> **MORE INFO** **CONTROLLING ANONYMOUS ACCESS**
>
> To control anonymous access to containers and blobs, follow the instructions provided at *http://msdn.microsoft.com/en-us/library/azure/dd179354.aspx.*

> **MORE INFO** **CONSTRUCTING AN SAS URI**
>
> SAS tokens are typically used to authorize access to the Storage Client Library when interacting with storage resources, but you can also use it directly with the storage resource URI and use HTTP requests directly. For details regarding the format of an SAS URI, see *http://msdn.microsoft.com/en-us/library/azure/dn140255.aspx.*

Creating an SAS token (Blobs)

The following code shows how to create an SAS token for a blob container. Note that it is created with a start time and an expiration time. It is then applied to a blob container:

```
SharedAccessBlobPolicy sasPolicy = new SharedAccessBlobPolicy();
sasPolicy.SharedAccessExpiryTime = DateTime.UtcNow.AddHours(1);
sasPolicy.SharedAccessStartTime = DateTime.UtcNow.Subtract(new TimeSpan(0, 5, 0));
sasPolicy.Permissions = SharedAccessBlobPermissions.Read | SharedAccessBlobPermissions.
Write | SharedAccessBlobPermissions.Delete | SharedAccessBlobPermissions.List;
CloudBlobContainer files = blobClient.GetContainerReference("files");
string sasContainerToken = files.GetSharedAccessSignature(sasPolicy);
```

The SAS token grants read, write, delete, and list permissions to the container (rwdl). It looks like this:

```
?sv=2014-02-14&sr=c&sig=B6bi4xKkdgOXhWg3RWIDO5peekq%2FRjvnuo5o41hj1pA%3D&st=2014
 -12-24T14%3A16%3A07Z&se=2014-12-24T15%3A21%3A07Z&sp=rwdl
```

You can use this token as follows to gain access to the blob container without a storage account key:

```
StorageCredentials creds = new StorageCredentials(sasContainerToken);
CloudStorageAccount accountWithSAS = new CloudStorageAccount(accountSAS, "account-name",
endpointSuffix: null, useHttps: true);

CloudBlobClientCloudBlobContainer sasFiles = sasClient.GetContainerReference("files");
```

With this container reference, if you have write permissions, you can interact with the container as you normally would assuming you have the correct permissions.

Creating an SAS token (Queues)

Assuming the same account reference as created in the previous section, the following code shows how to create an SAS token for a queue:

```
CloudQueueClient queueClient = account.CreateCloudQueueClient();
CloudQueue queue = queueClient.GetQueueReference("queue");
SharedAccessQueuePolicy sasPolicy = new SharedAccessQueuePolicy();
sasPolicy.SharedAccessExpiryTime = DateTime.UtcNow.AddHours(1);
sasPolicy.Permissions = SharedAccessQueuePermissions.Read |
SharedAccessQueuePermissions.Add | SharedAccessQueuePermissions.Update |
SharedAccessQueuePermissions.ProcessMessages;
sasPolicy.SharedAccessStartTime = DateTime.UtcNow.Subtract(new TimeSpan(0, 5, 0));
string sasToken = queue.GetSharedAccessSignature(sasPolicy);
```

The SAS token grants read, add, update, and process messages permissions to the container (raup). It looks like this:

```
?sv=2014-02-14&sig=wE5oAUYHcGJ8chwyZZd3Byp5jK1Po8uKu2t%2FYzQsIhY%3D&st=2014-12-2
4T14%3A23%3A22Z&se=2014-12-24T15%3A28%3A22Z&sp=raup
```

You can use this token as follows to gain access to the queue and add messages:

```
StorageCredentials creds = new StorageCredentials(sasContainerToken);
CloudQueueClient sasClient = new CloudQueueClient(new
Uri("https://dataike1.queue.core.windows.net/"), creds);
CloudQueue sasQueue = sasClient.GetQueueReference("queue");
sasQueue.AddMessage(new CloudQueueMessage("new message"));
Console.ReadKey();
```

> **IMPORTANT** **SECURE USE OF SAS**
>
> Always use a secure HTTPS connection to generate an SAS token to protect the exchange of the URI, which grants access to protected storage resources.

Creating an SAS token (Tables)

The following code shows how to create an SAS token for a table:

```
SharedAccessTablePolicy sasPolicy = new SharedAccessTablePolicy();
sasPolicy.SharedAccessExpiryTime = DateTime.UtcNow.AddHours(1);
sasPolicy.Permissions = SharedAccessTablePermissions.Query |
SharedAccessTablePermissions.Add | SharedAccessTablePermissions.Update |
SharedAccessTablePermissions.Delete;
sasPolicy.SharedAccessStartTime = DateTime.UtcNow.Subtract(new TimeSpan(0, 5, 0));
string sasToken = table.GetSharedAccessSignature(sasPolicy);
```

The SAS token grants query, add, update, and delete permissions to the container (raud). It looks like this:

```
?sv=2014-02-14&tn=%24logs&sig=dsnI7RBA1xYQVr%2FTlpDEZMO2H8YtSGwtyUUntVmxstA%3D&s
t=2014-12-24T14%3A48%3A09Z&se=2014-12-24T15%3A53%3A09Z&sp=raud
```

Renewing an SAS token

SAS tokens have a limited period of validity based on the start and expiration times requested. You should limit the duration of an SAS token to limit access to controlled periods of time. You can extend access to the same application or user by issuing new SAS tokens on request. This should be done with appropriate authentication and authorization in place.

Validating data

When you extend write access to storage resources with SAS, the contents of those resources can potentially be made corrupt or even be tampered with by a malicious party, particularly if the SAS was leaked. Be sure to validate system use of all resources exposed with SAS keys.

Create stored access policies

Stored access policies provide greater control over how you grant access to storage resources using SAS tokens. With a stored access policy, you can do the following after releasing an SAS token for resource access:

- Change the start and end time for a signature's validity
- Control permissions for the signature
- Revoke access

The stored access policy can be used to control all issued SAS tokens that are based on the policy. For a step-by-step tutorial for creating and testing stored access policies for blobs, queues, and tables, *see http://azure.microsoft.com/en-us/documentation/articles/storage-dot-net-shared-access-signature-part-2.*

> **IMPORTANT RECOMMENDATION FOR SAS TOKENS**
>
> Use stored access policies wherever possible, or limit the lifetime of SAS tokens to avoid malicious use.

> **MORE INFO   STORED ACCESS POLICY FORMAT**
>
> For more information on the HTTP request format for creating stored access policies, see: *https://docs.microsoft.com/en-us/rest/api/storageservices/establishing-a-stored-access-policy.*

Regenerate storage account keys

When you create a storage account, two 512-bit storage access keys are generated for authentication to the storage account. This makes it possible to regenerate keys without impacting application access to storage.

The process for managing keys typically follows this pattern:

1. When you create your storage account, the primary and secondary keys are generated for you. You typically use the primary key when you first deploy applications that access the storage account.

2. When it is time to regenerate keys, you first switch all application configurations to use the secondary key.

3. Next, you regenerate the primary key, and switch all application configurations to use this primary key.

4. Next, you regenerate the secondary key.

> *IMPORTANT* **MANAGING KEY REGENERATION**
>
> It is imperative that you have a sound key management strategy. In particular, you must be certain that all applications are using the primary key at a given point in time to facilitate the regeneration process.

Regenerating storage account keys

To regenerate storage account keys using the portal, complete the following steps:

1. Navigate to the management portal accessed via *https://portal.azure.com*.

2. Select your storage account from your dashboard or your All Resources list.

3. Click the Keys box.

4. On the Manage Keys blade, click Regenerate Primary or Regenerate Secondary on the command bar, depending on which key you want to regenerate.

5. In the confirmation dialog box, click Yes to confirm the key regeneration.

Configure and use Cross-Origin Resource Sharing

Cross-Origin Resource Sharing (CORS) enables web applications running in the browser to call web APIs that are hosted by a different domain. Azure Storage blobs, tables, and queues all support CORS to allow for access to the Storage API from the browser. By default, CORS is disabled, but you can explicitly enable it for a specific storage service within your storage account.

> *MORE* **INFO ENABLING CORS**
>
> For additional information about enabling CORS for your storage accounts, see: *http://msdn. microsoft.com/en-us/library/azure/dn535601.aspx.*

Configure storage metrics

Storage Analytics metrics provide insight into transactions and capacity for your storage accounts. You can think of them as the equivalent of Windows Performance Monitor counters. By default, storage metrics are not enabled, but you can enable them through the management portal, using Windows PowerShell, or by calling the management API directly.

When you configure storage metrics for a storage account, tables are generated to store the output of metrics collection. You determine the level of metrics collection for transactions and the retention level for each service: Blob, Table, and Queue.

Transaction metrics record request access to each service for the storage account. You specify the interval for metric collection (hourly or by minute). In addition, there are two levels of metrics collection:

- **Service level** These metrics include aggregate statistics for all requests, aggregated at the specified interval. Even if no requests are made to the service, an aggregate entry is created for the interval, indicating no requests for that period.

- **API level** These metrics record every request to each service only if a request is made within the hour interval.

> **NOTE** **METRICS COLLECTED**
>
> All requests are included in the metrics collected, including any requests made by Storage Analytics.

Capacity metrics are only recorded for the Blob service for the account. Metrics include total storage in bytes, the container count, and the object count (committed and uncommitted).

Table 2-1 summarizes the tables automatically created for the storage account when Storage Analytics metrics are enabled.

TABLE 2-1 Storage metrics tables

METRICS	TABLE NAMES
Hourly metrics	$MetricsHourPrimaryTransactionsBlob $MetricsHourPrimaryTransactionsTable $MetricsHourPrimaryTransactionsQueue $MetricsHourPrimaryTransactionsFile
Minute metrics (cannot set through the management portal)	$MetricsMinutePrimaryTransactionsBlob $MetricsMinutePrimaryTransactionsTable $MetricsMinutePrimaryTransactionsQueue $MetricsMinutePrimaryTransactionsFile
Capacity (only for the Blob service)	$MetricsCapacityBlob

Retention can be configured for each service in the storage account. By default, Storage Analytics will not delete any metrics data. When the shared 20-terabyte limit is reached, new data cannot be written until space is freed. This limit is independent of the storage limit of the account. You can specify a retention period from 0 to 365 days. Metrics data is automatically deleted when the retention period is reached for the entry.

When metrics are disabled, existing metrics that have been collected are persisted up to their retention policy.

Configuring storage metrics and retention

To enable storage metrics and associated retention levels for Blob, Table, and Queue services in the portal, follow these steps:

1. Navigate to the management portal accessed via *https://portal.azure.com*.

   A. Select your storage account from your dashboard or your All resources list.

   B. Scroll down to the Usage section, and click the Capacity graph check box.

   C. On the Metric blade, click Diagnostics Settings on the command bar.

   D. Click the On button under Status. This shows the options for metrics and logging.

   - If this storage account uses blobs, select Blob Aggregate Metrics to enable service level metrics. Select Blob Per API Metrics for API level metrics.

   - If this storage account uses tables, select Table Aggregate Metrics to enable service level metrics. Select Table Per API Metrics for API level metrics.

   - If this storage account uses queues, select Queue Aggregate Metrics to enable service level metrics. Select Queue Per API Metrics for API level metrics.

2. Provide a value for retention according to your retention policy. Through the portal, this will apply to all services. It will also apply to Storage Analytics Logging if that is enabled. Select one of the available retention settings from the slider-bar , or enter a number from 0 to 365.

Analyze storage metrics

Storage Analytics metrics are collected in tables as discussed in the previous section. You can access the tables directly to analyze metrics, but you can also review metrics in both Azure management portals. This section discusses various ways to access metrics and review or analyze them.

> **MORE INFO   STORAGE MONITORING, DIAGNOSING, AND TROUBLESHOOTING**
>
> For more details on how to work with storage metrics and logs, see: *http://azure.microsoft. com/en-us/documentation/articles/storage-monitoring-diagnosing-troubleshooting.*

Monitor metrics

At the time of this writing, the portal features for monitoring metrics is limited to some pre-defined metrics, including total requests, total egress, average latency, and availability (see Figure 2-4). Click each box to see a Metric blade that provides additional detail.

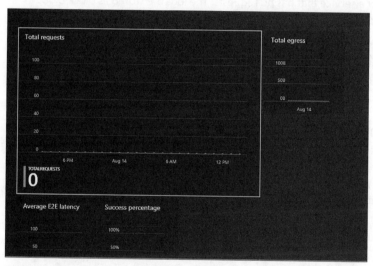

FIGURE 2-4 Monitoring overview from the portal

To monitor the metrics available in the portal, complete the following steps:

1. Navigate to the management portal accessed via *https://portal.azure.com.*
2. Select your storage account from your dashboard or your All Resources list.
3. Scroll down to the Monitor section, and view the monitoring boxes summarizing statistics. You'll see TotalRequests, TotalEgress, AverageE2ELatency, and AvailabilityToday by default.
4. Click each metric box to view additional details for each metric. You'll see metrics for blobs, tables, and queues if all three metrics are being collected.

Configure Storage Analytics Logging

Storage Analytics Logging provides details about successful and failed requests to each storage service that has activity across the account's blobs, tables, and queues. By default, storage logging is not enabled, but you can enable it through the management portal, by using Windows PowerShell, or by calling the management API directly.

When you configure Storage Analytics Logging for a storage account, a blob container named $logs is automatically created to store the output of the logs. You choose which services you want to log for the storage account. You can log any or all of the Blob, Table, or Queue servicesLogs are created only for those services that have activity, so you will not be charged if you enable logging for a service that has no requests. The logs are stored as block blobs as requests are logged and are periodically committed so that they are available as blobs.

Retention can be configured for each service in the storage account. By default, Storage Analytics will not delete any logging data. When the shared 20-terabyte limit is reached, new data cannot be written until space is freed. This limit is independent of the storage limit of the account. You can specify a retention period from 0 to 365 days. Logging data is automatically deleted when the retention period is reached for the entry.

Set retention policies and logging levels To enable storage logging and associated retention levels for Blob, Table, and Queue services in the portal, follow these steps:

1. Navigate to the management portal accessed via *https://portal.azure.com*.

2. Select your storage account from your dashboard or your All resources list.

3. Under the Metrics section, click Diagnostics.

4. Click the On button under Status. This shows the options for enabling monitoring features.

5. If this storage account uses blobs, select Blob Logs to log all activity.

6. If this storage account uses tables, select Table Logs to log all activity.

7. If this storage account uses queues, select Queue Logs to log all activity.

8. Provide a value for retention according to your retention policy. Through the portal, this will apply to all services. It will also apply to Storage Analytics Metrics if that is enabled. Select one of the available retention settings from the drop-down list, or enter a number from 0 to 365.

> **NOTE CONTROLLING LOGGED ACTIVITIES**
>
> From the portal, when you enable or disable logging for each service, you enable read, write, and delete logging. To log only specific activities, use Windows PowerShell cmdlets.

Enable client-side logging

You can enable client-side logging using Microsoft Azure storage libraries to log activity from client applications to your storage accounts. For information on the .NET Storage Client Library, see: *http://msdn.microsoft.com/en-us/library/azure/dn782839.aspx*. For information on the Storage SDK for Java, see: *http://msdn.microsoft.com/en-us/library/azure/dn782844.aspx*.

Analyze logs

Logs are stored as block blobs in delimited text format. When you access the container, you can download logs for review and analysis using any tool compatible with that format. Within the logs, you'll find entries for authenticated and anonymous requests, as listed in Table 2-2.

TABLE 2-2 Authenticated and anonymous logs

Request type	Logged requests
Authenticated requests	■ Successful requests ■ Failed requests such as timeouts, authorization, throttling issues, and other errors ■ Requests that use an SAS ■ Requests for analytics data
Anonymous requests	■ Successful requests ■ Server errors ■ Timeouts for client or server ■ Failed GET requests with error code 304 (Not Modified)

Logs include status messages and operation logs. Status message columns include those shown in Table 2-3. Some status messages are also reported with storage metrics data. There are many operation logs for the Blob, Table, and Queue services.

> **MORE INFO** **STATUS MESSAGES AND OPERATION LOGS**
>
> For a detailed list ofx specific logs and log format specifics, see: *http://msdn.microsoft.com/en-us/library/azure/hh343260.aspx* and *http://msdn.microsoft.com/en-us/library/hh343259.aspx*.

TABLE 2-3 Information included in logged status messages

Column	Description
Status Message	Indicates a value for the type of status message, indicating type of success or failure
Description	Describes the status, including any HTTP verbs or status codes
Billable	Indicates whether the request was billable
Availability	Indicates whether the request is included in the availability calculation for storage metrics

Finding your logs

When storage logging is configured, log data is saved to blobs in the $logs container created for your storage account. You can't see this container by listing containers, but you can navigate directly to the container to access, view, or download the logs.

To view analytics logs produced for a storage account, do the following:

Using a storage browsing tool, navigate to the $logs container within the storage account you have enabled Storage Analytics Logging for using this convention: *https://<accountname>. blob.core.windows.net/$logs*.

View the list of log files with the convention *<servicetype>/YYYY/MM/DD/ HHMM/<counter>.log*.

Select the log file you want to review, and download it using the storage browsing tool.

> **MORE INFO**   **LOG METADATA**
>
> The blob name for each log file does not provide an indication of the time range for the logs. You can search this information in the blob metadata using storage browsing tools or Windows PowerShell.

View logs with Microsoft Excel

Storage logs are recorded in a delimited format so that you can use any compatible tool to view logs. To view logs data in Excel, follow these steps:

1. Open Excel, and on the Data menu, click From Text.

2. Find the log file and click Import.

3. During import, select Delimited format. Select Semicolon as the only delimiter, and Double-Quote (") as the text qualifier.

Analyze logs

After you load your logs into a viewer like Excel, you can analyze and gather information such as the following:

- Number of requests from a specific IP range

- Which tables or containers are being accessed and the frequency of those requests

- Which user issued a request, in particular, any requests of concern

- Slow requests

- How many times a particular blob is being accessed with an SAS URL

- Details to assist in investigating network errors

> **MORE INFO**   **LOG ANALYSIS**
>
> You can run the Azure HDInsight Log Analysis Toolkit (LAT) for a deeper analysis of your storage logs. For more information, see: *https://hadoopsdk.codeplex.com/releases/ view/117906*.

Skill 2.4: Implement Azure SQL databases

In this section, you learn about Microsoft Azure SQL Database, a PaaS offering for relational data.

> **This skill covers how to:**
> - Choose the appropriate database tier and performance level
> - Configure and perform point in time recovery
> - Enable geo-replication
> - Import and export data and schema
> - Scale Azure SQL databases
> - Manage elastic pools, including DTUs and eDTUs
> - Manage limits and resource governor
> - Implement Azure SQL Data Sync
> - Implement graph database functionality in Azure SQL

Choosing the appropriate database tier and performance level

Choosing a SQL Database tier used to be simply a matter of storage space. Recently, Microsoft added new tiers that also affect the performance of SQL Database. This tiered pricing is called Service Tiers. There are three service tiers to choose from, and while they still each have restrictions on storage space, they also have some differences that might affect your choice. The major difference is in a measurement called database throughput units (DTUs). A DTU is a blended measure of CPU, memory, disk reads, and disk writes. Because SQL Database is a shared resource with other Azure customers, sometimes performance is not stable or predictable. As you go up in performance tiers, you also get better predictability in performance.

- **Basic** Basic tier is meant for light workloads. There is only one performance level of the basic service tier. This level is good for small use, new projects, testing, development, or learning.

- **Standard** Standard tier is used for most production online transaction processing (OLTP) databases. The performance is more predictable than the basic tier. In addition, there are four performance levels under this tier, levels S0 to S3 (S4 – S12 are currently in preview).

- **Premium** Premium tier continues to scale at the same level as the standard tier. In addition, performance is typically measured in seconds. For instance, the basic tier can handle 16,600 transactions per hour. The standard/S2 level can handle 2,570 transactions per minute. The top tier of premium can handle 735 transactions per second. That translates to 2,645,000 per hour in basic tier terminology.

There are many similarities between the various tiers. Each tier has a 99.99 percent up-time SLA, backup and restore capabilities, access to the same tooling, and the same database engine features. Fortunately, the levels are adjustable, and you can change your tier as your scaling requirements change.

The management portal can help you select the appropriate level. You can review the metrics on the Metrics tab to see the current load of your database and decide whether to scale up or down.

1. Click the SQL database you want to monitor.

2. Click the DTU tab, as shown in Figure 2-5.

3. Add the following metrics:

- CPU Percentage

- Physical Data Reads Percentage

- Log Writes Percentage

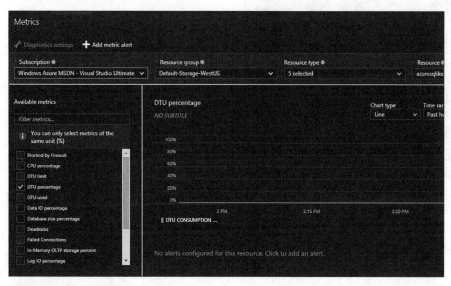

FIGURE 2-5 The Metrics tab

All three of these metrics are shown relative to the DTU of your database. If you reach 80 percent of your performance metrics, it's time to consider increasing your service tier or performance level. If you're consistently below 10 percent of the DTU, you might consider decreasing your service tier or performance level. Be aware of momentary spikes in usage when making your choice.

In addition, you can configure an email alert for when your metrics are 80 percent of your selected DTU by completing the following steps:

1. Click the metric.

2. Click Add Rule.

3. The first page of the Create Alert Rule dialog box is shown in Figure 2-6. Add a name and description, and then click the right arrow.

FIGURE 2-6 The first page of the Add An Alert Rule dialog box

4. Scroll down for the rest of the page of the Create Alert Rule dialog box, shown in Figure 2-7, select the condition and the threshold value.

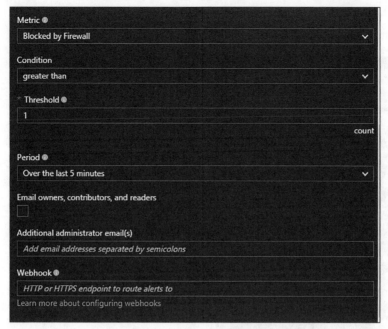

Metric ⓘ

Blocked by Firewall ⌄

Condition

greater than ⌄

Threshold ⓘ

1

count

Period ⓘ

Over the last 5 minutes ⌄

Email owners, contributors, and readers

☐

Additional administrator email(s)

Add email addresses separated by semicolons

Webhook ⓘ

HTTP or HTTPS endpoint to route alerts to

Learn more about configuring webhooks

FIGURE 2-7 The second page of the Create Alert Rule dialog box

5. Select your alert evaluation window. An email will be generated if the event happens over a specific duration. You should indicate at least 10 minutes.

6. Select the action. You can choose to send an email either to the service administrator(s) or to a specific email address.

Configuring and performing point in time recovery

Azure SQL Database does a full backup every week, a differential backup each day, and an incremental log backup every five minutes. The incremental log backup allows for a point in time restore, which means the database can be restored to any specific time of day. This means that if you accidentally delete a customer's table from your database, you will be able to recover it with minimal data loss if you know the timeframe to restore from that has the most recent copy.

The length of time it takes to do a restore varies. The further away you get from the last differential backup determines the longer the restore operation takes because there are more log backups to restore. When you restore a new database, the service tier stays the same, but the performance level changes to the minimum level of that tier.

Depending on your service tier, you will have different backup retention periods. Basic retains backups for 7 days. Standard and premium retains for 35 days.

You can restore a database that was deleted as long as you are within the retention period. Follow these steps to restore a database:

1. Select the database you want to restore, and then click Restore.

2. The Restore dialog box opens, as shown in Figure 2-8.

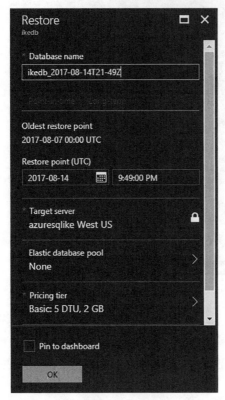

FIGURE 2-8 The Restore dialog box

3. Select a database name.

4. Select a restore point. You can use the slider bar or manually enter a date and time.

5. You can also restore a deleted database. Click on the SQL Server (not the database) that once held the database you wish to restore. Select the Deleted Databases tab, as shown in Figure 2-9.

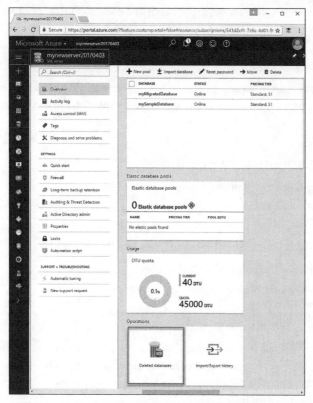

FIGURE 2-9 The Deleted Databases tab for SQL databases in the management portal

6. Select the database you want to restore.

7. Click Restore as you did in Step 1.

8. Specify a database name for the new database.

9. Click Submit.

Enabling geo-replication

Every Azure SQL Database subscription has built-in redundancy. Three copies of your data are stored across fault domains in the datacenter to protect against server and hardware failure. This is built in to the subscription price and is not configurable.

In addition, you can configure active geo-replication. This allows your data to be replicated between Azure data centers. Active geo-replication has the following benefits:

- Database-level disaster recovery goes quickly when you've replicated transactions to databases on different SQL Database servers in the same or different regions.

- You can fail over to a different data center in the event of a natural disaster or other intentionally malicious act.
- Online secondary databases are readable, and they can be used as load balancers for read-only workloads such as reporting.
- With automatic asynchronous replication, after an online secondary database has been seeded, updates to the primary database are automatically copied to the secondary database.

Creating an offline secondary database

To create an offline secondary database in the portal, follow these steps:

1. Navigate to your SQL database in the management portal accessed via *https://portal.azure.com*.
2. Scroll to the Geo Replication section, and click the Configure Geo Replication box.
3. On the Geo Replication blade, select your target region.
4. On the Create Secondary blade, click Create.

> *NOTE* **USES FOR CREATING AN OFFLINE SECONDARY**
>
> Another use for this feature has to do with the ability to terminate the continuous copy relationship between a primary and secondary database. You can terminate the relationship and then upgrade the primary database to a different schema to support a software upgrade. The secondary database gives you a rollback option.

Creating an online secondary database

Before you create an online secondary, the following requirements must be met:

- The secondary database must have the same name as the primary.
- They must be on separate servers.
- They both must be on the same subscription.
- The secondary server cannot be a lower performance tier than the primary.

The steps for configuring an active secondary is the same as creating an offline secondary, except you can select the target region, as shown in Figure 2-10.

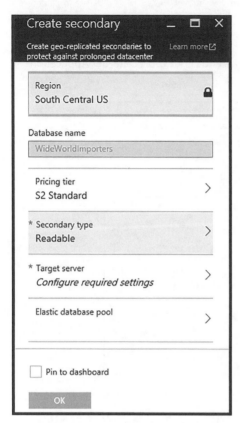

FIGURE 2-10 The New Secondary For Geo Replication dialog box for creating an active secondary

Creating an online secondary database

1. To create an online secondary in the portal, follow these steps:Navigate to your SQL database in the management portal accessed via *https://portal.azure.com*.

2. On the Create Secondary blade, change the Secondary Type to Readable.

3. Click Create to create the secondary.

Import and export schema and data

The on-premise version of Microsoft SQL Server has long had the ability to export and import data using a BACPAC file. This file will also work with Azure SQL Database. A BACPAC file is just a ZIP file that contains all of the metadata and state data of a SQL Server database.

The easiest way to import schema and data from an on-premise SQL Server into an Azure SQL Database is to use SQL Server Management Studio (SSMS). The general steps are:

1. Export source database using SSMS

2. Import database to a new destination using SSMS.

Export source database

1. Open SQL Server Management Studio

2. Right-click on the source database, click Tasks, and click Export Data-tier Application (see Figure 2-11).

Export Data-tier Application...

FIGURE 2-11 SSMS Export Data-tier right-click menu

3. Click Next on the Welcome screen (Figure 2-12).

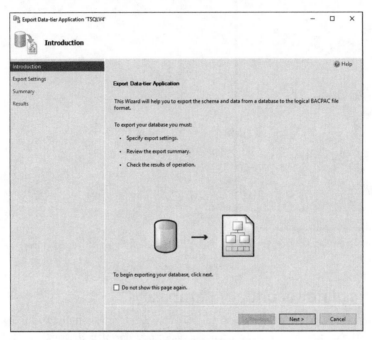

FIGURE 2-12 Welcome screen for BACPAC process

4. In the Export Settings screen, you can choose where the BACPAC file should be stored. You can either save it to a local disk or save it in an Azure Storage blob container. Either method is easy to use when you import the BACPAC file (Figure 2-13).

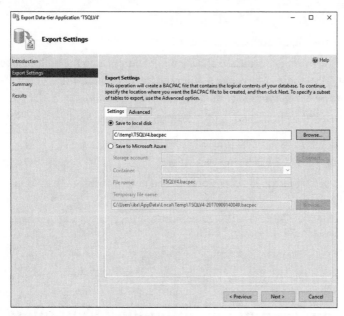

FIGURE 2-13 Location for BACPAC file

5. On the Advanced tab (Figure 2-14), you can selective choose specific tables or schemas or the entire database.

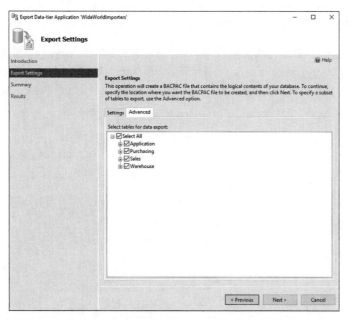

FIGURE 2-14 The advanced tab for selecting the correct tables and schema

6. Then click Finish and we're all done.

Import BACPAC file into Azure SQL Database

1. Connect to your Azure SQL Database using SSMS.

2. You may need to log into the portal and allow your IP address in to the built-in firewall used by Azure SQL Database. More information can be found here: *https://docs.micro-soft.com/en-us/azure/sql-database/sql-database-firewall-configure*.

    A. Right-click on the database folder and click Import Data-tier Application.

    B. Click Next.

    C. Choose the correct BACPAC file and click Next.

    D. In the next screen (Figure 2-15), click Connect and enter your storage account name and account key.

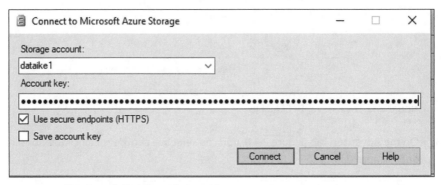

FIGURE 2-15 The Connect To Microsoft Azure Storage screen

3. Name the new database and select the pricing tier (see Figure 2-16). Warning: this option determines pricing. If you are just experimenting, choose Basic under the Edition of Microsoft Azure SQL Database.

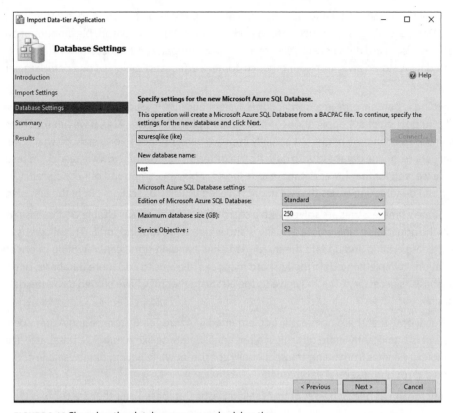

FIGURE 2-16 Choosing the database name and pricing tier

4. Click Next and Finish.

5. The schema and data will import into the new database that you've named.

Scale Azure SQL databases

There are two methods for preparing a relational database for a high transaction load. First, we can scale-up. This means that we will add CPU, memory, and better disk i/o to handle the load. In Azure SQL Database, scaling up is very simple: we just move the slider bar over to the right or choose a new pricing tier. This will give us the ability to handle more DTUs. Under a very high load, we might not be able to scale-up much futher. That would mean we'd have to use our second method, scale-out.

Scaling out a database means that we would break apart a large database into small portions. This is called sharding. We would put one portion of our data in one database and another portion of our data in a different database. We can do this by function, by date, by geo-location of our brand offices, by business unit, or some other method.

We may also shard a database simply because it is too large to be stored in a single Azure SQL Database. Or it is too much data to backup and restore in a reasonable amount of time. We may also shard data because we are a software company and our customers require that their data is stored away from our other customers, effectively giving us one database per customer.

Sharding is burdensome in a transactional system because it usually involves rewriting a significant portion of our applications to handle multiple databases. Also, if we get the sharding boundaries wrong, we might not actually improve performance. For instance, what if we often join data from one database with data from a different database? Now we're locking resources while we wait for the slower database to respond. This can compound our concurrency, blocking, and deadlocking issues that we might have led us towards scaling-out in the first place.

Some of these issues are solved with a shard map. This is usually a table or database that tells the application where data actually is and where to go looking for it. This allows us to move data around and update the shard map, thus avoiding significant rewriting of our application. If implemented correctly, shard maps can allow us to add more databases or delete database as necessary. This may give us the elasticity that may have eluded us on the database thus far.

You'll note that sharding is easily implemented in Azure Table Storage and Azure Cosmos DB, but is significantly more difficult in a relational database like Azure SQL Database. The complexity comes from being transactionally consistent while having data available and spread throughout several databases.

Microsoft has released a set of tools called Elastic Database Tools that are compatible with Azure SQL Database. This client library can be used in your application to create sharded databases. It has a split-merge tool that will allow you to create new nodes or drop nodes without data loss. It also includes a tool that will keep schema consistent across all the nodes by running scripts on each node individually.

The main power of the Elastic Database Tools is the ability to fan-out queries across multiple shards without a lot of code changes. Follow these general steps to use a sharded database:

1. Get a Shard Map.
   - There are several different types of shard maps, for instance range shard map will tell you what range of values exist in which databases. If we were to divide our data by customer ID, then we would make sure all tables in our database included a customer ID. We could grab anything about that customer, including their contacts, orders, invoices, payments, customer service disputes, and employees as long as we have the correct customer ID. A shard map might look like this:
     - 1 – 100   = Database1
     - 101 – 200 = Database2
     - 202 – 300 = Database 3
2. Create a MultiShareConnection Object

- This is similar to a regular SqlConnection object, except in represents a connection to a set of shards.

3. Create a multi-shard command.

4. Set the CommandText property

5. ExecuteReader

6. View the results using the MultiShardDataReader class.

7. Assuming you had a ShardMap object, the query would look like this:

```
using (MultiShardConnection conn = new MultiShardConnection(
                              myShardMap.GetShards(),
                              myShardConnectionString)
    )
{
using (MultiShardCommand cmd = conn.CreateCommand())
    {
      cmd.CommandText = "SELECT c1, c2, c3 FROM ShardedTable";
      cmd.CommandType = CommandType.Text;
      cmd.ExecutionOptions = MultiShardExecutionOptions.IncludeShardNameColumn;
      cmd.ExecutionPolicy = MultiShardExecutionPolicy.PartialResults;

      using (MultiShardDataReader sdr = cmd.ExecuteReader())
        {
            while (sdr.Read())
              {
                  var c1Field = sdr.GetString(0);
                  var c2Field = sdr.GetFieldValue<int>(1);
                  var c3Field = sdr.GetFieldValue<Int64>(2);
              }
        }
    }
}
```

Managed elastic pools, including DTUs and eDTUs

A single SQL Database server can have several databases on it. Those databases can each have their own size and pricing tier. This might work out well if we always know exactly how large each database will be and how many DTUs are needed for them individually. What happens if we don't really know that? Or we'd like the databases on a single server to share a DTU pool? Elastic pools (not to be confused with the last topic, Elastic Tools) are used to do exactly this: share DTUs across databases on a single server.

Elastic pools enable the user to purchase elastic Database Transaction Units (eDTUs) for a pool of multiple databases. The user adds databases to the pool, sets the minimum and maximum eDTUS for each database, and sets the eDTU limit of the pool based on their budget. This means that within the pool, each database is given the ability to auto-scale in a set range.

In Figure 2-17, you will see a database that spends most of its time idle, but occasionally spikes in activity. This database is a good candidate for an Elastic pool.

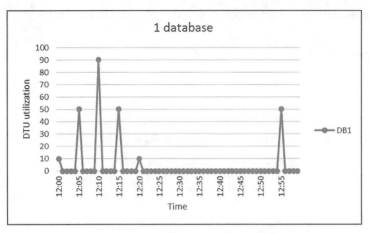

FIGURE 2-17 Choosing the right database to participate in the pool

To create an Elastic pool, follow these steps:

1. Click on your database server and click New Pool.

   ■ The new pool pane appears (Figure 2-18).

FIGURE 2-18 Creating an Elastic pool

2. Name the pool a unique name.

3. Choose a pricing tier for the pool.

4. To choose the databases you want to participate in the pool, click Configure Pool. This pane appears in Figure 2-19.

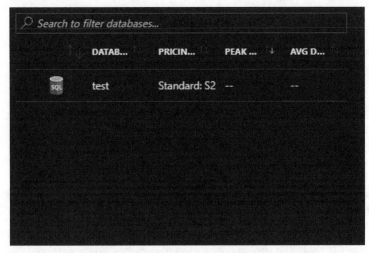

FIGURE 2-19 Choosing the databases that participate in the Elastic pool

Implement Azure SQL Data Sync

SQL Data Sync is a new service for Azure SQL Database. It allows you to bi-directionally replicate data between two Azure SQL Databases or between an Azure SQL Database and an on-premise SQL Server.

A Sync Group is a group of databases that you want to synchronize using Azure SQL Data Sync. A Sync Schema is the data you want to synchronize. Sync Direction allows you to synchronize data in either one direction or bi-directionally. Sync Interval controls how often synchronization occurs. Finally, a Conflict Resolution Policy determines who wins if data conflicts with one another.

The following diagram (Figure 2-20) shows how Azure Data Sync keeps multiple databases consistent with each other.

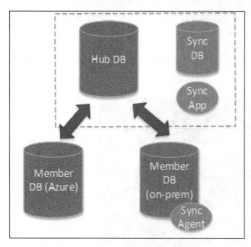

FIGURE 2-20 Azure Data Sync diagram

The hub database must always be an Azure SQL Database. A member database can either be Azure SQL Database or an on-premise SQL Server.

It is important to note that this is a method to of keeping data consistent across multiple databases, it is not an ETL tool. This should not be used to populate a data warehouse or to migrate an on-premise SQL Server to the cloud. This can be used to populate a read-only version of the database for reporting, but only if the schema will be 100% consistent.

> **MORE INFO AZURE SQL DATA SYNC**
>
> Here's a tutorial for creating a Data Sync Group: *https://docs.microsoft.com/en-us/azure/sql-database/sql-database-get-started-sql-data-sync*.

Implement graph database functionality in Azure SQL Database

SQL Server 2017 introduces a new graph database feature. This feature hasn't been released in the on-premise edition as of this writing, but should be available in Azure SQL Database by the time this book is released. We discuss graph databases in the next section on Azure Cosmos DB as well.

So far, we've discussed a NoSQL solution when we covered Azure Storage Tables. That was a key-value store. We will cover a different type of NoSQL solution, JSON document storage, when we examine Azure Cosmos DB DocumentDB. Graph databases are yet another NoSQL solution. Graph database introduce two new vocabulary words: nodes and relationships.

Nodes are entities in relational database terms. Each node is popularly a noun, like a person, an event, an employee, a product, or a car. A relationship is similar to a relationship in SQL Server in that it defines that a connection exists between nouns. Where the relationship in graph databases differ is that it is hierarchal in nature, where it tends to be flat in SQL Server, PostgresSQL, and other relational storage engines.

A graph is an abstract representation of a set of objects where nodes are linked with relationships in a hierarchy. A graph database is a database with an explicit and enforceable graph structure. Another key difference between a relational storage engine and a graph database storage engine is that as the number of nodes increase, the performance cost stays the same. Any relational database professional will tell you that joining tables will burden the engine and be a common source of performance issues when scaling. Graph databases don't suffer from that issue. Also, entities can be connected with each other through several different paths.

So where relational databases are optimized for aggregation, graph databases are optimized for having plenty of connections between nodes. Graph databases are popularly traversed through a domain specific language (DSL) called Gremlin.

In Azure SQL Database, graph-like capabilities are implemented through T-SQL. Graph databases popularly have several different relationship types that are possible between nodes. Azure SQL Database only has many-to-many relationships.

You can create graph objects in T-SQL with the following syntax:

```
CREATE TABLE Person (ID INTEGER PRIMARY KEY, Name VARCHAR(100), Age INT) AS NODE;
CREATE TABLE friends (StartDate date) AS EDGE;
```

This is very similar to the standard CREATE TABLE syntax, with the added "AS NODE" or "AS EDGE" at the end.

Azure SQL Database supports new query syntax for traversing the graph hierarchy. This query looks something like this:

```
SELECT Restaurant.name
FROM Person, likes, Restaurant
WHERE MATCH (Person-(likes)->Restaurant)
AND Person.name = 'John';
```

Notice the MATCH keyword in the T-SQL WHERE clause. This will show us every person that likes a restaurant named John.

MORE INFO **AZURE SQL GRAPH**

Here's a tutorial for creating a graph relationships that currently works with Azure SQL Database: *https://docs.microsoft.com/en-us/sql/relational-databases/graphs/sql-graph-sample.*

Skill 2.5: Implement Azure Cosmos DB DocumentDB

Azure Cosmos DB DocumentDB is a JSON document store database, similar to MongoDB. JSON document stores are quite a bit different than traditional relational database engines, and any attempt to map concepts will likely be futile. With that in mind, we'll do our best to use your existing knowledge of RDBMS's while discussing this topic. JSON document stores are the fastest growing NoSQL solutions. Developers gravitate towards it because it doesn't require assembling or disassembling object hierarchies into a flat relational design. Azure Cosmos DB was originally designed as a JSON document storage product. It has since added support for key-value (Table API) and graph (Gremlin).

JSON has been the lingua franca of data exchange on the internet for over a decade. Here is an example of JSON:

```
{
    "glossary": {
        "title": "example glossary",
        "GlossDiv": {
            "title": "S",
            "GlossList": {
                "GlossEntry": {
                    "ID": "SGML",
                    "SortAs": "SGML",
                    "GlossTerm": "Standard Generalized Markup Language",
                    "Acronym": "SGML",
                    "Abbrev": "ISO 8879:1986",
                    "GlossDef": {
                        "para": "A meta-markup language, used to create markup
                         languages such as DocBook.",
                        "GlossSeeAlso": ["GML", "XML"]
                    },
                    "GlossSee": "markup"
                }
            }
        }
    }
}
```

Notice the hierarchal nature of JSON. One of the key advantages of JSON is that it can express an object model that developers often create in code. Object models have parent nodes and child nodes. In our above example, GlossTerm is a child object of GlossEntry. JSON can also express arrays: GlossSeeAlso has two values in it. When relational database developers create an API to store JSON, they have to undergo a process called shredding where they remove each individual element and store them in flat tables that have relationships with each other. This process was time-consuming, offered little in real business value, and was prone to errors. Because of these drawbacks, developers often turn towards JSON document stores, where saving a document is as easy as pressing the Save icon in Microsoft Word. In this section we'll show how to create an object model, save it, and query it using Azure Cosmos DB DocumentDB.

This skill covers how to:

- Choose the Cosmos DB API surface
- Create Cosmos DB API Databases and Collections
- Query documents
- Run Cosmos DB queries
- Create Graph API databases
- Execute GraphDB queries

Choose the Cosmos DB API surface

Like previously mentioned, Azure Cosmos DB is a multi-model database that has several different APIs you can choose between: Table, DocumentDB, and GraphDB.

Azure Cosmos DB Table API provides the same functionality and the same API surface as Azure Storage tables. If you have an existing application that uses Azure Storage tables, you can easily migrate that application to use Azure Cosmos DB. This will allow you to take advantage of better performance, global data distribution, and automatic indexing of all fields, thus reducing significant management overhead of your existing Azure Storage table application.

Azure Cosmos DB Document DB is an easy-to-implement JSON document storage API. It is an excellent choice for mobile applications, web application, and IoT applications. It allows for rapid software development by cutting down the code the developer has to write to either shred their object model into a relational store, or manage the consistency of manual indexing in Azure Storage Tables. It also is compatible with MongoDB, another JSON document storage product. You can migrate an existing MongoDB application to Azure Cosmos DB Document-DB.

Azure Cosmos DB supports the Gremlin, a popular graph API. This allows developers to write applications that take advantage of Graph traversal of their data structures. Graph databases allow us to define the relationship between entities that are stored. For instance, we can declare that one entity works for another one, is married to a different one, and owns even a different one. Entities are not people, rather they are entries defined in our data store. We can say Paula works for Sally and is married to Rick. Paula owns a vintage Chevy Corvette. Knowing these, we can write a simple line of code in Gremlin to find out what car Paula owns. Graph databases excel at defining relationships and exploring the network of those relationships. As a result, they have been popular as engines for social media applications. Because Azure Cosmos DB supports the Gremlin API, it is easy to port existing applications that use it to Azure Cosmos DB.

Create Cosmos DB API Database and Collections

Each Cosmos DB account must have at least one database. A database is a logical container that can contain collections of documents and users. Users are the mechanism that get permissions to Cosmos DB resources. Collections primarily contain JSON documents. Collections should store JSON documents of the same type and purpose, just like a SQL Server table. Collections are different than tables because they don't enforce that documents have a particular schema. This can be very foreign to the relational database developer who assumes that every record in a table will have the same number of columns with the same data types. Collections *should* have documents of the same properties and data types, but they aren't required to. Azure Cosmos DB DocumentDB gracefully handles if columns don't exist on a document. For instance, if we are looking for all customers in zip code 92101, and a customer JSON document doesn't happen to have that property, Azure Cosmos DB just ignores the document and doesn't return it.

Collections can also store stored procedures, triggers, and functions. These concepts are also similar to relational databases, like Microsoft SQL Server. Stored procedures are application logic that are registered with a collection and repeatedly executed. Triggers are application logic that execute either before or after an insert, update (replace), or delete operation. Functions allow you to model a custom query operator and extend the core DocumentDB API query language. Unlike SQL Server, where these components are written in Transact-SQL, Azure DocumentDB stored procedures, triggers, and functions are written in JavaScript.

Before we can begin writing code against Azure Cosmos DB, we must first create an Azure Cosmos DB account. Follow these steps:

1. Sign in to the Azure portal.

2. On the left pane, click New, Databases, and then click Azure Cosmos DB.

3. On the New account blade, choose your programming model. For our example, click SQL (DocumentDB).

4. Choose a unique ID for this account. It must be globally unique, such as developazure1, but then you should call yours developazure(your given name here). This will be prepended to documents.azure.com to create the URI you will use to gain access to your account.

5. Choose the Subscription, Resource Group, and Location of your account.

6. Click Create.

7. Now let's create a Visual Studio solution.

8. Open Visual Studio 2015 or 2017.

9. Create a New Project.

10. Select Templates, Visual C#, Console Application.

11. Name your project.

12. Click OK.

13. Open Nuget Package Manager.

14. In the Browse tab, look for Azure DocumentDB. Add the Microsoft.Azure.DocumentDB client to your project.

15. In order to use the code, you may need a using statement like this:

```
using Microsoft.Azure.Documents.Client;
using Microsoft.Azure.Documents;
using Newtonsoft.Json;
```

Azure Cosmos DB requires two things in order to create and query documents, an account name and an access key. This should be familiar to you if you read the section on Azure Storage blobs or Azure Storage tables. You should store them in constants in your application like this:

```
private const string account = "<your account URI>";

private const string key = "<your key>";
```

Azure DocumentDB SDK also has several async calls, so we'll create our own async function called TestDocDb. We'll call it in the Main function of the console app.

```
static void Main(string[] args)
{
    TestDocDb().Wait();
}
```

You can find both of these things in Azure portal for your Azure Cosmos DB account. To create a database named SalesDB, use the following code:

```
private static async Task TestDocDb()
{
string id = "SalesDB";
var database = _client.CreateDatabaseQuery().Where(db => db.Id == id).AsEnumerable().
FirstOrDefault();

if (database == null)
{
database = await client.CreateDatabaseAsync(new Database { Id = id });
}
```

Now that we have a database for our sales data, we'll want to store our customers. We'll do that in our Customers collection. We'll create that collection with the following code:

```
string collectionName = "Customers";
var collection = client.CreateDocumentCollectionQuery(database.CollectionsLink).
Where(c => c.Id == collectionName).AsEnumerable().FirstOrDefault();
if (collection == null)
{
collection = await client.CreateDocumentCollectionAsync(database.CollectionsLink,
 new DocumentCollection { Id = collectionName});
}
```

Now let's add a few documents to our collection. Before we can do that, let's create a couple of plain-old CLR objects (POCOs). We want a little complexity to see what those documents look like when serialized out to Azure Cosmos DB. First we'll create a phone number POCO:

```
public class PhoneNumber
{
public string CountryCode { get; set; }
public string AreaCode { get; set; }
public string MainNumber { get; set; }
}
```

And now we add another POCO for each customer and their phone numbers:

```
public class Customer
{
    public string CustomerName { get; set; }
    public PhoneNumber[] PhoneNumbers { get; set; }
}
```

Now let's instantiate a few customers:

```
var contoso = new Customer
{
CustomerName = "Contoso Corp",
        PhoneNumbers = new PhoneNumber[]
            {
                new PhoneNumber
                    {
                        CountryCode = "1",
    AreaCode = "619",
    MainNumber = "555-1212"                              },
                new PhoneNumber
                    {
                        CountryCode = "1",
    AreaCode = "760",
    MainNumber = "555-2442"                              },
                }
};

var wwi = new Customer
{
CustomerName = "World Wide Importers",
        PhoneNumbers = new PhoneNumber[]
            {
                new PhoneNumber
                    {
                        CountryCode = "1",
    AreaCode = "858",
    MainNumber = "555-7756"                              },
                new PhoneNumber
                    {
                        CountryCode = "1",
    AreaCode = "858",
    MainNumber = "555-9142"                              },
                }
};
```

Once the customers are created, it becomes really easy to save them in Azure Cosmos DB DocumentDB. In order to serialize the object model to JSON and save it, it is really only once line of code:

```
await client.CreateDocumentAsync(collection.DocumentsLink, contoso);
```

And, to save the other document:

```
await _client.CreateDocumentAsync(collection.DocumentsLink, wwi);
```

Now that the documents are saved, you can log into your Cosmos DB account in the Azure portal, open Document Explorer and view them. Document Explorer is accessible on the top menu toolbar of your Cosmos DB configuration pane.

Query documents

Retrieving documents from Azure Cosmos DB DocumentDB is where the magic really happens. The SDK allows you to call a query to retrieve a JSON document and store the return in an object model. The SDK wires up any properties with the same name and data type automatically. This will sound amazing to a relational database developer who might be used to writing all of that code by hand. With Cosmos DB, the wiring up of persistence store to the object model happens without any data layer code.

In addition, the main way to retrieve data from Azure Cosmos DB is through LINQ, the popular C# feature that allows developers to interact with objects, Entity Framework, XML, and SQL Server.

Run Cosmos DB queries

There are three main ways you can query documents using the Azure Cosmos DB SDK: lambda LINQ, query LINQ, and SQL (a SQL-like language that's compatible with Cosmos DB).

A query of documents using lambda LINQ looks like this:

```
var customers = client.CreateDocumentQuery<Customer>(collection.DocumentsLink).
Where(c => c.CustomerName == "Contoso Corp").ToList();
```

A query of documents using LINQ queries looks like this:

```
        var linqCustomers = from c in
client.CreateDocumentQuery<Customer>(collection.DocumentsLink)

            select c;
```

A query for documents using SQL looks like this:

```
var customers = client.CreateDocumentQuery<Customer>(collection.DocumentsLink,
"SELECT * FROM Customers c WHERE c.CustomerName = 'Contoso Corp'");
```

Create Graph API databases

In order to create a Graph API database, you should follow the exact steps at the beginning of this objective. The difference would be that in the creation blade of Azure Cosmos DB, instead of choosing SQL as the API, choose Gremlin Graph API.

Use the following code to create a document client to your new Azure Cosmos DB Graph API account:

```
using (DocumentClient client = new DocumentClient(
    new Uri(endpoint),
    authKey,
    new ConnectionPolicy { ConnectionMode = ConnectionMode.Direct, ConnectionProtocol
= Protocol.Tcp }))
```

Once you have a client instantiated, you can create a new graph database with this code:

```
Database database = await client.CreateDatabaseIfNotExistsAsync(new Database
{ Id = "graphdb" });
```

Just like before, we need a collection for our data, so we'll create it like this:

```
DocumentCollection graph = await client.CreateDocumentCollectionIfNotExistsAsync(
    UriFactory.CreateDatabaseUri("graphdb"),
    new DocumentCollection { Id = "graph" },
    new RequestOptions { OfferThroughput = 1000 });
```

Execute GraphDB queries

GraphDB API queries are executed very similarly to the queries we looked at before.   GraphDB queries are defined through a series of Gremlin steps. Here is a simple version of that query:

```
IDocumentQuery<dynamic> query = client.CreateGremlinQuery<dynamic>
(graph, "g.V().count()");
while (query.HasMoreResults)
{
    foreach (dynamic result in await query.ExecuteNextAsync())
    {
        Console.WriteLine($"\t {JsonConvert.SerializeObject(result)}");
    }
}
```

Implement MongoDB database

Azure Cosmos DB can be used with applications that were originally written in MongoDB. Existing MongoDB drivers are compatible with Azure Cosmos DB. Ideally, you would switch between from MongoDB to Azure Cosmos DB by just changing a connection string (after loading the documents, of course).

You can even use existing MongoDB tooling with Azure Cosmos DB.

Manage scaling of Cosmos DB, including managing partitioning, consistency, and RUs

The main method for scaling performance in Azure Cosmos DB is the collection. Collections are assigned a specific amount of storage space and transactional throughput. Transactional throughput is measured in Request Units(RUs). Collections are also used to store similar documents together. An organization can choose to organize their documents into collections in any manner that logically makes sense to them. A software company might create a single collection per customer. A different company may choose to put heavy load documents in their own collection so they can scale them separately from other collections.

We described sharding in the last section and when we discussed Azure Storage Tables. Sharding is a feature of Azure Cosmos DB also. We can shard automatically by using a partition key. Azure Cosmos DB will automatically create multiple partitions for us. Partitioning is completely transparent to your application. All documents with the same partition key value will always be stored on the same partition. Cosmos DB may store different partition keys on the same partition or it may not. The provisioned throughput of a collection is distributed evenly among the partitions within a collection.

You can also have a single partition collection. It's important to remember that partitioning is always done at the collection, not at the Cosmos DB account level. You can have a collection that is a single partition alongside multiple partition collections. Single partition collections have a 10GB storage limit and can only have up to 10,000 RUs. When you create them, you do not have to specify a partition key. To create a single partition collection, follow these steps:

1. On you Cosmos DB account, click the overview tab and click Add Collection (Figure 2-21).

FIGURE 2-21 Creating a collection in the Azure Portal

2. On the Add Collection pane, name the collection and click Fixed for Storage Capacity. Notice how the partition key textbox automatically has a green check next to it indicating that it doesn't need to be filled out.

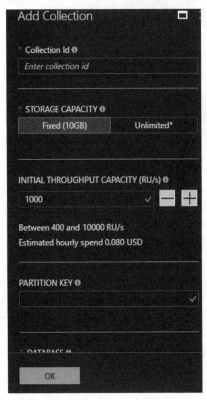

FIGURE 2-22 The Azure Portal

For multiple partition collections, it is important that you choose the right partition key. A good partition key will have a high number of distinct values without being unique to each individual document. Partitioning based on geographic location, a large date range, department, or customer type is a good idea. The storage size for documents with the same partition key is 10GB. The partition key should also be in your filters frequently.

A partition key is also the transaction boundary for stored procedures. Choose a key on documents that often get updated together with the same partition key value.

Consistency

Traditional relational databases have a little bit of baggage as it relates to data consistency. Users of those systems have the expectation that when they write data, all readers of that data will see the latest version of it. That strong consistency level is great for data integrity and notifying users when data changes, but creates problems with concurrency. Writers have to lock data as they write, blocking readers of the data until the write is over. This creates a line of readers waiting to read until the write is over. In most transactional applications, reads outnumber writes 10 to 1. Having writes block readers gives the readers the impression that the application is slow.

This has particularly created issues when scaling out relational databases. If a write occurs on one partition and it hasn't replicated to another partition, readers are frustrated that they are seeing bad or out of date data. It is important to note that consistency has long had an inverse relationship with concurrency.

Many JSON document storage products have solved that tradeoff by having a tunable consistency model. This allows the application developer to choose between strong consistency and eventual consistency. Strong consistency slows down reads and writes while giving the best data consistency between users. Eventual consistency allows the readers to read data while writes happen on a different replica, but isn't guaranteed to return current data. Things are faster because replicas don't wait to get the latest updates from a different replica.

In DocumentDB, there are five tunable consistency levels:

- **Strong** Mentioned in the previous paragraph.
- **Bounded Staleness** Tolerates inconsistent query results, but with a freshness guarantee that the results are at least as current as a specified period of time.
- **Session** The default in DocumentDB. Writers are guaranteed strong consistency on writers that they have written. Readers and other writer sessions are eventually consistent.
- **Consistent Prefix** Guarantees that readers do not see out of order writes. Meaning the writes may not have arrived yet, but when they do, they'll be in the correct order.
- **Eventual** Mentioned in the previous paragraph.

Manage multiple regions

It is possible to globally distribute data in Azure Cosmos DB. Most people think of global distribution as an high availability/disaster recovery (HADR) scenario. Although that is a side effect in Cosmos DB, it is primarily to get data closer to the users with lower network latency. European customers consume data housed in a data center in Europe. Indian customers consume data housed in India. At this writing, there are 30 data centers that can house Cosmos DB data.

Each replica will add to your Cosmos DB costs.

In a single geo-location Cosmos DB collection, you cannot really see the difference in consistency choices from the previous section. Data replicates so fast that the user always sees the latest copy of the data with few exceptions. When replicating data around the globe, choosing the correct consistency level becomes more important.

To choose to globally distribute your data, follow these steps:

1. In the Azure portal, click on your Cosmos DB account.
2. On the account blade, click Replicate data globally (Figure 2-23).

FIGURE 2-23 The Replicate data globally blade

3. In the Replicate data globally blade, select the regions to add or remove by clicking the regions on the map.

    - One region is flagged as the write region. The other regions are read regions. This consolidates the writes while distributing the reads, and since reads often outnumber writes significantly, this can drastically improve the perceived performance of your application.

4. You can now set that region for either manual or automatic failover (Figure 2-24). Automatic failover will switch the write region in order of priority.

FIGURE 2-24 The Automatic Failover pane

It is also possible to choose your preferred region in your application by using the Docu-mentDB API. The code looks like this in C#:

```
ConnectionPolicy connectionPolicy = new ConnectionPolicy();

//Setting read region selection preference
connectionPolicy.PreferredLocations.Add(LocationNames.WestUS); // first preference
connectionPolicy.PreferredLocations.Add(LocationNames.EastUS); // second preference
connectionPolicy.PreferredLocations.Add(LocationNames.NorthEurope); // third preference

// initialize connection
DocumentClient docClient = new DocumentClient(
    accountEndPoint,
    accountKey,
    connectionPolicy);
```

Implement stored procedures

Cosmos DB collections can have stored procedures, triggers, and user defined functions (UDFs), just like traditional database engines. In SQL Server, these objects are written using T-SQL. In Cosmos DB, they are written in JavaScript. This code will be executed directly in the collection's partition itself. Batch operations executed on the server will avoid network latency and will be fully atomic across multiple documents in that collection's partition. Operations in a stored procedure either all succeed or none succeed.

In order to create a Cosmos DB stored procedure in C#, you would use code that looked something like this.

```
var mySproc = new StoredProcedure
            {
                Id = "createDocs",
                Body = "function(documentToCreate) {" +
                  "var context = getContext();" +
                  "var collection = context.getCollection();" +
 "var accepted = collection.createDocument(collection.getSelfLink()," +
                  "documentToCreate," +
                  "function (err, documentCreated) {" +
                  "if (err) throw new Error('Error oh ' + documentToCreate.Name +
'- ' + err.message);" +
                      "context.getResponse().setBody(documentCreated.id)" +
                          "});" +
                  "if (!accepted) return;" +
                      "}"
            };
var response = await client.CreateStoredProcedureAsync(conferenceCollection.
SelfLink, mySproc);
```

This code creates a stored procedure using a string literal. It takes a document in as a pa-rameter and saves it in the collection. It does that by using the context object inside the stored procedure.

Access Cosmos DB from REST interface

Cosmos DB has a REST API that provides a programmatic interface to create, query, and delete databases, collections, and documents. So far, we've been using the Azure Document DB SDK in C#, but it's possible to call the REST URIs directly without the SDK. The SDK makes these calls simpler and easier to implement, but are not strictly necessary. SDKs are available for Python, JavaScript, Java, Node.js, and Xamarin. These SDKs all call the REST API underneath. Using the REST API allows you to use a language that might not have an SDK, like Elixir. Other people have created SDKs for Cosmos DB, like Swift developers for use in creating iPhone applications. If you choose other APIs, there are SDKs in even more langauges. For instance, the MongoDB API supports Golang.

The REST API allows you to send HTTPS requests using GET, POST, PUT, or DELETE to a specific endpoint.

Manage Cosmos DB security

Here are the various types of Cosmos DB security.

Encryption at rest

Encryption at rest means that all physical files used to implement Cosmos DB are encrypted on the hard drives they are using. Anyone with direct access to those files would have to unencrypt them in order to read the data. This also applies to all backups of Cosmos DB databases. There is no need for configuration of this option.

Encryption in flight

Encryption in flight is also required when using Cosmos DB. All REST URI calls are done over HTTPS. This means that anyone sniffing a network will only see encryption round trips and not clear text data.

Network firewall

Azure Cosmos DB implements an inbound firewall. This firewall is off by default and needs to be enabled. You can provide a list of IP addresses that are authorized to use Azure Cosmos DB. You can specify the IP addresses one at a time or in a range. This ensures that only an approved set of machines can access Cosmos DB. These machines will still need to provide the right access key in order to gain access. Follow these steps to enable the firewall:

1. Navigate to your Cosmos DB account.

2. Click Firewall.

3. Enable the firewall and specify the current IP address range.

4. Click Save (see Figure 2-25).

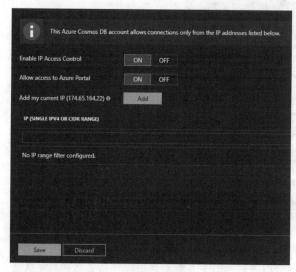

FIGURE 2-25 The Cosmos DB firewall pane

Users and permissions

Azure Cosmos DB support giving access to users in the database to specific resources or using Active Directory users.

Users can be granted permissions to an application resource. They can have two different access levels, either All or Read. All means they have full permission to the resource. Read means they can only read the resource, but not write or delete.

> **MORE INFO** **AZURE USERS AND PERMISSIONS**
>
> More information on creating permissions for database users can be found here: *https://docs.microsoft.com/en-us/azure/cosmos-db/secure-access-to-data/*.

Active Directory

You can use Active Directory users and give them access to the entire Cosmos DB database by using the Azure portal. Follow these steps to grant access:

1. Click on your Cosmos DB account and click Access Control (IAM).

2. Click Add to add a new Active Directory user.

FIGURE 2-26 The Cosmos DB Add permission pane

3. Choose the appropriate role for the user and enter the user's name or email address (Figure 2-27).

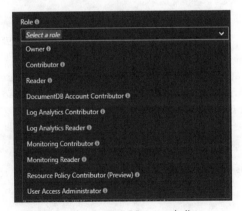

FIGURE 2-27 The Cosmos DB user role list

Now you've given permission to another user to that database. Note that you can give them reader access which will stop them from writing over documents. This might be good for ETL accounts, business/data analysts, or report authors.

Skill 2.6: Implement Redis caching

Redis is a key-value store, NoSQL database. Its implementation is very similar to Azure Table Storage. The main difference is Redis is very high performing by keeping the data in memory most of the time. By default, Redis also doesn't persist the data between reboots. There are exceptions to this, but the main purpose of keeping Redis cache in memory is for fast data retrieval and fast aggregations. This allows important data to be easily accessible to an application without loading the backend data store. As a result, Redis is typically not used as a data store for an application, but used to augment the data store you've already selected. Imagine using Azure SQL Database as your main data repository. Your application constantly looks up sales tax for all 50 states. Some cities even have their own sales tax that's higher than the state's sales tax. Constantly looking this up can compete with I/O for the rest of your application's functions. Offloading the sales tax lookup to a pinned Redis cache will not only make that lookup much faster, but will free up resources for your data repository for things like taking orders, updating addresses, awarding sales commission, and general reporting.

This is just one example of how Redis can be used. Redis has many uses, but primarily it's a temporary storage location of data that has a longer lifespan. That data needs to be expired when it's out of date and re-populated.

Azure Redis Cache is the Azure product built around Redis and offering it as a Platform-as-a-Service (PAAS) product.

> **This skill covers how to:**
> - Choose a cache tier
> - Implement data persistence
> - Implement security and network isolation
> - Tune cluster performance
> - Integrate Redis caching with ASP.NET session and cache providers

Choose a cache tier

First we need to create an Azure Redis Cache account using the Azure portal.

1. Log in to the Azure portal.
2. Click New, Databases, Redis Cache. Click Create.
3. In the New Redis Cache blade, specify configuration parameters (Figure 2-28).

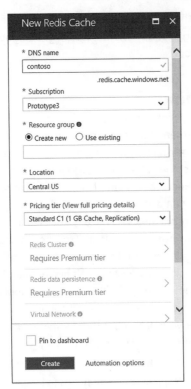

FIGURE 2-28 Azure Redis Cache Panel

4. Choose a DNS name for your cache. It must be globally unique.

5. Choose a Subscription, Resource group, and Location for the Redis Cache. Remember to keep it close to the application that will be using it.

6. Choose a Pricing tier for Redis Cache.

There are three tiers of Azure Redis Cache: Basic, Standard, and Premium. Basic is the cheapest tier and allows up to 53GB of Redis Cache database size. Standard has the same storage limit, but includes replication and failover with master/slave replication. This replication is automatic between two nodes. Premium increases ten times to 530GB. It also offers data persistence, meaning that data will survive power outages. It also includes much better network performance, topping out at 40,000 client connections. Obviously, the pricing increases as you move up from Basic through Premium.

Implement data persistence

Redis peristance allows you to save data to disk instead of just memory. Additionally, you can take snapshots of your data for backup purposes. This allows your Redis cache to survive hardware failure. Redis persistence is implemented through the RDB model, where data is streamed out to binary into Azure Storage blobs. Azure Redis Cache persistence is configured through the following pane shown in Figure 2-29.

FIGURE 2-29 Redis data persistence

On this pane, you can configure the frequency of the RDB snapshot, as well as the storage account that will be the storage target.

> **MORE INFO   IMPORT/EXPORT RDB**
>
> You can also manually import and export the RDB snapshot.   More information is found here: *https://docs.microsoft.com/en-us/azure/redis-cache/cache-how-to-import-export-data*.

Implement security and network isolation

Azure Redis Cache's primary security mechanism is done through access keys. We've used access keys in Azure Storage blobs, Azure Storage tables, and Azure Cosmos DB. In addition to access keys, Azure Redis Cache offers enhanced security when you use the premium offering. This is done primarily through the Virtual Network (VNET). This allows you to hide Redis Cache behind your application and not have a public URL that is open to the internet.

The VNET is configured at the bottom of the New Redis Cache pane (pictured earlier.) You can configure the virtual network when creating the Azure Redis Cache account. You cannot configure it after it has been created. Also, you can only use a VNET that exists in the same data center as your Azure Redis Cache account. Azure Redis Cache must be created in an empty subnet.

When creating an Azure Redis Cache account, select Virtual Network towards the bottom. You will see the following pane shown in Figure 2-30.

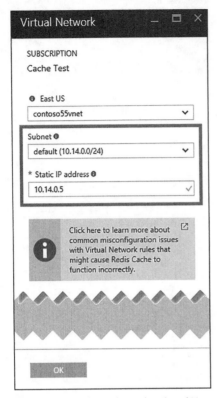

FIGURE 2-30 Azure Redis Cache Virtual Network pane

This is where you can configure your static IP address and subnet.

MORE INFO   **VIRTUAL NETWORKING**

For more information on Azure Virtual Networking, see here: *https://docs.microsoft.com/en-us/azure/virtual-network/virtual-networks-overview.*

Doing this isolates your Azure Redis Cache service behind your virtual network and keeps it from being accessed from the internet.

Tune cluster performance

Also with the premium service, you can implement a Redis Cluster. Redis clusters allow you to split the dataset among multiple nodes, allowing you to continue operations when a subset of the nodes experience failure, give more throughput, and increase memory (and there for total database) size as you increase the number of shards. Redis clustering is configured when you create the Azure Redis Cache account (Figure 2-31). The reason why Premium can store 10 times the data as the other two tiers is because clustering allows you to choose the number of nodes in the cluster, from 1 to 10.

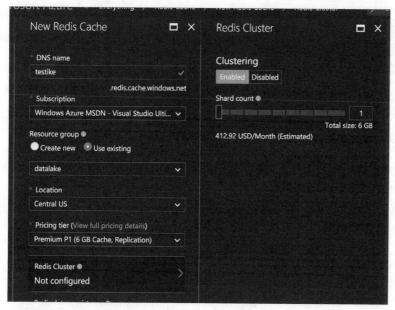

FIGURE 2-31 Redis Cache Clustering

Once the cache is created, you use it just like a non-clustered cache. Redis distributes your data for you.

Integrate Redis caching with ASP.NET session and cache providers

Session state in an ASP.NET applications is traditionally stored in either memory or a SQL Server database. Session state in memory is difficult to implement if the server is a member of a server farm and the user changes which server they're attached to. Session state would be lost in that case. Storing session state in a SQL database solves that problem, but introduces database management of performance, latency, and license management. Often databases are already under high load and don't need the added load of managing a high amount of session state.

Redis cache is an excellent place to store session state. To implement this, use the Redis Cache Session State Nuget package. Once added to the project, you just have to add the following line to your web.config file under the providers section:

```
<add name="MySessionStateStore"
        host = "127.0.0.1"
      port = ""
      accessKey = ""
      ssl = "false"
      throwOnError = "true"
      retryTimeoutInMilliseconds = "0"
      databaseId = "0"
      applicationName = ""
```

```
            connectionTimeoutInMilliseconds = "5000"
            operationTimeoutInMilliseconds = "5000"
    />
<add name="MySessionStateStore" type="Microsoft.Web.Redis.RedisSessionStateProvider"
 host="127.0.0.1" accessKey="" ssl="false"/>
```

The host attribute points to the endpoint of your Azure Redis account. ApplicationName allows multiple applications to use the same Redis database. Every other attribute is self-explanatory.

There is a different Nuget packaged called the Redis Output Cache Provider. This will store page output in Redis cache for future use. It's configured in a similar manner as the previous product.

Skill 2.7: Implement Azure Search

Azure Search is a Platform-as-a-Service (PAAS) offering that gives developers APIs needed to add search functionality in their applications. Primarily this mean full text search. The typical example is how Google and Bing search works. Bing doesn't care what tense you use, it spell checks for you, and finds similar topics based on search terms. It also offers term highlighting and can ignore noise words, as well as many other search-related features. Applying these features inside your application can give your users a rich and comforting search experience.

> **This skill covers how to:**
> - Create a service index
> - Add data
> - Search an index
> - Handle Search results

Create a service index

There are several types of Azure Search accounts: free, basic, standard, and high-density. The free tier only allows 50MB of data storage and 10,000 documents. As you increase from basic to high-density, you increase how many documents you can index as well as how quickly searches return. Compute resources for Azure Search are sold through Search Units (SUs). The basic level allows 3 search units. The high-density level goes up to 36 SUs. In addition, all of the paid pricing tiers offer load-balancing over three replicas or more replicas. To create an Azure Search service, follow these steps:

1. Log on to the Azure portal.
2. Add a new item. Look up Azure Search Service.
3. In the New Search Service pane, choose a unique URL, Subscription, Resource group, and Location.

FIGURE 2-32 Azure Search pane

4. Carefully choose an Azure Search pricing tier. Make a note of the search URI (your search name).search.windows.net.

As you use Azure Search, you can scale it if you need more SUs or have more documents to search. On your Azure Search pane, click Scale. The Scale blade is supported in Standard level and above, not basic. From there you can choose how many replicas handle your workload and how many partitions you have. Replicas distribute workloads across multiple nodes. Partitions allow for scaling the document count as well as faster data ingestion by spanning your index over multiple Azure Search Units. Both of these are only offered in the paid service tiers.

Add data

You add data to Azure Search through creating an index. An index contains documents used by Azure Search. For instance, a hotel chain might have a document describing each hotel they own, a home builder might have a document for each house they have on the market. An index is similar to a SQL Server table and documents are similar to rows in those tables.

In our examples, we'll use C# and the Microsoft .NET Framework to add data to an index and search it. To use the .NET SDK for Azure Search with our examples, you must meet the following requirements:

- Visual Studio 2017.

- Create an Azure Search service with the Azure portal. The free version will work for these code samples.

- Download the Azure Search SDK Nuget package.

Just like with our other services, we must first create a Search service client, like this:

```
string searchServiceName = "your search service name;
string accesskey = "your access key"
SearchServiceClient serviceClient = new SearchServiceClient(searchServiceName,
new SearchCredentials(accesskey));
```

Let's assume we build homes and we have a POCO for the home class. That class would have properties like RetailPrice, SquareFootage, Description, and FlooringType.

The home class might look like this:

```
using System;
using Microsoft.Azure.Search;
using Microsoft.Azure.Search.Models;
using Microsoft.Spatial;
using Newtonsoft.Json;

// The SerializePropertyNamesAsCamelCase attribute is defined in the Azure
// Search .NET SDK.
// It ensures that Pascal-case property names in the model class are mapped to
// camel-case field names in the index.
[SerializePropertyNamesAsCamelCase]
public partial class Home
{
    [System.ComponentModel.DataAnnotations.Key]
    [IsFilterable]
    public string HomeID { get; set; }

    [IsFilterable, IsSortable, IsFacetable]
    public double? RetailPrice { get; set; }

    [IsFilterable, IsSortable, IsFacetable]
    public int? SquareFootage { get; set; }

    [IsSearchable]
    public string Description { get; set; }

    [IsFilterable, IsSortable]
    public GeographyPoint Location { get; set; }
}
```

The properties all have attributes on them that tell Azure Search how to construct field definitions for them in the index. Notice how these are all public properties. Azure Search will only create definitions for public properties.

First, we create an index with the following code:

```
var definition = new Index()
{
```

```
    Name = "homes",
    Fields = FieldBuilder.BuildForType<Home>()
};
serviceClient.Indexes.Create(definition);
```

This will create an index object with field objects that define the correct schema based on our POCO. The FieldBuilder class iterates over the properties of the Home POCO using reflection.

First, create a batch of homes to upload.

```
var homes = new Home[]
{
    new Home()
    {
        RetailPrice = Convert.ToDouble("459999.00"),
        SquareFootage = 3200,
        Description = "Single floor, ranch style on 1 acre of property.  4 bedroom,
        large living room with open kitchen, dining area.",
        Location = GeographyPoint.Create(47.678581, -122.131577)
    };
```

Then create a batch object, declaring that you intend to upload a document:

```
ISearchIndexClient indexClient = serviceClient.Indexes.GetClient("homes");

var batch = IndexBatch.Upload(homes);
```

Then upload the document:

```
indexClient.Documents.Index(batch);
```

Search an index

In order to search documents, we must first declare a SearchParameters object and DocumentSearchResult object of type Home in our example.

```
SearchParameters parameters;
DocumentSearchResult<Home> searchResults;
```

Now we look for any home that has the word ranch in the document. We return only the HomeID field. We save the results.

```
parameters =
    new SearchParameters()
    {
        Select = new[] { "SquareFootage" }
    };
searchResults = indexClient.Documents.Search<Home>("3200", parameters);
```

Handle Search results

After we have the search results saved in the results variable, we can iterate through them like this:

```
foreach (SearchResult<Home> result in searchResults.Results)
{
    Console.WriteLine(result.Document);
}
```

We have covered many different areas that data can be stored in Microsoft Azure. These different storage products can be overwhelming and make choosing correctly difficult.

It is important to note that the same data can be stored in any of these solutions just fine, and your application will likely succeed no matter which storage product you use. You can store data in a key-value store, a document store, a graph database, a relational store, or any combination of these products. Functionally, they are very similar with similar features. There is also no specific set of problems that can only be stored in a graph database or only be stored in a relational engine. Understanding the different features, problems, advantages, and query languages will help you choose the correct data store for your application, but you will always feel uncertain that you chose the right one.

Anyone who looks at your problem and definitely knows the perfect storage product is likely either trying to sell you something, only knows that product and therefore has a vested interest in choosing it, has bought in to a specific buzz word or new trend, or is underinformed about the drawbacks of their preferred product. This author's advice is to inform yourself the best you can and make a decision while accepting the fact that every product has trade-offs.

Thought experiment

In this thought experiment, apply what you've learned about this skill. You can find answers to these questions in the next section.

Contoso Limited creates lasers that etch patterns for processors and memory. Their customers include large chip manufacturers around the world

Contoso is in the process of moving several applications to Azure. You are the data architect contracted by Contoso to help them make the good decisions for these applications regarding storage products and features. Contoso has a mobile application their sales people use to create quotes to email to their customers. The product catalog is in several languages and contains detailed product images. You are localizing a mobile application for multiple languages.

1. How will you structure the files in Blob storage so that you can retrieve them easily?

2. What can you do to make access to these images quick for users around the world?

   On a regular interval, a Contoso laser sends the shot count of how many times the laser fired to your application. The shot count is cumulative by day. Contoso built more than 500 of these lasers and distributed them around the world. Each laser has its own machine identifier. Each time the shot count is sent, it includes a time stamp. The analysts are mostly concerned with the most recent shot count sent. It's been decided to store the shot count in Azure Table Storage.

3. What should you use for the partition key? How many partitions should you create?

4. How should you create the row key?

5. How many tables should you build? What's in each table?

Contoso also wants to write a third application, a web application, that executives can use to show the relationship between customers of your company. Contoso knows that some of their customers purchase chips from other Contoso customers. Your company feels like it's in a perfect position to examine global business relationships since it has all of the laser records that occur in the global enterprise. Your company uses a variety of relational databases, like Oracle and Microsoft SQL Server. You have heard a lot about JSON Document storage engines, like Azure Cosmos DB, and feel like it would be a perfect fit for this project. Contoso is concerned that this application will have a significant load considering the amount of data that will be processed for each laser. You've decided to help them by implementing Redis Cache.

6. What are some advantages that Azure Cosmos DB has over traditional relational data stores?

7. What are disadvantages your enterprise will face in implementing a store like this?

8. How will your organization's data analyst query data from Azure Cosmos DB?

9. Where do you think Redis Cache can help them?

10. How will Redis Cache lessen the load on their database server?

11. What are some considerations when implementing Redis Cache?

Thought experiment answers

This section contains the solution to the thought experiment.

1. You would consider structuring the blob hierarchy so that one of the portions of the path represented the language or region.

2. You would consider creating a CDN on a publicly available container to cache those files locally around the world.

3. Machine ID seems like a logical candidate for PartitionKey.

4. Shot count time stamp, ordered descending.

5. There might be two tables, one for the machine metadata and one for the shots. You could also make an argument for consolidating both pieces of data into one table for speed in querying.

6. Cosmos DB will be easier to maintain because the schema is declared inside the application. As the application matures, the schema can mature. This will keep the schema

fresh and new and changeable. Cosmos DB doesn't really need a complicated data layer or an ORM, thus saving hours of development as we write and release. CosmosDB keeps the data in the same structure as the object model, keeping the data easy for developers to learn and navigate.

7. There is a learning curve for document stores and graph stores. Traditional relational developers might have a difficult time keeping up with it.

8. Business analysts and data analysts might need to learn a new query language in order to gain access to the data in Cosmos DB. ETL processes might need to be written to pipe document data into a traditional data store for reporting and visualizations. Otherwise the reporting burden of the application will rest on the original developers, which also may be an acceptable solution.

9. They can cache their entire product catalog. They can cache each session so that the session can be saved before it's committed to the database. They can cache location information, shipping information, etc.

10. All of the above items will greatly alleviate the load of their applications. Basically, you are stopping the relational database read locks from blocking the writing transactions. Also, by caching the reads, you are stopping them from competing for I/O with the writes.

11. Caching is memory intensive, so make sure you are using memory effectively. Caching rarely used things is not effective. Caching needs data management. Knowing when to expire cache, refresh cache, and populate cache are all things that should be thought of ahead of time.

Chapter summary

- A blob container has several options for access permissions. When set to Private, all access requires credentials. When set to Public Container, no credentials are required to access the container and its blobs. When set to Public Blob, only blobs can be accessed without credentials if the full URL is known.

- To access secure containers and blobs, you can use the storage account key or shared access signatures.

- Block blobs allow you to upload, store, and download large blobs in blocks up to 4 MB each. The size of the blob can be up to 200 GB.

- You can use a blob naming convention akin to folder paths to create a logical hierarchy for blobs, which is useful for query operations.

- All file copies with Azure Storage blobs are done asynchronously.

- Table storage is a non-relational database implementation (NoSQL) following the key-value database pattern.

- Table entries each have a partition key and row key. The partition key is used to logically group rows that are related; the row key is a unique entry for the row.

- The Table service uses the partition key for distributing collections of rows across physical partitions in Azure to automatically scale out the database as needed.

- A Table storage query returns up to 1,000 records per request, and will time out after five seconds.

- Querying Table storage with both the partition and row key results in fast queries. A table scan is required for queries that do not use these keys.

- Applications can add messages to a queue programmatically using the .NET Storage Client Library or equivalent for other languages, or you can directly call the Storage API.

- Messages are stored in a storage queue for up to seven days based on the expiry setting for the message. Message expiry can be modified while the message is in the queue.

- An application can retrieve messages from a queue in batch to increase throughput and process messages in parallel.

- Each queue has a target of approximately 2,000 messages per second. You can increase this throughput by partitioning messages across multiple queues.

- You can use SAS tokens to delegate access to storage account resources without sharing the account key.

- With SAS tokens, you can generate a link to a container, blob, table, table entity, or queue. You can control the permissions granted to the resource.

- Using Shared Access Policies, you can remotely control the lifetime of a SAS token grant to one or more resources. You can extend the lifetime of the policy or cause it to expire.

- Storage Analytics metrics provide the equivalent of Windows Performance Monitor counters for storage services.

- You can determine which services to collect metrics for (Blob, Table, or Queue), whether to collect metrics for the service or API level, and whether to collect metrics by the minute or hour.

- Capacity metrics are only applicable to the Blob service.

- Storage Analytics Logging provides details about the success or failure of requests to storage services.

- Storage logs are stored in blob services for the account, in the $logs container for the service.

- You can specify up to 365 days for retention of storage metrics or logs, or you can set retention to 0 to retain metrics indefinitely. Metrics and logs are removed automatically from storage when the retention period expires.

- Storage metrics can be viewed in the management portal. Storage logs can be downloaded and viewed in a reporting tool such as Excel.

- The different editions of Azure SQL Database affect performance, SLAs, backup/restore policies, pricing, geo-replication options, and database size.

- The edition of Azure SQL Database determines the retention period for point in time restores. This should factor into your backup and restore policies.

- It is possible to create an online secondary when you configure Azure SQL Database geo-replication. It requires the Premium Edition.

- If you are migrating an existing database to the cloud, you can use the BACPACs to move schema and data into your Azure SQL database.

- Elastic pools will help you share DTUs with multiple databases on the same server.

- Sharding and scale-out can be easier to manage by using the Elastic Tools from Microsoft.

- Azure SQL Database introduces new graph features and graph query syntax.

- The different types of APIs available in Azure Cosmos DB, including table, graph, and document.

- Why developers find document storage easy to use in web, mobile, and IoT applications because saving and retrieving data does not require a complex data layer or an ORM.

- The different ways to query Azure Cosmos DB, including LINQ lambda, LINQ query, and SQL.

- Why graph databases are a great solution for certain problems, particularly showing relationships between entities.

- Cosmos DB scaling is in large part automatic and requires little to no management. The most important thing is to correctly choose which documents will go in which collections and which partition key to use with them.

- Cosmos DB supports multiple regions for disaster recovery and to keep the data close to the users for improved network latency.

- Cosmos DB has several different security mechanisms, including encryption at rest, network firewalls, and users and permissions.

- What Redis Cache is and how it can help speed up applications.

- How to choose between the different tiers of Azure Redis Cache

- The importance of data persistence in maintaining state in case of power or hardware failure.

- How to scale Azure Redis Cache for better performance or larger data sets.

- Create an Azure Search Service using the Azure portal.

- Create an Azure Search index and populate it with documents using C# and the .NET SDK.

- Search the index for a keyword and handle the results.

## CHAPTER 3

Manage identity, application and network services

Beyond compute and storage features, Microsoft Azure also provides a number of infrastructure services for security and communication mechanisms to support many messaging patterns. In this chapter you learn about these core services.

Skills in this chapter:

- Skill 3.1: Integrate an app with Azure Active Directory (Azure AD)
- Skill 3.2: Develop apps that use Azure AD B2C and Azure AD B2B
- Skill 3.3: Manage Secrets using Azure Key Vault
- Skill 3.4: Design and implement a messaging strategy

Skill 3.1: Integrate an app with Azure AD

Azure Active Directory (Azure AD) provides a cloud-based identity management service for application authentication, Single Sign-On (SSO), and user management. Azure AD can be used for the following core scenarios:

- A standalone cloud directory service
- Corporate access to Software-as-a-Service (SaaS) applications with directory synchronization
- SSO between corporate and SaaS applications
- Application integration for SaaS applications using different identity protocols
- User management through a Graph API
- Manage multi-factor authentication settings for a directory

In this section, you learn how to do the following:

- Set up a directory
- How to integrate applications with Azure AD using WS-Federation, OAuth and SAML-P
- How to query the user directory with the Microsoft Graph API
- How to work with multi-factor authentication (MFA) features

> **This skill covers how to:**
> - Develop apps that use WS-Federation, SAML-P, and OpenID Connect and OAuth endpoints
> - Query the directory using Microsoft Graph API, MFA and MFA API

Preparing to integrate an app with Azure AD

There are several common scenarios for application integration with Azure AD, including the following:

- Users sign in to web applications
- Users sign in to JavaScript application (for example, single page applications or SPAs)
- Browser-based applications call Web APIs from JavaScript
- Users sign in to native / mobile applications that call Web APIs
- Web applications call Web APIs
- Server applications or processes call Web APIs

Where a user is present, the user must first be authenticated at Azure AD, thus presenting proof of authentication back to the application in the form of a token. You can choose from a few protocols to authenticate the user: WS-Federation, SAML-P, or OpenID Connect. OpenID Connect is the recommended path because it is the most modern protocol available, and is based on OAuth 2.0. Scenarios that involve API security are typically based on OAuth 2.0 flows, though this is not a strict requirement.

Authentication workflows involve details at the protocol level, but Figure 3-1 illustrates from a high level the OpenID Connect workflow for authenticating users to a web app. The user typically starts by navigating to a protected area of the web app, or electing to login (1). The application then sends an OpenID Connect sign in request (2) to Azure AD. If the user does not yet have a session at Azure AD (usually represented by a cookie), they are prompted to login (3). After successfully authenticating the user's credential (4) Azure AD writes a single sign-on (SSO) session cookie to establish the user session, and sends the OpenID Connect sign in response back to the browser (5), including an id token to identify the user. This is posted to the web app (6). The application validates the response and establishes the user session at the application (7).

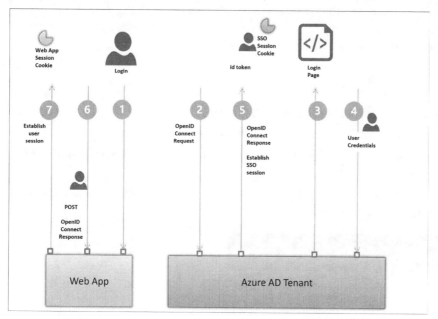

FIGURE 3-1 The high-level workflow for an OpenID Connect sign-in request

---

MORE INFO   AUTHENTICATION SCENARIOS

See the following reference for a review of these key authentication scenarios with related sample applications: *https://docs.microsoft.com/en-us/azure/active-directory/develop/ active-directory-authentication-scenarios.*

The following steps are involved in application integration scenarios with Azure AD:

1. Create your Azure AD directory. This is your tenant.

2. Create your application.

3. Register the application with Azure AD with information about your application.

4. Write code in your application to satisfy one of the scenarios for user authentication or token requests to call APIs.

5. Receive protocol-specific responses to your application from Azure AD, including a valid token for proof of authentication or for authorization purposes.

In this section, you'll learn how to create a directory, register an application in the Azure portal, and learn how to find integration endpoints for each protocol.

Creating a directory

To create a new Azure AD directory, follow these steps:

1. Navigate to the Azure portal accessed via *https://portal.azure.com.*

2. Click New and select Security + Identity, then select Azure Active Directory from the list of choices.

3. From the Create Directory blade, (Figure 3-2) enter your Organization name and your domain name. Select the country or region and click Create.

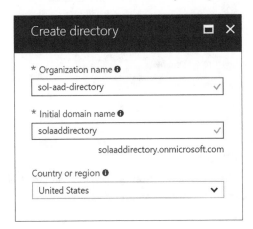

FIGURE 3-2 The Create Directory blade

4. Once created there will be a link shown on the same blade, that you can click to navigate to the directory. You can also navigate to the directory by selecting More Services from the navigate panel, then from the search textbox type **active,** then select Azure Active Directory. The blade for the new directory that you have created will be shown.

5. If the Azure Active Directory blade shown is not your new directory, you can switch directories by selecting the Switch Directories link from the directory blade (Figure 3-3). This drops down the directory selection menu from which you can choose the directory you want to navigate to.

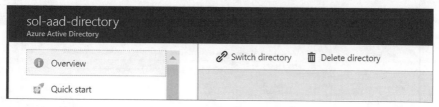

FIGURE 3-3 The Switch directory link available from an Azure Active Directory blade

MORE INFO   CREATING A PREMIUM DIRECTORY

See the following reference for setting up a premium directory: *https://docs.microsoft.com/en-us/azure/active-directory/active-directory-get-started-premium*.

MORE INFO   AZURE AD CONNECT

See the following reference for how to use Azure AD Connect to integrate your on-premises directories with your Azure AD directory: *https://docs.microsoft.com/en-us/azure/active-directory/connect/active-directory-aadconnect*.

Registering an application

You can register Web/API or Native applications with your directory. Web/API applications require setting up a URL for sign in responses. Native applications require setting up an application URI for OAuth2 responses to be redirected to. Visual Studio has tooling integration that supports automating the creation of applications if you configure your directory authentication while setting up the project with a template that supports this. This removes the need to manually register applications, and it initializes the configuration of the application for you as well, using middleware that understands how to integrate with Azure Active Directory.

You can manually add a Web/API application using the Azure portal by following these steps:

1. Navigate to the Azure portal accessed via *https://portal.azure.com*.

2. Select Azure Active Directory from the navigation panel and navigate to your directory.

3. Select App registrations (Figure 3-4) from the navigation pane, and click New Application Registration from the command bar at the top of the blade.

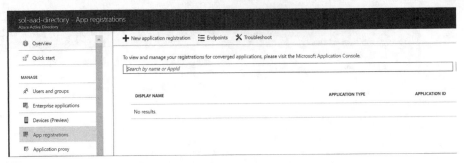

FIGURE 3-4 The App registrations blade

4. From the Create application blade (Figure 3-5), supply a name for the application. Choose the application type Web/API and supply the Sign-on URL, which is the address where the sign in response can be posted to the application. If you are using the OpenID Connect middleware for aspnetcore, the address will end with /signin-oidc and the middleware knows to look for responses arriving with that path.

FIGURE 3-5 The Create application blade

5. Click Create to register the application.

6. Select App registrations from the navigation pane for the directory. The new application will be listed in the blade.

7. Select your application by clicking it. From here you can customize additional settings such as the following:

   A. Uploading a logo for login branding

   B. Indicating if the application is single or multi-tenant

   C. Managing keys for OAuth scenarios

   D. Controlling consent settings

   E. Granting permissions

Viewing integration endpoints

You can integrate applications with Azure AD through several protocol endpoints including:

- WS-Federation metadata and sign-on endpoints
- SAML-P sign-on and sign-out endpoints
- OAuth 2.0 token and authorization endpoints
- Azure AD Graph API endpoint

EXAM TIP

The graph endpoint exposed in the Azure Portal for Azure AD directories and applications is the Azure AD Graph API, which relates to Azure AD v1 capabilities. This chapter covers the Microsoft Graph API which is the preferred way to integrate, so a different endpoint will be discussed later.

To view the endpoints (Figure 3-6) available to your directory, do the following:

1. Navigate to the Azure portal accessed via *https://portal.azure.com*.

2. Select Azure Active Directory from the navigation panel and navigate to your directory.

3. Select App registrations from the navigation pane for the directory, and click Endpoints from the command bar.

4. The endpoints blade (see Figure 3-2) lists protocol endpoints, such as the following:

   - *https://login.microsoftonline.com/c6cad604-0f11-4c1c-bdc0-44150037bfd9/federationmetadata/2007-06/federationmetadata.xml*

   - *https://login.microsoftonline.com/c6cad604-0f11-4c1c-bdc0-44150037bfd9/wsfed*

   - *https://login.microsoftonline.com/c6cad604-0f11-4c1c-bdc0-44150037bfd9/saml2*

   - *https://graph.windows.net/c6cad604-0f11-4c1c-bdc0-44150037bfd9*

   - *https://login.microsoftonline.com/c6cad604-0f11-4c1c-bdc0-44150037bfd9/oauth2/ token*

   - *https://login.microsoftonline.com/c6cad604-0f11-4c1c-bdc0-44150037bfd9/oauth2/ authorize*

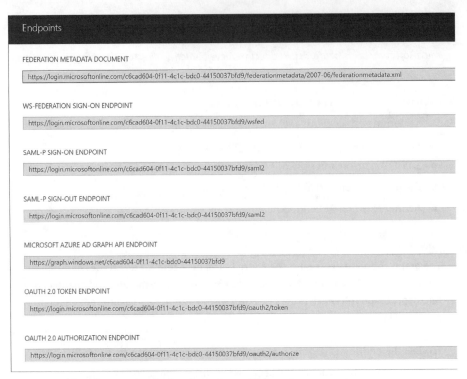

Endpoints

FEDERATION METADATA DOCUMENT

https://login.microsoftonline.com/c6cad604-0f11-4c1c-bdc0-44150037bfd9/federationmetadata/2007-06/federationmetadata.xml

WS-FEDERATION SIGN-ON ENDPOINT

https://login.microsoftonline.com/c6cad604-0f11-4c1c-bdc0-44150037bfd9/wsfed

SAML-P SIGN-ON ENDPOINT

https://login.microsoftonline.com/c6cad604-0f11-4c1c-bdc0-44150037bfd9/saml2

SAML-P SIGN-OUT ENDPOINT

https://login.microsoftonline.com/c6cad604-0f11-4c1c-bdc0-44150037bfd9/saml2

MICROSOFT AZURE AD GRAPH API ENDPOINT

https://graph.windows.net/c6cad604-0f11-4c1c-bdc0-44150037bfd9

OAUTH 2.0 TOKEN ENDPOINT

https://login.microsoftonline.com/c6cad604-0f11-4c1c-bdc0-44150037bfd9/oauth2/token

OAUTH 2.0 AUTHORIZATION ENDPOINT

https://login.microsoftonline.com/c6cad604-0f11-4c1c-bdc0-44150037bfd9/oauth2/authorize

FIGURE 3-6 A list of protocol endpoints for an Azure AD tenant

Develop apps that use WS-Federation, SAML-P, OpenID Connect and OAuth endpoints

You can integrate your applications for authentication and authorization workflows using WS-Federation, SAML Protocol (SAML-P), OpenID Connect and OAuth 2.0. Azure AD OAuth 2.0 and endpoints support both OpenID Connect and OAuth 2.0 integration for authentication or authorization requests. If your applications require support for WS-Federation or SAML 2.0 protocol you can use those endpoints to achieve the integration. This section discusses integration using these protocols.

> *NOTE* **OPENID CONNECT**
>
> OpenID Connect extends the features of OAuth 2.0 protocol to support user authentication workflows and session management. The OAuth 2.0 authorization endpoint is the endpoint used by OpenID Connect to perform authentication, and some new endpoints are introduced with OpenID Connect that also support session management, although you may not see all of these endpoints exposed directly by Azure AD. The endpoints exposed by an identity service are often implementation specific while they still (should) follow the protocols at their core.

Integrating with OpenID Connect

OAuth 2.0 is an authorization protocol, not an authentication protocol. OpenID Connect extends OAuth 2.0 with standard flows for user authentication and session management. Today's applications typically use OpenID Connect workflows authenticating users from web, JavaScript, or mobile applications (via the browser). OpenID Connect authentication involves the application sending a sign in request to the directory, and receiving a sign in response at the application. The sign in response includes an id token representing proof of authentication, and the application uses this to establish the user session at the application.

To create an aspnetcore application that authenticates users with OpenID Connect, do the following from Visual Studio 2017:

1. Open Visual Studio 2017 and create a new project based on the ASP.NET Core Web Application project template (Figure 3-7). Select Web Application for the style of application on the second dialog and then click Change Authentication.

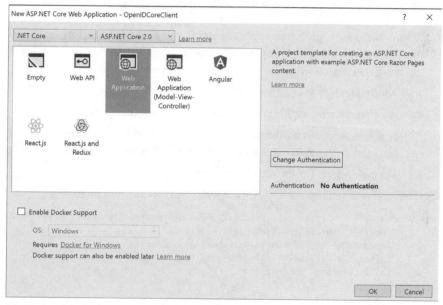

FIGURE 3-7 The new ASP.NET Core Web Application dialog

2. Select Work or School Accounts and enter your Azure AD domain into the textbox provided (if you are signed in, this will also be available in the drop-down list). Click OK to return to the previous dialog, and again click OK to accept the settings and create the project (Figure 3-8).

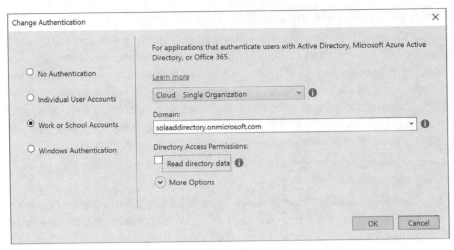

FIGURE 3-8 The Change Authentication dialog

3. Visual Studio will register this application with your Azure AD directory, and configure the project with the correct application settings in the appsettings.json file. These settings provide the following key information to the middleware:

   A. Which directory to communicate with (Domain and TenantId).

   B. Which registered application is making the request (ClientId).

   C. Which redirect URI should be provided with the sign in request, so that Azure AD can validate this in its list of approved redirect URIs (built from the CallbackPath).

   D. The base address of the Azure AD instance to send requests to (Instance).

4. The following settings are found in the web.config for the new project:

```
"AzureAd": {    "Instance": "https://login.microsoftonline.com/",
    "Domain": "solaaddirectory.onmicrosoft.com",
    "TenantId": "c6cad604-0f11-4c1c-bdc0-44150037bfd9",
    "ClientId": "483db32c-f517-495d-a7b5-03d6453c939c",
    "CallbackPath": "/signin-oidc"
  },
```

5. Navigate to your Azure AD directory (Figure 3-9) at the Azure portal and view the App registrations. Select your new application to view its properties. The properties show the App ID URI used to uniquely identify your application at the directory, and the home page URL used to send protocol responses post sign in.

FIGURE 3-9 Azure AD application settings blade

When you run the new project from Visual Studio you will see a workflow like this:

1. A user navigates to the application.

2. When the user browses to a protected page or selects Login, the application redirects anonymous users to sign in at Azure AD, sending an OpenID Connect sign in request to the OAuth endpoint.

3. The user is presented with a login page, unless she has previously signed in and established a user session at the Azure AD tenant.

4. When authenticated, an OpenID Connect response is returned via HTTP POST to the application URL, and this response includes an id token showing proof of user authentication.

5. The application processes this response, using the configured middleware that supports OpenID Connect protocol, and verifies the token is signed by the specified trusted issuer (your Azure AD tenant), onfirming that the token is still valid.

6. The application can optionally use claims in the token to personalize the application experience for the logged in user.

7. The application can also optionally query Azure AD for groups for authorization purposes.

Integrating with OAuth

OAuth 2.0 is an authorization protocol that is typically used for delegated authorization scenarios where user consent is required to access resources, and for access token requests. The desired response from an OAuth 2.0 authorization request is an access token, which is typically used to call APIs protecting resources.

Before an application can request tokens, it must be registered with the Azure AD tenant and have both a client id and secret (key) that can be used to make OAuth requests on behalf of the application.

To generate a secret for an application, complete the following steps:

1. Navigate to the directory from the Azure portal accessed via *https://portal.azure.com*.

2. Click App registrations in the navigation pane, and select the application you want to enable for token requests via OAuth.

3. Select Keys in the navigation pane. Provide a friendly name for the key and select a duration for the key to be valid (Figure 3-10).

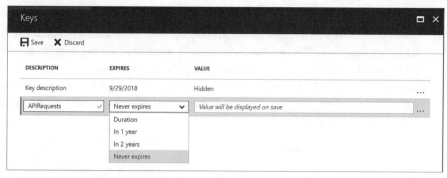

FIGURE 3-10 The Keys blade for an application in Azure AD

4. Click Save on the command bar and the value for the key appears.

5. Copy the key somewhere safe; it will not be presented again.

6. You can now use the client id and secret (key) to perform OAuth token requests from your application.

A later section, "Query the Graph API," covers an example of an OAuth token request authorizing an application to use the Graph API.

MORE INFO **OAUTH TOKEN REQUEST SAMPLES**

The following samples illustrate authorizing users and applications for OAuth token requests: *https://github.com/Azure-Samples/active-directory-dotnet-webapp-webapi-oauth2-useridentity* and *https://github.com/Azure-Samples/active-directory-dotnet-webapp-webapi-oauth2-appidentity*.

Integrating with WS-Federation

WS-Federation is an identity protocol used for browser-based applications for user authentication. To create a new ASP.NET MVC application that integrates with the WS-Federation endpoint there are a number of custom coding steps that are required since the templates do not support this directly. Those steps are discussed at the following reference: *https://github.com/Azure-Samples/active-directory-dotnet-webapp-wsfederation*.

NOTE **VISUAL STUDIO**

The reference uses Visual Studio 2013 but the steps work for Visual Studio 2017.

A few key points to call out about the setup for WS-Federation are as follows:

1. When you create a new project using Visual Studio (for example, based on the ASP. NET Web Application project template) you will select MVC for the style of application on the second dialog and leave No Authentication as the authentication option for the template (Figure 3-11). If you choose other authentication options, the generated code will always use OpenID Connect as the protocol, and this will not work for WS-Federation or other protocols.

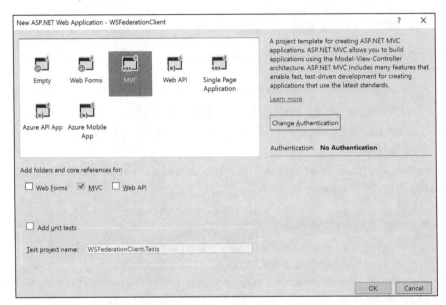

FIGURE 3-11 The new ASP.NET Web Application dialog with no authentication option selected

2. You will have to add code per the above reference to communicate using WS-Federation protocol and set up the application settings required to match your Azure AD setup for the application.

3. You will register an Azure AD application following the steps shown earlier in this skill. Here is an example for a WS-Federation application setup (Figure 3-12).

FIGURE 3-12 The settings for a registered WS-Federation compatible application in Azure AD

4. The details for connecting an MVC application with the registered Azure AD application for WS-Federation are covered in the reference. It shows you how to setup the OWIN middleware for WS-Federation: WsFederationAuthenticationMiddleware. In addition to following those steps, note the following:

   A. Ensure that the App ID URI matches the wtrealm parameter that will be passed in the WS-Federation request from the client application.

   B. Ensure SSL is enabled for your application.

   C. Ensure that the Home page URL is an HTTPS endpoint and matches the application SSL path.

When you run a WS-Federation client you will see the following workflow:

1. A user navigates to the application.

2. When the user browses to a protected page or selects Login, the application redirects anonymous users to sign in at Azure AD, sending a WS-Federation protocol request that indicates the application URI for the realm parameter. The URI matches the App ID URI shown in the registered application settings.

3. The request is sent to the tenant WS-Federation endpoint.

4. The user is presented with a login page, unless she has previously signed in and established a user session at the Azure AD tenant.

5. When authenticated, a WS-Federation response is returned via HTTP POST to the application URL - and this response includes a SAML token showing proof of user authentication.

6. The application processes this response, using the configured OWIN middleware that supports WS-Federation, and verifies the token is signed by the specified trusted issuer (your Azure AD tenant), and confirms that the token is still valid.

7. The application can optionally use claims in the token to personalize the application experience for the logged in user.

8. The application can optionally query Azure AD for groups for authorization purposes.

> **NOTE FEDERATION METADATA**
>
> WS-Federation exposes two endpoints: one for metadata and one for sign-in and sign-out. The metadata endpoint exposes the standard federation metadata document that many identity middleware know how to consume to discover the address of the sign-in and sign-out endpoint, the certificate required to validate signatures in a response, and other endpoints available at the service, such as SAML-P endpoints. If you use the metadata endpoint, your application should dynamically receive updates, such as new certificates used by the service. The sign-in and sign-out endpoint expects parameters indicating the purpose of the request.

Integrating with SAML-P

SAML 2.0 Protocol (SAML-P) can be used like WS-Federation to support user authentication to browser-based applications. For example, SAML-P integration with Azure AD might follow steps like this:

1. A user navigates to your application.

2. Your application redirects anonymous users to authenticate at Azure AD, sending a SAML-P request that indicates the application URI for the ConsumerServiceURL element in the request.

3. The request is sent to your tenant SAML2 sign in endpoint.

4. The user is presented with a login page, unless she has previously signed in and established a user session at the Azure AD tenant.

5. When authenticated, a SAML-P response is returned via HTTP POST to the application URL. The URL to use is specified in the single sign-on settings as the Reply URL. This response contains a SAML token.

6. The application processes this response, verifies the token is signed by a trusted issuer (Azure AD), and confirms that the token is still valid.

7. The application can optionally use claims in the token to personalize the application experience for the logged in user.

8. The application can optionally query Azure AD for groups for authorization purposes.

> **NOTE SAML-P ENDPOINTS**
>
> SAML-P support in Azure AD includes a sign-on and sign-out endpoint, and they are both the same URL. The protocol describes how to format each request so that the endpoint knows which action is requested.

> **MORE INFO SAML PROTOCOL**
>
> SAML-P tools are not provided as part of the .NET Framework libraries; however, there are a few third-party libraries available for building applications based on this protocol. Typically, support for SAML-P becomes important when you are integrating other SaaS applications with your Azure AD because some applications do not support WS-Federation or OpenID Connect. For more information on SAML-P and Azure AD, see *https://docs.microsoft.com/en-us/azure/active-directory/active-directory-saml-protocol-reference*.

Query the directory using Microsoft Graph API, MFA and MFA API

Beyond authentication and authorization workflows for your applications, you can also interact with the Microsoft Graph API to manage users and request information about users, and integrate multi-factor authentication scenarios into your solutions. This section discusses those capabilities.

> **NOTE MICROSOFT GRAPH VS. AZURE AD GRAPH**
>
> Microsoft Graph is the recommended API to be used over Azure AD Graph API - as it is where future investments in functionality are being made. Microsoft Graph already supports most everything that is exposed today through Azure AD graph and will ultimately support all of Azure AD Graph functionality. In the meantime, both APIs are supported for those applications that were already implemented against Azure AD Graph. New applications are recommended to use Microsoft Graph unless there is a feature that only Azure AD Graph exposes. See this reference for the roadmap: *https://dev.office.com/blogs/microsoft-graph-or-azure-ad-graph*.

Query the Microsoft Graph API

Using the Microsoft Graph API, you can interact with your Azure AD tenant to manage users, groups, and more. If the application is limited to read access only, query activity will be allowed. With read and write access, the application can perform additional management activities:

- Add, update, and delete users and groups
- Find users
- Request a user's group and role membership
- Manage group membership
- Create applications
- Query and create directory properties

> *MORE INFO* **MICROSOFT GRAPH API REFERENCE**
>
> See this reference for documentation regarding the Microsoft Graph: *https://developer. microsoft.com/en-us/graph/docs*.

EXAM TIP

The Microsoft Graph API is accessible via the Azure AD v2 endpoint. The Azure AD v2 endpoint is an evolution of the Azure AD v1 endpoint that modernizes some of the protocol payloads, allows you to use a single endpoint for both Azure AD and Microsoft Account users, and also adds other features. At the time of this writing, the only way to use the Azure AD v2 endpoint is to register applications at the new Microsoft Application Registry at *https://apps.dev.microsoft.com.* **For more details on this see:** *https://docs.microsoft.com/en-us/ azure/active-directory/develop/active-directory-appmodel-v2-overview*.

Before you can interact with the Microsoft Graph API programmatically, you must create an application with the Microsoft Application Registry as follows (Figure 3-13):

1. Navigate to the Microsoft Application Registry accessed via *https://apps.dev.microsoft. com.*

2. Click Add an app, and from the app registration page enter a friendly name for your application and supply your contact email for administering the applications. You can optionally select the Guided Setup checkbox for a walkthrough to complete additional settings. Click to create the application.

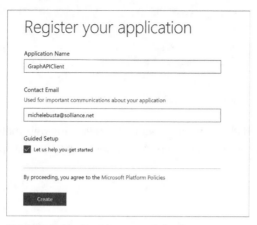

FIGURE 3-13 The Register your application page

3. If you do not select the guided setup, you will see the registration details for your new application and be able to view and manage those details, for example:

   A. View the application id (a GUID) identifying your application.

   B. Generate a password or set up a key pair for the application to support token requests.

   C. Supply web application integration details such as redirect URL and single sign-out URL.

   D. Supply mobile application integration details such as redirect URI.

   E. Set any delegated or application permissions that the application requires.

   F. Provide other application customization details that are relevant during sign in such as the logo, home page URL, terms of service URL, and privacy statement URL.

An application can query the Microsoft Graph API in a few ways:

- The application can directly query the graph API with the application id and secret, to access information that the application has direct access to (without user consent being required).

- The application can request information about the user through delegated permissions, which implies that the user must first authenticate to the application, grant consent (or at least have consent automatically granted at the administrative level), and then make requests on behalf of that user.

To set up a web application to support user authentication, consent and delegated permissions to user information exposed via the Graph API:

1. Create an application password. Click Generate New Password from the Application secrets section. In the dialog presented save the generated password somewhere safe as it will not be presented again (Figure 3-14).

FIGURE 3-14 The Application Secrets section of the registered application

2. From Platforms section, select Add Platform and select Web. Provide the web application sign in URL and for single sign-out scenarios you can optionally provide the application sign out URL (Figure 3-15).

FIGURE 3-15 The web application configuration for sign in and sign out

3. By default, the Microsoft Graph Permissions will have delegated permissions for User. Read selected. You may choose to change the delegated permissions, or add application permissions, based on the type of requests your application may make to the Graph API.

> **MORE INFO** **AZURE SAMPLES FOR MICROSOFT GRAPH**
>
> See the Azure Samples on GitHub for more examples for calling the Microsoft Graph API including the following examples for web apps and JavaScript based applications:
>
> *https://github.com/Azure-Samples/active-directory-dotnet-webapp-openidconnect-v2* and *https://github.com/Azure-Samples/active-directory-javascript-singlepageapp-dotnet-webapi-v2.*

Working with MFA

Multi-factor authentication (MFA) requires that users provide more than one verification method during the authentication process, including two or more of the following:

- A password (something you know)
- An email account or phone (something you have)
- Biometric input like a thumbprint (something you are)

Azure Multi-Factor Authentication (MFA) is the Microsoft solution for two-step verification workflows that can work with phone, text messages or mobile app verification methods.

> **NOTE** **MFA SETTINGS**
>
> At the time of this writing, you must still navigate to the (old) management portal to enable MFA for users in your directory, and to configure MFA settings. This will change in the near future.

You can enable MFA for users in your directory by doing the following:

1. Navigate to the Azure portal accessed via *https://portal.azure.com*.

2. Click New and select Security + Identity, then select Multi-Factor Authentication from the list of choices (Figure 3-16).

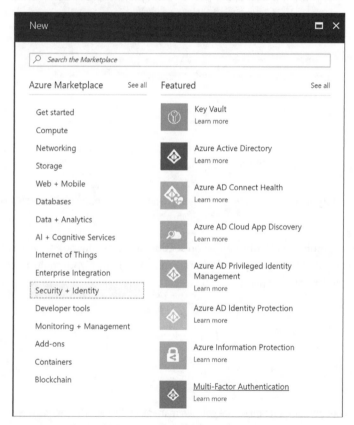

FIGURE 3-16 The Multi-Factor Authentication selection in the Azure Portal

3. You will see a link that will take you to the (old) management portal. Click Go to navigate to that portal (Figure 3-17).

FIGURE 3-17 The Coming Soon screen that links to the old management portal for managing Multi-Factor Authentication

4. From the (old) management portal select your directory and click the Configure tab (Figure 3-18).

FIGURE 3-18 A directory view in the (old) management portal where you can configure MFA settings

5. Scroll down to the multi-factor authentication section and click Manage service settings. You will navigate to another portal where you can configure your multi-factor authentication service settings (Figure 3-19).

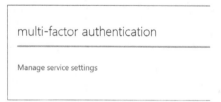

FIGURE 3-19 The configuration section where you can manage multi-factor authentication

6. From the multi-factor authentication portal, select the service settings tab. You can optionally customize settings for the following:

    A. App passwords

    B. Trusted IPs to bypass multi-factor authentication

C. Enabled multi-factor verification options such as call or text to phone, mobile notifications or mobile apps

D. Device remember-me settings

7. Select the users tab. From here you can select users and enable multi-factor authentication (Figure 3-20). Select a user from your directory who does not yet have multi-factor enabled, and click Enable from the action pane to the right.

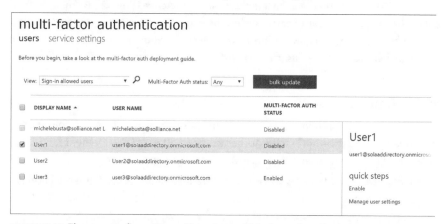

FIGURE 3-20 The user configuration settings for multi-factor authentication

Users with multi-factor authentication enabled will be prompted to set up their multi-factor authentication settings during their next login. The login workflow will follow these steps:

1. First, the user is taken to the directory login where they are prompted to login with their username and password.

2. Once authenticated, they are presented with a request to set up their multi-factor settings (Figure 3-21).

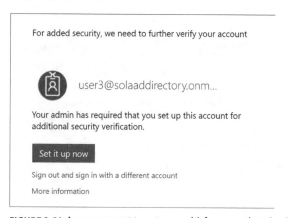

FIGURE 3-21 A user prompt to set up multi-factor authentication

3. If the user has not yet supplied their email address or phone number for multi-factor authentication, they will be asked to provide this information now. In addition, they will be taken through the process of verifying this information to ensure they can be used safely for future multi-factor authentication workflows.

EXAM TIP

Azure Multi-Factor Authentication is included inAzure Active Directory Premium plans and Enterprise Mobility + Security plans, and can be deployed either in the cloud or on-premises. See the following documentation for the full details about Microsoft's MFA solution: *https://docs.microsoft.com/en-us/azure/multi-factor-authentication*.

Work with the MFA API

You may choose to integrate multi-factor authentication directly into your applications. This can be done by using the Multi-factor Authentication Software Development Kit (SDK), which provides an API for interacting with Azure MFA from your application.

In order to use these MFA APIs you must first create a Multi-factor Authentication Provider from the Azure portal following these steps:

1. Navigate to the Azure portal accessed via *https://portal.azure.com*.

2. Click New and select Security + Identity, then select Multi-Factor Authentication from the list of choices. You will see a link that will take you to the (old) management portal (Figure 3-22). Click Go to navigate to that portal.

3. Select Active Directory from the navigation pane and select the Multi-factor Auth Providers tab.

FIGURE 3-22 The list of directories in the (old) management portal

4. Create a new provider and set these values (Figure 3-23):

   A. Name for the provider.

   B. Usage model, choosing between Per Enabled User or Per Authentication.

   C. Associate the provider with one of your directories.

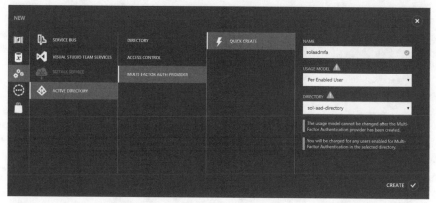

FIGURE 3-23 Creating a new multi-factor auth provider in the (old) management portal

5. Click Create to create the new multi-factor authentication provider (Figure 3-24). You will see it in the list of the providers once it's created.

FIGURE 3-24 The list of multi-factor authentication providers

6. To manage settings for the multi-factor authentication provider, select it and click Manage from the command bar below. You will be taken to the Azure Multi-Factor Authentication portal (Figure 3-25).

7. Select Downloads to view the available MFA SDK downloads and choose the one for your development environment for download.

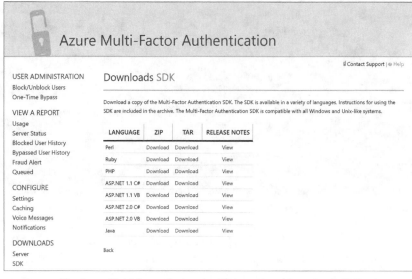

FIGURE 3-25 The Azure Multi-factor Authentication portal and Downloads SDK area

---

Skill 3.2: Develop apps that use Azure AD B2C and Azure AD B2B

Azure AD supports user sign-in with social identity providers such as Google and Facebook as part of Azure AD B2C. Azure AD also enables access to applications from external partners as part of Azure B2B collaboration. This section discusses these features.

> **This skill covers how to:**
> - Design and implement .NET MVC, Web API, and Windows desktop apps that leverage social identity provider authentication
> - Leverage Azure AD B2B to design and implement applications that support partner-managed identities and enforce multi-factor authentication

Design and implement apps that leverage social identity provider authentication

Azure AD B2C makes it possible for users of your applications to authenticate with social identity providers, enterprise accounts using open standards, and local accounts where users are managed by Azure AD. Fundamentally this means that the user signs in at the identity provider, and therefore, credentials are managed by the identity provider.

Figure 3-26 illustrates the workflow assuming OpenID Connect protocol for communication between a web application and the Azure AD B2C tenant. The user navigates to the application to login (1) and is redirected to Azure AD with an OpenID Connect sign in request (2). Azure AD redirects the user to the third party identity provider (3) with the protocol that is established for communication between Azure AD and that provider (it may not be OpenID Connect). If the user does not yet have an active session at the identity provider, they are typically presented with a login page to enter credentials (4), and upon successful authentication (5), the identity provider issues a protocol response and sets up the user session (6) possibly in the form of an SSO session cookie. The response is posted to Azure AD (7) and validated. Upon successful validation of the response (and user identity) Azure AD establishes a user session (SSO session cookie) and issues an OpenID Connect response to the calling web app (8). This response is posted to the web app (9) and validated to establish the user session at the web app (10).

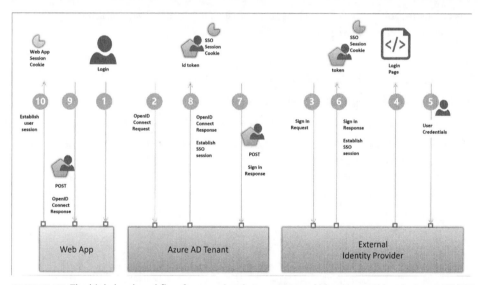

FIGURE 3-26 The high-level workflow for user sign-in to an external identity provider via Azure AD B2C

There are a few important things to point out about this workflow:

- Applications need not be aware of the identity provider where the user signs in, since the application trusts the response from Azure AD.
- The trust relationships are between applications and Azure AD, and between Azure AD and the identity provider(s) that are configured (see Figure 3-27).

- The protocols to be used between Azure AD and identity provider can vary per identity provider. This has no relationship to how the application communicates with Azure AD.

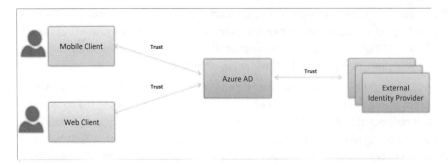

FIGURE 3-27 Trust relationships between Applications and Azure AD, and between Azure AD and external identity providers

This section covers how to set up Azure AD B2C to enable users to login with their preferred social identity provider such as Microsoft Account, Facebook, Google+, Amazon or Linked In.

> *MORE INFO* **AZURE AD B2C OVERVIEW**
>
> For a complete look at Azure AD B2C see this overview: *https://docs.microsoft.com/en-us/azure/active-directory-b2c/active-directory-b2c-overview*.

Create an Azure AD B2C tenant

To create a new Azure AD B2C tenant follow these steps:

1. Navigate to the Azure portal accessed via *https://portal.azure.com*.
2. Click New and select Security + Identity, then select Azure Active Directory B2C from the list of choices (Figure 3-28).

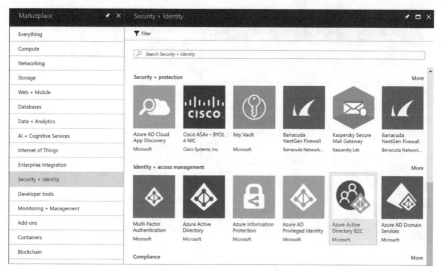

FIGURE 3-28 The list of options under Security + Identity in the Azure portal where Azure Active Directory B2C can be found

3. Click Create from the Azure Active Directory B2C blade.

    You may be prompted to switch to a directory with a subscription attached. If so, click Switch directories and select the correct subscription where you want to create the new B2C tenant. You may also have to repeat steps 1-3.

4. From the Create new B2C tenant or Link to existing tenant blade, select Create a new Azure AD B2C tenant (Figure 3-29).

5. Enter a name for the organization, a domain name, and select the country or region for the new tenant.

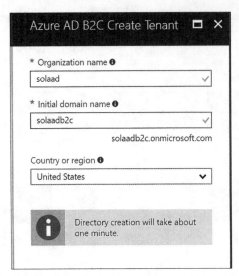

FIGURE 3-29 Settings for creating a new Azure AD B2C tenant.

6. You can navigate to your directory by clicking the link supplied in the create blade, after the directory is created. Or, you can navigate to More Services from the navigation menu and type **Azure AD** to filter the list and find Azure AD B2C, then select it (Figure 3-30).

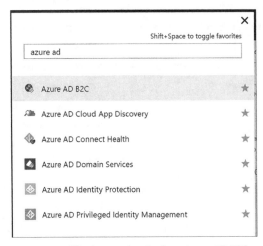

FIGURE 3-30 Filtering services to show Azure AD B2C

7. Your tenant will appear in the B2C Tenant dashboard and may show a notification indicating that it is not attached to a subscription. If this happens, switch directories again, select your subscription from the list, and repeat steps 1-3. At step 4 select Link to existing tenant and choose your tenant. This will remove the warning.

8. Repeat step 6 to return to your Azure B2C tenant dashboard and click the tenant settings component. From here you will be able to manage your tenant settings.

Register an application

A given solution may have one or more applications that will integrate with Azure AD B2C. Integration requires an application be registered with the B2C tenant. When you register an application, you can configure how the application will integrate with the tenant, for example:

- Indicate if the application is a web or API application, or a native application
- Indicate if OpenID Connect will be used to authenticate users interactively
- Indicate any required redirect URLs or URIs

Follow these steps to register a web application:

1. Navigate to your B2C tenant settings (Figure 3-31) as described in the previous section
2. Select Applications and click Add from the command bar

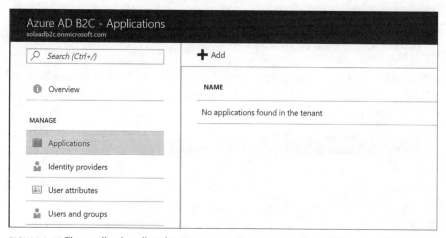

FIGURE 3-31 The applications list where you can register a new application

3. In the New application blade, provide the following settings (Figure 3-32):
    A. Enter a name for the application
    B. Select Yes for Web App / Web API
    C. Select Yes for Allow implicit flow
    D. Provide a reply URL authentication responses should be posted

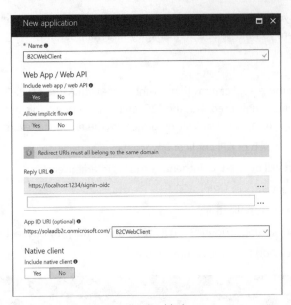

FIGURE 3-32 The New application blade

4. An application ID is created for the application once you create it (Figure 3-33). Select the application from the applications list and you can review its settings including this new application ID.

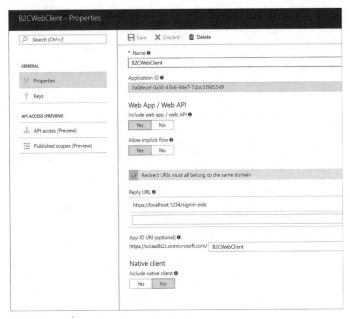

FIGURE 3-33 The settings for an application

Now you can set up your application with the following settings:

- Configure any external identity providers to be supported for sign in
- Manage user attributes
- Manage users and groups
- Manage policies

Configure identity providers

You may want to give your users a choice between one or more external identity providers to sign in. Azure AD supports a pre-defined set of well-known social identity providers to choose from (Figure 3-34).

To configure an external identity provider, follow these steps:

1. Navigate to your directory settings as discussed previously.
2. Select identity providers from the navigation pane.
3. Enter a name for the identity provider, something that matches the provider you will configure such as "google" or "facebook."
4. Select the identity provider to configure and click OK.

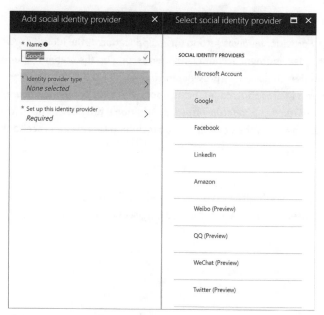

FIGURE 3-34 The identity providers supported by Azure B2C tenants

5. Set up the identity provider in the final tab. Based on the selected identity provider, you will be presented with required settings that typically include a client id and secret for the provider. You must have previously set up an application with the identity provider,

in order to have the required settings for this configuration. Once you have entered the required settings, click OK (see Figure 3-35).

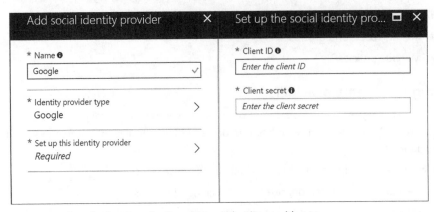

FIGURE 3-35 Required settings for Google as an identity provider

6.   Click Create to complete the configuration of the identity provider. You will see your new provider listed in the identity providers blade.

> **MORE INFO** **CONFIGURING IDENTITY PROVIDERS**
>
> The setup for each identity provider involves setting up an application at the identity provider, sometimes through a development account, and then setting up the credentials and related information required by that identity provider in your Azure AD B2C settings. See this reference for setting up a Microsoft Account: *https://docs.microsoft.com/en-us/azure/active-directory-b2c/active-directory-b2c-setup-msa-app*. Additional provider setup instructions can be found in the same area of the documentation including Google and Facebook.

Configuring policies

There are several policies you can configure for your Azure AD B2C tenant. These policies enable features and govern the user experience for the following scenarios:

- Sign-up
- Sign-in
- Profile editing
- Password reset

These policies all provide default UI templates but allow for overriding those templates for further customization. You can also determine which identity provider shall be supported, support for multi-factor authentication, and control over which claims shall be returned with the id token post authentication. For sign-up, you can also configure which profile attributes you want to collect for the user.

MORE INFO   **B2C APPLICATION SAMPLES**

Once you have set up your Azure B2C tenant, configuring applications to integrate involves similar steps to those described earlier for OpenID Connect application integration. See the following samples from the Azure Samples GitHub repository, specifically related to B2C applications:

https://github.com/Azure-Samples/active-directory-b2c-dotnetcore-webapp https://github. com/Azure-Samples/active-directory-b2c-xamarin-native

https://github.com/Azure-Samples/active-directory-b2c-dotnet-webapp-and-webapi

Leverage Azure AD B2B to design and implement applications that support partner-managed identities and enforce multi-factor authentication

Azure AD B2B collaboration capabilities enable organizations using Azure AD to allow users from other organizations, with or without Azure AD, to have limited access to documents, resources and applications.

From your Azure AD tenant you can:

- Set up single sign-on to enterprise applications such as Salesforce and Dropbox through Azure AD

- Support user authentication via Azure AD for your own applications

- Enable access to these applications to users outside of your directory

- Enforce multi-factor authentication for these users

MORE INFO   **AZURE AD B2B**

For details on Azure AD B2B collaboration and adding guest users to access applications, see this reference: *https://docs.microsoft.com/en-us/azure/active-directory/active-directory-b2b-what-is-azure-ad-b2b.*

Skill 3.3: Manage Secrets using Azure Key Vault

Cloud applications typically need a safe workflow for secret management. Azure Key Vault provides a secure service for Azure applications and services for:

- Encrypting storage account keys, data encryption keys, certificates, passwords and other keys and secrets

- Protecting those keys using hardware security modules (HSMs)

Azure Key Vault supports importing and generating keys in HSMs. This means that keys are processed in FIPS 140-2 Level 2 validated HSMs.

Developers can easily create keys to support development efforts, while administrators are able to grant or revoke access to keys as needed. This section covers how to manage secrets with Azure Key Vault.

This skill covers how to:

- Configure Azure Key Vault
- Manage access, including tenants
- Implement HSM protected keys
- Manage service limits
- Implement logging
- Implement key rotation

MORE INFO **KEY VAULT OVERVIEW**

For detailed documentation on Azure Key Vault, see this reference: *https://docs.microsoft. com/en-us/azure/key-vault/key-vault-whatis.*

Configure Azure Key Vault

You can create one or more key vault in a subscription, according to your needs for management isolation. To create a new key vault, follow these steps:

1. Navigate to the Azure portal accessed via *https://portal.azure.com*.
2. Click New and select Security + Identity, then select Key Vault from the list of choices (Figure 3-36).

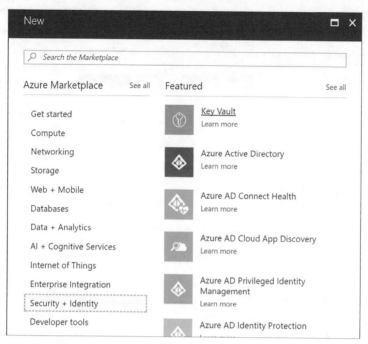

FIGURE 3-36 Selecting Key Vault from the Security + Identity features

3. From the Create key vault blade, enter the following values (Figure 3-37):

A. A name for the key vault

B. Choose the subscription

C. Create or choose a resource group

D. A location

E. Choose a pricing tier - primarily based on your requirements for HSM

F. Set up policies for user access to keys, secrets and certificates

G. Optionally grant access for Azure Virtual Machines, Azure Resource Manager or Azure Disk Encryption

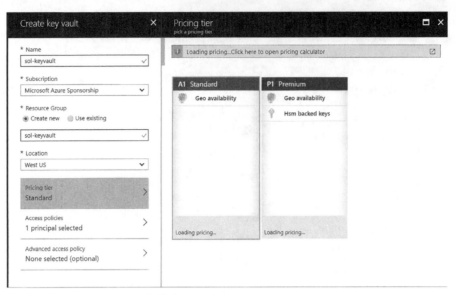

FIGURE 3-37 The Create key vault blade

4. Click Create to create the key vault.

Manage access, including tenants

There are two ways to access the key vault - through the management plane or the data plane. The management plane exposes an interface for managing the key vault settings and policies, and the data plane exposes an interface for managing the actual secrets and policies related directly to managing those secrets. You can set up policies that control access through each of these planes, granting users, applications or devices access to specific functionality (service principals). These service principals must be associated with the same Azure AD tenant as the key vault.

To create policies for your key vault, navigate to the key vault Overview and do the following (Figure 3-38):

1. Select Access policies from the navigation pane.

2. Select Add new from the Access policies blade.

3. Select Configure from template and select Key, Secret & Certificate Management. This will initialize a set of permissions based on the template, which you can later adjust.

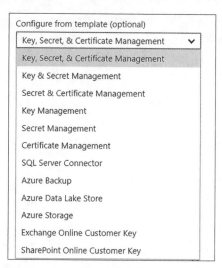

FIGURE 3-38 Options for configuring a policy

4. Click Select a principal and enter a username, application id or device id from your directory.

5. Review key permissions selected by the template-modify them as needed according to the requirements for the principal selected (Figure 3-39).

FIGURE 3-39 The options for customizing key permissions for a policy

6. Review secret permissions selected by the template, modify them as needed according to the requirements for the principal selected (Figure 3-40).

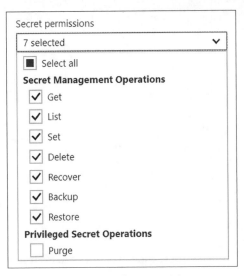

FIGURE 3-40 The options for customizing secret permissions for a policy

7. Review certificate permissions selected by the template, and modify them as needed according to the requirements for the principal selected (Figure 3-41).

FIGURE 3-41 The options for customizing certificate permissions for a policy

8. Click OK to save the policy settings (Figure 3-42).

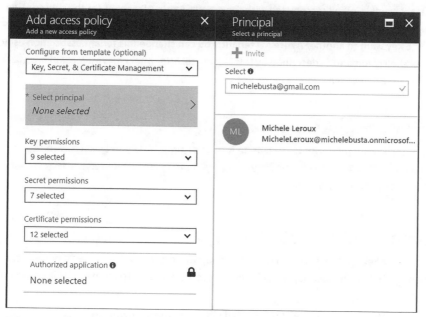

FIGURE 3-42 The options for customizing key permissions for a policy

9. From the key vault blade, click Save from the command bar to commit the changes.

In addition to granting access to service principals, you can also set advance access policies to allow access to Azure Virtual Machines, Azure Resource Manager, or Azure Disk Encryption as follows (Figure 3-43):

1. Select the Advanced access policies tab from the navigation pane.

2. Enable access by Azure Virtual Machines, Azure Resource Manager or Azure Disk Encryption as appropriate.

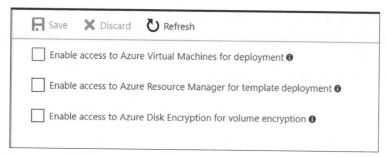

FIGURE 3-43 The options for setting advanced rules for a policy

Implement HSM protected keys

If you create a key vault based on a premium subscription, you will be able to generate, store and manage Hardware Security Module (HSM) protected keys. To create an HSM protected key follow these steps:

1. Navigate to the Azure portal accessed via *https://portal.azure.com*.

2. Navigate to More Services from the navigation menu and type **key vault** to filter the list and find Key Vaults and then select it.

3. From the Key vaults blade, select a previously created key vault that supports HSM.

4. Select the Keys tab from the navigation pane, and click Add from the command bar.

5. From the Create key blade, enter the following information (Figure 3-44):

   A. For Options, select Generate. You can also upload a key or restore a key from a backup.

   B. Provide a name for the key.

   C. For key type, select HSM protected key.

   D. Optionally provide an activation and expiry date for the key. Otherwise there is no set expiry.

   E. Indicate if the key should be enabled now.

FIGURE 3-44 The Create a key blade

6. Click Create to complete the creation of the key.

> **MORE INFO MANAGING HSM KEYS WITH POWERSHELL**
>
> See this reference for more on managing HSM keys with PowerShell: *https://docs.microsoft. com/en-us/azure/key-vault/key-vault-hsm-protected-keys*.

EXAM TIP

Software keys (not protected by HSM) can be later exported from the key vault. HSM keys, on the other hand, can never be exported. In addition, all cryptographic operations using HSM keys are always performed within the HSM boundary.

Implement logging

You can monitor access to Key Vault by enabling logging. Logs include:

- All REST API requests including failed, unauthenticated or unauthorized requests
- Key vault operations to create, delete or change settings
- Operations that involve keys, secrets, and certificates in the key vault

Logs are saved to an Azure storage account of your choice, in a new container (generated for you) named insights-logs-auditevent. To set up diagnostic logging, follow these steps:

1. Navigate to the Azure portal accessed via *https://portal.azure.com*.

2. Navigate to More Services from the navigation menu and type "key vault " to filter the list and find Key Vaults, and then select it.

3. From the Key vaults blade, select the key vault to enable logging for.

4. From the Key vault blade, select the Diagnostics logs tab from the navigation pane.

5. From the Diagnostics logs blade, select the Turn on diagnostics link.

6. From the Diagnostics settings blade enter the following settings (Figure 3-45):

   A. Provide a name for the diagnostics settings.

   B. One of the following optional settings must be chosen:

   ■ Select Archive to a storage account and configure a storage account where the logs should be stored. This storage account must be previously created using the Resource Manager deployment model (not Classic), and a new container for key vault logs will be created in this storage account.

   ■ Optionally select Stream to an event hub if you want logs to be part of your holistic log streaming solution.

   ■ Optionally select Send logs to Log Analytics and configure an OMS workspace for the logs to be sent to.

   C. Select AuditEvent (the only category for key vault logging) and configure retention preferences for storage. If you configure retention settings, older logs will be deleted.

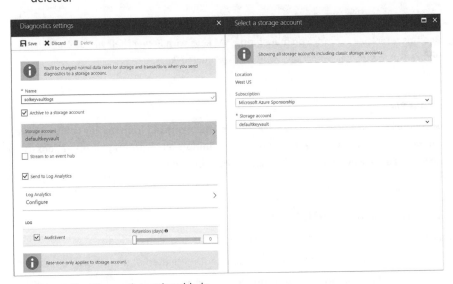

FIGURE 3-45 The Diagnostics settings blade

7. Click Save from the command bar to save these diagnostics settings.

8. You will now be able to see logs from the Diagnostics output.

MORE INFO **MANAGE KEY VAULT LOGGING WITH POWERSHELL**

See this reference for more on how to set up key vault logging including the use of Power-Shell: *https://docs.microsoft.com/en-us/azure/key-vault/key-vault-logging*.

Implement key rotation

The beauty of working with a key vault is the ability to roll keys without impact to applications. Applications do not hold on to key material, and they reference keys indirectly through the key vault. Keys are updated without affecting this reference and so application configuration updates are no longer necessary when keys are updated. This opens the door to simplified key update procedures and the ability to embrace regular or ad-hoc key rotation schedules.

Each key, secret or certificate stored in Azure Key Vault can have one or more versions associated. The first version is created when you first create the key. Subsequent versions can be created through the Azure Portal, through key vault management interfaces, or through automation procedures.

To rotate a key from the Azure Portal, navigate to the key vault and follow these steps:

1. Select the Keys tab from the navigation pane.
2. Select the key to rotate.
3. From the key's Versions blade (Figure 3-46), you will see the first version of the key that was created.

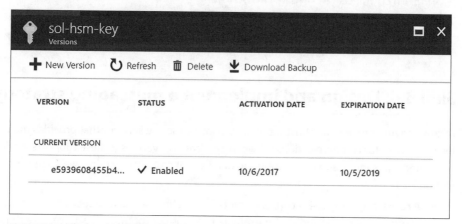

FIGURE 3-46 The Versions blade where you can create a new version

4. Click New Version from the command bar and you will be presented with the Create A Key Blade where you can generate or upload a new key to be associated with the same key name. You can choose the type of key (Software key or HSM protected key) and optionally indicate an activation and expiry timeframe. Click Create to replace the key.

5. You will now see two versions of the key on the Versions blade (Figure 3-47). Applications querying for the key will now retrieve the new version.

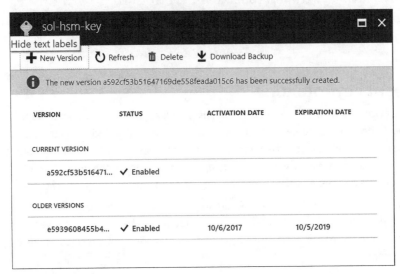

FIGURE 3-47 The Versions blade showing a new version and older versions

This key rotation procedure works similarly for secrets and certificates. Applications will now retrieve the newer version when contacting the key vault for the specified key.

> **MORE INFO   IMPLEMENTING KEY ROTATION**
>
> See this reference for more details on managing a key rotation process with PowerShell: *https://docs.microsoft.com/en-us/azure/key-vault/key-vault-key-rotation-log-monitoring.*

Skill 3.4: Design and implement a messaging strategy

MicrosoftAzure provides a robust set of hosted infrastructure services that provides multi-tenant services for communications between applications. Variously, these supports service publishing, messaging, and the distribution of events at scale. The services we focus on in this section include:

- **Azure Relay** Expose secure endpoints for synchronous calls to service endpoints across a network boundary, for example to expose on-premises resources to a remote client without requiring a VPN.

- **Azure Service Bus Queues**   Implement brokered messaging patterns where the message sender can deliver a message even if the receiver is temporarily offline.

- **Azure Service Bus Topics and subscriptions**   Implement brokered messaging patterns for publish and subscribe where messages can be received by more than one receiver (subscriber), and conditions can be applied to message delivery.

- **Azure Event Hubs**   Implement scenarios that support high-volume message ingest and where receivers can pull messages to perform processing at scale.

- **Azure Notification Hubs**   Implement scenarios for sending app-centric push notifications to mobile devices.

Relays are used for relayed, synchronous messaging. The remaining scenarios are a form of brokered, asynchronous messaging patterns. In this section, you learn how to implement, scale and monitor each Service Bus resource.

MORE INFO   **SERVICE BUS RESOURCES AND SAMPLES**

See these references for a collection of overviews, tutorials, and samples related to Service Bus:

- **Azure Relay**   *https://docs.microsoft.com/en-us/azure/service-bus-relay/*

- **Service Bus Messaging**   *https://docs.microsoft.com/en-us/azure/service-bus-messaging/*

- **Event Hubs**   *https://docs.microsoft.com/en-us/azure/event-hubs/*

- **Notification Hubs**   *https://docs.microsoft.com/en-us/azure/notification-hubs/*

This skill covers how to:

- Develop and scale messaging solutions using Service Bus queues, topics, relays and Notification Hubs

- Scale and monitor messaging

- Determine when to use Event Hubs, Service Bus, IoT Hub, Stream Analytics and Notification Hubs

Develop and scale messaging solutions using Service Bus queues, topics, relays and Notification Hubs

A namespace is a container for Service Bus resources including queues, topics, Relays, Notification Hubs, and Event Hubs. With namespaces, you can group resources of the same type into a single namespace, and you can choose to further separate resources according to management and scale requirements. You don't create a namespace directly, instead you will typically create a namespace as a first step in deploying a Service Bus queue, topic, Relay, Notification Hubs or Event Hubs instance. Once you have a namespace for a particular service, you can add other service instances of the same type to it (a Service Bus namespace supports the addition of queues and topics, so a Notification Hubs namespace supports only Notification Hubs instances). You can also manage access policies and adjust the pricing tier (for scaling purposes), both of which apply to all the services in the namespace.

The steps for creating a Service Bus namespace are as follows:

1. In the Azure Portal, select + New, then search for the type of namespace you want to create: Service Bus, Relay, Notification Hubs or Event Hubs.

2. Select Create.

3. In the Create namespace blade (Figure 3-48), enter a unique prefix for the namespace name.

4. Choose your Azure Subscription, Resource group and Location.

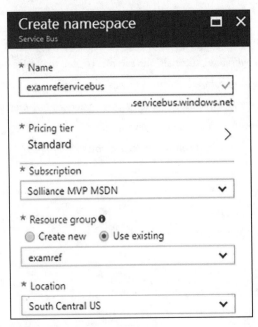

FIGURE 3-48 Creating a Service Bus namespace

5. Select Create to deploy the namespace.

Selecting a protocol for messaging

By default, Service Bus supports several communication protocols. Table 3-1 lists the protocol options and required ports.

TABLE 3-1 Service Bus protocols and ports

Protocol	PORTS	Description
SBMP	9350-9354 (for relay) 9354 (for brokered messaging)	Service Bus Messaging Protocol (SBMP), is a proprietary SOAP-based protocol that typically relies on WCF under the covers to implement messaging with between applications through Service Bus. Relay services use this protocol by default when non-HTTP relay bindings are chosen. environment is set to use HTTP. This protocol is being phased out in favor of AMQP.
HTTP	80, 443	HTTP protocol can be used for relay services when one of the HTTP relay bindings are selected and the Service Bus environment is set to use HTTP connectivity. The brokered messaging client library uses this if you do not specify AMQP protocol and set the Service Bus environment to HTTP as follows: ServiceBusEnvironment.SystemConnectivity.Mode = ConnectivityMode.Http;
AMQP	5671, 5672	Advanced Message Queuing Protocol (AMQP) is a modern, cross-platform asynchronous messaging standard. The brokered messaging client library uses this protocol if the connection string indicates TransportType of Amqp.
WebSockets	80, 443	WebSockets provide a standards compliant way to establish bi-directional communication channels, and can be used for Service Bus queues, topics and the Relay.

> **MORE INFO   AMQP PROTOCOL**
>
> Advanced Message Queuing Protocol (AMQP) is the recommended protocol to use for brokered message exchange if firewall rules are not an issue. For additional information, see *https://docs.microsoft.com/azure/service-bus-messaging/service-bus-amqp-overview*.

EXAM TIP

Connectivity issues are common for on-premises environments that disable ports other than 80 and 443. For this reason, it is still often necessary for portability to use HTTP protocol for brokered messaging.

Introducing the Azure Relay

The Azure Relay service supports applications that need to communicate by providing an Azure hosted rendezvous endpoint where listeners (the server process that exposes functionality) and senders (the application that consumes the server process functionality) can connect, and then the Azure Relay service itself takes care of relaying the data between the two cloud-side connections. The Azure Relay has two distinct ways that you can choose from to securely achieve this form of connectivity:

- **Hybrid Connections**   With Hybrid Connections your applications communicate by establishing Web Sockets connections with relay endpoints. This approach is standards based, meaning it is useable from almost any platform containing basic Web Socket capabilities.
- **WCF Relays**   With WCF relays, your applications use Windows Communication Foundation to enable communication across relay endpoints. This approach is only useable with applications leveraging WCF and .NET.

Using Hybrid Connections

At a high level, to use Hybrid Connections involves these steps:

1. Deploy an Azure Relay namespace
2. Deploy a Hybrid Connection within the namespace
3. Retrieve the connection configuration (connection details and credentials)
4. Create a listener application that uses the configuration to provide service-side functionality
5. Create a sender application that uses the configuration to communicate with the listener
6. Run the applications

The following sections walk through creating a simple solution where the listener simply echoes the text sent from the sender. The sender itself takes input typed from the user in a console application and sends it to the listener by way of a Hybrid Connection.

> *MORE INFO*   **CREATING LISTENER AND SENDER APPLICATIONS**
>
> The following steps detail how to create listener and sender applications using .NET. For an equivalent example that uses Node.js, see *https://docs.microsoft.com/azure/service-bus-relay/relay-hybrid-connections-node-get-started*.

DEPLOY AN AZURE RELAY NAMESPACE

The following steps are needed to deploy a new Azure Relay namespace:

1. In the Azure Portal, select + NEW and then search for "Relay". Select the item labeled Relay by Microsoft.
2. In the Create namespace blade, enter a unique prefix for the namespace name.
3. Choose your Azure Subscription, Resource group and Location.
4. Select Create to deploy the namespace.

DEPLOY A HYBRID CONNECTION

The following steps are needed to deploy a new Hybrid Connection within the Azure Relay namespace:

1. Using the Portal, navigate to the blade of your deployed Relay namespace.
2. Select + Hybrid Connection from the command bar.

3. On the Create Hybrid Connection blade, enter a name for your new Hybrid Connection.

4. Select Create.

RETRIEVE THE CONNECTION CONFIGURATION

Your applications will need at minimum the following configuration in order to communicate with the Hybrid Connection:

- Namespace URI
- Hybrid Connection Name
- Shared access policy name
- Shared access policy key

Follow these steps to retrieve these values for use in your listener and sender applications:

1. Using the Portal, navigate to the blade of your deployed Relay namespace.

2. From the menu, select Shared access policies to retrieve the policies available at the namespace level.

3. In the list of policies, select a policy. For example, by default the RootManageSharedAccessKey policy is available.

4. On the Policy blade, take note of the policy name and the value of the Primary key. Also note the connection string values you can use with SDKs that support these as inputs (Figure 3-49).

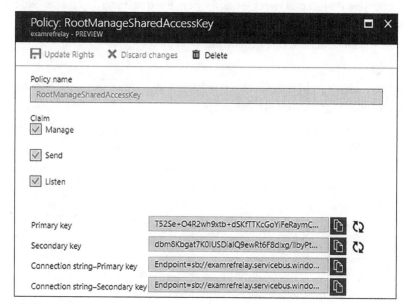

FIGURE 3-49 Examining a Policy

5. Close the Policy blade.

6. From the menu, select Hybrid Connections.

7. In the listing, select your deployed Hybrid Connection.

8. From the Essentials panel, take note of the value for Namespace. This is the namespace name.

9. Also, take note of the Hybrid Connection URL (Figure 3-50). It is of the form
https://<namespace>.servicebus.windows.net/<hybridconnectionname>

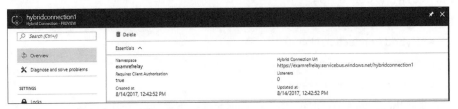

FIGURE 3-50 Obtaining the Hybrid Connection URL

10. You can get the name of your Hybrid Connection either from the title of the blade, or by looking at the Hybrid Connection URL and copying the value after the slash (/).

CREATE A LISTENER APPLICATION

Follow these steps to create simple listener application that echoes any text transmitted by a sender application:

1. Launch Visual Studio.

2. Select File, New, Project and select Visual C# from the tree under Templates, and then the Console App (.NET Framework) template.

3. Provide the name and location of your choice.

4. Select OK.

5. In Solution Explorer, right click the new project and select Manage NuGet Packages.

6. In the document that appears, select Browse.

7. Search for "Microsoft.Azure.Relay" and then select the Microsoft Azure Relay item in the list (Figure 3-51).

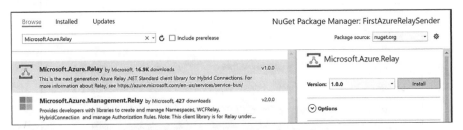

FIGURE 3-51 Selecting the Microsoft.Azure.Relay NuGet package

8. Select Install to begin the installation and follow the prompts.

9. Open program.cs.

10. Replace the using statements at the top of the document with the following:

```
using System;
using System.IO;
using System.Threading;
using System.Threading.Tasks;
using Microsoft.Azure.Relay;
```

11. Replace the Program class with the following:

```
class Program
{
    private const string RelayNamespace = "<namespace>.servicebus.windows.net";
    private const string ConnectionName = "<hybridconnectionname>";
    private const string KeyName = "<sharedaccesskeyname> ";
    private const string Key = "<sharedaccesskeyvalue>";


    static void Main(string[] args)
    {
        RunAsync().GetAwaiter().GetResult();
    }

    private static async void ProcessMessagesOnConnection(
                            HybridConnectionStream relayConnection,
                            CancellationTokenSource cts)
    {
        Console.WriteLine("New session");

        // The connection is a fully bidirectional stream, enabling the Listener
    to echo the text from the Sender.
        var reader = new StreamReader(relayConnection);
        var writer = new StreamWriter(relayConnection) { AutoFlush = true };
        while (!cts.IsCancellationRequested)
        {
            try
            {
                // Read a line of input until a newline is encountered
                var line = await reader.ReadLineAsync();

                if (string.IsNullOrEmpty(line))
                {
                    await relayConnection.ShutdownAsync(cts.Token);
                    break;
                }
                Console.WriteLine(line);

                // Echo the line back to the client
                await writer.WriteLineAsync($"Echo: {line}");
            }
            catch (IOException)
            {
                Console.WriteLine("Client closed connection");
                break;
            }
        }
```

```
                Console.WriteLine("End session");

                // Close the connection
                await relayConnection.CloseAsync(cts.Token);
        }

        private static async Task RunAsync()
        {
            var cts = new CancellationTokenSource();
            var tokenProvider =
                        TokenProvider.CreateSharedAccessSignatureTokenProvider(KeyNa
me, Key);
            var listener = new HybridConnectionListener(
                                new Uri(string.Format("sb://{0}/{1}",
    RelayNamespace, ConnectionName)),
                                tokenProvider);

            // Subscribe to the status events
            listener.Connecting += (o, e) => { Console.WriteLine("Connecting"); };
            listener.Offline += (o, e) => { Console.WriteLine("Offline"); };
            listener.Online += (o, e) => { Console.WriteLine("Online"); };

            // Establish the control channel to the Azure Relay service
            await listener.OpenAsync(cts.Token);
            Console.WriteLine("Server listening");

            // Providing callback for cancellation token that will close the listener.
            cts.Token.Register(() => listener.CloseAsync(CancellationToken.None));

            // Start a new thread that will continuously read the console.
            new Task(() => Console.In.ReadLineAsync().ContinueWith((s) => {
    cts.Cancel(); })).Start();

            // Accept the next available, pending connection request.
            while (true)
            {
                var relayConnection = await listener.AcceptConnectionAsync();
                if (relayConnection == null)
                {
                    break;
                }

                ProcessMessagesOnConnection(relayConnection, cts);
            }

            // Close the listener after we exit the processing loop
            await listener.CloseAsync(cts.Token);
        }
    }
```

12. In the aforementioned code, replace the values as follows:

- **<namespace>**   Your Azure Relay namespace name.

- **<hybridconnectionname>**   The name of your Hybrid Connection.

- **<sharedaccesskeyname>** The name of your Shared Access Key as acquired from the Policy blade in the Portal.

- **<sharedaccesskeyvalue>** The value of your Shared Access Key as acquired from the Policy blade in the Portal.

CREATE A SENDER APPLICATION

Next, add another Console Application project that will contain the code for the sender application by following these steps:

1. In Solution Explorer, right click your solution and select Add, New Project and then choose Console App (.NET Framework).

2. Provide the name and location of your choice.

3. Select OK.

4. In Solution Explorer, right click the new project and select Manage NuGet Packages.

5. In the document that appears, select Browse.

6. Search for "Microsoft.Azure.Relay" and then select the Microsoft Azure Relay item in the list.

7. Select Install to begin the installation and follow the prompts.

8. Open program.cs.

9. Replace the using statements at the top of the document with the following:

```
using System;
using System.IO;
using System.Threading;
using System.Threading.Tasks;
using Microsoft.Azure.Relay;
Replace the Program class with the following:
class Program
{
    private const string RelayNamespace = "<namespace>.servicebus.windows.net";
    private const string ConnectionName = "<hybridconnectionname>";
    private const string KeyName = "<sharedaccesskeyname> ";
    private const string Key = "<sharedaccesskeyvalue>";

    static void Main(string[] args)
    {
        RunAsync().GetAwaiter().GetResult();
    }
private static async Task RunAsync()
    {
        Console.WriteLine("Enter lines of text to send to the server with
 ENTER");
        // Create a new hybrid connection client
        var tokenProvider = TokenProvider.CreateSharedAccessSignatureTokenProv
ider(KeyName, Key);
        var client = new HybridConnectionClient(new
Uri(String.Format("sb://{0}/{1}", RelayNamespace, ConnectionName)),
tokenProvider);
```

```
// Initiate the connection
var relayConnection = await client.CreateConnectionAsync();
var reads = Task.Run(async () => {
    var reader = new StreamReader(relayConnection);
    var writer = Console.Out;
    do
    {
        // Read a full line of UTF-8 text up to newline
        string line = await reader.ReadLineAsync();
        // if the string is empty or null, we are done.
        if (String.IsNullOrEmpty(line))
            break;
        // Write to the console
        await writer.WriteLineAsync(line);
    }
    while (true);
});

// Read from the console and write to the hybrid connection
var writes = Task.Run(async () => {
    var reader = Console.In;
    var writer = new StreamWriter(relayConnection) { AutoFlush = true
};

    do
    {
        // Read a line form the console
        string line = await reader.ReadLineAsync();
        await writer.WriteLineAsync(line);
        if (String.IsNullOrEmpty(line))
            break;
    }
    while (true);
});
await Task.WhenAll(reads, writes);
await relayConnection.CloseAsync(CancellationToken.None);
}
```

10. In the aforementioned code, replace the values as follows:

- **<namespace>** Your Azure Relay namespace name.

- **<hybridconnectionname>** The name of your Hybrid Connection.

- **<sharedaccesskeyname>** Tthe name of your Shared Access Key.

- **<sharedaccesskeyvalue>** Tthe value of your Shared Access Key.

RUN THE APPLICATIONS

Finally, run the applications to exercise the relay functionality:

1. Using Solution Explorer, right click your solution and select Set Startup Projects.

2. In the dialog, select Multiple startup projects.

3. Set the action to Start for both projects, making sure that your listener is above your sender so that it starts first.

4. Select OK.

5. From the Debug menu, select Start without debugging.

6. On the sender console screen (Figure 3-52), respond to the prompt by typing some text to send to the listener and pressing enter.

7. Verify in the other console screen (the listener), that the text was received and that it was echoed back to the sender.

FIGURE 3-52 The console output of the Listener and Sender applications

Using the WCF Relay

The WCF Relay service is frequently used to expose on-premises resources to remote client applications located in the cloud or across network boundaries, in other words it facilitates hybrid applications. It involves creating a Service Bus namespace for the Relay service, creating shared access policies to secure access to management, and following these high level implementation steps:

1. Create a service contract defining the messages to be processed by the Relay service.

2. Create a service implementation for that contract. This implementation includes the code to run when messages are received.

3. Host the service in any compatible WCF hosting environment, expose an endpoint using one of the available WCF relay bindings, and provide the appropriate credentials for the service listener.

4. Create a client reference to the relay using typical WCF client channel features, providing the appropriate relay binding and address to the service, with the appropriate credentials for the client sender.

5. Use the client reference to call methods on the service contract to invoke the service through the Service Bus relay.

The WCF Relay service supports different transport protocols and Web services standards. The choice of protocol and standard is determined by the WCF relay binding selected for service endpoints. The list of bindings supporting these options are as follows:

- BasicHttpRelayBinding
- WS2007HttpRelayBinding
- WebHttpRelayBinding
- NetTcpRelayBinding

- NetOneWayRelayBinding
- NetEventRelayBinding

Clients must select from the available endpoints exposed by the service for compatible communication. HTTP services support two-way calls using SOAP protocol (optionally with extended WS* protocols) or classic HTTP protocol requests (also referred to as REST services). For TCP services, you can use synchronous two-way calls, one-way calls, or one-way event publishing to multiple services.

EXAM TIP

The NetTcpRelayBinding relay supports two connection modes: relayed (the default) or hybrid. In hybrid mode, communications are initially relayed, but if possible, a direct socket connection is established between client and service, thus removing the relay from communications for the session.

Deploy a WCF Relay

The following steps are needed to deploy a new WCF Relay within the Azure Relay namespace:

1. Using the Portal, navigate to the blade of your deployed Relay namespace.
2. Select + WCF Relay from the command bar.
3. On the Create WCF Relay blade (Figure 3-53), enter a name for your new WCF Relay.
4. Select the Relay Type (NetTcp or HTTP).

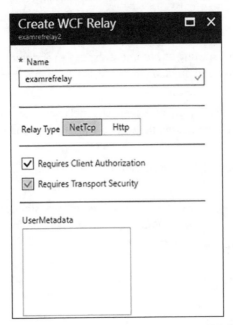

FIGURE 3-53 Using the Portal to create a WCF Relay

5. Select Create.

6. Once deployment completes, select your new WCF Relay from the list (Figure 3-54).

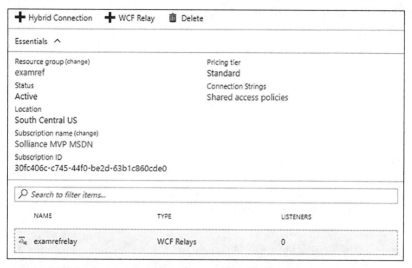

FIGURE 3-54 Selecting the newly created Relay in the Portal

7. In the Essentials blade, take note of your WCF Relay URL and namespace (Figure 3-55).

Essentials ⌃	
Namespace	WCF Relay Url
examrefrelay2	https://examrefrelay2.servicebus.windows.net/ex...
Relay Type	Requires Client Authorization
NetTcp	true
Requires Transport Security	Is Dynamic
true	false

FIGURE 3-55 Viewing the Namespace and WCF Relay URL

Managing relay credentials

WCF Relay credentials are managed on the Shared access policies blade for the namespace as follows:

1. Make sure you have created a Service Bus namespace as described in the section "Create a Service Bus namespace."

2. Navigate to the blade for your Service Bus namespace in the Azure Portal.

3. From the menu, select Shared access.

4. To create a new shared access policy for the namespace, select + Add.

5. Provide a name for the Policy and select what permissions (Manage, Send, Listen) it should have (Figure 3-56).

6. Select Create.

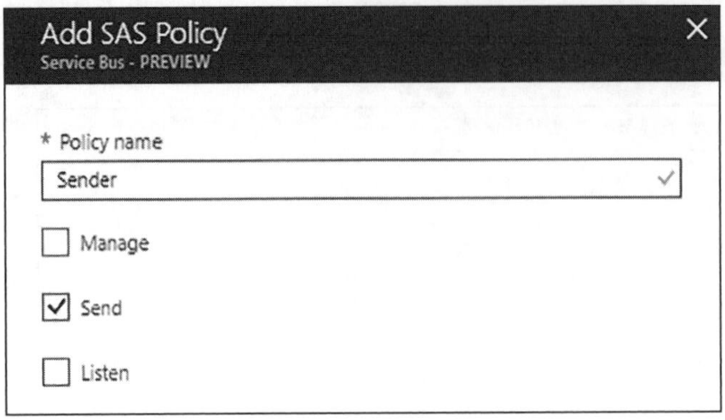

FIGURE 3-56 Using the Portal to add a new SAS policy.

7. You can view the Keys after the policy has been created by selecting Shared access polices and then choosing your newly created policy.

> **MORE INFO**   **SENDER AND RECEIVER KEYS**
>
> It is considered a best practice to create separate keys for the sender and receiver, and possibly multiple keys according to different groups of senders and receivers. This allows you to more granularly control which applications have send, receive, and management rights to Service Bus relays created in the namespace. It also not recommended that you use the RootManageSharedAccessKey in production application configuration. You should treat this policy like you would an administrator account.

CREATING A RELAY AND LISTENER ENDPOINT

After you have created the namespace and noted the listener policy name and key, you can write code to create a relay service endpoint. Here is a simple example, it assumes you have deployed a relay of type NetTcp:

1. Open Visual Studio and create a new console application.

2. Add the Microsoft Azure Service Bus NuGet package (WindowsAzure.ServiceBus) to the console application.

3. Create a WCF service definition to be used as a definition for the relay contract and an implementation for the relay listener service. Add a class file to the project with the following service contract and implementation. Include the using statement at the top of the file:

```
using System.ServiceModel;
[ServiceContract]
public interface IrelayService
{
  [OperationContract]
  string EchoMessage(string message);
}
```

```
public class RelayService:IrelayService
{
  public string EchoMessage(string message)
  {
    Console.WriteLine(message);
    return message;
  }
}
```

4. Host the WCF service in the console application by creating an instance of the WCF Ser-
   viceHost for the service. Add an endpoint using NetTcpRelayBinding, passing the name
   of the Service Bus namespace, policy name, and key. Include the using statements at the
   top of the file:

```
using System.ServiceModel;
using Microsoft.ServiceBus;
    class Program
    {
        static void Main(string[] args)
        {
            string serviceBusNamespace = "<namespace>";
            string listenerPolicyName = "<sharedaccesspolicykeyname>";
            string listenerPolicyKey = "<sharedaccesspolicykeyvalue>";
            string serviceRelativePath = "<relayname>";
            ServiceHost host = new ServiceHost(typeof(RelayService));

            host.AddServiceEndpoint(typeof(IrelayService), new
NetTcpRelayBinding(){ IsDynamic = false },
                ServiceBusEnvironment.CreateServiceUri("sb", serviceBusNamespace,
serviceRelativePath))
                .Behaviors.Add(new TransportClientEndpointBehavior
                {
                    TokenProvider = TokenProvider. CreateSharedAccessSignatureToke
nProvider(listenerPolicyName, listenerPolicyKey)
                });

            host.Open();

            Console.WriteLine("Service is running. Press ENTER to stop the
service.");
            Console.ReadLine();

            host.Close();
        }
    }
```

5. In the aforementioned code, replace the values as follows:

   - **<namespace>**   Your WCF Relay namespace name.

   - **<sharedaccesskeyname>**   The name of your Shared Access Key.

   - **<sharedaccesskeyvalue>**   The value of your Shared Access Key.

   - **<relayname>**   The name of your WCF Relay.

6. Run the console, and the WCF service listener is now waiting for messages.

EXAM TIP

You can configure WCF Relay endpoints programmatically or by using application configuration in the <system.servicemodel> section. The latter is more appropriate for dynamically configuring the host environment for production applications.

SENDING MESSAGES THROUGH RELAY

After you have created the relay service, defined the endpoint and related protocols, and noted the sender policy name and key, you can create a client to send messages to the relay service. Here is a simple example with steps building on the previous sections:

1. In the existing Visual Studio solution created in the previous section, add another console application called RelayClient.

2. Add the Microsoft Azure Service Bus NuGet package to the client console application.

3. Add a new class to the project, copy the WCF service interface, and create a new interface to be used by the WCF client channel creation code. Include the using statement at the top of the file:

```
using System.ServiceModel;
[ServiceContract]
public interface IrelayService
{
  [OperationContract]
  string EchoMessage(string message);
}
public interface IrelayServiceChannel:IrelayService,IClientChannel {}
```

4. Add code in the main entry point to call the relay service. You will create a WCF client channel for the client channel interface, provide an instance of the NetTcpRelayBinding for the client endpoint, and provide an EndpointAddress for the namespace and relative path to the service. You will also provide the sender policy name and key. Include the using statement at the top of the file:

```
using Microsoft.ServiceBus;
using System.ServiceModel;
    class Program
    {
        static void Main(string[] args)
        {
            string serviceBusNamespace = "<namespace>";
            string senderPolicyName = "<sharedaccesspolicykeyname>";
            string senderPolicyKey = "<sharedaccesspolicykeyvalue>";
            string serviceRelativePath = "<relayname>";

            var client = new ChannelFactory<IrelayServiceChannel>(
                new NetTcpRelayBinding(){ IsDynamic = false },
                new EndpointAddress(
                    ServiceBusEnvironment.CreateServiceUri("sb",
```

```
            serviceBusNamespace, serviceRelativePath)));

                client.Endpoint.Behaviors.Add(
                    new TransportClientEndpointBehavior { TokenProvider =
        TokenProvider.CreateSharedAccessSignatureTokenProvider(senderPolicyName,
        senderPolicyKey) });

                using (var channel = client.CreateChannel())
                {
                    string message = channel.EchoMessage("hello from the relay!");
                    Console.WriteLine(message);
                }
                Console.ReadLine();
            }
        }
```

5. In the aforementioned code, replace the values as follows:

   - **<namespace>** your WCF Relay namespace name.
   - **<sharedaccesskeyname>** the name of your Shared Access Key.
   - **<sharedaccesskeyvalue>** the value of your Shared Access Key.
   - **<relayname>** the name of your WCF Relay.

6. To test sending messages to the service created in the previous section, first run the service listener console, and then the client console. You will see the message written to both consoles.

> **NOTE   RELAY ALTERNATIVES**
>
> Practically speaking, most systems today employ an asynchronous architecture that involves queues, topics, or event hubs as a way to queue work for on-premises processing from a remote application.

Using Service Bus queues

Service Bus queues provide a brokered messaging service that supports physical and temporal decoupling of a message producer (sender) and message consumer (receiver). Queues are based on the brokered messaging infrastructure of Service Bus and provide a First In First Out (FIFO) buffer to the first receiver that removes the message. There is only one receiver per message.

> **MORE INFO   AZURE QUEUES VS. SERVICE BUS QUEUES**
>
> Azure queues are built on top of storage, while Service Bus queues are built on top of a broader messaging infrastructure. For more information on how the two compare, and how to choose between them, see *https://docs.microsoft.com/azure/service-bus-messaging/ service-bus-azure-and-service-bus-queues-compared-contrasted*.

Properties of the Service Bus queue influence its behavior, including the size and partitions for scale out, message handling for expiry and locking, and support for sessions. Table 3-2 shows the core properties of a Service Bus queue. Properties prefixed with an asterisk (*) indicate a property not shown in the portal while creating the queue, but can be edited in the portal after they are created.

TABLE 3-2 Queue properties

Property	Description
Max Size	The size of the queue in terms of capacity for messages. Can be from 1 GB to 5 GB without partitioning, and 80 GB when partitioning is enabled.
Default message time to live	Time after which a message will expire and be removed from the queue. Defaults to 14 days in the Portal.
Move expired messages to dead-letter sub-queue	If enabled, automatically moves expired messages to the dead letter queue.
Lock duration	Duration of time a message is inaccessible to other receivers when a receiver requests a peek lock on the message. Defaults to 1 minute. Can be set to a value up to 5 minutes.
Enable duplicate detection	If enabled, the queue will retain a buffer and ignore messages with the same message identifier (provided by the sender). The window for this buffer can be set to a value up to 7 days.
*Duplicate detection history	Window of time for measuring duplicate detection. Defaults to 10 minutes.
Enable sessions	If enabled, messages can be grouped into sequential batches to guarantee ordered delivery of a set of messages.
Enable partitioning	If enabled, messages will be distributed across multiple message brokers and can be grouped by partition key. Up to 100 partitioned queues are supported within a Basic or Standard tier namespace. Premium tier namespaces support 1,000 partitions per messaging unit.
*Maximum delivery count	The maximum number of times Service Bus will try to deliver the message before moving it to the dead-letter sub-queue.
*Queue status	Allows for disabling publishing or consumption without removing the queue. Valid choices are Active, Disabled, Receive Disabled (send only mode) or Send Disabled (receive only mode).

> **MORE INFO   QUEUE PROPERTIES**
>
> For a comprehensive list of all Service Bus queue properties, see the QueueDescription class documentation available at *https://docs.microsoft.com/dotnet/api/microsoft.servicebus.messaging.queuedescription.*

In this section you learn how to create a queue, send messages to a queue, and retrieve messages from a queue.

CREATING A QUEUE

You can create a queue directly from the portal by following these steps:

1. Navigate to the Service Bus namespace (Figure 3-57) you provisioned in the portal.

2. In the command bar, select + Queue.

3. Provide a name for the new queue.

4. Select Create to deploy the queue.

FIGURE 3-57 Creating a new Service Bus queue in the Portal

Managing queue credentials

Queue credentials are managed either at the namespace level. To manage the Shared access policies blade for the namespace, follow these steps:

1. Navigate to the blade for your Service Bus namespace in the Azure Portal.

2. From the menu, select Shared access policies under the Settings header.

3. To create a new shared access policy for the queue, select + Add.

4. Provide a name for the Policy and select what permissions (Manage, Send, Listen) it should have.

5. Select Create.

6. You can view the Keys after the policy has been created by selecting Shared access polices and then choosing your newly created policy.

FINDING QUEUE CONNECTION STRINGS

To communicate with a queue, you provide connection information including the queue URL and shared access credentials. The portal provides a connection string for each shared access policy you have created. For example, the following are the connection strings for the Receiver and Sender policies created at the namespace level in the previous section:

```
Endpoint=sb://<namespace>.servicebus.windows.net/;SharedAccessKeyName=<policyname>;Share
dAccessKey=B2bwP15EErkuF2NHJ17wlNKUiCHrersCcag08/K0U8w=;
```

You can access this information as follows:

1. Navigate to the blade for your Service Bus namespace in the Azure Portal.

2. Select Shared access polices and then choosing the desired policy.

3. The connection strings are displayed on the blade that appears.

EXAM TIP

The connection string shown in the management portal for queues, topics, notification hubs, and event hubs does not use AMQP protocol by default. You must add a TransportType=Amqp string as follows to tell the client library to use this recommended protocol:

```
Endpoint=sb://<namespace>.servicebus.windows.net/;SharedAccessKeyName=
Receiver;SharedAccessKey=N1Qt3CQyha1BxVFpTTJXMGkG/OOh14WTJbe1+M84tho=;
TransportType=Amqp.
```

SENDING MESSAGES TO A QUEUE

After you have created the namespace and queue and you've noted the sender connection string, you can write code to create a queue client that sends message to that queue. Here is a simple example with steps:

1. Open Visual Studio and create a new console application called QueueSender.

2. Add the Microsoft Azure Service Bus NuGet package to the console application.

3. In the main entry point, add code to send messages to the queue. Get the connection string with a TransportType setting for AMQP, create an instance of the Messaging-Factory, and create a reference to the queue with QueueClient. You can then create a BrokeredMessage (in this case, a string) and send that using the queue reference. The following listing shows the entire implementation, including required namespaces:

```
using Microsoft.ServiceBus;
using Microsoft.ServiceBus.Messaging;
class Program
{
    static void Main(string[] args)
    {
        string queueName = "<queuename>";
        string connection = "Endpoint=sb://<namespace>.servicebus.windows.net/;
SharedAccessKeyName=<sharedaccesskeyname>;
SharedAccessKey=<sharedaccesskeyvalue>;TransportType=Amqp";
        MessagingFactory factory = MessagingFactory.CreateFromConnectionString(
connection);
        QueueClient queue = factory.CreateQueueClient(queueName);
        string message = "queue message over amqp";
        BrokeredMessage bm = new BrokeredMessage(message);
        queue.Send(bm);
    }
}
```

4. In the aforementioned code, replace the values as follows:

- **<namespace>**   Your Service Bus namespace name.

- **<sharedaccesskeyname>**   The name of your Shared Access Key.

- **<sharedaccesskeyvalue>**   The value of your Shared Access Key.

- **<queuename>**   The name of your queue.

5. Run the project to send a message to the queue.

EXAM TIP

The BrokeredMessage type can accept any serializable object or a stream to be included in the body of the message. You can also set additional custom properties on the message and provide settings relevant to partitions and sessions.

RECEIVING MESSAGES FROM A QUEUE

There are two modes for processing queue messages:

- **ReceiveAndDelete**   Messages are delivered once, regardless of whether the receiver fails to process the message.

- **PeekLock**   Messages are locked after they are delivered to a receiver so that other receivers do not process them unless they are unlocked through timeout or if the receiver that locked the message abandons processing.

By default, PeekLock mode is used, and this is preferred unless the system can tolerate lost messages. The receiver should manage aborting the message if it can't be processed to allow another receiver to try to process the message more quickly.

After you have created the namespace and queue and you've noted the receiver connection string, you can write code to read messages from the queue using the client library. Here is a simple example with steps:

1. In the existing Visual Studio solution created in the previous section, add another console application called QueueListener.

2. Add the Microsoft Azure Service Bus NuGet package to the console application.

3. In the main entry point, add code to read messages from the queue. Get the connection string with a TransportType setting for AMQP, create an instance of the Messaging-Factory, and create a reference to the queue with QueueClient. You can then use that QueueClient to receive messages. The following listing shows the entire implementation, including required namespaces:

```
using System;
using Microsoft.ServiceBus.Messaging;
class Program
{
    static void Main(string[] args)
    {
        string queueName = "<queuename>";
        string connection = "Endpoint=sb://<namespace>.servicebus.windows.net/;
SharedAccessKeyName=<sharedaccesskeyname>;
SharedAccessKey=<sharedaccesskeyvalue>=;TransportType=Amqp";

        MessagingFactory factory = MessagingFactory.CreateFromConnectionString(
connection);
        QueueClient queue = factory.CreateQueueClient(queueName);
        while (true)
        {
            BrokeredMessage message = queue.Receive();
            if (message != null)
            {
                try
                {
                    Console.WriteLine("MessageId {0}", message.MessageId);
                    Console.WriteLine("Delivery {0}", message.DeliveryCount);
                    Console.WriteLine("Size {0}", message.Size);
                    Console.WriteLine(message.GetBody<string>());
                     message.Complete();
                }
                catch (Exception ex)
                {
                    Console.WriteLine(ex.ToString());
                    message.Abandon();
                }
            }
        }
    }
}
```

4. In the aforementioned code, replace the values as follows:

- **<namespace>** Your Service Bus namespace name.
- **<sharedaccesskeyname>** The name of your Shared Access Key.
- **<sharedaccesskeyvalue>** The value of your Shared Access Key.
- **<queuename>** The name of your queue.

NOTE **DUPLICATE MESSAGES**

Service Bus queues support at-least-once processing. This means that under certain circumstances, a message might be redelivered and processed twice. To avoid duplicate messages, you can use the MessageId of the message to verify that a message was not already processed by your system.

MORE INFO **DEAD LETTER QUEUES**

Messages that cannot be processed are considered poison messages and should be removed from the queue and handled separately. This is typically done with a dead letter queue. Service Bus queues have a dead letter sub-queue available for this purpose. You write to the dead letter sub-squeue when you detect a poison message and provide a separate service to process those failures. Messages written to the dead letter sub-queue do not expire. For a sample, see *https://docs.microsoft.com/en-us/azure/service-bus-messaging/service-bus-dead-letter-queues*.

Using Service Bus topics and subscriptions

Service Bus queues support one-to-one delivery from a sender to a single receiver. Service Bus topics and subscriptions support one-to-many communication in support of traditional publish and subscribe patterns in brokered messaging. When messages are sent to a topic, a copy is made for each subscription, depending on filtering rules applied to the subscription. Messages are not received from the topic; they are received from the subscription. Receivers can listen to one or more subscriptions to retrieve messages.

Properties of the Service Bus topic influence its behavior, including the size and partitions for scale out and message handling for expiry. Table 3-3 and Table 3-4 respectively show the core properties of a Service Bus topic and subscription. Properties prefixed with an asterisk (*) indicate a property not shown in the management portal while creating the topic or subscription, but can be edited in the management portal after they are created.

TABLE 3-3 Topic properties

Property	Description
Max size	The size of the topic buffer in terms of capacity for messages. Can be from 1 GB to 5 GB, and 80 GB when partitioning is enabled.
Default message time to live	Time after which a message will expire and be removed from the topic buffer. Defaults to 14 days in the portal.
Enable duplicate detection	If enabled, the topic will retain a buffer and ignore messages with the same message identifier (provided by the sender). The window for this can be set to a value up to 7 days.
*Duplicate detection history	Window of time for measuring duplicate detection. Defaults to 10 minutes.
*Filter message before publishing	If enabled, the publisher will fail to publish a message that will not reach a subscriber.
*Topic status	Allows for disabling publishing without removing the topic. Valid choices are Enabled, Disabled, or Send Disabled (receive only mode).
Enable partitioning	If enabled, messages will be distributed across multiple message brokers and can be grouped by partition key. Up to 100 partitioned topics are supported within a Basic or Standard tier namespace. Premium tier namespaces support 1,000 partitions per messaging unit.

TABLE 3-4 Subscription properties

Property	Description
Default message time to live	Time after which a message will expire and be removed from the subscription buffer.
Move expired messages to dead-letter sub-queue	If enabled, automatically moves expired messages to the dead letter topic path.
Move messages that cause filter evaluation exceptions to the dead-letter sub-queue	If enabled, automatically moves messages that fail filter evaluation to the dead letter sub-queue.
Lock duration	Duration of time a message is inaccessible to other receivers when a receiver requests a peek lock on the message. Defaults to 30 seconds. Can be set to a value up to 5 minutes.
Enable sessions	If enabled, messages can be grouped into sequential batches to guarantee ordered delivery of a set of messages.
Enable batched operations	If enabled, server-side batch operations are supported.
Maximum delivery count	The maximum number of times Service Bus will try to deliver the message before moving it to the dead-letter sub-queue.
*Topic subscription state	Allows for disabling consumption without removing the subscription. Valid choices are Enabled, Disabled, or Receive Disabled (send only mode).

MORE INFO **TOPIC & SUBSCRIPTION PROPERTIES**

For a comprehensive list of all Service Bus topic properties, see the TopicDescription class documentation available at: *https://docs.microsoft.com/dotnet/api/microsoft.servicebus. messaging.topicdescription.* Similarly, for subscription properties, see:*https://docs.microsoft. com/dotnet/api/microsoft.servicebus.messaging.subscriptiondescription.*

CREATING A TOPIC AND SUBSCRIPTION

You can create a topic directly from the portal by following these steps:

1. Navigate to the Service Bus namespace (Figure 3-58) you provisioned in the portal.
2. In the command bar, select + Topic.
3. Provide a name for the new topic.
4. Select Create to deploy the topic.
5. To create subscriptions for the topic, select the topic in the portal.
6. Select + Subscription in the command bar.
7. Provide a name for the subscription.

FIGURE 3-58 Creating a new Service Bus subscription against a selected topic in the Portal

8. Select Create to deploy the subscription.

MANAGING TOPIC CREDENTIALS

Service Bus topic credentials can be managed from the portal. The following example illustrates creating a sender and receiver policy:

1. Navigate to the blade for your Service Bus namespace in the Azure Portal.

2. From the menu, select Shared access policies.

3. To create a new shared access policy for the topic, select + Add.

4. Provide a name for the Policy and select what permissions (Manage, Send, Listen) it should have. For a Sender policy, select only the Sender permission. For a Receiver policy, select only the Listen permission.

5. Select Create.

6. You can view the Keys and connection strings after the policy has been created by selecting Shared access polices and then choosing your newly created policy.

> **NOTE SHARED ACCESS POLICIES FOR TOPICS**
>
> You will usually create at least one policy per subscriber to isolate access keys and one for send permissions to separate key access between clients and services.

SENDING MESSAGES TO A TOPIC

With topics and subscriptions, you send messages to a topic and retrieve them from a subscription. After you have created the namespace, the topic, and one or more subscriptions, and you've noted the sender connection string, you can write code to create a topic client that sends messages to that topic. Here is a simple example with steps:

1. Open Visual Studio and create a new console application called TopicSender.

2. Add the Microsoft Azure Service Bus NuGet package to the console application.

3. In Program.cs, add code to send messages to the topic. Begin by adding the following namespace:

```
using Microsoft.ServiceBus.Messaging;
```

4. Create an instance of the MessagingFactory, and create a reference to the topic with TopicClient. You can then create a BrokeredMessage and send that using the topic reference. Here is the body of the main method:

```
string topicName = "<topicname>";
string connection =
"Endpoint=sb://<namespace>.servicebus.windows.net/;SharedAccessKeyName=
<sharedaccesskeyname>;SharedAccessKey=<shareaccesskeyvalue>";
MessagingFactory factory =
MessagingFactory.CreateFromConnectionString(connection);
TopicClient topic = factory.CreateTopicClient(topicName);
topic.Send(new BrokeredMessage("topic message"));
```

5. In the aforementioned code, replace the values as follows:

- **<namespace>** **Y**our Service Bus namespace name.
- **<sharedaccesskeyname>** The name of your Shared Access Key.
- **<sharedaccesskeyvalue>** The value of your Shared Access Key.
- **<topicname>** The name of your topic.

6. Run the project to send a message to the topic.

RECEIVING MESSAGES FROM A SUBSCRIPTION

Processing messages from a subscription is similar to processing messages from a queue. You can use ReceiveAndDelete or PeekLock mode. The latter is the preferred mode and the default.

After you have created the namespace, topic, and subscriptions, and you've noted the subscription connection string, you can write code to read messages from the subscription using the client library. Here is a simple example with steps:

1. In the existing Visual Studio solution created in the previous section, add another console application called TopicListener.

2. Add the Microsoft Azure Service Bus NuGet package to the console application.

3. In Program.cs, add code to receive messages from the subscription. Begin by adding the following namespace:

```
using Microsoft.ServiceBus.Messaging;
```

4. In the main entry point, add code to read messages from a subscription. Get the connection string for the subscription, create an instance of the MessagingFactory, and create a reference to the subscription with SubscriptionClient. You can then call Receive() to get the next BrokeredMessage from the subscription for processing. Here is the body of the main method:

```
string topicName = "<topicname>";
string subA = "<subscriptioname>";
string connection = "Endpoint=sb://<namespace>.servicebus.windows.
net/;SharedAccessKeyName=
<sharedaccesskeyname>;SharedAccessKey=<sharedaccesskeyvalue>";
MessagingFactory factory =
MessagingFactory.CreateFromConnectionString(connection);
SubscriptionClient clientA = factory.CreateSubscriptionClient(topicName, subA);
while (true)
{
    BrokeredMessage message = clientA.Receive();
    if (message != null)
    {
        try
        {
            Console.WriteLine("MessageId {0}", message.MessageId);
            Console.WriteLine("Delivery {0}", message.DeliveryCount);
            Console.WriteLine("Size {0}", message.Size);
            Console.WriteLine(message.GetBody<string>());
            message.Complete();
        }
}
```

```
        catch (Exception ex)
        {
            Console.WriteLine(ex.ToString());
            message.Abandon();
        }
    }
```

5. In the aforementioned code, replace the values as follows:

   ■ **<namespace>**   Your Service Bus namespace name.

   ■ **<sharedaccesskeyname>**   The name of your Shared Access Key.

   ■ **<sharedaccesskeyvalue>**   The value of your Shared Access Key.

   ■ **<topicname>**   The name of your topic.

   ■ **<subscriptionname>**   The name of your Service Bus subscription to the topic.

6. Run both the sender and the receiver projects to see the message exchange.

EXAM TIP

If you enable batch processing for the subscription, you can receive a batch of messages in a single call using ReceiveBatch() or ReceiveBatchAsync(). This will pull messages in the subscription up to the number you specify, or fewer if applicable. Note that you must be aware of the potential lock timeout while processing the batch.

MORE INFO   **ATCHING AND PREFETCH**

You can batch messages from a queue or topic client to avoid multiple calls to send messages to Service Bus, including them in a single call. You can also batch receive messages from a queue or subscription to process messages in batch. For more information on batch processing and prefetch, an alternative to batch, see *https://docs.microsoft.com/azure/ service-bus-messaging/service-bus-performance-improvements*.

FILTERING MESSAGES

One of the powerful features of topics and subscriptions is the ability to filter messages based on certain criteria, such as the value of specific message properties. Based on criteria, you can determine which subscription should receive a copy of each message. In addition, you can configure the topic to validate that every message has a valid destination subscription as part of publishing.

By default, subscriptions are created with a "match all" criteria, meaning all topic messages are copied to the subscription. You cannot create a subscription with filter criteria through the portal, but you can create it programmatically using the NamespaceManager object and its CreateSubscription() method. The following code illustrates creating an instance of the NamespaceManager for a topic and creating a subscription with a filter based on a custom message property:

```
string topicName = "<topicname>";
string connection = "Endpoint=sb://<namespace>.servicebus.windows.
net/;SharedAccessKeyName=
<sharedaccesskeyname>;
SharedAccessKey=<sharedacceskeyvalue>";
var ns = NamespaceManager.CreateFromConnectionString(connectionString);
SqlFilter filter = new SqlFilter("Priority == 1");
ns.CreateSubscription(topicName, "PrioritySubscription", filter);
To send messages to the topic, targeting the priority subscription, set
the Priority property to one on each message:
BrokeredMessage message = new BrokeredMessage("priority message");
message.Properties["Priority"] = 1;
```

Using Event Hubs

Event Hubs support very high-volume message streaming as is typical of enterprise application logging solutions or Internet of Things (IoT) scenarios. With Event Hubs, your application can support the following:

- Ingesting message data at scale
- Consuming message data in parallel by multiple consumers
- Re-processing messages by restarting at any point in time within the message stream

Messages to Event Hubs are FIFO and durable for up to seven days. Consumers can reconnect to an Event Hub and choose where to begin processing, allowing for the re-processing scenario (sometimes referred to as message replay) or for reconnecting after failure. Event Hubs differ from queues and topics in that there are no enterprise messaging features. Instead there is very high throughput and volume. For example, there isn't a Time-to-Live (TTL) feature for messages, no dead-letter sub-queue, no transactions or acknowledgements. The focus is low latency, highly reliable, message streaming with order preservation and replay. Event Hubs also differ in their model from traditional queues, which use a competing consumer pattern (whereby a message goes to at most one consumer and the service tracks the state of messages sent to consumer) and instead use a multi-consumer pattern where each consumer is responsible for tracking the state of its own progress thru the messages.

Table 3-5 shows the core properties of an event hub. Properties prefixed with an asterisk (*) indicate a property not shown in the management portal while creating the queue, but they can be edited in the management portal after they are created.

MORE INFO **EVENT HUBS OVERVIEW**

For more details on the event hubs architecture, see *http://msdn.microsoft.com/en-us/library/azure/dn836025.aspx.*

TABLE 3-5 Event Hub properties

Property	Description
Partition count	Determines the number of partitions across which messages are distributed. Can be set to a value between 2 and 32 and cannot be modified after it is created.
Message retention	Determines the number of days a message will be retained before it is removed from the event hub. Can be between 1 and 7 days.
Capture	Enables the Capture feature that automatically writes messages ingested to the Event Hub to an Azure Storage blob container. The data is written as block blobs in the Apache Avro format. Can be On or Off.
Capture Time window	Defines the time window that triggers a capture event. The default is 5 minutes.
Capture Size window	Defines the size in bytes that once reached triggers a capture event. The default is 300 MB.
Capture Container	The Azure Storage container that will store the capture files.
Capture Storage Account	The Azure Storage Account that will store the capture files.
Capture file name format	The template used for creating the blob name of the capture files, typically used with path segments for the namespace, Event Hub name, partition id, and timestamp.
*Event hub state	Allows for disabling the hub without removing it. Valid choices are Enabled or Disabled.

CREATING AN EVENT HUB

You can create an event hub directly from the portal by following these steps:

1. Using the portal, navigate to the blade for your deployed Event Hub namespace.

2. From the command bar, select + Event Hub.

3. Provide a name for your Event Hub (Figure3-59) and select Create.

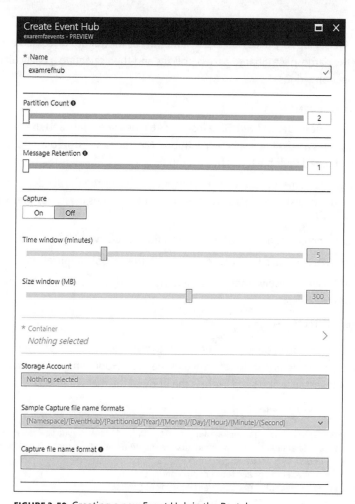

FIGURE 3-59 Creating a new Event Hub in the Portal

MANAGING EVENT HUB CREDENTIALS

Event Hub credentials can be managed from the portal at the namespace level in the same way as was shown for Service Bus queues.

FINDING EVENT HUB CONNECTION STRINGS

Connection strings for Event Hubs are accessed in the same way as for queues discussed earlier and are located under the namespace, Shared access policies and then selecting a particular policy to view the connection strings.

SENDING MESSAGES TO AN EVENT HUB

With Event Hubs, you send messages as EventData instances to the Event Hub, and the service will distribute those messages across the available partitions. Messages are stored for up to seven days and can be retrieved multiple times by consumers.

After you have created the namespace and Event Hub and you've noted the sender connection string, you can write code to create an Event Hub client that sends messages. Here is a simple example with steps:

1. Open Visual Studio and create a new console application called EventHubSender.

2. Add the Microsoft Azure Service Bus NuGet package to the console application.

3. In Program.cs, add code to receive messages from the subscription. Begin by adding the following namespace:

   ```
   using Microsoft.ServiceBus.Messaging;
   ```

4. In the main entry point, add code to send messages to the Event Hub. Create an instance of the MessagingFactory and a reference to the EventHubClient. You can then create an EventData instance and send. Here is the body of the main method:

   ```
   string ehName = "<eventhubname>";
   string connection =
   "Endpoint=sb://<namespace>.servicebus.windows.net/;SharedAccessKeyName=
   <sharedaccesskeyname>;SharedAccessKey=<sharedaccesskeyvalue>;TransportType=Amqp";
   MessagingFactory factory =
    MessagingFactory.CreateFromConnectionString(connection);
   EventHubClient client = factory.CreateEventHubClient(ehName);
   string message = "event hub message";
   EventData data = new EventData(Encoding.UTF8.GetBytes(message));
   client.Send(data);
   ```

5. In the aforementioned code, replace the values as follows:

   - **<namespace>** Your Event Hub namespace name.
   - **<sharedaccesskeyname>** The name of your Shared Access Key.
   - **<sharedaccesskeyvalue>** The value of your Shared Access Key.
   - **<eventhubname>** The name of your Event Hub.

6. Run the sender project to send a message.

RECEIVING MESSAGES FROM A CONSUMER GROUP

When you create the Event Hub, you allocate a number of partitions to distribute message ingestion. This helps you to scale the Event Hub ingress alongside settings for throughput (to be discussed in the next section). To consume messages, consumers connect to a single partition. In this example, a default consumer group is created to consume events, and within that consumer group there is typically one consumer application process for each partition. You can think of the consumer process like a subscription to a Service Bus topic that is specific to a partition, and the consumer group as a logical entity that represents the stream processing application all-up, inclusive of all the individual processes that together handle all messages.

After you have created the namespace, and Event Hub, and you've noted the Event Hub connection string, you can write code to read messages from the consumer group using the client library. Here is a simple example with steps:

1. In the existing Visual Studio solution created in the previous section, add another console application called EventHubListener.

2. Add the Microsoft Azure Service Bus NuGet package to the console application.

3. In Program.cs, add code to receive messages from the subscription. Begin by adding the following namespace:

   ```
   using Microsoft.ServiceBus.Messaging;
   ```

4. In the main entry point, add code to read data from the Event Hub using the default consumer group. You can then call Receive() to get the next event from the partition with ID "0" for processing. Here is the body of the main method:

```
string ehName = "<eventhubname>";
string connection =
"Endpoint=sb://<namespace>.servicebus.windows.net/;SharedAccessKeyName=
<sharedaccesskeyname>;
SharedAccessKey=<sharedaccesskeyvalue>;TransportType=Amqp";
MessagingFactory factory =
 MessagingFactory.CreateFromConnectionString(connection);
EventHubClient ehub = factory.CreateEventHubClient(ehName);
EventHubConsumerGroup group = ehub.GetDefaultConsumerGroup();
EventHubReceiver receiver = group.CreateReceiver("0");
while (true)
{
    EventData data = receiver.Receive();
    if (data != null)
    {
        try
        {
```

```
            string message = Encoding.UTF8.GetString(data.GetBytes());
            Console.WriteLine("EnqueuedTimeUtc: {0}", data.EnqueuedTimeUtc);
            Console.WriteLine("PartitionKey: {0}", data.PartitionKey);
            Console.WriteLine("SequenceNumber: {0}", data.SequenceNumber);
            Console.WriteLine(message);
        }
        catch (Exception ex)
        {
            Console.WriteLine(ex.ToString());
            }
    }
}
```

5. In the aforementioned code, replace the values as follows:

    ■ **<namespace>**   Your Event Hub namespace name.

    ■ **<sharedaccesskeyname>**   The name of your Shared Access Key.

    ■ **<sharedaccesskeyvalue>**   The value of your Shared Access Key.

    ■ **<eventhubname>**   The name of your Event Hub.

6. Run both projects to send and receive a message.

> **MORE INFO**   **EVENTPROCESSORHOST**
>
> To simplify scaling event hub consumers for .NET developers, there is a NuGet package that supplies a hosting feature for event hubs called EventProcessorHost which can easily be hosted within an Azure Web Job. For more information, see: *https://www.nuget.org/pack-ages/Microsoft.Azure.ServiceBus.EventProcessorHost/.*

> **NOTE**   **CONSUMER GROUPS**
>
> A default consumer group is created for each new event hub, but you can optionally create multiple consumer groups (receivers) to consume events in parallel.

Using Notification Hubs

Notification hubs provide a service for push notifications to mobile devices, at scale. If you are implementing applications that are a source of events to mobile applications, Notification Hubs simplify the effort to send platform-compatible notifications to all the applications and devices in your ecosystem.

CREATING A NOTIFICATION HUB

You can create a notification hub directly from portal by following these steps:

1. Using the portal, select + NEW and search for Notification Hub.

2. Provide a name for the Notification Hub and the new Event Hub Namespace.

3. Select a location, resource group, subscription and pricing tier.

4. Select Create.

IMPLEMENTING SOLUTIONS WITH NOTIFICATION HUBS

A solution that involves Notification Hubs typically has the following moving parts:

- A mobile application deployed to a device and able to receive push notifications
- A back-end application or other event source that will publish notifications to the mobile application
- A platform notification service, compatible with the application platform
- A Notification Hub to receive messages from the publisher and handle pushing those events in a platform-specific format to the mobile device

The implementation requirements vary based on the target platform for the mobile application. For a set of tutorials with steps for each platform supported, including the steps for setting up the mobile application, the back-end application, and the notification hub, see *http://azure.microsoft.com/documentation/articles/notification-hubs-windows-store-dotnet-get-started.*

> **MORE INFO NOTIFICATION HUB GUIDES**
>
> The following references provide additional background and programming guidance for Notification Hubs and mobile services:
>
> - Notification hubs overview and tutorials: *http://msdn.microsoft.com/en-us/library/azure/jj891130.aspx*
> - Notification hubs documentation: *http://azure.microsoft.com/documentation/services/notification-hubs/*
> - Mobile Apps documentation: *https://azure.microsoft.com/en-us/documentation/learning-paths/appservice-mobileapps/*

Scale and monitor messaging

In this section, you learn how to choose a Service Bus pricing tier, scale Service Bus features, and monitor communication.

Choosing a pricing tier

When you create a Service Bus namespace, you choose a messaging tier for all entities that will belong to that namespace. The tier you choose controls which entities you have access to as follows:

- **Basic tier**   Queues (up to 100 connections)
- **Standard tier**   Queues, topics and related messaging features (up to 1000 connections)
- **Premium tier**   All features in Standard, plus larger message sizes, resource isolation and linear scalability (1,000 brokered connections per messaging unit)

Standard and Premium tiers support advance brokered messaging features such as transactions, de-duplication, sessions, and forwarding, so if you need these features for your solution, select from these tiers.

MORE INFO   **SERVICE BUS TIERS**

For information on Service Bus tier pricing, see: *http://azure.microsoft.com/pricing/details/service-bus/.*

Event Hubs have their own tiering approach. The basic tier only supports a single consumer group, so if you want to support parallelized processing across partitions, choose a standard or dedicated messaging tier. In addition, standard tier provides additional storage up to seven days for event hubs. The dedicated tier is sold at a fixed price per daily capacity unit instead of charged million events as is done by the basic and standard tiers.

MORE INFO   **EVENT HUB TIERS**

For information on event hub tier pricing, see: *http://azure.microsoft.com/pricing/details/event-hubs/.*

Notification Hubs have a separate tier selection strategy. When you create a namespace that supports Notification Hubs, you choose a messaging tier for brokered messaging entities, if applicable, and select a Notification Hub tier appropriate to your expected push notification strategy.

- **Free tier**   Up to 1 million messages per month and up to 500 active devices per Namespace; no support for auto-scale nor a number of other enterprise features
- **Basic tier**   10 million messages per month and up to 200,000 active devices per namespace plus unlimited overage for a fee; support for auto-scale; no support for other enterprise features
- **Standard tier**   The same as basic tier, but supporting up to 10 million devices per namespace, with all enterprise features

MORE INFO   **NOTIFICATION HUB TIERS**

For information on notification hub tier pricing, see: *http://azure.microsoft.com/pricing/details/notification-hubs/.*

Scaling Service Bus features

Service Bus entities scale based on a variety of properties, including:

- Namespaces
- Partitions
- Message size

- Throughput units
- Entity instances

Not all of these properties impact every Service Bus entity in the same manner.

A Service Bus namespace is a container for one or more entities, such as relays, queues, topics, event hubs, and notification hubs. In most cases, the namespace itself is not a unit of scale, with some exceptions specifically related to pricing (referenced earlier), event hub throughput (to be discussed), and the following:

- For relays, there is a limit to the number of endpoints, connections overall, and listeners.
- The number of topics and queues are limited, and separately a smaller number of partitioned topics and queues are supported.

Since pricing is not directly related to namespace allocation between relays, queues, topics, and event hubs, you can avoid reaching some of these limits by isolating entities that could be impacted into separate namespaces. For example, consider isolating individual relays that might grow their connection requirements, or consider isolating partitioned queues and topics.

> **MORE INFO   SERVICE BUS QUOTAS**
>
> For the latest information related to namespace and other quotas for individual Service Bus entities, see: *https://docs.microsoft.com/azure/service-bus-messaging/service-bus-quotas.*

Beyond namespace selection, each entity has slightly different requirements for scale as is discussed in this section.

Scaling relays

This section discusses how to scale relays for potential namespace limitations.

NAMESPACE

As mentioned previously, relay endpoints have a limited number of overall connections and listeners that can be supported per namespace. When you are considering the design for a relay service, you should consider the number of concurrent connections that might be required for communicating with the endpoint.

If the scale of the solution has the potential to exceed the quota per namespace, the following approach can help to mitigate the limitation:

- Design the solution to support publishing an instance of each relay service into multiple namespaces. This will allow for growth so that additional listeners can be added by adding namespaces with a new relay service instance.
- Design the solution so that clients sending messages to the relay service can distribute calls across a selection of service instances. This implies building a service registry.

Scaling queues and topics

This section discusses how to scale queues and topics for potential namespace or storage limitations and discusses the use of batching and partitions to help with scaling.

NAMESPACE

Queues and topics are similar in their scale triggers. Neither is particularly bound by the namespace it belongs to except in the total number of queues or topics supported and the limited number of partitioned queues and topics. Ideally, you will have a pattern for your solution in terms of namespace allocations by Service Bus entities.

STORAGE

When you create a new queue or topic, you must choose the maximum expected storage from one GB to five GBs, and this cannot be resized. This impacts the amount of concurrent storage supported as messages flow through Service Bus.

BATCHING

To increase throughput for a queue or topic, you can have senders batch messages to Service Bus and listeners batch receive or pre-fetch from Service Bus. This increases overall throughput across all connected senders and listeners and can help reduce the number of messages taking up storage.

> **MORE INFO   BATCHING AND PRE-FETCHING**
>
> For more information on batch send, batch receive, or pre-fetch, see: *https://docs.microsoft. com/en-us/azure/service-bus-messaging/service-bus-performance-improvements*.

PARTITIONS

Adding partitions increases the number of message brokers available for incoming messages, as well as the number available for consuming messages. For high throughput queues and topics, you should enable partitioning when you create the queue or topic.

> **MORE INFO   PARTITIONED ENTITIES**
>
> For more information on partitions, see: *https://docs.microsoft.com/en-us/azure/service-bus-messaging/service-bus-partitioning*.

Scaling Event Hubs

This section discusses how to scale event hubs for potential namespace limitations and discusses how to set throughput units or use partitions to help with scaling.

NAMESPACE

Each namespace can have multiple Event Hubs, but those Event Hubs share the throughput units allocated to the namespace. This means that multiple Event Hubs can share a single throughput unit to conserve cost, but conversely, if a single Event Hub has the potential of scaling beyond the available throughput units for a namespace, you might consider creating a separate namespace for it.

EXAM TIP

You can request additional throughput by navigating to your Event Hub namespace in the Azure Portal, selecting Scale, adjusting the slider to the desired number of units and selecting Save.

THROUGHPUT UNITS

The primary unit of scale for Event Hubs is throughput units. This value is controlled at the namespace level and thus applies to all Event Hubs in the namespace. By default, you get a single throughput unit which provides ingress up to one MB per second, or 1,000 events per second, and egress up to two MB per second. You pre-purchase units and can by default configure up to 20 units.

PARTITIONS

A single Event Hub partition can scale to utilize a maximum of one throughput unit; therefore, the number of partitions across Event Hubs in the namespace should be equal to or greater than the number of throughput units selected.

Scaling Notification Hubs

There is no equivalent notion of throughput units in Notification Hubs. The scaling capacity is dictated by the selected pricing tier.

Monitoring Service Bus features

In this section you learn how to monitor queues, topics, event hubs, and notification hubs.

MONITORING QUEUES

To monitor a Service Bus queue from the portal, complete the following steps:

1. Navigate to the blade for the queue and select the Overview tab.
2. The metrics shown for a queue includes message counts, the max storage size of the queue and the current storage used by the queue.

MONITORING TOPICS

To monitor a Service Bus topic from existing portal, complete the following steps:

1. Navigate to the blade for the topic and select the Overview tab.

2. The metrics shown for a queue includes message counts, or the max storage size of the queue and the current storage used by the queue.

MONITORING EVENT HUBS

To monitor Event Hub from the portal, follow these steps (Figure 3-60):

1. Navigate to the blade Event Hub Namespace blade and select the Overview tab. From this tab you are viewing a summary of activity across all Event Hub instances in the namespace, including statistics about incoming messages, incoming send requests, outgoing messages and internal server errors.

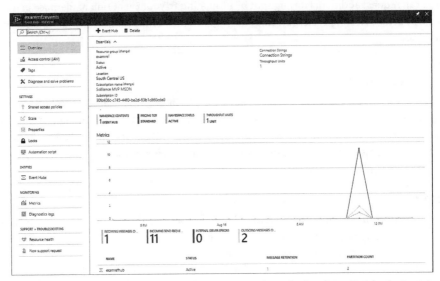

FIGURE 3-60 Viewing Event Hub metrics from the Overview tab of an Event Hub in the Portal

2. Select the chart to view the Metric blade.

3. Select Edit Chart from the command bar to view customize the time range plotted in the chart, the style (Bar or Line) and the metrics to display (Figure 3-61).

FIGURE 3-61 Viewing the list of available Event Hub metrics from Edit Chart blade for an Event Hub

4. Select OK to apply the changes to the chart.

MONITORING NOTIFICATION HUBS

To monitor a Notification Hub from the portal:

1. Navigate to the blade for your Notification Hub in the portal.
2. From the menu on the left, select Metrics under the Monitoring header.
3. Choose from the list of metrics the set of metrics you wish to chart and the chart on the right will update with the corresponding metric.

Determine when to use Event Hubs, Service Bus, IoT Hub, Stream Analytics and Notification Hubs

To help you better recall when to use which service, the following table summarizes when to use each of the services discussed in this chapter, as well as some of the related services that help in message processing.

TABLE 3-6 Services and related services for message processing help

Service	Purpose	Comment
Service Bus Queue	Messaging	Best for first in, first out messaging.
Service Bus Topics/Subscriptions	Broadcast messaging	Best for publish/subscribe scenarios or when you need multiple consumers to be able to read the same message conditionally.
Event Hubs	High-scale message ingest	Best for massive scale message ingest scenarios, such as telemetry
IoT Hub	Device messaging	Best for scenarios that have high scale messaging requirements but also need device management capabilities
Notification Hubs	Push notifications	Best for sending push notifications for mobile apps.
Stream Analytics	Message processing	Best for processing messages from Event Hubs, IoT Hub using SQL queries
EventProcessorHost	Message processing	Best for processing messages from Event Hubs, IoT Hub using .NET custom code

Thought experiment

In this thought experiment, apply what you've learned about implementing Azure AD, Azure Key Vault, and selecting a messaging strategy. Apply this to a scenario with an appropriate selection across each Azure feature. This will require you to choose the Azure AD configuration, the Key Vault configuration, and the messaging features, which are best suited to the solution. You can find answers to this thought experiment in the "Thought Experiment Answers" section at the end of this chapter. The following paragraphs describe the solution and the questions to answer.

You are designing a multi-tenant solution that sells widgets. The system tracks your products, each customer, and the orders.

There are several applications that comprise the system:

- The internal web application (Corporate Portal) that allows the corporate employees to manage available widgets and manage customers and orders.

  - All corporate employees should be able to use this portal, their access restricted by the groups they belong to.

  - There isn't an existing directory to work with, so the user store will be a green field setup.

  - Corporate users are expected to use multi-factor authentication.

  - It is expected that the corporate users will be setup by an administrator to the organization.

- The external web application (Customer Portal) that allows customers to view their orders, manage their profiles and preferences, and place new orders.

  - Customers can sign up for access to this portal, but access to tenants is managed by the Corporate Portal.

- Customer users should be able to sign-in by creating a user account, or by signing up with their Google or Microsoft Account.

These applications will not only authenticate users, but also request access tokens to call secure APIs. This will require storing client id and secret settings for each client application that will request access tokens.

Each customer also expects a report of his or her own activity each month, and on demand as needed. These reports require sifting through large amounts of data and generating a PDF file for the customer, to be emailed when it is generated. In addition, since it is a multi-tenant site, you want to track detailed logs for insights into individual customer activity at any given time to troubleshoot or gather intelligence on usage patterns.

1. How would you go about setting up corporate users in Azure AD?

2. How would you go about supporting self-registration and social login for customer users in Azure AD?

3. Which features of Azure AD would you use to support user authentication and token issuance for APIs?

4. How can Azure Key Vault be used in this solution?

5. What kind of communication architecture might fit the reporting strategy and why?

Thought experiment answers

This section contains the solution to the thought experiment.

1. Consider setting up an Azure AD tenant dedicated to corporate users for the Corporate Portal. Add users via the portal, or programmatically and assign users to appropriate groups that align with application permissions.

2. Consider adding customer users as Azure AD B2C collaboration users - guest users - who can register and sign-in with Microsoft Account or Google identity providers.

3. Configure applications for the Azure AD tenant, and create keys for access token requests for APIs. Applications can request access tokens during sign-in if the application will use the token from a SPA or from the web application, or individually request access tokens. Any protocol flows that require a secret will use the client id and secret for the application.

4. Create a Key Vault in the same subscription as the Azure AD tenant. Create secrets to hold the Azure AD application secrets that are necessary for token requests.

5. Consider using Service Bus queues to offload processing of report generation from the main website to a separate compute tier that can be scaled as needed. Since this is not a publish-and-subscribe scenario, queues can satisfy this requirement. Actual processing can be performed by any compute tier, including a VM, cloud service worker role, or web job in an isolated VM.

Chapter summary

- You can easily create new Azure AD directories and manage users and registered applications via the Azure Portal.

- Azure AD supports WS-Federation, SAML-P, OpenID Connect and OAuth 2 protocols for application integration. Registered applications can integrate with Azure AD using any of these protocol endpoints.

- You can manage users programmatically using the Microsoft Graph API at the Azure AD v2 endpoint, but this also requires registering application at the new Microsoft Application Registry separate from the applications registered from within the Azure Portal (today).

- You can use the Microsoft Graph API to query directories; to find and manage users, groups and role assignment; and to create applications for integration with Azure AD directories.

- You can enable multi-factor authentication for users individually or in batch. This requires additional licenses for your users.

- You can integrate multi-factor authentication directly to your applications by using the MFA SDK which exposes APIs for this purpose.

- Azure AD B2C enables users to register and sign-in using social identity providers.

- Azure AD B2B enables organizations to allow access to applications and resources by external users.

- Azure Key Vault provides a secure way to manage keys, secrets and certificates including support for HSM protected assets.

- A Service Bus namespace is a container for relay and message broker communication through relays, queues, topics and subscriptions, event hubs, and notification hubs.

- Relay enables access to on-premises resources without exposing on-premises services to the public Internet. By default, all relay messages are sent through Service Bus (relay mode), but connections might be promoted to a direct connection (hybrid mode).

- Queues and topics are message brokering features of Service Bus that provide a buffer for messages, partitioning options for scalability, and a dead letter feature for messages that can't be processed.

- Queues support one-to-one message delivery while topics support one-to-many delivery.

- Event hubs support high-volume message streaming and can ingest message data at scale. Messages are stored in a buffer and can be processed multiple times.

- Service Bus features can require authentication using a key. You can create multiple keys to isolate the key used for management and usage patterns, such as send and receive.

## CHAPTER 4

Design and implement Azure PaaS compute and web and mobile services

The Azure platform provides a rich set of Platform-as-a-Service (PaaS) capabilities for hosting web applications and services. The platform approach provides more than just a host for running your application logic; it also includes robust mechanisms for managing all aspects of your web application lifecycle, from configuring continuous and staged deployments to managing runtime configuration, monitoring health and diagnostic data, and of course, helping with scale and resilience. Azure Apps Services includes a number of features to manage web applications and services including Web Apps, Logic Apps, Mobile Apps and API Apps. API Management provides additional features with first class integration to APIs hosted in Azure. Azure Functions and Azure Service Fabric enable modern microservices architectures for your solutions, in addition to several third-party platforms that can be provisioned via Azure Quickstart Templates. These key features are of prime importance to the modern web application, and this chapter explores how to leverage them.

Skills in this chapter:

- Skill 4.1: Design Azure App Service Web Apps
- Skill 4.2: Design Azure App Service API Apps
- Skill 4.3: Develop Azure App Service Logic Apps
- Skill 4.4: Develop Azure App Service Mobile Apps
- Skill 4.5: Implement API Management
- Skill 4.6: Implement Azure Functions and WebJobs
- Skill 4.7: Design and implement Azure Service Fabric Apps
- Skill 4.8: Design and implement third-party Platform as a Service (PaaS)
- Skill 4.9: Design and implement DevOps

Skill 4.1: Design Azure App Service Web Apps

Azure App Service Web Apps (or, just Web Apps) provides a managed service for hosting your web applications and APIs with infrastructure services such as security, load balancing, and scaling provided as part of the service. In addition, Web Apps has an integrated DevOps experience from code repositories and from Docker image repositories. You pay for compute resources according to your App Service Plan and scale settings. This section covers key considerations for designing and deploying your applications as Web Apps.

> **This skill covers how to:**
> - Define and manage App Service plans
> - Configure Web App settings
> - Configure Web App certificates and custom domains
> - Manage Web Apps by using the API, Azure PowerShell, and Xplat-CLI
> - Implement diagnostics, monitoring, and analytics
> - Design and configure Web Apps for scale and resilience

Define and manage App Service plans

An App Service plan defines the supported feature set and capacity of a group of virtual machine resources that are hosting one or more web apps, logic apps, mobile apps, or API apps (this section discusses web apps specifically, and the other resources are covered in later sections in this chapter).

Each App Service plan is configured with a pricing tier (for example, Free, Shared, Basic, and Standard), and each tier describes its own set of capabilities and cost. An App Service plan is unique to the region, resource group, and subscription. In other words, two web apps can participate in the same App Service plan only when they are created in the same subscription, resource group, and region (with the same pricing tier requirements).

This section describes how to create a new App Service plan without creating a web app, and how to create a new App Service plan while creating a web app. It also reviews some of the settings that can be useful for managing the App Service plan.

> **MORE INFO APP SERVICES OVERVIEW**
>
> For an overview of App Services and Web App development see *https://docs.microsoft.com/en-us/azure/app-service/*.

Creating a new App Service plan

To create a new App Service plan in the portal, complete the following steps:

1. Navigate to the portal accessed via *https://portal.azure.com*.

2. Select New on the command bar.

3. Within the Marketplace (Figure 4-1) search text box, type **App Service Plan** and press Enter.

FIGURE 4-1 The Marketplace search for App Service Plan.

4. Select App Service Plan from the results.

5. On the App Service Plan blade, select Create.

6. On the New App Service Plan blade (Figure 4-2), provide a name for your App Service plan, choose the subscription, resource group, operating system (Windows or Linux), and location into which you want to deploy. You should also confirm and select the desired pricing tier.

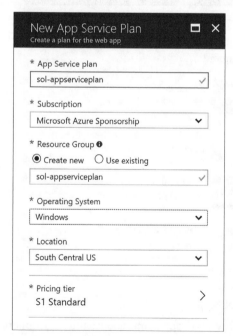

FIGURE 4-2 The settings for a new App Service Plan

7. Click Create to create the new App Service plan.

Following the creation of the new App Service plan, you can create a new web app and associate this with the previously created App Service plan. Or, as discussed in the next section, you can create a new App Service plan as you create a new web app.

> **MORE INFO   APP SERVICE PRICING TIERS**
>
> App Service plan pricing tiers range from Free, Shared, Basic, Standard, Premium, and Isolated tiers. It is important to understand the features offered by each tier related to custom domains, certificates, scale, deployment slots, and more. For more information see *https://azure.microsoft.com/en-us/pricing/details/app-service*.

Creating a new Web App and App Service plan

To create a new Web App and a new App Service plan in the portal, complete the following steps:

1. Navigate to the portal accessed via *https://portal.azure.com*.
2. Select New on the command bar.
3. Within the Marketplace list (Figure 4-3), select the Web + Mobile option.

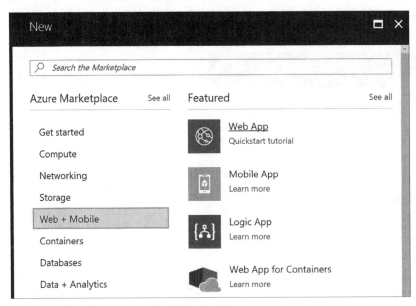

FIGURE 4-3 The Marketplace list for Web + Mobile

4. On the Web + Mobile blade, select Web App.
5. On the Web App blade (Figure 4-4), provide an app name, choose the subscription, resource group, operating system (Windows or Linux), and choose a setting for Application Insights. You also select the App Service plan into which you want to deploy.

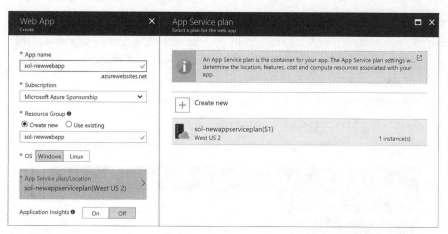

FIGURE 4-4 The selections for a new App Service.

6. When you click the App Service plan selection, you can choose an existing App Service plan, or create a new App Service plan. To create a new App Service plan, click Create New from the App Service Plan blade.

7. From the New App Service Plan blade (Figure 4-5), choose a name for the App Service plan, select a location, and select a pricing tier. Click OK and the new App Service plan is created with these settings.

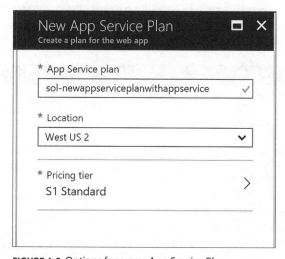

FIGURE 4-5 Options for a new App Service Plan.

8. From the Web App blade, click Create to create the web app and associate it with the new App Service plan.

Review App Service plan settings

Once you've created a new App Service plan, you can select the App Service plan in the portal and manage relevant settings including managing web apps and adjusting scale.

To manage an App Service plan, complete the following steps:

1. Navigate to the portal accessed via *https://portal.azure.com*.

2. Select More Services on the command bar.

3. In the filter text box, type **App Service Plans**, and select App Service Plans (Figure 4-6).

FIGURE 4-6 Search results for App Service plans

4. Review the list of App Service plans (Figure 4-7). Note the number of apps deployed to each is shown in the list. You can also see the pricing tiers. Select an App Service plan from the list to navigate to the App Service Plan blade.

FIGURE 4-7 List of App Service plans

5. From the left navigation pane, select Apps to view the apps that are deployed to the App Service plan (Figure 4-8). You can select from the list of apps to navigate to the app blade and manage its settings.

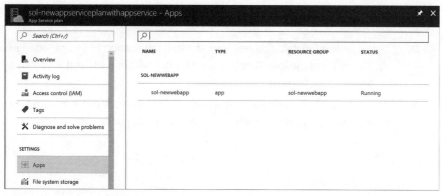

FIGURE 4-8 List of apps deployed to the App Service plan.

6. From the left navigation pane, select Scale Up to choose a new pricing tier for the App Service plan.

7. From the left navigation pane, select Scale Out to increase or decrease the number of instances of the App Service plan, or to configure Autoscale settings.

Configure Web App settings

Azure Web Apps provide a comprehensive collection of settings that you can adjust to establish the environment in which your web application runs, as well as tools to define and manage the values of settings used by your web application code. You can configure the following groups of settings for your applications:

- Application type and library versions
- Load balancing
- Slot management
- Debugging
- App settings and connection strings
- IIS related settings

To manage Web App settings follow these steps:

1. Navigate to the blade of your web app in the portal accessed via *https://portal.azure. com*.

2. Select the Application settings tab from the left navigation pane. The setting blade appears to the right.

3. Choose from the general settings required for the application:

   A. Choose the required language support from .NET Framework, PHP, Java, or Python, and their associated versions.

   B. Choose between 32bit and 64bit runtime execution.

C. Choose web sockets if you are building a web application that leverages this feature from the browser.

D. Choose Always On if you do not want the web application to be unloaded when idle. This reduces the load time required for the next request and is a required setting for web jobs to run effectively.

E. Choose the type of managed pipeline for IIS. Integrated is the more modern pipeline and Classic would only be used for legacy applications (Figure 4-9).

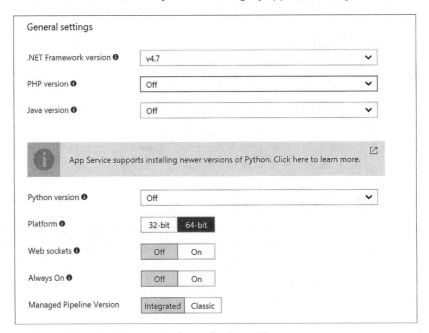

FIGURE 4-9 General settings section for application settings

4. Choose your setting for ARR affinity (Figure 4-10). If you choose to enable ARR affinity your users will be tied to a particular host machine (creating a sticky session) for the duration of their session. If you disable this, your application will not create a sticky session and your application is expected to support load balancing between machines within a session.

FIGURE 4-10 ARR affinity settings

5. When you first create your web app, the auto swap settings are not available to configure. You must first create a new slot, and from the slot you may configure auto swap to another slot (Figure 4-11).

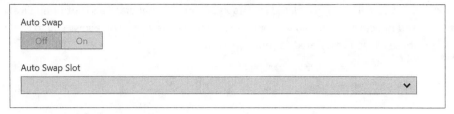

FIGURE 4-11 Auto Swap settings

6. Enable remote debugging (Figure 4-12) if you run into situations where deployed applications are not functioning as expected. You can enable remote debugging for Visual Studio versions 2012, 2013, 2015, and 2017.

FIGURE 4-12 Remote debugging settings for the web app

7. Configure the app settings required for your application. These app settings (Figure 4-13) override any settings matching the same name from your application.

FIGURE 4-13 Application settings

8. Configure any connection strings for your application (Figure 4-14). These connection string settings override any settings matching the same key name from your application configuration. For connection strings, once you create the settings, save, and later return to the application settings blade; those settings are hidden unless you select it to show the value again.

FIGURE 4-14 Connection string settings

9. Configure IIS settings related to default documents, handlers, and virtual applications and directories required for your application (Figure 4-15). This allows you to control these IIS features related to your application.

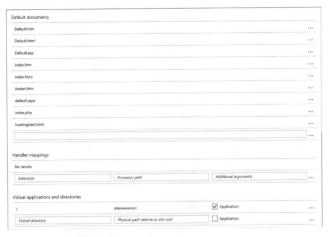

FIGURE 4-15 IIS settings

Configure Web App certificates and custom domains

When you first create your web app, it is accessible through the subdomain you specified in the web app creation process, where it takes the form <yourwebappname>.azurewebsites.net. To map to a more user-friendly domain name (such as contoso.com), you must set up a custom domain name.

If your website will use HTTPS to secure communication between it and the browser using Transport Layer Security (TLS), more commonly (but less accurately) referred to in the industry as Secure Socket Layer (SSL), you need to utilize an SSL certificate. With Azure Web Apps, you can use an SSL certificate with your web app in one of two ways:

- You can use the "built-in" wildcard SSL certificate that is associated with the *.azurewebsites.net domain.
- More commonly you use a certificate you purchase for your custom domain from a third-party certificate authority.

> **NOTE**
>
> There are multiple types of SSL certificates, but the one you choose primarily depends on the number of different custom domains (or subdomains) that the certificate secures. Some certificates apply to only a single fully qualified domain name (sometimes referred to as *basic certs*), some certificates apply to a list of fully qualified domain names (also called *subjectAltName* or *UC certs*), and other certificates apply across an unlimited number of subdomains for a given domain name (usually referred to as *wildcard certs*).

Mapping custom domain names

Web Apps support mapping to a custom domain that you purchase from a third-party registrar either by mapping the custom domain name to the virtual IP address of your website or by mapping it to the <yourwebappname>.azurewebsites.net address of your website. This mapping is captured in domain name system (DNS) records that are maintained by your domain registrar. Two types of DNS records effectively express this purpose:

- A records (or, address records) map your domain name to the IP address of your website.
- CNAME records (or, alias records) map a subdomain of your custom domain name to the canonical name of your website, expressed as <yourwebappname>.azurewebsites.net.

Table 4-1 shows some common scenarios along with the type of record, the typical record name, and an example value based on the requirements of the mapping.

TABLE 4-1 Mapping domain name requirements to DNS record types, names, and values

Requirement	Type of Record	Record Name	Record Value
contoso.com should map to my web app IP address	A	@	138.91.240.81 IP address
contoso.com and all subdomains demo.contoso.com and www.contoso.com should map to my web app IP address	A	*	138.91.240.81 IP address
www.contoso.com should map to my web app IP address	A	www	138.91.240.81 IP address
www.contoso.com should map to my web app canonical name in Azure	CNAME	www	contoso.azurewebsites.net Canonical name in Azure

Note that whereas A records enable you to map the root of the domain (like *contoso.com*) and provide a wildcard mapping for all subdomains below the root (like *www.contoso.com* and *demo.contoso.com*), CNAME records enable you to map only subdomains (like the www in *www.contoso.com*).

Configuring a custom domain

To configure a custom domain, you need access to your domain name registrar setup for the domain while also editing configuration for your web app in the Azure portal.

EXAM TIP

Use of a custom domain name is not supported by the Free App Service plan pricing tier. All other pricing tiers including Shared, Basic, Standard, and Premium support custom domains.

These are the high-level steps for creating a custom domain name for your web app:

1. Navigate to the blade of your web app in the portal accessed via *https://portal.azure. com*.

2. Ensure your web app uses an App Service plan that supports custom domains.

3. Click Custom Domains from the left navigation pane.

4. On the Custom Domains blade (Figure 4-16) note the external IP address of your web app.

FIGURE 4-16 Part of the custom domain blade for the web app

5. Select Add Hostname to open the Add Hostname blade. Enter the hostname and click Validate for the portal to validate the state of the registrar setup with respect to your web app. You can then choose to set up an A record or CNAME record (Figure 4-17).

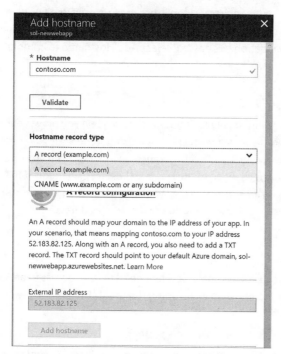

FIGURE 4-17 Part of the Add hostname blade

6. To set up an A record, select A Record and follow the instructions provided in the blade. It guides you through the following steps for an A record setup:

A. You first add a TXT record at your domain name registrar, pointing to the default Azure domain for your web app, to verify you own the domain name. The new TXT record should point to <yourwebappname>.azurewebsites.net.

B. In addition, you add an A record pointing to the IP address shown in the blade, for your web app.

7. To set up a CNAME record, select CNAME record, and follow the instructions provided in the blade.

A. If using a CNAME record, following the instructions provided by your domain name registrar, add a new CNAME record with the name of the subdomain, and for the value, specify your web app's default Azure domain with <yourwebappname>.azurewebsites.net.

8. Save your DNS changes. Note that it may take some time for the changes to propagate across DNS. In most cases, your changes are visible within minutes, but in some cases, it may take up to 48 hours. You can check the status of your DNS changes by doing a DNS lookup using third-party websites like *http://mxtoolbox.com/DNSLookup.aspx*.

9. After completing the domain name registrar setup, from the Custom Domains blade, click Add Hostname again to configure your custom domain. Enter the domain name and select Validate again. If validation has passed, select Add Hostname to complete the assignment.

> *IMPORTANT* **IP ADDRESS CHANGES**
>
> The IP address that you get by following the preceding steps will change if you move your web app to a Free web hosting plan, if you delete and recreate it, or potentially if you subsequently enable SSL with the IP Based type. This can also happen unintentionally if you reach your spending limit and the web app is changed to the Free web hosting plan mode. If the IP address changes and you are using an A record to map your custom domain to your web app, you will need to update the value of the A record to use the new IP address.

Configuring SSL certificates

To configure SSL certificates for your custom domain, you first need to have access to an SSL certificate that includes your custom domain name, including the CNAME if it is not a wildcard certificate.

To assign an SSL certificate to your web app, follow these steps:

1. Navigate to the blade of your web app in the portal accessed via *https://portal.azure.com*.

2. Click SSL certificates from the left navigation pane.

3. From the SSL certificates (Figure 4-18) blade you may choose to import an existing app service certificate, or upload a new certificate.

FIGURE 4-18 SSL certificates blade

4. You can then select Add Binding to set up the correct binding. You can set up bindings that point at your naked domain (contoso.com), or to a particular CNAME (www.contoso.com, demo.contoso.com), so long as the certificate supports it.

5. You can choose between Server Name Indication (SNI) or IP based SSL when you create the binding for your custom domain (Figure 4-19).

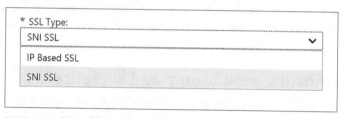

FIGURE 4-19 Part of the Add Binding blade

> **MORE INFO** **SSL CERTIFICATES AND BINDINGS**
>
> For more information on purchasing SSL certificates and setting up Web App certificates see *https://docs.microsoft.com/en-us/azure/app-service/web-sites-purchase-ssl-web-site*.

Manage Web Apps by using the API, Azure PowerShell, and Xplat-CLI

In addition to configuring and managing Web Apps via the Azure portal, programmatic or script-based access is available for much of this functionality and can satisfy many development requirements.

The options for this include the following:

- **Azure Resource Manager (ARM)** Azure Resource Manager provides a consistent management layer for the management tasks you can perform using Azure PowerShell, Azure CLI, Azure portal, REST API, and other development tools. For more information on this see *https://docs.microsoft.com/en-us/azure/azure-resource-manager/*.

- **REST API** The REST API enables you to deploy and manage Azure infrastructure resources using HTTP request and JSON payloads. For more details on this see *https://docs.microsoft.com/en-us/rest/api/resources/*.

- **Azure PowerShell** Azure PowerShell provides cmdlets for interacting with Azure Resource Manager to manage infrastructure resources. The PowerShell modules can be installed to Windows, macOS, or Linux. For additional details see *https://docs.microsoft.com/en-us/powershell/azure/overview*.

- **Azure CLI** Azure CLI (also known as XplatCLI) is a command line experience for managing Azure resources. This is an open source SDK that works on Windows, macOS, and Linux platforms to create, manage, and monitor web apps. For details see *https://docs.microsoft.com/en-us/cli/azure/overview*.

> **MORE INFO** **MANAGING APP SERVICES**
>
> See the following links that provide samples for managing App Services using Azure and Azure CLI at: *https://docs.microsoft.com/en-us/azure/app-service/app-service-powershell-samples* and *https://docs.microsoft.com/en-us/azure/app-service/app-service-cli-samples*.

Implement diagnostics, monitoring, and analytics

Without diagnostics, monitoring, and analytics, you cannot effectively investigate the cause of a failure, nor can you proactively prevent potential problems before your users experience them. Web Apps provide multiple forms of logs, features for monitoring availability and automatically sending email alerts when the availability crosses a threshold, features for monitoring your web app resource usage, and integration with Azure Analytics via Application Insights.

EXAM TIP

App Services are also governed by quotas depending on the App Service plan you have chosen. Free and Shared apps have CPU, memory, bandwidth, and filesystem quotas; when reached the web app no longer runs until the next cycle, or the App Service plan is changed. Basic, Standard, and Premium App Services are only limited by filesystem quotas based on the SKU size selected for the host.

> **MORE INFO** **QUOTAS**
>
> For the latest listing of specific quotas, limits, and features, visit *https://docs.microsoft.com/azure/azure-subscription-service-limits#app-service-limits*.

Configure diagnostics logs

A web app can produce many different types of logs, each focused on presenting a particular source and format of diagnostic data. The following list describes each of these logs:

- **Event Log** The equivalent of the logs typically found in the Windows Event Log on a Windows Server machine, this is a single XML file on the local file system of the web application. In the context of web apps, the Event Log is particularly useful for capturing unhandled exceptions that may have escaped the application's exception handling logic and surfaced to the web server. Only one XML file is created per web app.

- **Web server logs** Web server logs are textual files that create a text entry for each HTTP request to the web app.

- **Detailed error message logs** These HTML files are generated by the web server and log the error messages for failed requests that result in an HTTP status code of 400 or higher. One error message is captured per HTML file.

- **Failed request tracing logs** In addition to the error message (captured by detailed error message logs), the stack trace that led to a failed HTTP request is captured in these XML documents that are presented with an XSL style sheet for in-browser consumption. One failed request trace is captured per XML file.

- **Application diagnostic logs** These text-based trace logs are created by web application code in a manner specific to the platform the application is built in using logging or tracing utilities.

To enable these diagnostic settings from the Azure portal, follow these steps:

1. Navigate to the blade of your web app in the portal accessed via *https://portal.azure. com*.

2. Select the Diagnostics Logs tab from the left navigation pane. The Diagnostics Logs blade (Figure 4-20) will appear to the right. From this blade you can choose to configure the following:

   A. Enable application logging to the file system for easy access through the portal.
   B. Enable storing application logs to blob storage for longer term access.
   C. Enable Web Server logging to the file system or to blob storage for longer term access.
   D. Enable logging detailed error messages.
   E. Enable logging failed request messages.

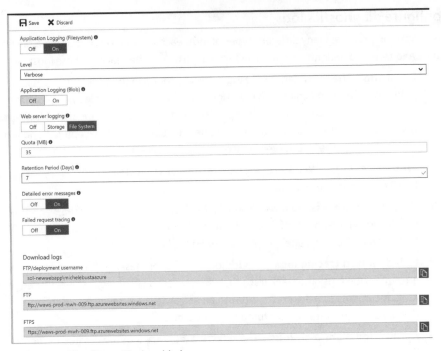

FIGURE 4-20 The diagnostics logs blade

3. If you enable files system logs for application and Web Server logs, you can view those from the Log Streaming tab (Figure 4-21).

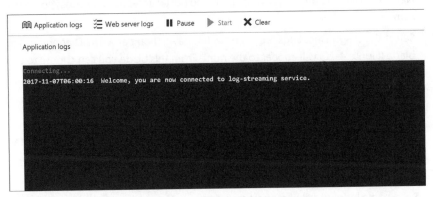

FIGURE 4-21 The log streaming blade

4. You can access more advanced debugging and diagnostics tools from the Advanced Tools tab (Figure 4-22).

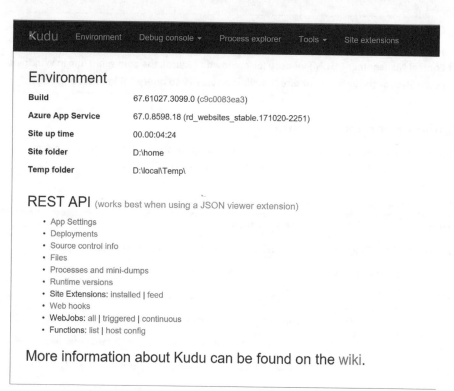

FIGURE 4-22 The Kudu web site

Table 4-2 describes where to find each type of log when retrieving diagnostic data stored in the web app's local file system. The Log Files folder is physically located at D:\home\LogFiles.

TABLE 4-2 Locations of the various logs on the web app's local file system

Log Type	Location
Event Log	\LogFiles\eventlog.xml
Web server logs	\LogFiles\http\RawLogs*.log
Detailed error message logs	\LogFiles\DetailedErrors\ErrorPage######.htm
Failed request tracing logs	\LogFiles\W3SVC**.xml
Application diagnostic logs (.NET)	\LogFiles\Application*.txt
Deployment logs	\LogFiles\Git. This folder contains logs generated by the internal deployment processes used by Azure web apps, as well as logs for Git deployments

EXAM TIP

You can retrieve diagnostics logs data by using Visual Studio Server Explorer, the Site Control Management (SCM) website (also known as Kudu), the command line in Windows PowerShell or the xplat-cli, or direct download via FTP to query Table or Blob storage.

Configure endpoint monitoring

App Services provide features for monitoring your applications directly from the Azure portal. There are many metrics available for monitoring, as listed in Table 4-3.

TABLE 4-3 List of available metrics that are monitored for your web apps

METRIC	DESCRIPTION
Average Response Time	The average time taken for the app to serve requests in ms.
Average memory working set	The average amount of memory in MiBs used by the app.
CPU Time	The amount of CPU in seconds consumed by the app.
Data In	The amount of incoming bandwidth consumed by the app in MiBs.
Data Out	The amount of outgoing bandwidth consumed by the app in MiBs.
Http 2xx	Count of requests resulting in a http status code >= 200 but < 300.
Http 3xx	Count of requests resulting in a http status code >= 300 but < 400.
Http 401	Count of requests resulting in HTTP 401 status code.
Http 403	Count of requests resulting in HTTP 403 status code.
Http 404	Count of requests resulting in HTTP 404 status code.
Http 406	Count of requests resulting in HTTP 406 status code.
Http 4xx	Count of requests resulting in a http status code >= 400 but < 500.
Http Server Errors	Count of requests resulting in a http status code >= 500 but < 600.
Memory working set	Current amount of memory used by the app in MiBs.
Requests	Total number of requests regardless of their resulting HTTP status code.

You can monitor metrics from the portal and customize which metrics should be shown by following these steps:

1. Navigate to the blade of your web app in the portal accessed via *https://portal.azure. com*.

2. Select the Overview tab from the left navigation pane. This pane shows a few default charts for metrics including server errors, data in and out, requests, and average response time (Figure 4-23 and 4-24).

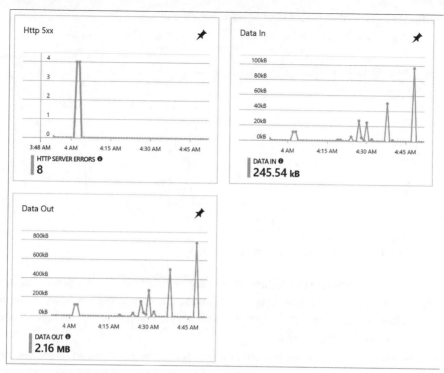

FIGURE 4-23 Metrics showing http server errors, data in, and data out

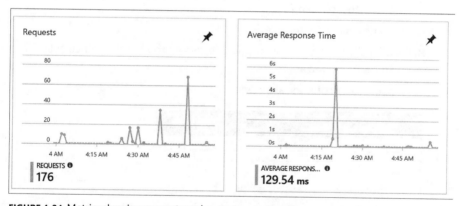

FIGURE 4-24 Metrics showing requests and average response time

3. You can customize the metrics (Figure 4-25) shown by creating new graphs and pinning those to your dashboard.

   A. Click one of the graphs. You'll be taken to edit the metrics blade for the graph, limited to compatible metrics for the selection.

B. Select the metrics to add or remove from the graph.

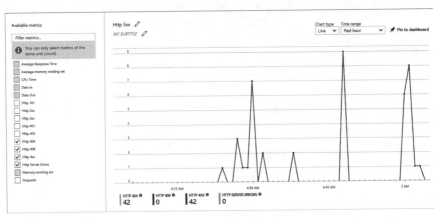

FIGURE 4-25 Selecting metrics to show on the graph

C. Save the graph to the dashboard. You can now navigate to your portal dashboard to view the selected metrics without having to navigate to the web app directly. From here you can also edit the graph by selecting it, editing metrics, and saving back to the same pinned graph.

4. You can also add alerts for metrics. From the Metrics blade click Add Metric alert from the command bar at the top of the blade. This takes you to the Add Rule blade (Figure 4-26) where you can configure the alert. To configure an alert for slow requests, as an example, do the following:

A. Provide a name for the rule.

B. Optionally change the subscription, resource group, and resource but it will default to the current web app.

C. Choose Metrics for the alert type.

FIGURE 4-26 Part of the Add rule blade

D. Choose the metric from the drop-down list (Figure 4-27), in this case Average Response Time with a condition greater than a threshold of 2 seconds over a 15 minute period.

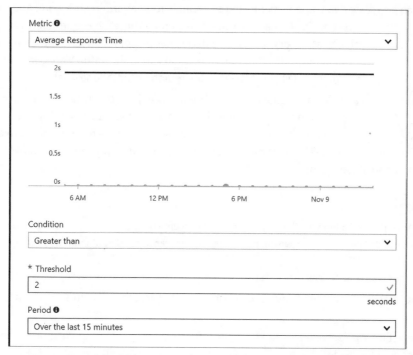

FIGURE 4-27 Part of the Add rule blade where you can set the metric values

E. From the same blade you can also indicate who to notify, configure a web hook, or even configure a Logic App to produce a workflow based on the alert.

5. Click OK to complete the alert configuration.

6. You can view the alerts from the Alerts tab of the navigation pane.

> **NOTE** **MONITORING QUOTAS**
>
> You can also monitor quotas by selecting the Quotas tab from the left navigation pane. This gives you an indication of where you stand with your quotas based on the App Service plan.

Design and configure Web Apps for scale and resilience

App Services provide various mechanisms to scale your web apps up and down by adjusting the number of instances serving requests and by adjusting the instance size. You can, for example, increase the number of instances (scale out) to support the load you experience during business hours, but then decrease (scale in) the number of instances during less busy hours to save costs. Web Apps enable you to scale the instance count manually, automatically via a schedule, or automatically according to key performance metrics. Within a datacenter, Azure load balances traffic between all of your Web Apps instances using a round-robin approach.

You can also scale a web app by deploying to multiple regions around the world and then utilizing Microsoft Azure Traffic Manager to direct web app traffic to the appropriate region based on a round robin strategy or according to performance (approximating the latency perceived by clients of your application). Alternately, you can configure Traffic Manager to use the alternate regions as targets for failover if the primary region becomes unavailable.

In addition to scaling instance counts, you can manually adjust your instance size (scale up or down). For example, you can scale up your web app to utilize more powerful VMs that have more RAM memory and more CPU cores to serve applications that are more demanding of memory consumption or CPU utilization, or scale down your VMs if you later discover your requirements are not as great.

EXAM TIP

Web Apps provide a high availability SLA of 99.9 percent using only a single standard instance. You do not need to provision more than one instance to benefit from this SLA.

To scale your web app, follow these steps:

1. Navigate to the blade of your web app in the portal accessed via *https://portal.azure. com*.

2. Select the App Service plan tab from the left navigation pane. This takes you to the App Service Plan blade.

3. Select the Scale Up tab from the left navigation pane and you'll be taken to a blade to select the new pricing tier for your web app VMs.

4. Select the Scale Out tab and you'll be taken to the Scale Out blade to choose the number of instances to scale out or into (Figure 4-28).

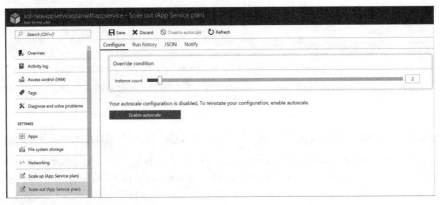

FIGURE 4-28 The scale out blade.

5. If you select Enable autoscale, you can create conditions based on metrics and rules in order for the site to automatically adjust instance count.

> **MORE INFO**   **MONITORING, ANALYTICS, AND AUTOSCALING**
>
> For more information on monitoring web apps, analytics, and setting up autoscale, see:
>
> *https://docs.microsoft.com/en-us/azure/log-analytics/log-analytics-azure-web-apps-analytics*, *https://docs.microsoft.com/en-us/azure/application-insights/app-insights-analytics*, *https://docs.microsoft.com/en-us/Azure/monitoring-and-diagnostics/insights-autoscale-best-practices*, and *https://docs.microsoft.com/en-us/Azure/monitoring-and-diagnostics/insights-how-to-scale*.

Skill 4.2: Design Azure App Service API Apps

Azure API Apps provide a quick and easy way to create and consume scalable RESTful APIs, using the language of your choice, in the cloud. As part of the Azure infrastructure, you can integrate API Apps with many Azure services such as API Management, Logic Apps, Functions, and many more. Securing your APIs can be done with a few clicks, whether you are using Azure Active Directory, OAuth, or social networks for single sign-on.

If you have existing APIs written in .NET, Node.js, Java, Python, or PHP, they can be brought into App Services as API Apps. When you need to consume these APIs, enable CORS support so you can access them from any client. Swagger support makes generating client code to use your API simple. Once you have your API App set up, and clients are consuming it, it is important to know how to monitor it to detect any issues early on.

> **This skill covers how to:**
> - Create and deploy API Apps
> - Automate API discovery by using Swashbuckle
> - Use Swagger API metadata to generate client code for an API app
> - Monitor API Apps

Create and deploy API Apps

There are different ways you can create and deploy API Apps, depending on the language and development environment of choice. For instance, if you are using Visual Studio, you can create a new API Apps project and publish to a new API app, which provisions the service in Azure. If you are not using Visual Studio, you can provision a new API App service using the Azure portal, Azure CLI, or PowerShell.

Creating a new API App from the portal

To create a new API app in the portal, complete the following steps:

1. Navigate to the portal accessed via *https://portal.azure.com*.

2. Select New on the command bar.

3. Within the Marketplace (Figure 4-29) search text box, type **API App**, and press Enter.

FIGURE 4-29 Marketplace search for API App

4. Select API App from the results.

5. On the API App blade, select Create.

6. On the Create API App blade, choose your Azure subscription, select a Resource Group, select or create an App Service Plan, select whether you want to enable Application Insights, and then click Create.

> *NOTE* **SERVER-SIDE AND CLIENT-SIDE PROJECTS**
>
> After creating your API App service, you can quickly create sample ASP.NET, Node.js, or Java server-side and client-side projects using your new service, by selecting Quickstart from your API App blade in the portal.

Creating and deploying a new API app with Visual Studio 2017

Visual Studio 2017 comes preconfigured with the ability to create an API app when you have installed the ASP.NET and web development, as well as Azure development workloads. Follow these steps to create a new API app with Visual Studio 2017:

1. Launch Visual Studio, and then select File > New > Project.

2. In the New Project dialog, select ASP.NET Web Application (.NET Framework) within the Cloud category (Figure 4-30). Provide a name and location for your new project, and then click OK.

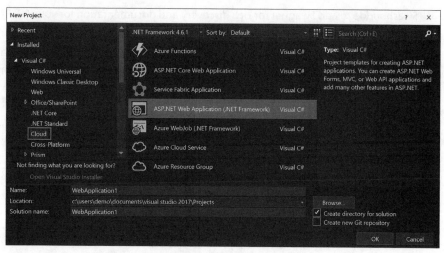

FIGURE 4-30 The ASP.NET Web Application Cloud project type

3. Select the Azure API App template (Figure 4-31), and then click OK.

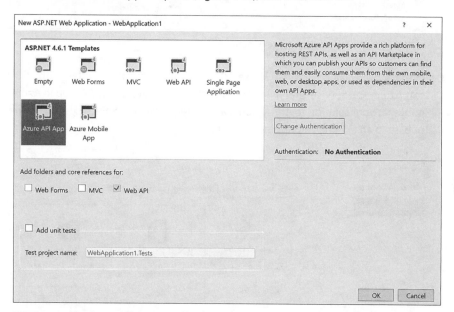

FIGURE 4-31 The Azure API App template

Visual Studio creates a new API App project within the specified directory, adding useful NuGet packages, such as:

- Newtonsoft.Json for deserializing requests and serializing responses to and from your API app.

- Swashbuckle to add Swagger for rich discovery and documentation for your API REST endpoints.

In addition, Web API and Swagger configuration classes are created in the project's startup folder. All you need to do from this point, to deploy your API app is to complete your Controller actions, and publish from Visual Studio.

Follow these steps to deploy your API app from Visual Studio:

1. Right-click your project in the Visual Studio Solution Explorer (Figure 4-32), then click Publish.

FIGURE 4-32 Publish solution context menu

2. In the Publish dialog (Figure 4-33), select the Create New option underneath Microsoft Azure App Service, and then click Publish. This creates a new API app in Azure and publishes your solution to it. You could alternately select the Select Existing option to publish to an existing API App service.

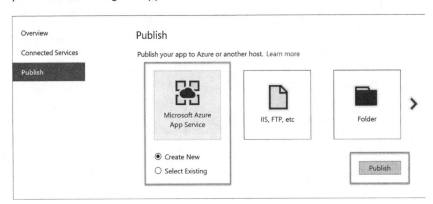

FIGURE 4-33 The Publish dialog

3. In the Create App Service dialog (Figure 4-34), provide a unique App name, select your Azure subscription and resource group, select or create an App Service Plan, and then click Create.

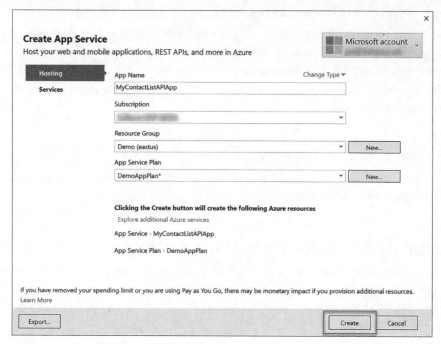

FIGURE 4-34 Create App Service dialog

4. When your API app is finished publishing, it will open in a new web browser. When the page is displayed, navigate to the /swagger path to view your generated API details, and to try out the REST methods. For example *http://<YOUR-API-APP>.azurewebsites.net/swagger/* (Figure 4-35).

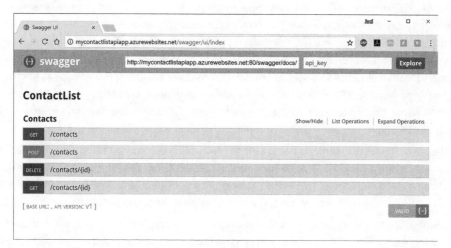

FIGURE 4-35 The Swagger interface for the published API App

Automate API discovery by using Swashbuckle

Swagger is a popular, open source framework backed by a large ecosystem of tools that helps you design, build, document, and consume your RESTful APIs. The previous section included a screenshot of the Swagger page generated for an API App. This was generated by the Swashbuckle NuGet package.

The core component of Swagger is the Swagger Specification, which is the API description metadata in the form of a JSON or YAML file. The specification creates the RESTful contract for your API, detailing all its resources and operations in a human and machine-readable format to simplify development, discovery, and integration with other services. This is a standardized OpenAPI Specification (OAS) for defining RESTful interfaces, which makes the generated metadata valuable when working with a wide range of consumers. Included in the list of consumers that can read the Swagger API metadata are several Azure services, such as Microsoft PowerApps, Microsoft Flow, and Logic Apps. Meaning, when you publish your API App service with Swagger, these Azure services and more immediately know how to interact with your API endpoints with no further effort on your part.

Beyond other Azure services being able to more easily use your API App, Swagger RESTful interfaces make it easier for other developers to consume your API endpoints. The API explorer that comes with swagger-ui makes it easy for other developers (and you) to test the endpoints and know what the data format looks like that need to be sent and should be returned in kind.

Generating this Swagger metadata manually can be a very tedious process. If you build your API using ASP.NET or ASP.NET Core, you can use the Swashbuckle NuGet package to automatically do this for you, saving a lot of time initially creating the metadata, and maintaining it. In addition to its Swagger metadata generator engine, Swashbuckle also contains an embedded version of swagger-ui, which it will automatically serve up once Swashbuckle is installed.

Use Swashbuckle in your API App project

Swashbuckle is provided by way of a set of NuGet packages: Swashbuckle and Swashbuckle. Core. When you create a new API App project using the Visual Studio template, these NuGet packages are already included. If you don't have them installed, follow these steps to add Swashbuckle to your API App project:

1. Install the Swashbuckle NuGet package, which includes Swashbuckle.Core as a dependency, by using the following command from the NuGet Package Manager Console:

   ```
   Install-Package Swashbuckle
   ```

2. The NuGet package also installs a bootstrapper (App_Start/SwaggerConfig.cs) that enables the Swagger routes on app start-up using WebActivatorEx. You can configure Swashbuckle's options by modifying the GlobalConfiguration.Configuration. EnableSwagger extension method in SwaggerConfig.cs. For example, to exclude API actions that are marked as Obsolete, add the following configuration:

   ```
   public static void Register()
   {
           var thisAssembly = typeof(SwaggerConfig).Assembly;
           GlobalConfiguration.Configuration
             .EnableSwagger(c =>
                 {
                     …
                     …
                     // Set this flag to omit descriptions for any actions
                     decorated with the Obsolete attribute
                         c.IgnoreObsoleteActions();
                     …
                     …
                 });
   }
   ```

3. Modify your project's controller actions to include Swagger attributes to aid the generator in building your Swagger metadata. Listing 4-1 illustrates the use of the SwaggerResponseAttribute at each controller method.

4. Swashbuckle is now configured to generate Swagger metadata for your API endpoints with a simple UI to explore that metadata. For example, the controller in Listing 4-1 may produce the UI shown in Figure 4-36.

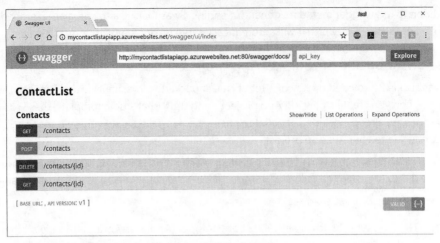

FIGURE 4-36 The Swagger interface for the published API App

LISTING 4-1 C# code showing Swagger attributes added to the API App's controller actions

```csharp
/// <summary>
/// Gets the list of contacts
/// </summary>
/// <returns>The contacts</returns>
[HttpGet]
[SwaggerResponse(HttpStatusCode.OK,
    Type = typeof(IEnumerable<Contact>))]
[Route("~/contacts")]
public async Task<IEnumerable<Contact>> Get()
{
    …
}


/// <summary>
/// Gets a specific contact
/// </summary>
/// <param name="id">Identifier for the contact</param>
/// <returns>The requested contact</returns>
[HttpGet]
[SwaggerResponse(HttpStatusCode.OK,
    Description = "OK",
    Type = typeof(IEnumerable<Contact>))]
[SwaggerResponse(HttpStatusCode.NotFound,
    Description = "Contact not found",
    Type = typeof(IEnumerable<Contact>))]
[SwaggerOperation("GetContactById")]
[Route("~/contacts/{id}")]
public async Task<Contact> Get([FromUri] int id)
{
    …
}

/// <summary>
```

```
/// Creates a new contact
/// </summary>
/// <param name="contact">The new contact</param>
/// <returns>The saved contact</returns>
[HttpPost]
[SwaggerResponse(HttpStatusCode.Created,
    Description = "Created",
    Type = typeof(Contact))]
[Route("~/contacts")]
public async Task<Contact> Post([FromBody] Contact contact)
{
    ...
}
```

You can test any of the API methods by selecting it from the list. Here we selected the /contacts/{id} GET method and tested it by entering a value of 2 in the id parameter, and clicking the Try It Out! button. Notice that Swagger details the return model schema, shows a Curl command and a Request URL for invoking the method, and shows the actual response body after clicking the button (Figure 4-37).

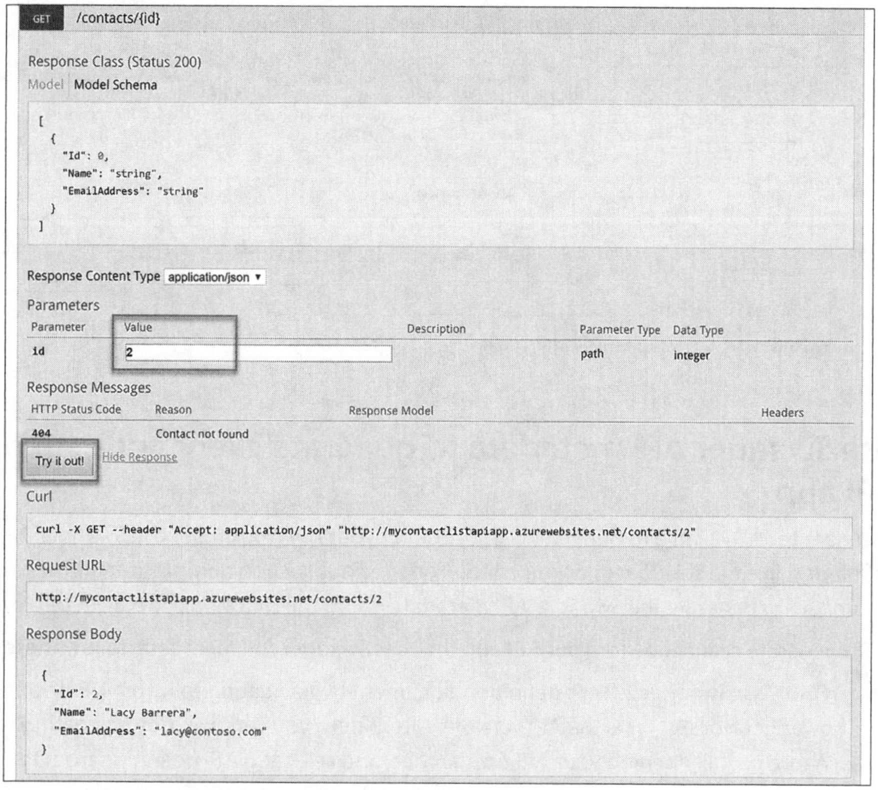

FIGURE 4-37 An API method and result after testing with Swagger

Enable CORS to allow clients to consume API and Swagger interface

Before clients, such as other web services or client code generators, can consume your API endpoints and Swagger interface, you need to enable CORS on the API App in Azure. To enable CORS, follow these steps:

1. Navigate to the portal accessed via *https://portal.azure.com*.

2. Open your API App service. You can find this by navigating to the Resource Group in which you published your service.

3. Select CORS from the left-hand menu (Figure 4-38). Enter one or more allowed origins, then select Save. To allow all origins, enter an asterisk (*) in the Allowed Origins field and remove all other origins from the list.

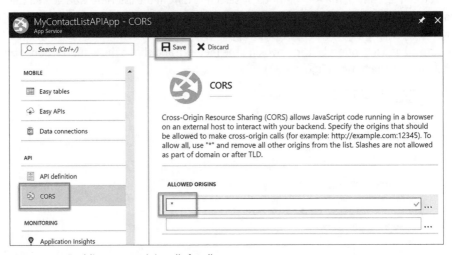

FIGURE 4-38 Enabling cross-origin calls for all sources

Use Swagger API metadata to generate client code for an API app

There are tools available to generate client code for your API Apps that have Swagger API definitions, like the swagger.io online editor. The previous section demonstrated how you can automatically generate the Swagger API metadata, using the Swashbuckle NuGet package.

To generate client code for your API app that has Swagger API metadata, follow these steps:

1. Find your Swagger 2.0 API definition document by navigating to http://<your-api-app/swagger/docs/v1 (v1 is the API version). Alternately, you can find it by navigating to the Azure portal, opening your API App service, and selecting API definition from the left-hand menu. This displays your Swagger 2.0 API definition URL (Figure 4-39).

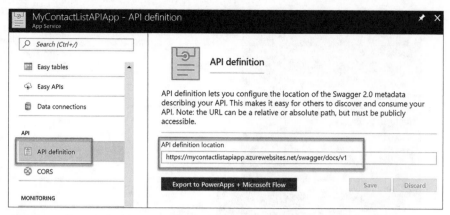

FIGURE 4-39 Steps to find the API App's Swagger 2.0 metadata URL

2. Navigate to *https://editor.swagger.io* to use the Swagger.io Online Editor.

3. Select File > Import URL. Enter your Swagger 2.0 metadata URL in the dialog box and click OK (Figure 4-40).

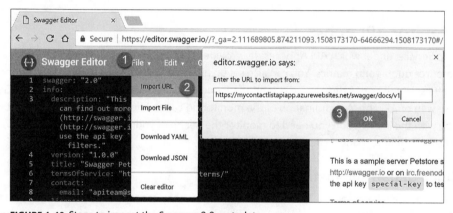

FIGURE 4-40 Steps to import the Swagger 2.0 metadata

4. After a few moments, your Swagger metadata appears on the left-hand side of the editor, and the discovered API endpoints will be displayed on the right. Verify that all desired API endpoints appear, and then select Generate Client from the top menu. Select the desired language or platform for the generated client app. This initiates a download of a zip file containing the client app (Figure 4-41).

FIGURE 4-41 Steps to generate client code in Swagger.io

Monitor API Apps

App Service, under which API Apps reside, provides built-in monitoring capabilities, such as resource quotas and metrics. You can also set up alerts and automatic scaling based on these metrics. In addition, Azure provides built-in diagnostics to assist with debugging an App Service web or API app. A combination of the monitoring capabilities and logging should provide you with the information you need to monitor the health of your API app, and determine whether it is able to meet capacity demands.

Using quotas and metrics

API Apps are subject to certain limits on the resources they can use. The limits are defined by the App Service plan associated with the app. If the application is hosted in a Free or Shared plan, and then the limits on the resources the app can use are defined by Quotas, as discussed earlier for Web Apps.

If you exceed the CPU and bandwidth quotas, your app will respond with a 403 HTTP error, so it's best to keep an eye on your resource usage. Exceeding memory quotas causes an application reset, and exceeding the filesystem quota will cause write operations to fail, even to logs. If you need to increase or remove any of these quotas, you can upgrade your App Service plan.

Metrics that you can view pertaining to your apps are the same as shown earlier in Table 4-3. As with Web Apps, metrics are accessed from the Overview blade of your API App within the Azure portal by clicking one of the metrics charts, such as Requests or Average Response Time. Once you click a chart, you can customize it by clicking it and selecting edit chart. From here you can change the time range, chart type, and metrics to display.

Enable and review diagnostics logs

By default, when you provision a new API App, diagnostics logs are disabled. These are detailed server logs you can use to troubleshoot and debug your app. To enable diagnostics logging, perform the following steps:

1. Navigate to the portal accessed via *https://portal.azure.com*.

2. Open your API App service. You can find this by navigating to the Resource Group in which you published your service.

3. Select Diagnostics logs from the left-hand menu (Figure 4-42). Turn on any logs you wish to capture. When you enable application diagnostics, you also choose the Level. This setting allows you to filter the information captured to informational, warning, or error information. Setting this to verbose will log all information produced by the application. This is also where you can go to retrieve FTP information for downloading the logs.

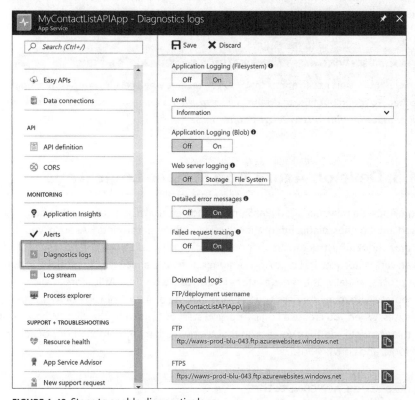

FIGURE 4-42 Steps to enable diagnostics logs

You can download the diagnostics logs via FTP, or they can be downloaded as a zip archive by using PowerShell or the Azure CLI.

The types of logs and structure for accessing logs follow that described for Web Apps and shown in Table 4-2.

> **MORE INFO   MONITOR AN API APP WITH WEB SERVER LOGS**
>
> For more information about monitoring API Apps with web server logs, see: *https://docs. microsoft.com/azure/app-service/web-sites-enable-diagnostic-log*. To view sample CLI scripts you can use to enable and download logs, see: *https://docs.microsoft.com/azure/app-service/scripts/app-service-cli-monitor*. For information on troubleshooting your API Apps with Visual Studio, refer to: *https://docs.microsoft.com/azure/app-service/web-sites-dotnet-troubleshoot-visual-studio*.

> **MORE INFO   VIEWING METRICS AND QUOTAS FOR YOUR APP SERVICE**
>
> For more information on viewing metrics and quotas for your App Service, such as an API App, see *https://docs.microsoft.com/azure/app-service/web-sites-monitor*.

> **MORE INFO   RECEIVING ALERT NOTIFICATIONS ON YOUR APP'S METRICS**
>
> You can configure alert notifications that you can receive when certain metrics thresholds are reached. To found out how to do this, see: *https://docs.microsoft.com/ azure/monitoring-and-diagnostics/insights-receive-alert-notifications*.

Skill 4.3: Develop Azure App Service Logic Apps

Azure Logic Apps is a fully managed iPaaS (integration Platform as a Service) that helps you simplify and implement scalable integrations and workflows in the cloud. As such, you don't have to worry about infrastructure, management, scalability, and availability because all of that is taken care of for you. Its Logic App Designer gives you a nice way to model and automate your process visually, as a series of steps known as a workflow. At its core, it allows you to quickly integrate with many services and protocols, inside of Azure, outside of Azure, as well as on-premises. When you create a Logic App, you start out with a trigger, like 'When an email arrives at this account,' and then you act on that trigger with many combinations of actions, condition logic, and conversions.

> **MORE INFO   LOGIC APP CONNECTORS**
>
> There is a large list of connectors you can use to integrate with services and protocols that can be found at *https://docs.microsoft.com/azure/connectors/apis-list*.

This skill covers how to:

- Create a Logic App connecting SaaS services
- Create a Logic App with B2B capabilities
- Create a Logic App with XML capabilities
- Trigger a Logic App from another app
- Create custom and long-running actions
- Monitor Logic Apps

Create a Logic App connecting SaaS services

One of the strengths of Logic Apps is its ability to connect a large number of SaaS (Software as a Service) services to create your own custom workflows. In this example, we will connect Twitter with an Outlook.com or hosted Office 365 mailbox to email certain tweets as they arrive.

To create a new Logic App in the portal, complete the following steps:

1. Navigate to the portal accessed via *https://portal.azure.com*.
2. Select New on the command bar.
3. Select Enterprise Integration, then Logic App (Figure 4-43).

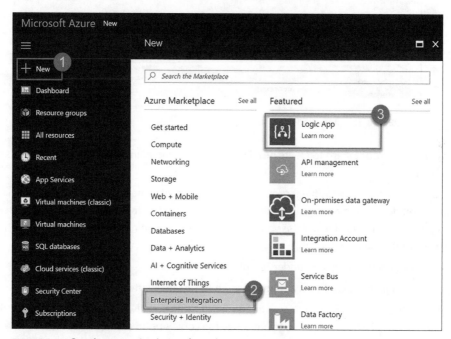

FIGURE 4-43 Creating a new Logic App from the Azure Portal

4. Provide a unique name, select a resource group and location, check Pin To Dashboard, and then click Create (Figure 4-44).

FIGURE 4-44 The Create logic app form

Follow the above steps to create new Logic Apps as needed in the remaining segments for this skill.

Once the Logic App has been provisioned, open it to view the Logic Apps Designer. This is where you design or modify your Logic App. You can select from a series of commonly used triggers, or from several templates you can use as a starting point. The following steps show how to create one from scratch.

1. Select Blank Logic App under Templates.

2. All Logic Apps start with a trigger. Search the list for Twitter, and then select it.

3. Click Sign in to create a connection to Twitter with your Twitter account. A dialog will appear where you sign in and authorize the Logic App to access your account.

4. In the Twitter trigger form on the designer (Figure 4-45), enter your search text to return certain tweets (such as #nasa), and select an interval and frequency, establishing how often you wish to check for items, returning all tweets during that time span.

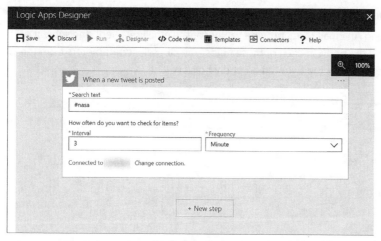

FIGURE 4-45 The Twitter trigger form in the Logic Apps Designer

5. Select the + New Step button, and then choose Add An Action.

6. Type **outlook** in the search box, and then select Office 365 Outlook (Send An Email) from the results. Alternately, you can select Outlook.com from the list (Figure 4-46).

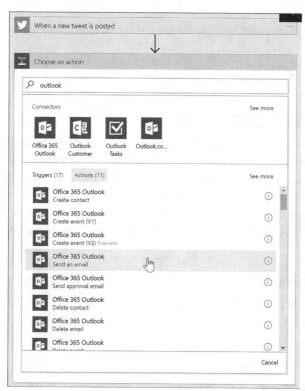

FIGURE 4-46 Adding a new Office 365 Outlook action in the Logic Apps Designer

7.   Click Sign In to create a connection to your Office 365 Outlook account (Figure 4-47).

8.   In the Send An Email form, provide values for the email recipient, the subject of the email, and the body. In each of these fields, you can select parameters from the Twitter Connector, such as the tweet's text and who posted it.

FIGURE 4-47 Adding details to a new Office 365 Outlook action in the Logic Apps Designer

9.   Click Save in the Logic Apps Designer menu. Your Logic App is now live. If you wish to test right away and not wait for your trigger interval, click Run.

Create a Logic App with B2B capabilities

Logic Apps support business-to-business (B2B) workflows and communication through the Enterprise Integration Pack. This allows organizations to exchange messages electronically, even if they use different protocols and formats. Enterprise integration allows you to store all your artifacts in one place, within your integration account, and secure messages through encryption and digital signatures. To access these artifacts from a logic app, you must first link it to your integration account. Your integration account needs both Partner and Agreement artifacts prior to creating B2B workflows for your logic app.

Create an integration account

To get started with the Enterprise Integration Pack so you can create B2B workflows, you must first create an integration account, following these steps:

1.   Navigate to the portal accessed via *https://portal.azure.com*.

2.   Select More Services on the command bar.

3.   In the filter box, type **integration**, and then select Integration Accounts in the results list (Figure 4-48).

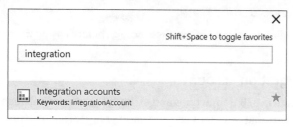

FIGURE 4-48 Navigating to the Integration accounts blade

4. At the top of the Integration Accounts blade, select + Add.

5. Provide a name for your Integration Account (Figure 4-49), select your resource group, location, and a pricing tier. Once validation has passed, click Create.

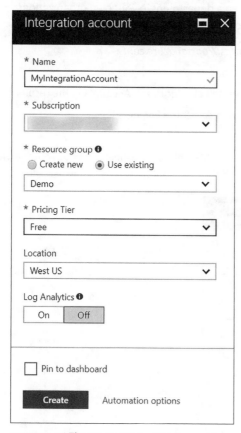

FIGURE 4-49 The create Integration account form

Add partners to your integration account

Partners are entities that participate in B2B transactions and exchange messages between each other. Before you can create partners that represent you and another organization in these transactions, you must both share information that identifies and validates messages sent by each other. After you discuss these details and are ready to start your business relationship, you can create partners in your integration account to represent you both. These message details are called agreements. You need at least two partners in your integration account to create an agreement. Your organization must be the host partner, and the other partner(s) guests. Guest partners can be outside organizations, or even a department in your own organization.

To add a partner to your integration account, follow these steps:

1. Navigate to the portal accessed via *https://portal.azure.com*.

2. Select More Services on the command bar.

3. In the filter box, type **integration**, then select Integration Accounts in the results list.

4. Select your integration account, and then select the Partners tile.

5. In the Partners blade, select + Add.

6. Provide a name for your partner (Figure 4-50), select a Qualifier, and then enter a Value to help identify documents that transfer through your apps. When finished, click OK.

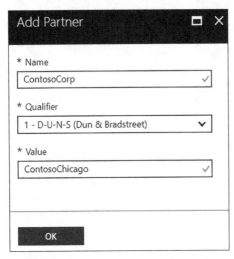

FIGURE 4-50 Adding a partner to an Integration account

7. After a few moments, the new partner (Figure 4-51) will appear in your list of partners.

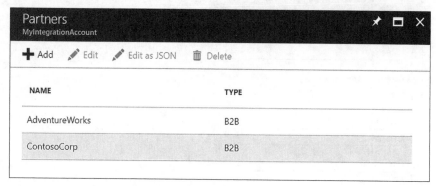

FIGURE 4-51 Partners added to an Integration account

Add an agreement

Now that you have partners associated with your integration account, you can allow them to communicate seamlessly using industry standard protocols through agreements. These agreements are based on the type of information exchanged, and through which protocol or transport standards they will communicate: AS2, X12, or EDIFACT.

Follow these steps to create an AS2 agreement:

1. Navigate to the portal accessed via *https://portal.azure.com*.

2. Select More Services on the command bar.

3. In the filter box, type **integration**, and then select Integration Accounts in the results list (Figure 4-52).

4. Select your integration account, and then select the Agreements tile.

5. In the Agreements blade, select + Add.

6. Provide a name for your agreement and select AS2 for the agreement type. Now select the Host Partner, Host Identity, Guest Partner, and Guest Identity. You can override send and receive settings as desired. Click OK.

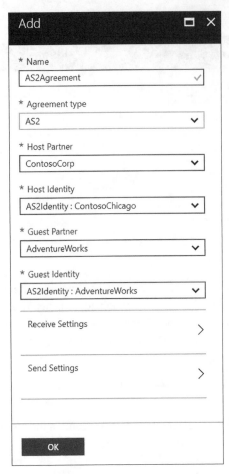

FIGURE 4-52 Adding an agreement to an Integration account

Link your Logic app to your Enterprise Integration account

You will need to link your Logic app to your integration account so you can create B2B workflows using the partners and agreements you've created in your integration account. You must make sure that both the integration account and Logic app are in the same Azure region before linking.

To link, follow these steps:

1. Navigate to the portal accessed via *https://portal.azure.com*.

2. Select More Services on the command bar.

3. In the filter box, type **logic**, and then select Logic Apps in the results list.

4. Select your logic app, and then select Workflow settings.

5. In the Workflow settings blade, select your integration account from the select list, and click Save (Figure 4-53).

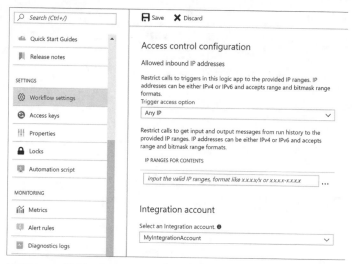

FIGURE 4-53 Linking an integration account with a logic app

Use B2B features to receive data in a Logic App

After creating an integration account, adding partners and agreements to it, and linking it to a Logic app, you can now create a B2B workflow using the Enterprise Integration Pack, following these steps:

1. Open the Logic App Designer on the Logic app that has a linked integration account.

2. Select Blank Logic App under Templates.

3. Search for "http request" in the trigger filter, and then select Request (When an HTTP request is received) from the list of results (Figure 4-54).

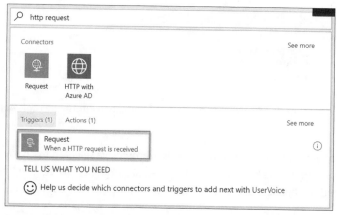

FIGURE 4-54 Selecting a Request trigger in the Logic App Designer

4. Select the + New Step button, and then choose Add An Action.

5. Type **as2** in the search box, and then select AS2 (Decode AS2 Message) from the results (Figure 4-55).

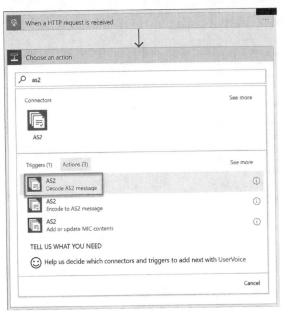

FIGURE 4-55 Selecting a Decode AS2 Message action in the Logic App Designer

6. In the form that follows, provide a connection name, and then select your integration account, and click Create (Figure 4-56).

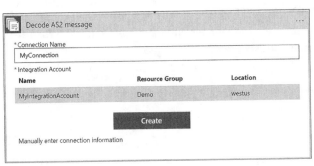

FIGURE 4-56 Setting the Decode AS2 Message connection information form in the Logic App Designer

7. Add the Body that you want to use as input. In this example, we selected the body of the HTTP request that triggers the Logic app. Add the required Headers for AS2. In this example, we selected the headers of the HTTP request that triggers the Logic app (Figure 4-57).

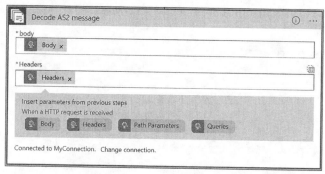

FIGURE 4-57 Setting the Decode AS2 Message body and headers information form in the Logic App Designer

8. Select the + New Step button, and then choose Add An Action.

9. Type **x12** in the search box, and then select X12 (Decode X12 Message) from the results (Figure 4-58).

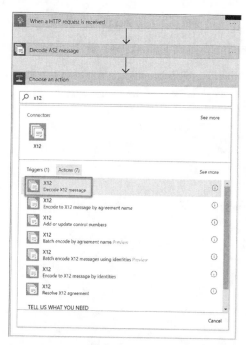

FIGURE 4-58 Selecting a Decode X12 Message action in the Logic App Designer

10. In the form that follows, provide a connection name, and then select your integration account as before, and click Create (Figure 4-59).

11. The input for this new action is the output for the previous AS2 action. Because the actual message content is JSON-formatted and base64-encoded, you must specify an expression as the input. To do this, you type the following into the X12 Flat File Message

to Decode field: **@base64ToString(body('Decode_AS2_Message')?['AS2Message']
?['Content'])**

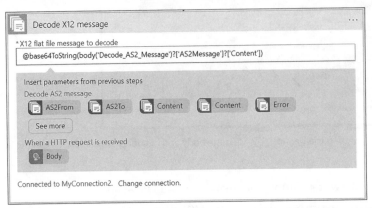

FIGURE 4-59 Setting the Decode X12 flat file message to decode the information form in the Logic App Designer

12. Select the + New Step button, and then choose Add An Action (Figure 4-60).

13. Type **response** in the search box, and then select Request (Response) from the results.

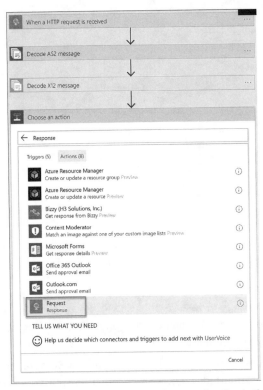

FIGURE 4-60 Selecting a Request (Response) action in the Logic App Designer

14. The response body should include the MDN from the output of the Decode X12 Message action (Figure 4-61). To do this, we type the following into the Body field: **@ base64ToString(body('Decode_AS2_message')?['OutgoingMdn']?['Content'])**

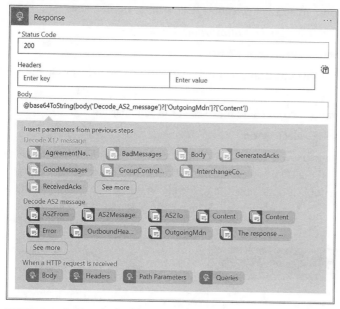

FIGURE 4-61 Setting the body in the Response form in the Logic App Designer

15. Click Save in the Logic Apps Designer menu.

Create a Logic App with XML capabilities

Oftentimes, businesses send and receive data between one or more organizations in XML format. Due to the dynamic nature of XML documents, schemas are used to confirm that the documents received are valid and are in the correct format. Schemas are also used to transform data from one format to another. Transforms are also known as maps, which consist of source and target XML schemas. When you link your logic app with an integration account, the schema and map artifacts within enable your Logic app to use these Enterprise Integration Pack XML capabilities.

The XML features included with the Enterprise Integration pack are:

- **XML validation**   Used to validate incoming and outgoing XML messages against a specific schema.
- **XML transform**   Used to convert data from one format to another.
- **Flat file encoding/decoding**   Used to encode XML content prior to sending, or to convert XML content to flat files.
- **XPath**   Used to extract specific properties from a message, using an xpath expression.

Add schemas to your integration account

Since schemas are used to validate and transform XML messages, you must add one or more to your integration account before working with the Enterprise Integration Pack XML features within your linked logic app. To add a new schema, follow these steps:

1. Navigate to the portal accessed via *https://portal.azure.com*.

2. Select More Services on the command bar.

3. In the filter box, type **integration**, and then select Integration Accounts in the results list (Figure 4-62).

4. Select your integration account, and then select the Schemas tile.

5. In the Schemas blade, select + Add.

6. Provide a name for your schema and select whether it is a small file (<= 2MB) or a large file (> 2MB). If it is a small file, you can upload it here. If you select Large file, then you need to provide a publicly accessible URI to the file. In this case, we're uploading a small file. Click the Browse button underneath Schema to select a local XSD file to upload. Click OK.

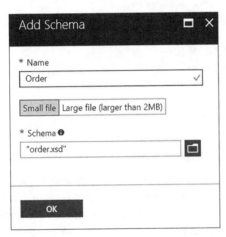

FIGURE 4-62 Adding a schema to an Integration account

Add maps to your Integration account

When you want to your Logic app to transform data from one format to another, you first add a map (schema) to your linked Integration account.

To add a new schema, follow these steps:

1. Navigate to the portal accessed via *https://portal.azure.com*.

2. Select More Services on the command bar.

3. In the filter box, type **integration**, then select Integration Accounts in the results list.

4. Select your integration account, and then select the Maps tile.

5. In the Maps blade, select + Add.

6. Provide a name for your map and click the Browse button underneath Map to select a local XSLT file to upload. Click OK (Figure 4-63).

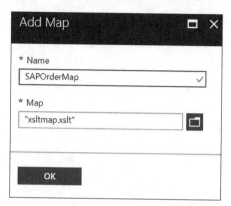

FIGURE 4-63 Adding a map to an Integration account

MORE INFO   **HOW TO CREATE A TRANSFORM/MAP**

You can create the map that you upload to your Integration account by using the Visual Studio Enterprise Integration SDK at *https://aka.ms/vsmapsandschemas.*

Add XML capabilities to the linked Logic App

After adding an XML schema and map to the Integration account, you are ready to use the Enterprise Integration Pack's XML validation, XPath Extract, and Transform XML operations in a Logic App.

Once your LogicAapp has been linked to the Integration account with these artifacts, follow these steps to use the XML capabilities in your Logic App:

1. Open the Logic App Designer on the Logic pp that has a linked Integration account.

2. Select Blank Logic App under Templates.

3. Search for "http request" in the trigger filter, and then select Request (When An HTTP Request Is Received) from the list of results (Figure 4-64).

4. Select the + New Step button, and then choose Add An Action.

5. Type **xml** in the search box, and then select XML (XML Validation) from the results.

FIGURE 4-64 Selecting an XML Validation action in the Logic App Designer

6. In the form that follows, select the Body parameter from the HTTP request trigger for the Content value. Select the Order schema in the Schema Name select list, which is the schema we added to the Integration account (Figure 4-65).

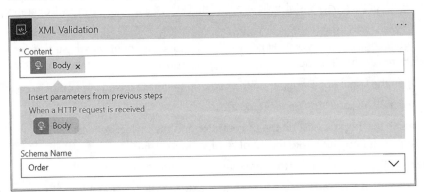

FIGURE 4-65 Selecting an XML Validation form values in the Logic App Designer

7. Select the + New Step button, and then choose Add An Action.

8. Type **xml** in the search box, and then select Transform XML from the results (Figure 4-66).

FIGURE 4-66 Selecting an Transform XML action in the Logic App Designer

9. In the form that follows, select the Body parameter from the HTTP request trigger for the Content value. Select the SAPOrderMap map in the Map select list, which is the map we added to the Integration account (Figure 4-67).

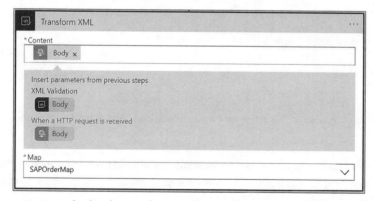

FIGURE 4-67 Setting the Transform XML form values in the Logic App Designer

10. In the Condition form that appears, select the Edit In Advanced Mode link, and then type in your XPath expression. In our case, we type in the following (Figure 4-68): **@equals(xpath(xml(body('Transform_XML')), 'string(count(/.))'), '1')**

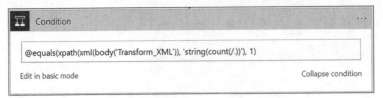

FIGURE 4-68 Setting the XPath expression for the new condition in the Logic App Designer

11. In the "If true" condition block beneath, select Add An Action. Search for "response," and then select Request (Response) from the resulting list of actions (Figure 4-69).

FIGURE 4-69 Selecting a Response action for the new condition's "If true" block in the Logic App Designer

12. In the Response form, select the Transformed XML parameter from the previous Transform XML step. This returns a 200 HTTP response containing the transformed XML (an SAP order) within the body (Figure 4-70).

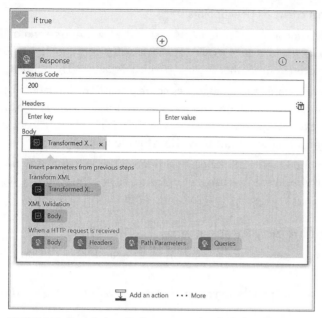

FIGURE 4-70 Completing the Response action form for the new condition's "If true" block in the Logic App Designer

13. Click Save in the Logic Apps Designer menu.

> **MORE INFO**   **DEPLOY THIS LOGIC APP**
>
> Visit the GitHub project page for this Azure Quickstart template to deploy the Logic App in your Azure account at: *https://github.com/Azure/azure-quickstart-templates/tree/master/201-logic-app-veter-pipeline.*

> **MORE INFO**   **USING XML CAPABILITIES IN LOGIC APPS**
>
> For more information about working with XML capabilities in Logic Apps, see: *https://docs.microsoft.com/azure/logic-apps/logic-apps-enterprise-integration-xml.*

Trigger a Logic App from another app

There are many triggers that can be added to a Logic App. Triggers are what kick off the workflow within. The most common type of triggers you can use to trigger, or call, your Logic Apps from another app, are those that create HTTP endpoints. Triggers based on HTTP endpoints tend to be more widely used due to the simplicity of making REST-based calls from practically any web-enabled development platform.

These are the triggers that create HTTP endpoints:

- **Request**   Responds to incoming HTTP requests to start the Logic App's workflow in real time. Very versatile, in that it can be called from any web-based application, external webhook events, even from another Logic App with a request and response action.

- **HTTP Webhook**   Event-based trigger that does not rely on polling for new items. Register subscribe and unsubscribe methods with a callback URL used to trigger the logic app. Whenever your external app or service makes an HTTP POST to the callback URL, the logic app fires, and includes any data passed into the request.

- **API Connection Webhook**   The API connection trigger is similar to the HTTP trigger in its basic functionality. However, the parameters for identifying the action are slightly different.

Create an HTTP endpoint for your logic app

To create an HTTP endpoint to receive incoming requests for a Request Trigger, follow these steps:

1. Open the Logic App Designer on the logic app to which you will be adding an HTTP endpoint.

2. Select Blank Logic App under Templates.

3. Search for "http request" in the trigger filter, and then select Request (When An HTTP Request Is Received) from the list of results.

4. You can optionally enter a JSON schema for the payload, or data, that you expect to be sent to the trigger. This schema can be added to the Request Body JSON Schema field. To generate the schema, select the Use Sample Payload To Generate Schema link at the bottom of the form. This displays a dialog where you can type in or paste a sample JSON payload. This generates the schema when you click Done. The advantage to having a schema defined is that the designer will use the schema to generate tokens that your logic app can use to consume, parse, and pass data from the trigger through your workflow (Figure 4-71).

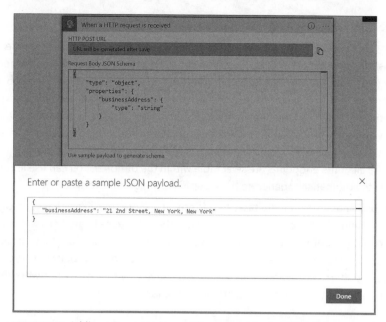

FIGURE 4-71 Adding a Request trigger with a request body JSON schema

5. Click Save in the Logic Apps Designer menu.

6. After saving, the HTTP POST URL is generated on the Receive trigger (Figure 4-72). This is the URL your app or service uses to trigger your logic app. The URL contains a Shared Access Signature (SAS) key used to authenticate the incoming requests.

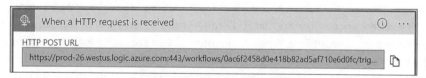

FIGURE 4-72 The generated HTTP POST URL on the Request trigger

---

MORE INFO **CALL, TRIGGER, OR NEST WORKFLOWS WITH HTTP ENDPOINTS IN LOGIC APPS**

For more information on the topic of using HTTP endpoints to call, trigger, or nest workflows in Logic Apps see: *https://docs.microsoft.com/azure/logic-apps/logic-apps-http-endpoint*.

MORE INFO **CREATE AN API THAT FOLLOWS THE WEBHOOK SUBSCRIBE/UNSUBSCRIBE PATTERN**

For more information on how to create an API that follows the webhook subscribe and unsubscribe pattern in logic apps see *https://docs.microsoft.com/azure/logic-apps/logic-apps-create-api-app#webhook-triggers*.

Create custom and long-running actions

You can create your own APIs that provide custom actions and triggers. Because these are web-based APIs that use REST HTTP endpoints, you can build them in any language framework like .NET, Node.js, or Java. You can also host your APIs on Azure App Service as either web apps or API apps. However, API apps are preferred because they will make it easier to build, host, and consume your APIs used by Logic Apps. Another recommendation is to provide an OpenAPI (previously Swagger) specification to describe your RESTful API endpoints, their operations, and parameters. This makes it much easier to reference your custom API from a logic app workflow because all of the endpoints are selectable within the designer. You can use libraries like Swashbuckle to automatically generate the OpenAPI (Swagger) file for you.

If your custom API has long-running tasks to perform, it is more than likely that your logic app will time out waiting for the operation to complete. This is because Logic Apps will only wait around two minutes before timing out a request. If your long-running task takes several minutes, or hours to complete, you need to implement a REST-based async pattern on your API. These types of patterns are already fully supported natively by the Logic Apps workflow engine, so you don't need to worry about the implementation there.

> **MORE INFO** **USE SWASHBUCKLE TO AUTOMATICALLY GENERATE OPENAPI (SWAGGER)**
>
> Swashbuckle makes it easy to automatically generate the OpenAPI (Swagger) specification file for you. For more information see *https://github.com/domaindrivendev/Swashbuckle*.

Long-running action patterns

Your custom API operations serve as endpoints for the actions in your Logic App's workflow. At a basic level, the endpoints accept an HTTP request and return an HTTP response within the Logic App's request timeout limit. When your custom action executes a long-running operation that will exceed this timeout, you can follow either the asynchronous polling pattern or the asynchronous webhook pattern. These patterns allow your logic app to wait for these long-running tasks to finish.

Asynchronous polling

The way the asynchronous polling pattern works is as follows:

1. When your API receives the initial request to start work, it starts a new thread with the long-running task, and immediately returns an HTTP Response "202 Accepted" with a location header. This immediate response prevents the request from timing out, and causes the workflow engine to start polling for changes.

2. The location header points to the URL for the Logic Apps to check the status of the long-running job. By default, the engine checks every 20 seconds, but you can also add a "Retry-after" header to specify the number of seconds until the next poll.

3. After the allotted time (20 seconds), the engine polls the URL on the location header. If the long-running job is still going, you should return another "202 Accepted" with a location header. If the job has completed, you should return a "200 OK" along with any relevant data. This is what the Logic Apps engine will continue the workflow with.

> **MORE INFO**   **ASYNCHRONOUS POLLING PATTERN**
>
> For more information on the asynchronous polling pattern see *https://docs.microsoft.com/azure/logic-apps/logic-apps-create-api-app#async-pattern*.

Asynchronous Webhooks

The asynchronous webhook pattern works by creating two endpoints on your API controller:

- **Subscribe**   The Logic Apps engine calls the subscribe endpoint defined in the workflow action for your API. Included in this call is a callback URL created by the logic app that your API stores for when work is complete. When your long-running task is complete, your API calls back with an HTTP POST method to the URL, along with any returned content and headers, as input to the logic app.
- **Unsubscribe**   This endpoint is called any time the logic app run is cancelled. When your API receives a request to this endpoint, it should unregister the callback URL and stop any running processes.

> **MORE INFO**   **ASYNCHRONOUS WEBHOOK PATTERN**
>
> For more information on the asynchronous webhook pattern see *https://docs.microsoft.com/azure/logic-apps/logic-apps-create-api-app#webhook-actions*.

Monitor Logic Apps

When you create a logic app, you can use out-of-the-box tools within Logic Apps to monitor your app and detect any issues it may have, such as failures. You can view runs and trigger history, overall status, and performance.

If you want real-time event monitoring, as well as richer debugging, you can enable diagnostics on your logic app and send events to OMS with Log Analytics, or to other services, such as Azure Storage and Event Hubs.

Select Metrics (Figure 4-73) under Monitoring in the left-hand menu of your logic app to view performance information and the overall state, such as how many actions succeeded or failed, over the specified time period. It will display an interactive chart based on the selected metrics.

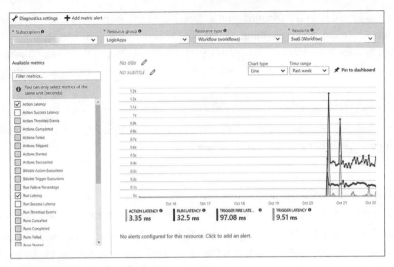

FIGURE 4-73 Metrics for a logic app

Select Alert Rules under Monitoring to create alerts based on metrics (such as any time failures occur over a 1-hour period), activity logs (with categories such as security, service health, autoscale, etc.), and near real time metrics, based on the data captured by your Logic App's metrics, in time periods spanning from one minute to 24 hours. Alerts can be emailed to one or more recipients, route alerts to a webhook, or run a logic app.

The overview blade of your logic app displays both Runs History and Trigger History (Figure 4-74). This view lets you see at a glance how often the app was called, and whether those operations succeeded. Select a run history to see its details, including any data it received.

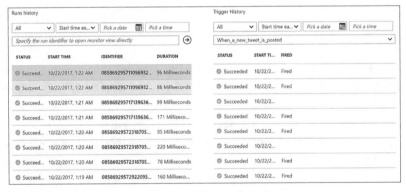

FIGURE 4-74 The Runs history and Trigger History of a logic app

---

MORE INFO **MONITOR STATUS AND SET UP DIAGNOSTICS LOGGING FOR LOGIC APPS**

To learn more about how to monitor status, set up diagnostics logging, and turn on alerts for Logic Apps see *https://docs.microsoft.com/azure/logic-apps/logic-apps-monitor-your-logic-apps.*

Skill 4.4: Develop Azure App Service Mobile Apps

Mobile Apps in Azure App Service provides a platform for the development of mobile applications, providing a combination of back-end Azure hosted services with device side development frameworks that streamline the integration of the back-end services.

> **This skill covers how to:**
> - Create a mobile app
> - Add authentication to a mobile app
> - Add offline sync to a mobile app
> - Add push notifications to a mobile app

Mobile Apps enables the development of applications across a variety of platforms, targeting native iOS, Android, and Windows apps, cross-platform Xamarin (Android, Forms and iOS) and Cordova. Mobile Apps includes a comprehensive set of open source SDKs for each of the aforementioned platforms, and together with the services provided in Azure provide functionality for:

- **Authentication and authorization** Enables integration with identity providers including Azure Active Directory, Facebook, Google, Twitter, and Microsoft Account.
- **Data access** Enables access to tabular data stored in an Azure SQL Database or an on-premises SQL Server (via a hybrid connection) via an automatically provisioned and mobile-friendly OData v3 data source.
- **Offline sync** Enables reads as well as create, update, and delete activity to happen against the supporting tables even when the device is not connected to a network, and coordinates the synchronization of data between local and cloud stores as dictated by the application logic (e.g., network connectivity is detected or the user presses a "Sync" button).
- **Push notifications** Enables the sending of push notifications to app users via Azure Notifications Hubs, which in turn supports the sending of notifications across the most popular push notifications services for Apple (APNS), Google (GCM), Windows (WNS), Windows Phone (MPNS), Amazon (ADM) and Baidu (Android China) devices.

Create a mobile app

From a high level, the process for creating a mobile app is as follows:

1. Identify the target device platforms you want your app to target.
2. Prepare your development environment.
3. Deploy an Azure Mobile App Service instance.
4. Configure the Azure Mobile App Service.
5. Configure your client application.

6. Augment your project with authentication/authorization, offline data sync, or push notification capabilities.

The sections that follow cover each of these steps in greater detail.

Identify the target device platforms

The first decision you make when creating an mobile app is choosing which device platforms to support. For device platforms, you can choose from the set that includes native Android, Cordova, native iOS (Objective-C or Swift), Windows (C#), Xamarin Android, Xamarin Forms and Xamarin iOS.

Because each device platform brings with it a set of requirements, it can make getting started an almost overwhelming setup experience. One way to approach this is to start with one device platform so that you can complete the end-to-end process, and then layer on additional platforms after you have laid the foundation for one platform. Additionally, if you choose to use Xamarin or Cordova as your starting platform you gain the advantage that these platforms can themselves target multiple device platforms, allowing you to write portable code libraries once that is shared by projects that are specific to each target device.

Prepare your development environment

The requirements for your development environment vary depending on the device platforms you wish to target. The pre-requisites here include the supported operating system (e.g., macOS, Windows), the integrated development environment (e.g., Android Studio, Visual Studio for Windows, Visual Studio for Mac or Xcode) and the devices (e.g., the emulators/simulators or physical devices used for testing your app from the development environment of your choice).

Table 4-4 summarizes key requirements by device platform.

TABLE 4-4 Requirements for each target platform

Target Platform	Requirements
Android	OS: macOS or Windows IDE: Android Studio Devices: Android emulator and devices
Cordova	OS: macOS and Windows IDE: Visual Studio for Windows Devices: Android, iOS*, Windows emulators and devices.
iOS	OS: macOS IDE: Xcode Devices: iOS simulator and devices
Windows	OS: Windows IDE: Visual Studio for Windows Devices: Windows desktop and phone
Xamarin.Android	OS: macOS or Windows IDE: Visual Studio for mac or Windows Devices: Android emulators and devices.
Xamarin.Forms	OS: macOS and Windows IDE: Visual Studio for mac or Windows Devices: Android, iOS*, Windows emulators and devices.
Xamarin.iOS	OS: macOS IDE: Visual Studio for mac or Windows Devices: iOS* simulator and devices

* Running the iOS simulator or connecting to an iOS device requires a computer running macOS that is reachable across the network from the Windows development computer, or running the indicated IDE on a macOS.

Deploy an Azure Mobile App Service

With the aforementioned decisions in place, you are now ready to deploy an Azure Mobile App Service instance to provide the backend services to your app. Follow these steps:

1. In the Azure Portal, select New, and search for Mobile App, and select the Mobile App entry.
2. Select Create.
3. Provide a unique name for your Mobile App.
4. Select an Azure subscription and Resource Group.
5. Select an existing App Service Plan or create a new one.
6. Select Create to deploy the mobile app.

Configure the mobile app

Once you have deployed your mobile app, you need to configure where it will store its tabular data and the language (your options are C# or Node.js) in which the backend APIs are implemented (which affects the programming language you use when customizing the backend behavior). The following steps walk you through preparing the quick start solution, which you can use as a starting point for your mobile app. Follow these steps:

1. In the Azure Portal, navigate to the blade for your mobile app.
2. From the menu, under the Deployment heading, select Quick Start.
3. On the General listing, select the platform you wish to target first.
4. On the Quick Start blade, select the button underneath the header 1 Connect a database that reads You Will Need A Database In Order To Complete This Quickstart. Click Here To Create One."
5. On the Data Connections blade, select + Add.
6. On the Add Data Connection blade, leave the Type drop-down at SQL Database.
7. Select SQL Database - Configure Required Settings.
8. On the Database blade, select an existing Azure SQL Database, or create a new database (and optionally a new SQL Database Server).
9. Back on the Add Data Connection blade, select Connection String.
10. Provide the name to use for referring to this connection string in configuration.
11. Select OK.
12. Select OK once more to add the data connection (and create the SQL Database if so configured).

13. In a few minutes (when creating a new SQL Database), the new entry appears in the Data Connections blade. When it does, close the Data Connections blade.

14. On the Quick Start blade, underneath the header, Create A Table API, choose Node.js and select the check box I Acknowledge That This Will Overwrite All Site Contents. Then select the Create TodoItem table button that is enabled. If you choose to use C#, note that you will have to download the zip provided, extract it, open it in Visual Studio, compile and then publish the App Service to your Mobile App instance. This is performed in the same way as you deploy Web Apps as described previously.

15. Leave the Quick Start blade open and continue to the next section.

Configure your client application

Now that you have a basic mobile app backend deployed, you are now ready to create the application that will run on your targeted devices. You can create a new application from a generated quick start project or by connecting an existing application:

1. From the Quick Start blade of your mobile app, underneath the header, Configure Your Client Application, set the toggle to create A New App If You Want To Create A Solution or Connect An Existing App If You Already Have A Solution Built and just need to connect it to the mobile app.

2. If you select Create A New App, you will be provided with instructions specific to the device platform you selected previously as well as a download link from which you can download a generated solution that includes the code customized for access to the deployed mobile app backend. For example, if you selected Xamarin.Forms as your platform, you are provided with a zip file that contains a personalized project that you can open in Visual Studio for Windows or Visual Studio for macOS, which has been pre-configured to connect to your mobile app backend.

3. If you select Connect An Existing App, you are provided with instructions and code you can copy and paste into your project to connect it to the mobile app backend.

4. Once you have completed the steps for either option, you can open and run the project in the IDE and start working against your mobile app backend.

Add authentication to a mobile app

Once you have your project in place and connected to your mobile app backend, you can enable authentication and authorization. Recall that this enables integration with identity providers including Azure Active Directory, Facebook, Google, Twitter and Microsoft Account such that your app users need to sign in using credentials from one of these providers. To do so, follow these steps.

1. Identify the set of identity providers you want to support.

2. For each identity provider, you need to follow the provider's specific instructions to register your app and retrieve the credentials needed to authenticate using that provider. The up-to-date instructions for each provider are available:

A. Azure Active Directory: *https://docs.microsoft.com/en-us/azure/app-service-mobile/app-service-mobile-how-to-configure-active-directory-authentication*

B. Facebook: *https://docs.microsoft.com/en-us/azure/app-service-mobile/app-service-mobile-how-to-configure-facebook-authentication*

C. Google: *https://docs.microsoft.com/en-us/azure/app-service-mobile/app-service-mobile-how-to-configure-google-authentication*

D. Microsoft: *https://docs.microsoft.com/en-us/azure/app-service-mobile/app-service-mobile-how-to-configure-microsoft-authentication*

E. Twitter: *https://docs.microsoft.com/en-us/azure/app-service-mobile/app-service-mobile-how-to-configure-twitter-authentication*

3. Configure authentication / authorization in your mobile app.

4. Navigate to the blade of your mobile app in the Azure Portal.

5. From the menu, under the Settings header, select Authentication / Authorization.

6. Under the Allowed External Redirect URLs header, in the text box provide a callback URL that will be used to invoke your application. It should be of the form [scheme]://easyauth.callback where the value of [scheme] is a string you specify that starts with a letter and consists of only letters and numbers. For example, myapp://easyauth.callback.

7. Select Save from the command bar.

8. Restrict permissions to authenticated users on the service side. The approach you take varies depending on how you configured your backend language and if you have deployed custom backend code.

9. If you are using the Node.js backend created through the quick start in the Azure Portal, you can control access to data on a table-by-table basis. From your Mobile App blade, in the menu select Easy Tables, and then select the table you want to secure. For all of the permission options, set the value to Authenticated Access Only and select Save.

10. If you deployed a C# backend, in the controller for your project that inherits from Table-Controller, decorate the class with the Authorize attribute. For example:

```
[Authorize]

  public class TodoItemController : TableController<TodoItem>
```

11. If you have deployed a customized Node.js backend, you need to modify the code accessing the table and set the access property to authenticated. For example:

```
table.access = 'authenticated';
```

12. Add the authentication logic to your app project. The specific steps to take vary based upon the target platform for your app, but in general they amount adding user interface elements to initiate sign-in and handling the authentication events. An important step in the configuration of the authentication is providing the value of your scheme you defined for the Allowed External Redirects URL (e.g., myapp).

13. Run your application in your local simulator or device to verify the authentication flow.

Add offline sync to a mobile app

The offline data sync capability comes from a mix of client-side SDK and service-side features. This capability enables reads as well as create, update and delete activity to happen against the supporting tables even when the device is not connected to a network, and coordinates the synchronization of data between local and cloud stores as dictated by the application logic (e.g., network connectivity is detected or the user presses a "Sync" button). The feature includes support for conflict detection when the same record is changed on both the client and the backend, and it allows for the conflicts to be resolved on either the client side or service side.

- On the Mobile App service side, you need a table that leverages Mobile App easy tables. This is typically a table in SQL Database that is exposed by Mobile Apps using the OData endpoint. Easy tables can be managed in the Mobile App blade in the portal, including adjusting their schema, setting permissions, and modifying the service side script (for Node.js backends) that processes the create, read, update, delete (CRUD) operations.

- On the client side, the Azure Mobile App SDKs provide an interface referred to as a SyncTable that wraps access to the remote easy table. When using a SyncTable all the CRUD operations work from a local store, whose implementation is device platform specific. The local store provides the data persistence capability on the client device. In iOS the local store is based on Core Data, and for Windows, Xamarin, and Android the local store is based on SQL lite.

Changes to the data are made through a sync context object that tracks the changes that are made across all of the tables. This sync context maintains an operation queue that is an ordered list of create, update and delete operations that have been performed against the data locally.

- To modify the backend table data with the changes performed against the local store, you have to perform a push. To populate the local store with data from the backend, you have to perform a pull. A push operation executes a series of REST calls to your mobile app backend that applies all the CUD changes since the last push. It's important to note that when you push changes, you are always pushing a set containing at least one operation; you are not pushing a specific table. This restriction ensures that multiple operations against the context that may span across multiple tables are replayed against the backend table in the correct order.

- There is a notion of an implicit push; this occurs when you execute a pull operation but have pending operations to push. In this case, the pull will first execute a push against the sync context.

- Offline sync supports incremental sync, whereby each time you pull records from the source only the source records that are new or have changed are retrieved (as opposed to downloading the entire table worth of data every time). You can clear the contents of the local store by performing a purge.

You can enable Offline Sync by following these high-level steps:

1. Modify the client code that accesses your easy tables to use objects of the SyncTable variety.

2. Implement a method that is run when your application first launches that defines the table schema and initializes the local store with data from the remote table.

3. Implement a method that launches initiate sync operation. This could be triggered from a button or refresh gesture.

4. You can test the offline behavior of your app by:

5. Running the application once as normal and adding data to your table.

6. Modifying the application's configuration so that it no longer points to the correct URI of your mobile app backend.

7. Run the application again. This time the offline behavior should take affect. Make some modifications to the data.

8. Restore the application's configuration.

9. Run the application again and verify that the changes you made while offline appear in your easy table. To do this, navigate to the blade of your mobile app, select Easy Tables from the menu, and then select your table to view its contents.

Add push notifications to a mobile app

Push notifications enable you to send app-specific messages to your app running across a variety of platforms. In Azure Mobile Apps, push notification capabilities are provided by Azure Notification Hubs, which is accessed using the Mobile Apps SDKs for the platform of choice. Notification Hubs, in turn, abstract your application from the complexities of dealing with the various push notification systems (PNS) that are specific to each platform, which includes challenges like device registration with the PNS, backend services to send messages to the PNS, and provides for routing of messages to targeted users or groups of users (which requires maintaining a mapping of users to devices), and scaling to support such functions across a huge base of devices. Notifications Hubs supports the sending of notifications across the most popular push notifications services for Apple (APNS), Google (GCM), Windows (WNS), Windows Phone (MPNS), Amazon (ADM), and Baidu (Android China) devices.

To add push notifications, follow these steps:

1. Deploy a Notification Hub with your mobile app.

2. Navigate to the blade of your mobile app, and on the menu under the Settings heading, select Push.

3. From the Command bar, select Connect.

4. On the Notification Hub blade, choose an existing Notification Hub or provision a new one. If you choose to provision a new Notification Hub, provide a name for the hub, a name for the new namespace, and select the desired pricing tier, and then select OK.

5. Select the link Configure Push Notification Services.

6. On the Push Notification Services blade, select the PNS to which you want to connect the Notification Hub.

7. On the blade for the PNS, enter the PNS specific configuration, and select Save.

8. Configure your backend server project to send push notifications.

9. Modify the app project to respond to push notifications.

> **MORE INFO**   **RECEIVING PUSH NOTIFICATIONS IN THE CLIENT APP**
>
> Coverage of the implementation details of receiving push notifications for every platform supported by Mobile Apps is out of scope for this book. To read the implementation details for your particular platform navigate to *https://docs.microsoft.com/ en-us/azure/app-service-mobile/app-service-mobile-xamarin-forms-get-started-push#configure-and-run-the-android-project-optional* and use the drop-down at the top of the article to select your platform.

Skill 4.5: Implement API Management

Azure API Management is a turnkey solution for publishing, managing, securing, and analyzing APIs to both external and internal customers in minutes. You can create an API gateway for back-end services hosted anywhere, not just those hosted on Azure. Many modern APIs protect themselves by rate-limiting consumers, meaning, limiting how many requests can be made in a certain amount of time. Traditionally, there is a lot of work that goes into that process. When you use API Management to manage your API, you can easily secure it and protect it from abuse and overuse with an API key, JWT validation, IP filtering, and through quotas and rate limits.

If you have several APIs as part of your solution, and they are hosted across several services or platforms, you can group them all behind a single static IP and domain, simplifying communication, protection, and reducing maintenance of consumer software due to API locations changing. You also can scale API Management on demand in one or more geographical locations. Its built-in response caching also helps with improving latency and scale.

Hosting your APIs on the API Management platform also makes it easier for developers to use your APIs, by offering self-service API key management, and an auto-generated API catalog through the developer portal. APIs are also documented and come with code examples, reducing developer on-boarding time using your APIs.

API Management is made up of the following components:

- The *API gateway* is the endpoint that:
    - Accepts API calls and routes them to your backends.
    - Verifies API keys, JWT tokens, certificates, and other credentials.
    - Enforces usage quotas and rate limits.
    - Transforms your API on the fly without code modifications.
    - Caches backend responses where set up.
    - Logs call metadata for analytics purposes.

- The *publisher portal* is the administrative interface where you set up your API program. Use it to:
  - Define or import API schema.
  - Package APIs into products.
  - Set up policies like quotas or transformations on the APIs.
  - Get insights from analytics.
  - Manage users.
- The *developer portal* serves as the main web presence for developers, where they can:
  - Read API documentation.
  - Try out an API via the interactive console.
  - Create an account and subscribe to get API keys.
  - Access analytics on their own usage.

This skill covers how to:
- Create managed APIs
- Configure API management policies
- Protect APIs with rate limits
- Add caching to improve performance
- Monitor APIs
- Customize the Developer Portal

Create managed APIs

The API Management service is the platform on which the API gateway, publisher portal, and developer portal are hosted. As such, before you can create APIs, you must first create a service instance.

Create an API Management service

1. Navigate to the portal accessed via *https://portal.azure.com*.
2. Select New on the command bar.
3. Select Developer Tools, and then API Management (Figure 4-75).

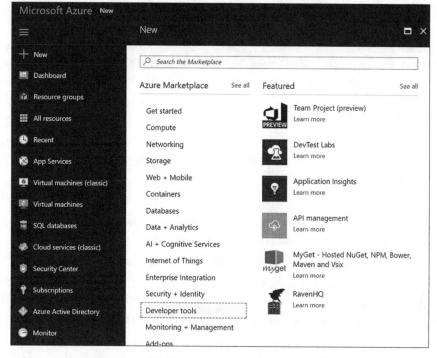

FIGURE 4-75 Creating a new API Management service instance from the Azure Portal

4. Provide a unique name, select a resource group and location, enter an organization name that will appear on the developer portal and emails, an administrator email, your pricing tier, select Pin To Dashboard, and then click Create.

Add a product

Before you can publish an API, it needs to be added to a product. A product in API Management contains one or more APIs, as well as constraints such as a usage quota and terms of use. This is a great way to add API access levels, like starter (limit to five calls/minute) or unlimited. You can create several products to group APIs with their own usage rules. Developers can subscribe to a product once it is published, and then begin using its APIs.

Follow these steps to add and publish a new product:

1. Navigate to your API Management service on the portal.

2. Select Publisher Portal on the top of the overview blade.

3. Select Products on the left-hand menu, and then click Add Product.

4. Within the new product form, provide a Title, which should be a descriptive name for your product that appears on the developer and admin portals. Provide a Description that explains the product's purpose and any other information you want to display. The remaining fields allow you to set your level of protection, meaning, whether your product requires a subscription, and if so, whether the subscription needs to be approved by

an administrator, and whether developers can subscribe more than once. Once finished, click Save.

5. Once the product has been added, you need to add one or more APIs to it before you can publish it. Select a product, and then click the Add API To Product link. This gives you a list of APIs that you can assign to the product.

Create a new API

1. Navigate to your API Management service on the portal.

2. Select Publisher Portal on the top of the overview blade.

3. Select APIs on the left-hand menu, and then click Add API.

4. Within the new product form (Figure 4-76):

   A. Provide a unique Web API Name, which should be a descriptive name for your API that appears on the developer and publisher portals.

   B. Enter the Web Service URL, which is the HTTP endpoint for your API.

   C. Enter the Web Service URL suffix, which is unique to your API, and is the last part of the API's public URL.

   D. Select the desired Web API URL Scheme (HTTP or HTTPS (default)).

   E. Select the product you created and any others you want to add it to.

   F. When finished, click OK.

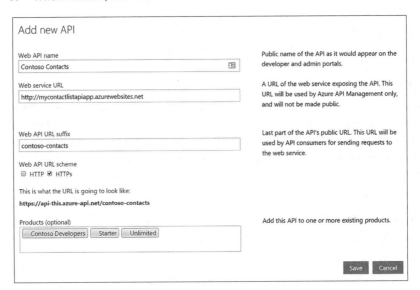

FIGURE 4-76 Completing the Response action form for the logic app

Add an operation to your API

Before you can use your new API, you must add one or more operations. These operations do things like enable service documentation, the interactive API console, set per operation limits, set request/response validation, and configure operation-level statistics.

1. Navigate to your API Management service on the portal.

2. Select Publisher Portal on the top of the overview blade.

3. Select APIs on the left-hand menu, select your API from the list, and then select the Operations tab.

4. Click + Add Operation.

5. By default, the Signature tab will be selected. The Signature is the URL template used to send requests to the underlying API. Here you select (Figure 4-77):

    A. The HTTP verb (GET, POST, etc.).

    B. Type in the URL template (e.g. /contacts/{id}).

    C. Type in a display name, and description.

    D. You can also add a rewrite URL template to call the back-end with a converted URL.

FIGURE 4-77 Adding a new operation to a managed API

6. Select the Parameters tab. New query parameters are automatically generated based on the URL template defined in the signature. In our case, an id template parameter was generated because the URL template of our signature for this operation is /contacts/{id}. Specify the type (string, number, etc.) and provide a description for each query parameter (Figure 4-78).

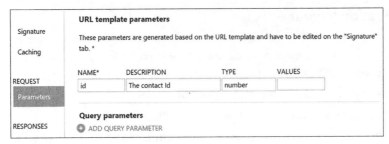

FIGURE 4-78 URL template parameters

7. You can optionally use the other tabs to specify caching and responses for the operation. Click Save when finished.

Publish your product to make your API available

The last step to making your API available to other developers is to publish your product to which this and any other APIs have been added.

To publish your product, follow these steps:

1. Navigate to your API Management service on the portal.
2. Select Publisher portal on the top of the overview blade.
3. Select Products on the left-hand menu, and then click select your product from the list.
4. The summary tab will indicate whether your product has been published, and any associated APIs. You must have at least one API added before you can publish. Click the Publish link.
5. When the confirmation appears, click Yes, and then publish it.
6. After publishing, select the Visibility tab. Choose which roles, such as developers, you want to be able to see the product on the developer portal and subscribe to the product. Click Save when finished.

> **MORE INFO   ADD AND PUBLISH AN API PRODUCT**
>
> To learn more about creating and publishing a product in API Management see *https://docs.microsoft.com/azure/api-management/api-management-howto-add-products*.

Configure API Management policies

API Management policies allow you, as the publisher, to determine the behavior of your APIs through configuration, requiring no code changes. You define a policy definition, which is a collection of statements that are executed sequentially on the request or response of your API. There are many policies you can select from, such as whether to allow cross domain calls, how to authenticate requests, find and replace strings in the body, setting rate limits, and many more.

Because the API gateway receives all requests to your APIs, the policies you defined are applied at this level. The policies statements you choose affect both inbound requests and outbound responses. Policies can be applied globally, or scoped to the Product, API, or Operation level.

To configure a policy, follow these steps:

1. Navigate to your API Management service on the portal.

2. Select Publisher Portal on the top of the overview blade.

3. Select Policies on the left-hand menu.

4. At the top of the policies page, you will find select lists to define the policy scope at the Product, API, and Operations levels. If you do not select a specific operation, all operations are included in this policy. To create a policy scoped globally, simply deselect any options from these select lists (Figure 4-79).

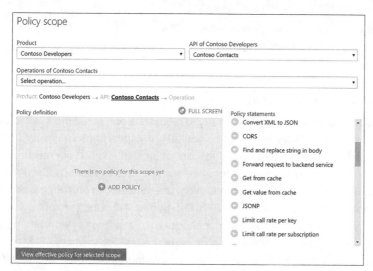

FIGURE 4-79 Policies page for an API Management service in the Publisher portal

5. To add a new policy to the selected policy scope, select + Add Policy link in the Policy definition area.

6. The policy definition will appear in XML format. To add an inbound policy that limits the call rate per key, place your cursor just inside the content of the inbound XML element, and then click the Limit Call Rate Per Key policy statement on the right. This adds the statement to rate limit inbound requests to the number of calls you specify within your defined period of time in seconds, and any other conditions you desire (Figure 4-80).

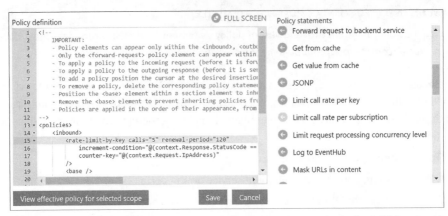

FIGURE 4-80 Editing the policy definition for an API Management service in the Publisher portal

7. When you are finished, click Save. Your changes will be immediately applied to the API Management gateway.

> **MORE INFO APPLYING POLICIES IN API MANAGEMENT**
>
> For more information about how to apply policies in API Management see: *https://docs. microsoft.com/azure/api-management/api-management-howto-policies*.

Protect APIs with rate limits

Protecting your published APIs by throttling incoming requests is one of the most attractive offerings of API Management. When you open up your API for others to use, it is difficult to guarantee a promised level of service if you cannot control the demand on your resources. Or, you may be interested in controlling your resource costs by limiting requests, preventing you from unnecessarily scaling up your services to meet unexpected demand. Rate limiting, or throttling, is common practice when providing APIs. Oftentimes, API publishers offer varying levels of access to their APIs. For instance, you may choose to offer a free tier with very restrictive rate limits, and various paid tiers offering higher request rates. This is where API Management's products come into play. Define products for your varying service levels, and apply rate limiting policies to each product, accordingly.

Create a product to scope rate limits to a group of APIs

The following steps show how to create a free trial, adding APIs that developers can use on a rate-limited free trial basis:

1. Navigate to your API Management service on the portal.
2. Select Publisher Portal on the top of the Overview blade.
3. Create a new product named Free Trial.

4. Set the description to Subscribers Will Be Able To Run 10 Calls/Minute Up To A Maximum Of 200 Calls/Week.

5. Set the visibility to Developers.

6. Add your APIs to the product and publish it.

7. Go to Policies and set the policy scope to the free trial product.

8. Click + Add Policy.

9. Position the cursor within the inbound element.

10. Scroll through the list of policy statements and select Limit Call Rate Per Subscription. Modify the XML to set calls to 10 and renewal-period to 60. You can delete the API and operation elements because they are not needed in this scenario.

11. Position your cursor immediately below the rate-limit element you added. Select Set Usage Quota Per Subscription in the list of policy statements. Modify the XML to set calls to 200 and renewal-period to 604800. You can delete the API and operation elements because they are not needed in this scenario.

12. Save your changes. In the end, your inbound policy should look as follows (Figure 4-81):

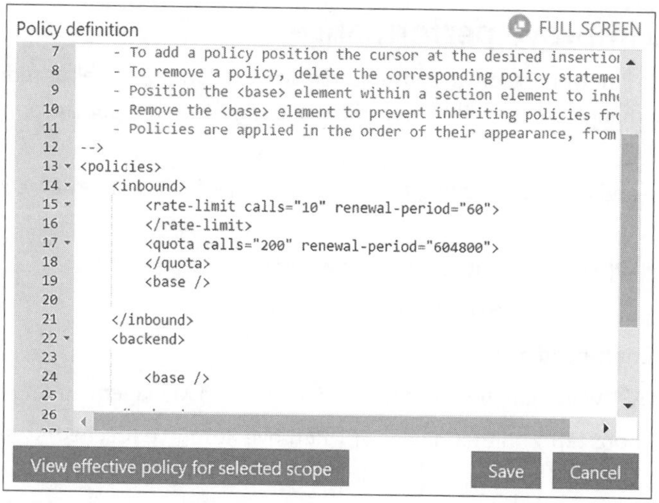

FIGURE 4-81 Editing the policy definition to set rate limits on a product

Advanced rate limiting

In its simplest implementation, you can control the rate of requests or the total requests/data transferred. These constraints do not help when individual end-users of your API consume exponentially more of the quota than other users. If you want to avoid having high-usage consumers limit access to occasional users, by using up the pool of available resources, consider using the new rate-limit-by-key and quota-by-key policies. These are more flexible rate limiting policies that allow you to define expressions to track traffic usage by user-level information, such as IP address and user identity.

Here is an example of rate and quota limiting by IP address:

```
<rate-limit-by-key  calls="10"
        renewal-period="60"
        counter-key="@(context.Request.IpAddress)" />

<quota-by-key calls="1000000"
        bandwidth="10000"
        renewal-period="2629800"
        counter-key="@(context.Request.IpAddress)" />
```

> **MORE INFO   ADVANCED RATE LIMITING**
>
> For more information about advanced rate limiting through flexible request throttling see *https://docs.microsoft.com/azure/api-management/api-management-sample-flexible-throttling*.

Add caching to improve performance

Caching is a great way to limit your resource consumption, like bandwidth, as well as reduce latency for infrequently changing data. API Management allows you to configure response caching on operations.

Follow these steps to add response caching for your API (Figure 4-82), and review caching policies:

1. Navigate to your API Management service on the portal.
2. Select Publisher portal on the top of the overview blade.
3. Select APIs on the left-hand menu.
4. Select the ECHO API, which is automatically added to new API Management services.
5. Select the Operations tab, and then select GET Retrieve Resource (Cached) from the list.

FIGURE 4-82 The API operations tab

6. Select the Caching tab (Figure 4-83) to view the caching settings. To enable cach-
    ing on an operation, select the Enable check box. You can modify the keyed operation
    responses by setting values in the Vary By Query String Parameters and Vary By Headers
    fields. In this case, cache keys are being computed on two different headers: Accept
    and Accept-Charset. Duration sets the cache duration in seconds. Here it is set to 3600
    seconds.

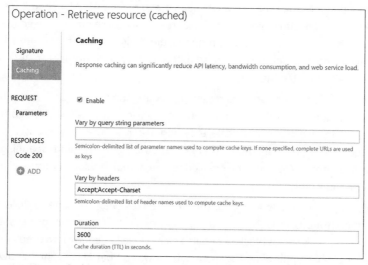

FIGURE 4-83 Caching settings for the GET operation of the Echo API

7. Select Policies from the left-hand menu of the publisher portal.

8. Select Echo API from the API select list, and then Retrieve Resource (Cached) from the Operation select list.

9. Here you see that the caching policies in the policy editor reflect the values in the Caching tab of the operation. Any changes here are reflected on the Caching tab, and vice-versa.

> ***MORE INFO*** **CUSTOM CACHING IN API MANAGEMENT**
>
> To learn how to implement custom caching see *https://docs.microsoft.com/azure/api-management/api-management-sample-cache-by-key.*

Monitor APIs

API Management provides a few methods by which you can monitor resource usage, service health, activities, and analytics. If you want real-time monitoring, as well as richer debugging, you can enable diagnostics on your logic app and send events to OMS with Log Analytics, or to other services, such as Azure Storage, and Event Hubs. Select Diagnostics Logs from the left-hand menu of your API Management service, and then select Turn On Diagnostics to archive your gateway logs and metrics to a storage account, stream to an event hub, or send to Log Analytics on OMS.

Activity logs provide insight into the operations that were performed on your API Management services, so you can determine the "what, who, and when" for any write operations taken on your API Management services. Select Activity Log from the left-hand menu to filter and view these logs. From here, you can select Export to archive these logs in a storage account or send them to an event hub. You can also select Log Analytics to send the logs to OMS.

- Select Metrics under Monitoring in the left-hand menu of your API Management service to view the state and health of your APIs in near real-time. These metrics are emitted every minute. You can monitor gateway requests, determine which of those were successful or failed, and also view unauthorized gateway requests. It displays an interactive chart based on the selected metrics.

- Select Alert rules under Monitoring to create alerts based on metrics (such as any time failed gateway requests occur over a one-hour period), activity logs (with categories such as security, service health, autoscale, etc.), and near real time metrics, based on the data captured by your API Management service's metrics, in time periods spanning from one minute to 24 hours. Alerts can be emailed to one or more recipients, route alerts to a webhook, or run a logic app.

Open the publisher portal to view Analytics. This shows an overview of usage by developers, top products, top subscriptions, top APIs, and top operations. Each of these categories show the number of successful calls versus blocked or failed calls, as well as bandwidth used and average response time, when applicable. The usage tab shows number of calls and bandwidth by region, highlighting countries on a map, corresponding with the origin of the requests. You can select any continent or country to drill down further into the selected region. The health tab shows statistics about status codes, caching, API response time, and Service response time. Finally, the activity tab shows more detailed information about requests by developers, on products, by subscriptions, for APIs, and on which operations.

> **MORE INFO**   **MONITOR API MANAGEMENT**
>
> To learn more about how to monitor an API Management service see *https://docs.microsoft. com/azure/api-management/api-management-howto-use-azure-monitor.*

Customize the developer portal

The API Management developer portal is built on top of a content management system (CMS), which gives you flexibility on ways you can customize its layout, content, and styles. Because this is the portal through which developers discover, subscribe to, and learn more about your APIs, you may wish to alter the look and feel to more closely match your company's website, or craft the experience for your end users in general.

There are three different methods by which you can customize the developer portal.

Edit static page content and layout elements

The layout of every page of the developer portal is based on small page elements called widgets (Figure 4-84).

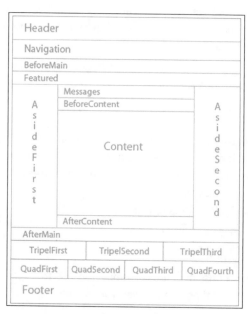

FIGURE 4-84 The widget layout of the developer portal

The content area on the page is specific to an individual page's contents. Any Contents widget can be edited to modify that page's content. The page layout elements are comprised of the remaining widgets. Any edits made to these layout widgets are applied to all pages within the portal.

To edit the contents of a layout widget, perform the following steps:

1. Navigate to your API Management service on the portal.
2. Select Publisher portal on the top of the overview blade.
3. Select Widgets on the left-hand menu, underneath the DEVELOPER PORTAL section.
4. Select the widget you wish to edit, such as Banner.
5. The Edit Widget form allows you to select the zone for the widget, layer, position, title, name (used for CSS), and its HTML.
6. Make changes as desired, and then click Save. You immediately see your changes on the developer portal.

To edit the contents of a page, perform the following steps:

1. Navigate to your API Management service on the portal.
2. Select Publisher portal on the top of the overview blade.
3. Select Content on the left-hand menu, underneath the DEVELOPER PORTAL section.
4. Select the page you wish to edit, such as Welcome.
5. The Edit Page form allows you change the page title, select whether you wish to display the title on the front-end, and its HTML.
6. Make changes as desired, and then click Save. When you are satisfied with your changes, click Publish Now to make those changes visible to everyone. You immediately see your changes on the developer portal.

Using these tools, you can add new layout widgets, as well as new pages. Use the Navigation area to create custom menu links or rearrange their order.

Customize the styling

Change the colors, fonts, spacing, and other styles by altering the style rules in the developer portal. For instance, change the colors and fonts to match your company's website. To change these style rules, you need to be logged in to the developer portal as an administrator. This requires opening the developer portal from the publisher portal.

1. Navigate to your API Management service on the portal.
2. Select Publisher portal on the top of the overview blade.
3. Select Developer portal from the top-right of the page.
4. On the developer portal, hover your mouse over the customization icon to display the customization toolbar (Figure 4-85), and then select Styles from the toolbar.

FIGURE 4-85 The customization toolbar in the developer portal

5. In the list of editable styles that appear, you can either look through the list and change style values as you see fit, or click the Select An Element On The Page button, and then select any element on the page to view only its styles.

6. When you are finished making edits, click the Publish button at the bottom of the customization toolbar. This will show a preview of your changes. When satisfied, click the Publish Customizations button to make your changes publicly available.

Customize using templates

Use templates to customize the system-generated developer pages, such as API docs, user authentication, products, etc. Template markup uses the DotLiquid syntax, based on Ruby's Liquid markup, to alter the appearance and behavior of the corresponding page. Dynamic content in the template is controlled through tokenized strings. When you select a template to edit, there are three panes that are displayed. The top pane is a preview of the corresponding page. On the bottom left is the template editing pane where you edit the markup, and on the bottom right is the template data pane. This pane serves as a guide to the data model for the entities available in the selected template. You can reference the template data when adding tokenized strings to the template beside it.

To edit templates, follow these steps:

1. Navigate to your API Management service on the portal.

2. Select Publisher portal on the top of the overview blade.

3. Select Developer portal from the top-right of the page.

4. On the developer portal, hover your mouse over the customization icon to display the customization toolbar, and then select Templates from the toolbar.

5. Select the template you wish to edit from the list.

6. Alter the template markup, using the bottom-left template editing pane. Here you can use a mix of HTML and tokenized strings. Reference the template data to the right to view tokenized strings you can add to the template, and the values they will display if you reference them. All changes will update the preview pane on top in real time.

7. When finished editing, click the save icon in the template editing pane.

8. Saved templates can be published either individually, or all together. To publish an individual template, click Publish in the template editor.

9. Click Yes to confirm and make your changes to the template live on the developer portal.

> **MORE INFO   EDIT STATIC PAGE CONTENT AND LAYOUT ELEMENTS**
>
> To learn more about editing static page content and layout elements on the developer portal see *https://docs.microsoft.com/azure/api-management/api-management-modify-content-layout*.

> **MORE INFO   CUSTOMIZE THE STYLING**
>
> For more information on how customize the styling of the developer portal, see *https://docs.microsoft.com/azure/api-management/api-management-customize-styles*.

> **MORE INFO   CUSTOMIZE USING TEMPLATES**
>
> For more information on how to customize the developer portal using templates see *https://docs.microsoft.com/azure/api-management/api-management-developer-portal-templates*.

Skill 4.6: Implement Azure Functions and WebJobs

Azure Functions is a serverless compute service that enables you to run code on-demand without having to explicitly provision or manage infrastructure. Use Azure Functions to run a script or piece of code in response to a variety of events from sources such as:

- HTTP requests
- Timers
- Webhooks
- Azure Cosmos DB
- Blob
- Queues
- Event Hub

When it comes to implementing background processing tasks, the main options in Azure are Azure Functions and WebJobs. It is important to mention, however, that Functions are actually built on top of WebJobs. The choice to use one or the other really depends on the problem you are trying to solve. For example, if you already have an app service running a website or a web API and you require a background process to run in the same context, a WebJob makes the most sense. Here are two examples that may drive you to using a WebJob:

- **The Service Plan** You want to share compute resources between the website or API and the WebJob.
- **Shared libraries** The WebJob should share libraries that run the website or API.

Otherwise, for situations where you want to externalize a process so that it runs and scales independently from your web application or API environment, or you are implementing an event handler in response to some external event (i.e., a Webhook); Azure Functions are the more modern serverless technology to choose.

MORE INFO **AZURE FUNCTIONS**

For a general references on Azure Functions see *https://docs.microsoft.com/en-us/azure/azure-functions/.*

This skill covers how to:

- Create Azure Functions
- Implement a webhook function
- Create an event processing function
- Implement an Azure-connected function
- Integrate a Function with storage
- Debug a Function
- Design and implement a custom binding
- Implement and configure proxies
- Integrate with App Service Plan

Create Azure Functions

The Azure portal gives you a quick and easy way to create a functions app, add functions based on a template and test the function.

NOTE **VISUAL STUDIO 2017**

You can also develop, test, and publish functions using Visual Studio 2017.

To create a function app in the portal follow these steps (Figure 4-86):

1. Navigate to the portal accessed via *https://portal.azure.com*.
2. Select New on the command bar.
3. Select Compute, and then Function App.
4. Click Create and supply the app name, subscription, resource group, hosting plan, location, and storage plan (if you select Consumption plan).

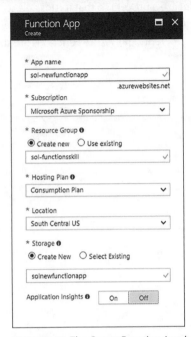

FIGURE 4-86 The Create Function App blade

5. After a few minutes, the Functions App is created (Figure 4-87).

FIGURE 4-87 A new function app

MORE INFO **CREATING FUNCTIONS WITH AZURE CLI**

You can also create functions using Azure CLI and from Visual Studio. See these references at: *https://docs.microsoft.com/en-us/azure/azure-functions/functions-create-first-azure-function-azure-cli* and *https://docs.microsoft.com/en-us/azure/azure-functions/functions-create-your-first-function-visual-studio*.

Implement a Webhook function

Visual Studio provides a complete development and debugging environment for Azure Functions with the addition of Azure Functions Extension. To create a Webhook function using Visual Studio 2017, follow these steps:

1. Ensure you have the Functions App Visual Studio Extension installed first (Figure 4-88).

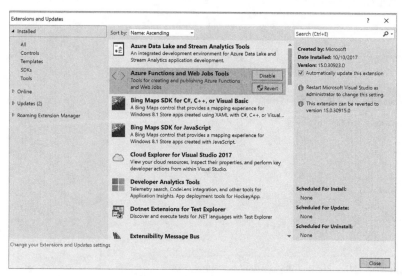

FIGURE 4-88 Azure Functions and WebJobs Tools

2. In the New Project dialog, expand Visual C# > Cloud node, select Azure Functions, type a Name for your project, and click OK (Figure 4-89).

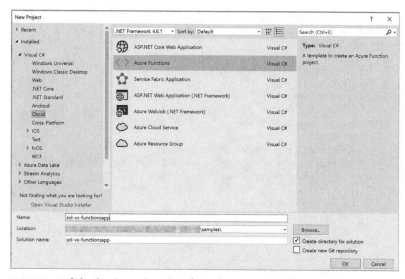

FIGURE 4-89 Selecting Azure Functions from the New Project dialog

3. This creates a new Functions App in your subscription. You may have to log in to the Azure portal to complete the process.

4. From Visual Studio, go to Solution Explorer, right-click the project node, and select Add > New Item. Select Azure Function, and click Add.

5. From the New Azure Function dialog, select Generic WebHook, type the function name, and click OK (Figure 4-90).

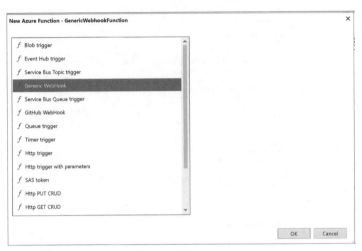

FIGURE 4-90 Selecting the type of Azure Function

6. This generates an initial implementation for your function. The FunctionName attribute sets the name of your function. The HttpTrigger(WebHookType = "genericJson") attribute indicates the message that triggers the function.

```
using Microsoft.Azure.WebJobs;
using Microsoft.Azure.WebJobs.Host;
using Newtonsoft.Json;
using System.Net;
using System.Net.Http;
using System.Threading.Tasks;
namespace SolVsFunctionapp
{
    public static class GenericWebhookFunction
    {
        [FunctionName("GenericWebhookFunction")]
        public static async Task<object> Run([HttpTrigger(WebHookType =
"genericJson")]HttpRequestMessage req, TraceWriter log)
        {
            log.Info($"Webhook was triggered!");

            string jsonContent = await req.Content.ReadAsStringAsync();
            dynamic data = JsonConvert.DeserializeObject(jsonContent);

            if (data.first == null || data.last == null)
            {
```

```
                return req.CreateResponse(HttpStatusCode.BadRequest, new
                {
                    error = "Please pass first/last properties in the input
object"
                });
            }

            return req.CreateResponse(HttpStatusCode.OK, new
            {
                greeting = $"Hello {data.first} {data.last}!"
            });
        }
    }
}
```

7. You ran run the function from Visual Studio directly using Azure Functions Tools. Press F5 to run. If prompted, accept the download and install Azure Functions Core tools.

8. You can copy the URL of your function from the Azure Function runtime output (Figure 4-91).

FIGURE 4-91 The console output after running a Webhook function from Visual Studio

9. You can now post a JSON payload to the function using any tool that an issue HTTP requests to test the function.

Create an event processing function

To create an event processing function, please complete these steps:

1. Navigate to the portal accessed via *https://portal.azure.com*.

2. Go to your Function App, such as the one created in the previous section, and click the + sign to create a new function (Figure 4-92).

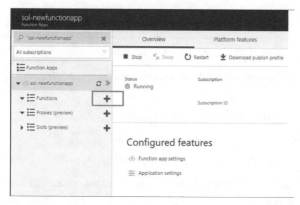

FIGURE 4-92 The Function Apps blade where you can create a new function

3. Select Timer and CSharp, and select Create This Function (Figure 4-93).

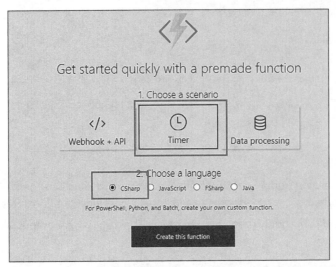

FIGURE 4-93 The Function Apps blade where you can choose the type of function

4. This creates a skeleton function that runs based on a timer. You can edit the function. json file to adjust settings for the function (Figure 4-94).

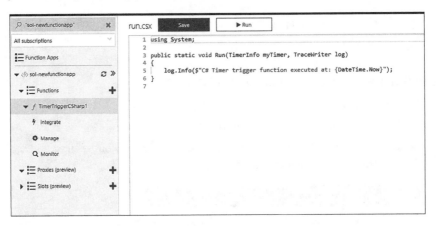

FIGURE 4-94 A new timer-based function

5. You can view the output of the function and any logs emitted as it executes.

Implement an Azure-connected function

To create an Azure-connected function using Azure Queues, follow these steps:

1. Navigate to the portal accessed via *https://portal.azure.com*.

2. Go to your Function App, such as the one used in the previous section, and click the + sign to create a new function.

3. Select QueueTrigger - C#, provide a name for the function, provide the name of the queue and the storage account that it belongs to. Click Create to create the function (Figure 4-95).

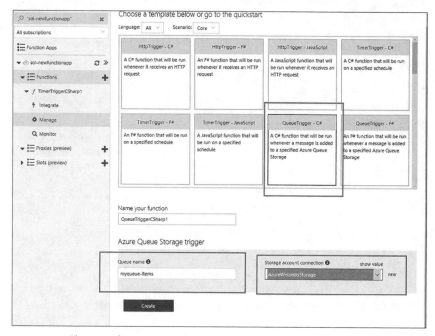

FIGURE 4-95 The setup for a QueueTrigger

4. A skeleton implementation for the function is created. This is triggered for each message written to the specified queue (Figure 4-96).

```csharp
run.csx         Save              ▶ Run

1  using System;
2
3  public static void Run(string myQueueItem, TraceWriter log)
4  {
5      log.Info($"C# Queue trigger function processed: {myQueueItem}");
6  }
7
```

FIGURE 4-96 The code behind the QueueTrigger function

5. To complete the integration, create the storage account and queue that you specified when creating the function. From the function app definition, select the Integrate tab, and select the storage queue under Triggers. Expand the Documentation link and enter the storage account name and key. The function will use these credentials to connect to the storage account (Figure 4-97).

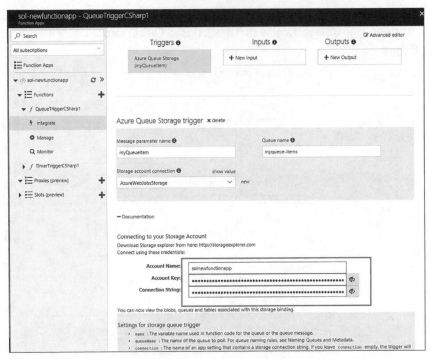

FIGURE 4-97 The integration blade for setting up the storage queue trigger credentials

To test the function, add a message to the queue. After a few seconds the function log in the portal shows output from processing the message (Figure 4-98).

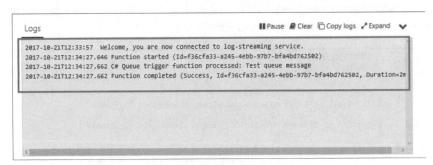

FIGURE 4-98 The log output for the function after processing a single message

Integrate a function with storage

To create a function integrated with Azure Storage Blobs, follow these steps:

1. Navigate to the portal accessed via *https://portal.azure.com*.

2. Go to your Function App, such as the one used in the previous section, and click the + sign to create a new function.

3. Select BlobTrigger - C#, provide a name for the function, provide the path to the blob container item and the storage account that it belongs to. Click Create to create the function (Figure 4-99).

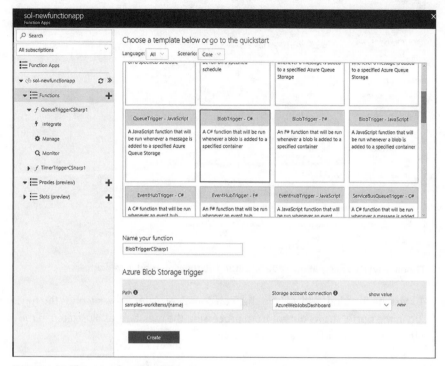

FIGURE 4-99 The setup for a BlobTrigger

4. A skeleton implementation for the function is created. This is triggered for each blob written to the specified storage container (Figure 4-100).

```
run.csx        Save           ▶ Run
1  public static void Run(Stream myBlob, string name, TraceWriter log)
2  {
3      log.Info($"C# Blob trigger function Processed blob\n Name:{name} \n Si
4  }
5
```

FIGURE 4-100 The code behind the BlobTrigger function

5. To complete the integration, create the storage account and blob container that you specified when creating the function. From the function app definition, select the Integrate tab, and select Azure Blob Storage under Triggers. Expand the Documentation link, and enter the storage account name and key. The function uses these credentials to connect to the storage account (Figure 4-101).

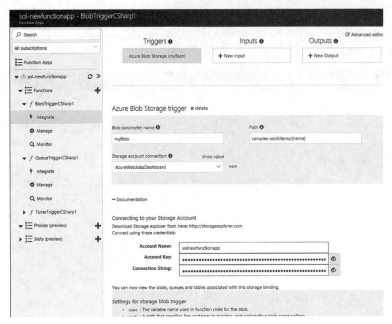

FIGURE 4-101 The integration blade for setting up the blob trigger credentials

6. To test the function, add a file to the blob container. After a few seconds the function log in the portal shows output from processing the message, as illustrated in the previous section for Azure storage queues.

Design and implement a custom binding

Function triggers indicate how a function is invoked. There are a number of predefined triggers, some already discussed in previous sections, including:

- HTTP triggers
- Event triggers
- Queues and topic triggers
- Storage triggers

Every function must have one trigger. The trigger is usually associated with a data payload that is supplied to the function. Bindings are a declarative way to map data to and from function code. Using the Integrate tab (as shown in previous sections to connect a Queue to a function, for example) you can provide connection settings for such a data binding activity.

> **MORE INFO TRIGGERS AND BINDINGS**
>
> For additional details on triggers and bindings available to Azure Functions, and how they work, see *https://docs.microsoft.com/en-us/azure/azure-functions/functions-triggers-bindings*.

Debug a Function

You can use VS Code or Visual Studio 2017 to debug an Azure Function. For more information on working with local Functions projects and local debugging, see: *https://docs.microsoft.com/en-us/azure/azure-functions/functions-run-local*.

Implement and configure proxies

If you have a solution with many functions you'll find it can become work to manage given the different URLs, naming, and versioning potentially related to each function. An API Proxy acts as a single point of entry to functions from the outside world. Instead of calling the individual function URLs, you provide a proxy as a facade to your different function URLs.

> **NOTE** **API PROXIES**
>
> API Proxies make sense in HTTP-bound Azure Functions. They may work for other event-driven functions, however, HTTP triggers are best suited for their functionality. In addition, API Proxies are in preview at the time of this writing and do not include any security features. As an alternative, you can use API Management for a fully featured solution.

To create a simple API Proxy, follow these steps (Figure 4-102):

1. Consider an existing function that includes the function code (API key) and any query string parameters in the URL such as the following example:

   ```
   https://sol-newfunctionapp.azurewebsites.net/api/
   AirplanesApi?code=N8eJPFEkD1MkOeQngOqRsaLVxeHRQ4QcxacFRdLtMDBdak3eeN/
   kNQ==&id=0099991
   ```

2. API proxies require two important pieces of information:

   A. **The Route Template**   Provides a template of how the proxies are triggered, for example a REST-compliant API path that removes the need for the function code and query string parameters:

   ```
   /api/airplanes/86327
   ```

   B. **The Backend URL**   The function URL to match to.

FIGURE 4-102 The settings while creating a new API proxy

3. Update the Backend URL too so that it uses the variables provided in the route template.

```
https://sol-newfunctionapp.azurewebsites.net/api/{rest}Api?code=q/
vTyTaw4wTzyFuY16wuMOnUPEhJLzRFqKRDXaChGz3/HzSOmyMaNw==&id={id}.
```

4. When you request the URL, the variables in the route template (i.e., {rest} and {id}) are replaced with whatever is passed in the request. For example, this URL:

```
https://sol-newfunctionapp.azurewebsites.net/api/airplanes/3434
```

Routes to this URL:

```
https://sol-newfunctionapp.azurewebsites.net/api/airplanesApi?code=q/
vTyTaw4wTzyFuY16wuMOnUPEhJLzRFqKRDXaChGz3/HzSOmyMaNw==&id=3434
```

EXAM TIP

API proxies have the ability to modify the requests and responses on the fly.

MORE INFO   API PROXIES

For more details about API Proxies see *https://docs.microsoft.com/en-us/azure/azure-functions/functions-proxies*.

Integrate with App Service Plan

Functions can operate in two different modes:

- **Consumption Plan**   Where your function is allocated dynamically to the amount of compute power required to execute under the current load.

- **App Service Plan**   Where your function is assigned a specific app service hosting plan and is limited to the resources available to that hosting plan.

For more information about the difference between Consumption and App Service Plans see: *https://docs.microsoft.com/en-us/azure/azure-functions/functions-scale*. For more information about setting up an App Service Plan see: *https://docs.microsoft.com/en-us/azure/app-service/azure-web-sites-web-hosting-plans-in-depth-overview*.

Skill 4.7: Design and Implement Azure Service Fabric apps

Azure Service Fabric is a platform that makes it easy to package, deploy, and manage distributed solutions at scale. It provides an easy programming model for building microservices solutions with a simple, familiar, and easy to understand development experience that supports stateless and stateful services, and actor patterns. In addition, to providing a packaging and deployment solution for these native components, Service Fabric also supports the deployment of guest executables and containers as part of the same managed and distributed system.

The following list summarizes these native and executable components:

- **Stateless Services**   Stateless Fabric-aware services that run without managed state.

- **Stateful Services**   Stateful Fabric-aware services that run with managed state where the state is close to the compute.

- **Actors**   A higher level programming model built on top of stateful services.

- **Guest Executable**   Can be any application or service that may be cognizant or not cognizant of Service Fabric.

- **Containers**   Both Linux and Windows containers are supported by Service Fabric and may be cognizant or not cognizant of Service Fabric.

This skill provides an overview of the Service Fabric programming experience.

> ***MORE INFO*   SERVICE FABRIC OVERVIEW**
>
> For an overview of Service Fabric see *https://docs.microsoft.com/en-us/azure/service-fabric*.

This skill covers how to:

- Create a Service Fabric application
- Add a web front end to a Service Fabric application
- Build an Actors-based service
- Monitor and diagnose services
- Deploy an application to a container
- Migrate apps from cloud services
- Scale a Service Fabric app
- Create, secure, upgrade, and scale Service Fabric Cluster in Azure

Create a Service Fabric application

A Service Fabric application can consist of one or more services. The application defines the deployment package for the services, and each service can have its own configuration, code, and data. A Service Fabric cluster can host multiple applications, and each has its own independent deployment and upgrade lifecycle.

> **MORE INFO** **SERVICE FABRIC APPLICATIONS**
>
> The following reference has additional information about the Service Fabric application and related concepts at *https://docs.microsoft.com/en-us/azure/service-fabric/service-fabric-application-model*.

In this skill you create a new Service Fabric application that has a stateful service. This service is reachable via RPC and is called by a web front end created in the next section. The service is called Lead Generator and returns the current count for the number of leads that have been generated and persisted with the service. Figure 4-103 illustrates the service endpoint.

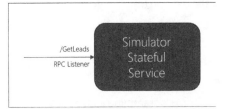

FIGURE 4-103 A simple stateful service endpoint supporting RPC communication

To create a new Service Fabric application, follow these steps:

1. Launch Visual Studio, and then select File > New > Project.
2. In the New Project dialog, select Service Fabric Application within the Cloud category. Provide a name and location for your new project, nd then click OK. In this example the name is LeadGenerator (Figure 4-104).

Microsoft.ServiceFabric.Services.Remoting by Microsoft, **236K** downloads   v2.8.219
This package contains the Service Framework Remoting APIs for building and connecting to reliable services on Microsoft Service Fabric.

FIGURE 4-104 The New Project dialog where you can select Service Fabric Application as the project type

3. Select Stateful Service from the list of service templates and provide a name, LeadGenerator.Simulator as shown here.

FIGURE 4-105 The New Service Fabric Service dialog where you can select Stateful Service as the service template

4. From Solution Explorer, expand the new LeadGenerator.Simulator node and expand the PackageRoot folder where you'll find ServiceManifest.xml. This file describes the service deployment package and related information. It includes a section that describes the service type that is initialized when the Service Fabric runtime starts the service:

```
<ServiceTypes>
  <StatefulServiceType ServiceTypeName="SimulatorType" HasPersistedState="true" />
</ServiceTypes>
```

5. A service type is created for the project; in this case the type is defined in the Simulator.cs file. This service type is registered when the program starts, in Program.cs, so that the Service Fabric runtime knows which type to initialize when it creates an instance of the service.

```
private static void Main()
{
    try
    {
        ServiceRuntime.RegisterServiceAsync("SimulatorType",
            context => new Simulator(context)).GetAwaiter().GetResult();
        ServiceEventSource.Current.ServiceTypeRegistered(Process.
GetCurrentProcess().Id,
 typeof(Simulator).Name);
        Thread.Sleep(Timeout.Infinite);
    }
    catch (Exception e)
    {
        ServiceEventSource.Current.ServiceHostInitializationFailed(e.ToString());
        throw;
    }
}
```

6. The template produces a default implementation for the service type, with a RunAsync method that increments a counter every second. This counter value is persisted with the service in a dictionary using the StateManager, available through the service base type StatefulService. This counter is used to represent the number of leads generated for the purpose of this example.

```
protected override async Task RunAsync(CancellationToken cancellationToken)
{
    var myDictionary = await this.StateManager.GetOrAddAsync<IReliableDictionary<s
tring, long>>("myDictionary");
    while (true)
    {
        cancellationToken.ThrowIfCancellationRequested();
        using (var tx = this.StateManager.CreateTransaction())
        {
            var result = await myDictionary.TryGetValueAsync(tx, "Counter");
            ServiceEventSource.Current.ServiceMessage(this.Context, "Current
Counter Value: {0}",
                result.HasValue ? result.Value.ToString() : "Value does not
exist.");
            await myDictionary.AddOrUpdateAsync(tx, "Counter", 0, (key, value)
 => ++value);
            await tx.CommitAsync();
        }
        await Task.Delay(TimeSpan.FromSeconds(1), cancellationToken);
    }
}
```

7. This service will run, and increment the counter as it runs persisting the value, but by default this service does not expose any methods for a client to call it. Before you can create an RPC listener you add the required nuget package, Microsoft.ServiceFabric. Services.Remoting.

8. Create a new service interface using the IService marker interface from the Microsoft. ServiceFabric.Services.Remoting namespace, that indicates this service can be called remotely:

```
using Microsoft.ServiceFabric.Services.Remoting;
using System.Threading.Tasks;
public interface ISimulatorService : IService
{
 Task<long> GetLeads();
}
```

9. Implement this interface on the Simulator service type, and include an implementation of the GetLeads method to return the value of the counter:

```
public async Task<long> GetLeads()
{
    var myDictionary = await StateManager.GetOrAddAsync<IReliableDictionary<stri
ng, long>>("myDictionary");
    using (var tx = StateManager.CreateTransaction())
  {
        var result = await myDictionary.TryGetValueAsync(tx, "Counter");
        await tx.CommitAsync();
        return result.HasValue ? result.Value : 0;
    }
}
```

10. To expose this method to clients, add an RPC listener to the service. Modify the Create-ServiceReplicaListeners() method in the Simulator service type implementation, to add a call to CreateServiceReplicaListeners() as shown here:

```
        protected override IEnumerable<ServiceReplicaListener>
CreateServiceReplicaListeners()          {
            yield return new ServiceReplicaListener(this.
CreateServiceRemotingListener);
        }
```

> **MORE INFO** **SERVICE FABRIC COMMUNICATION**
>
> For more information related to setting up listeners for Service Fabric stateful services see *https://docs.microsoft.com/en-us/azure/service-fabric/service-fabric-reliable-services-communication.*

Add a web front end to a Service Fabric application

The previous section reviewed creating a simple stateful service that returns the value of a counter over RPC. To illustrate calling this service from a client application, this section reviews how to create a web front end and call a stateful service endpoint, as illustrated in Figure 4-106.

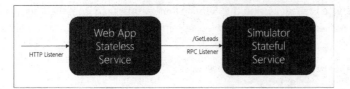

FIGURE 4-106 An HTTP listener-based web app calling a stateful service over RPC

Follow these steps to add a web app to an existing Service Fabric application:

1. From the Solution Explorer in Visual Studio, expand the Service Fabric application node. Right-click the Services node, and select New Service Fabric Service (Figure 4-107).

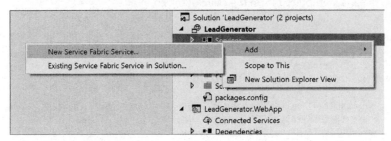

FIGURE 4-107 The context menu for adding a new Service Fabric service to the existing application services

2. From the New Service Fabric Service dialog, select Stateless ASP.NET Core for the service template. Supply the service name LeadGenerator.WebApp, and click OK (Figure 4-108).

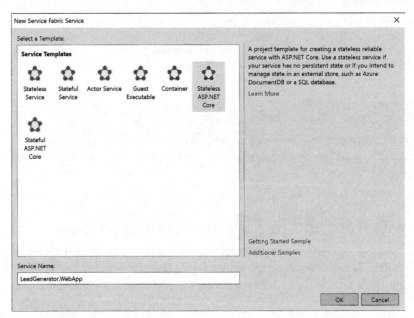

FIGURE 4-108 The New Service Fabric Service dialog where you can choose the Stateless ASP.NET Core template

3. From the New ASP.NET Core Web Application dialog select Web Application (Model-View-Controller) template. Click OK.

4. From Solution Explorer, expand the new LeadGenerator.WebApp node, and expand the PackageRoot folder where you'll find ServiceManifest.xml. Alongside the service type definition there is a section that describes the HTTP endpoint where the web app will listen for requests:

```
<Endpoints>"
  <Endpoint Protocol="http" Name="ServiceEndpoint" Type="Input" Port="8168" />
</Endpoints>
```

5. The new WebApp type is defined in WebApp.cs, which inherits StatelessService. For the service to listen for HTTP requests, the CreateServiceInstanceListeners() method sets up the WebListener as shown in this listing for the type:

```
internal sealed class WebApp : StatelessService
{
public WebApp(StatelessServiceContext context) : base(context)
{ }
protected override IEnumerable<ServiceInstanceListener>
CreateServiceInstanceListeners()
{
    return new ServiceInstanceListener[]
    {
        new ServiceInstanceListener(serviceContext =>
            new WebListenerCommunicationListener(serviceContext,
"ServiceEndpoint", (url, listener) =>
            {
                ServiceEventSource.Current.ServiceMessage(serviceContext,
$"Starting WebListener on {url}");
                return new WebHostBuilder().UseWebListener()
                    .ConfigureServices(services =>
                        services
                        .AddSingleton<StatelessServiceContext>(serviceCon
text))
                    .UseContentRoot(Directory.GetCurrentDirectory())
                    .UseStartup<Startup>()
                    .UseApplicationInsights()
                    .UseServiceFabricIntegration(listener,
ServiceFabricIntegrationOptions.None)
                    .UseUrls(url)
                    .Build();
            }))
    };
}
}
```

Next you call the stateful service that returns the leads counter value, from the stateless web application just created.

1. Make a copy of the service interface defined for the service type, in this case ISimulatorService:

```
public interface ISimulatorService : IService
{
 Task<long> GetLeads();
}
```

2. Modify the ConfigureServices instruction in WebApp.cs to inject an instance of the FabricClient type (change shown in bold):

```
return new WebHostBuilder().UseWebListener()
  .ConfigureServices(services => {
  services
  .AddSingleton<StatelessServiceContext>(serviceContext)
  .AddSingleton(new FabricClient());
})
```

3. Now that FabricClient is available for dependency injection, modify the HomeController to use it:

```
private FabricClient _fabricClient;
public HomeController(FabricClient client) { _fabricClient = client; }
```

4. Modify the Index method in the HomeController to use the FabricClient instance to call the Simulator service:

```
public async Task<IActionResult> Index()
{
    ViewData["Message"] = "Your home page.";
    var model = new Dictionary<Guid, long>();
    var serviceUrl = new Uri("fabric:/LeadGenerator/Simulator");
    foreach (var partition in await
_fabricClient.QueryManager.GetPartitionListAsync(serviceUrl))
    {
        var partitionKey = new ServicePartitionKey
(((Int64RangePartitionInformation)partition.PartitionInformation).LowKey);
        var proxy = ServiceProxy.Create<ISimulatorService>(serviceUrl,
partitionKey);
        var leads = await proxy.GetLeads();
        model.Add(partition.PartitionInformation.Id, leads);
    }
    return View(model);
}
```

5. Update Index.cshtml to display the counter for each partition:

```
@model IDictionary<Guid, long>
<h2>@ViewData["Title"].</h2>
<h3>@ViewData["Message"]</h3>
<table class="table-bordered">
    <tr>
        <td><strong>PARTITION ID</strong></td>
        <td><strong># LEADS</strong></td>
    </tr>
    @foreach (var partition in Model)
    {
        <tr>
```

```
        <td>@partition.Key.ToString()</td>
        <td>@partition.Value</td>
      </tr>
    }
</table>
```

6. To run the web app and stateful service, you can publish it to the local Service Fabric cluster. Right-click the Service Fabric application node from the Solution Explorer and select Publish. From the Publish Service Fabric Application dialog, select a target profile matching one of the local cluster options, and click Publish (Figure 4-109).

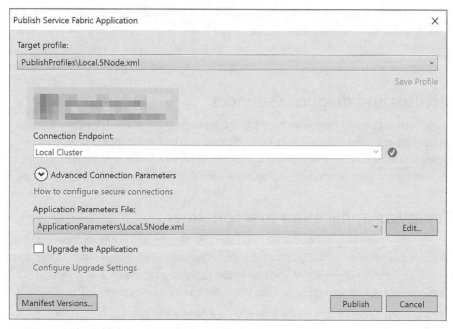

FIGURE 4-109 The Publish Service Fabric Application dialog

7. Once the application is deployed, you can access the web app at *http://localhost:8162* (or, whatever the indicated port is in the service manifest for the web app. The home page triggers a call to the stateful service, which will increment as the counter is updated while it runs.

Build an Actors-based service

The actor model is a superset of the Service Fabric stateful model. Actors are simple POCO objects that have many features that make them isolated, independent unit of compute and state with single-thread execution.

To create a new Service Fabric application based on the Actor service template, follow these steps:

1. Launch Visual Studio, then select File > New > Project.

2. In the New Project dialog, select Service Fabric Application within the Cloud category. Provide a name and location for your new project, and then click OK.

3. Select Actor Service from the list of service templates and provide a name, such as SimpleActor.

4. This generates a default implementation of the Actor Service.

MORE INFO   **SERVICE FABRIC RELIABLE ACTORS**

For more information on the implementation of the actor pattern in Service Fabric see *https://docs.microsoft.com/en-us/azure/service-fabric/service-fabric-reliable-actors-introduction*.

Monitor and diagnose services

All applications benefit from monitoring and diagnostics to assist with troubleshooting issues, evaluating performance or resource consumption, and gathering useful information about the application at runtime. For more information about Service Fabric specific approaches to this, see *https://docs.microsoft.com/en-us/azure/service-fabric/service-fabric-diagnostics-overview*.

Deploy an application to a container

Service Fabric can run processes and containers side by side, and containers can be Linux or Windows based containers. If you have an existing container image and wish to deploy this to an existing Service Fabric cluster, you can follow these steps to create a new Service Fabric application and set it up to deploy and run the container in your cluster:

1. Launch Visual Studio, nd then select File > New > Project.

2. In the New Project dialog, select Service Fabric Application within the Cloud category. Provide a name and location for your new project, and then click OK.

3. From the New Service Fabric Service dialog, choose Container for the list of templates and supply a container image and name for the guest executable to be created (Figure 4-110).

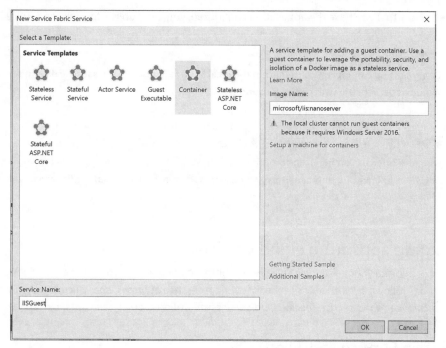

FIGURE 4-110 The New Service Fabric Service dialog with Container selected, and an image name specified

4. From Solution Explorer, open the ServiceManifest.xml file and modify the <Resources> section to provide a UriScheme, Port and Protocol setting for the service endpoint.

```
<Resources>
  <Endpoints>
    <Endpoint Name="IISGuestTypeEndpoint" UriScheme="http" Port="80"
Protocol="http"/>
  </Endpoints>
</Resources>
```

5. From Solution Explorer, open the ApplicationManifest.xml file. Create a policy for container to host <PortBinding> policy by adding this <Policies> section to the <ServiceManifestImports> section. Indicate the container port for your container. In this example the container port is 80.

```
<ServiceManifestImport>
  <ServiceManifestRef ServiceManifestName="IISGuestPkg"
ServiceManifestVersion="1.0.0" />
  <ConfigOverrides />
  <Policies>
    <ContainerHostPolicies CodePackageRef="Code">
      <PortBinding ContainerPort="80" EndpointRef="IISGuestTypeEndpoint"/>
    </ContainerHostPolicies>
  </Policies>
</ServiceManifestImport>
```

6. Now that you have the application configured, you can publish and run the service.

EXAM TIP

Currently, you cannot run containers in the local Service Fabric cluster because it requires Windows Server 2016 with container support.

> ***MORE INFO*** **WINDOWS CONTAINERS**
>
> For more information regarding working with Windows containers both locally and in Windows Server environments see *https://docs.microsoft.com/en-us/virtualization/windowscontainers/index.*

Migrate apps from cloud services

You can migrate your existing cloud services, both web and worker roles, to Service Fabric applications following instructions in the following reference at *https://docs.microsoft.com/en-us/azure/service-fabric/service-fabric-cloud-services-migration-worker-role-stateless-service.*

Scale a Service Fabric app

In order to scale a Service Fabric app, the following terms are important to understand: Instances, Partitions, and Replicas.

By default, the Service Fabric tooling produces three publish profiles that you can use to deploy your application:

- **Local.1Node.xml**   To deploy against the local 1-node cluster.
- **Local.5Node.xml**   To deploy against the local 5-node cluster.
- **Cloud.xml**   To deploy against a Cloud cluster.

These publish profiles indicate the settings for the number of instances and partitions for each service. Consider this example of the parameters to a Local.5Node.xml:

```
<Parameters>
  <Parameter Name="WebApp_InstanceCount" Value="3" />
  <Parameter Name="Simulator_PartitionCount" Value="3" />
  <Parameter Name="Simulator_MinReplicaSetSize" Value="3" />
  <Parameter Name="Simulator_TargetReplicaSetSize" Value="3" />
</Parameters>
```

- **WebApp_InstanceCount**   Specifies the number of instances the WebApp service must have within the cluster.
- **Simulator_PartitionCount**   Specifies the number of partitions (for the stateful service) the Simulator service must have within the cluster.
- **Simulator_MinReplicaSetSize**   Specifies the minimum number of replicas required for each partition that the WebApp service should have within the cluster.

- **Simulator_TargetReplicaSetSize** Specifies the number of target replicas required for each partition that the WebApp service should have within the cluster.

Consider the following diagram illustrating the instances and partitions associated with the stateless Web App and stateful simulator service, as shown in the Local.5Node.xml configuration (Figure 4-111).

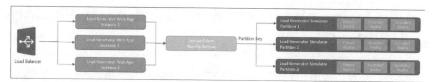

FIGURE 4-111 The instances for a stateless service, and partitions for a stateful service

- The Web App instance count is set to 3. As the diagram illustrates, when published to a Service Fabric cluster in Azure requests would be load balanced across those three instances.

- The Simulator service is assigned three partitions, each of which have replicas to ensure durability of each instance's state.

EXAM TIP

Sometimes the terms instances and replicas are used interchangeably, however, instances are for stateless services whereas replicas are for stateful services.

Create, secure, upgrade, and scale Service Fabric Cluster in Azure

To publish your Service Fabric application to the Azure in production, you'll create a cluster, learn how to secure it, learn how to upgrade applications with zero downtime, and configure the application to scale following some of the practices already discussed. The following references will start you off with these topics:

- For an introduction to creating a Service Fabric Cluster see:

  - *https://docs.microsoft.com/en-us/azure/service-fabric/service-fabric-get-started-azure-cluster*

  - *https://docs.microsoft.com/en-us/azure/service-fabric/service-fabric-deploy-any-where*

- For details on securing Azure Service Fabric Clusters in production, see this reference:

  - *https://docs.microsoft.com/en-us/azure/service-fabric/service-fabric-cluster-security*

- For details on upgrading clusters, see this reference:

  - *https://docs.microsoft.com/en-us/azure/service-fabric/service-fabric-cluster-upgrade*

- You can scale clusters manually or programmatically as described in these references:

- https://docs.microsoft.com/en-us/azure/service-fabric/service-fabric-cluster-scale-up-down

- https://docs.microsoft.com/en-us/azure/service-fabric/service-fabric-cluster-pro-grammatic-scaling

Skill 4.8: Design and implement third-party Platform as a Service (PaaS)

Azure supports many third-party PaaS offerings and services through the Azure Marketplace. These can be deployed through the Azure portal, using ARM, or using other CLI tools. This skill helps you navigate those offerings.

> **This skill covers how to:**
> - Implement Cloud Foundry
> - Implement OpenShift
> - Provision applications by using Azure Quickstart Templates
> - Build applications that leverage Azure Marketplace solutions and services

Implement Cloud Foundry

Cloud Foundry is an open-source PaaS for building, deploying, and operating 12-factor applications developed in various languages and frameworks. It is a mature container-based application platform allowing you to easily deploy and manage production-grade applications on a platform that supports continuous delivery and horizontal scale, and supports hybrid and multi-cloud scenarios.

There are two forms of Cloud Foundry available to run on Azure:

- **Open-source Cloud Foundry (OSS CF)**   An entirely open-source version of Cloud Foundry managed by the Cloud Foundry Foundation.

- **Pivotal Cloud Foundry** (PCF)   An enterprise distribution of Cloud Foundry from Pivotal Software Inc., which adds on a set of proprietary management tools and enterprise support.

> **MORE INFO**   **AZURE SERVICE PRINCIPALS**
>
> Before you can create a Cloud Foundry cluster in Azure you must first create an Azure Service Principal, following the instructions found at: *https://github.com/cloudfoundry-incubator/bosh-azure-cpi-release/blob/master/docs/get-started/create-service-principal.md.*

To deploy a basic Pivotal Cloud Foundry on Azure from the Azure Marketplace, follow these steps:

1. Navigate to the portal accessed via *https://portal.azure.com.*

2. Select Marketplace from the Azure Dashboard.

3. Search for "Pivotal Cloud Foundry," and select Pivotal Cloud Foundry On Azure.

4. From within the Pivotal Cloud Foundry On Azure blade, click Create (Figure 4-112).

5. On the Basics blade, provide a storage account name prefix, paste your SSH public key, upload the azure-credentials.json Service Principal file, enter the Pivotal Network API token, choose a resource group, and location for the cluster. Click OK.

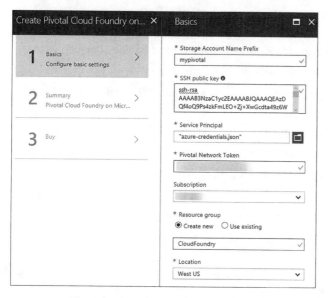

FIGURE 4-112 The selections for a new Pivotal Cloud Foundry cluster in the portal

6. On the Summary blade, wait for the validation to pas,s and click OK.

7. On the Buy blade, click Purchase.

To deploy the open-sourced version of Cloud Foundry on Azure, you deploy BOSH and then Cloud Foundry. The steps can be performed manually, or via Azure Resource Manager (ARM) templates. Detailed instructions can be found at *https://github.com/cloudfoundry-incubator/bosh-azure-cpi-release/tree/master/docs.*

> **MORE INFO   SSH KEYS**
>
> For more information about creating SSH keys for creating clusters see: *https://docs.micro-soft.com/en-us/azure/virtual-machines/linux/ssh-from-windows.*

> **MORE INFO   DEPLOYING AN APP TO CLOUD FOUNDRY**
>
> For more information about deploying apps to your Cloud Foundry cluster see: *https://docs.microsoft.com/azure/virtual-machines/linux/cloudfoundry-deploy-your-first-app.*

Implement OpenShift

The OpenShift Container Platform is a PaaS offering from Red Hat built on Kubernetes. It brings together Docker and Kubernetes, and provides an API to manage these services. OpenShift simplifies the process of deploying, scaling, and operating multi-tenant applications onto containers.

There are two forms of OpenShift that you can deploy to Azure:

- The open-source OpenShift Origin
- The enterprise-grade Red Hat OpenShift Container Platform

Both are built on the same open source technologies, with the Red Hat OpenShift Container Platform offering enterprise-grade security, compliance, and container management.

Prerequisites for installing both forms of OpenShift include:

1. Generate an SSH key pair (Public / Private), ensuring that you do not include a passphrase with the private key.
2. Create a Key Vault to store the SSH Private Key.
3. Create an Azure Active Directory Service Principal.
4. Install and configure the OpenShift CLI to manage the cluster.

Some specific prerequisites for deploying Red Hat OpenShift Container Platform include:

5. OpenShift Container Platform subscription eligible for use in Azure. You need to specify the Pool ID that contains your entitlements for OpenShift.
6. Red Hat Customer Portal login credentials. You may use either an Organization ID and Activation Key, or a Username and Password. It is more secure to use the Organization ID and Activation Key.

You can deploy both from the Azure Marketplace templates, or using ARM templates.

To deploy Red Hat OpenShift Container Platform on Azure from the Azure Marketplace, perform the following steps (Figure 4-113):

1. Navigate to the portal accessed via *https://portal.azure.com*.
2. Select Marketplace from the Azure Dashboard.
3. Search for "OpenShift," and select Red Hat OpenShift Container Platform (BYOL).
4. From within the Red Hat OpenShift Container Platform (BYOL) blade, click Create.
5. On the Basics blade, provide the VM Admin user name, paste the SSH public key, choose a resource group and location for the platform. Click OK.

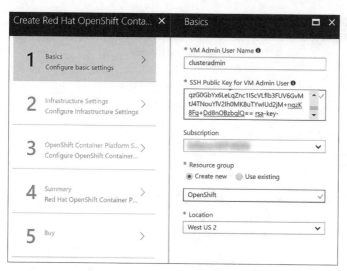

FIGURE 4-113 The selections in the Basics blade for a new Red Hat OpenShift Container Platform

6. On the Infrastructure Settings blade, provide an OCP cluster name prefix, select a cluster size, provide the resource group name for your Key Vault, as well as the Key Vault name and its secret name you specified in the prerequisites. Click OK (Figure 4-114).

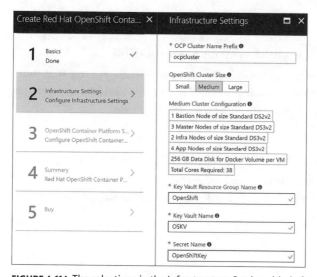

FIGURE 4-114 The selections in the Infrastructure Settings blade for a new Red Hat OpenShift Container Platform in the portal

7. On the OpenShift Container Platform Settings blade, provide an OpenShift Admin user password, enter your Red Hat subscription manager credentials, specify whether you want to configure an Azure Cloud Provider, and select your default router subdomain. Click OK (Figure 4-115).

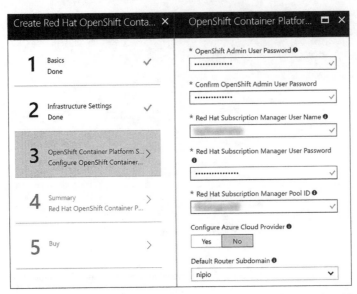

FIGURE 4-115 The selections in the OpenShift Container Platform Settings blade for a new Red Hat OpenShift Container Platform in the portal

8. On the Summary blade, wait for the validation to pass, and click OK.

9. On the Buy blade, click Purchase.

> **MORE INFO   OPENSHIFT CONTAINER PLATFORM PREREQUISITES**
>
> For an alternative method to deploy the OpenShift Container Platform using ARM templates instead of the marketplace, as well as detailed steps to complete the prerequisites see *https://github.com/Microsoft/openshift-container-platform*.

> **MORE INFO   DEPLOYING OPENSHIFT ORIGIN ON AZURE**
>
> For step-by-step instructions on how to deploy OpenShift Origin on Azure, including completing the prerequisites see *https://docs.microsoft.com/en-us/azure/virtual-machines/linux/openshift-get-started*.

Provision applications by using Azure Quickstart Templates

Azure Quickstart Templates are community-contributed Azure Resource Manager (ARM) templates that help you quickly provision applications and solutions with minimal effort. You can search available Quickstart Templates in the gallery located at *https://azure.microsoft.com/resources/templates*.

Resources that are deployed as part of a Quickstart template can be thought of as related and interdependent parts of a single entity. ARM templates allow you to deploy, update, or delete all of the resources within the solution in a single, coordinated operation. You use a template for deployment and that template can work for different environments such as testing, staging, and production, while ensuring your resources are deployed in a consistent state.

Depending on the Quickstart Template you select, you will provide a set of parameters that get passed into the deployment command.

You can deploy a Quickstart Template using one of these methods (based on the example at *https://azure.microsoft.com/resources/templates/101-hdinsight-hbase-replication-geo*):

1. Using PowerShell, use the New-AzureRmResourceGroupDeployment cmdlet. You are prompted to supply values for the parameters. For example:

```
New-AzureRmResourceGroupDeployment -Name <deployment-name> -ResourceGroupName
<resource-group-name> -TemplateUri https://raw.githubusercontent.com/azure/azure-
quickstart-templates/master/101-hdinsight-hbase-replication-geo/azuredeploy.json
```

2. Using the Azure Command-Line Interface (CLI), use the group deployment create command. You are prompted to supply values for the parameters. For example:

```
azure config mode arm

azure group deployment create <my-resource-group> <my-deployment-name> --template-
uri https://raw.githubusercontent.com/azure/azure-quickstart-templates/master/101-
hdinsight-hbase-replication-geo/azuredeploy.json
```

3. Click the Deploy to Azure button, if provided. This opens a form for the Quickstart template in Azure, allowing you to enter the parameter values from within the portal (Figure 4-116).

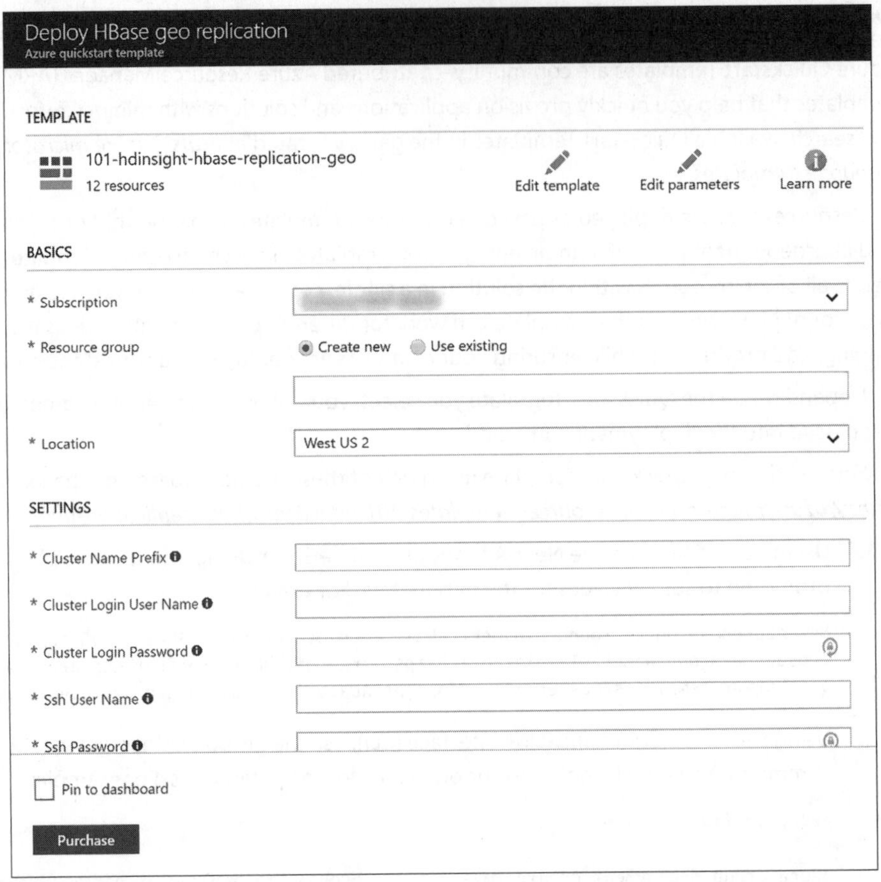

FIGURE 4-116 An Azure Quickstart Template form in the Azure Portal after clicking a Deploy to Azure button

> **MORE INFO** **AZURE QUICKSTART TEMPLATE GALLERY**
>
> Browse and search Quickstart Templates contributed by the community at *https://azure. microsoft.com/resources/templates*.

Build applications that leverage Azure Marketplace solutions and services

The Azure Marketplace is an online applications and services marketplace that enables start-ups and independent software vendors (ISVs) to offer their solutions to Azure customers around the world. The marketplace makes it easier for consumers to search, purchase, and de-ploy a wide range of applications and services in just a few clicks. Some such applications and services include virtual machine images and extensions, APIs, applications, Machine Learning services, and data services.

You can subscribe to and deploy a product from the Azure Marketplace by visiting *https://azuremarketplace.microsoft.com/* or by clicking the Marketplace tile on the Azure Portal dashboard.

Pricing varies based on product types. ISV software charges and Azure infrastructure costs are charged separately through your Azure subscription. Pricing models include:

- **BYOL Model**   Bring-your-own-license. You obtain outside of the Azure Marketplace the right to access or use the offering and are not charged Azure Marketplace fees for use of the offering in the Azure Marketplace.

- **Free**   Free SKU. Customers are not charged Azure Marketplace fees for use of the offering.

- **Free Software Trial (Try it now)**   Full-featured version of the offer that is promotionally free for a limited period of time. You are not charged Azure Marketplace fees for use of the offering through a trial period. Upon expiration of the trial period, customers are automatically be charged based on standard rates for use of the offering.

- **Usage-Based**   You are charged or billed based on the extent of your use of the offering. For Virtual Machines Images, you are charged an hourly Azure Marketplace fee. For Data Services, Developer services, and APIs, you are charged per unit of measurement as defined by the offering.

- **Monthly Fee**   You are charged or billed a fixed monthly fee for a subscription to the offering (from date of subscription start for that particular plan). The monthly fee is not prorated for mid-month cancellations or unused services.

You can find the offer-specific pricing details on the solution details page.

Skill 4.9: Design and implement DevOps

DevOps is a combination of Development (Dev) and information technology Operations (Ops). It describes a set of practices emphasizing the collaboration between both teams, while automating software delivery and infrastructure changes with the ultimate goal of reliability and repeatability of these processes. Automation and repeatability allows for increased deployment frequency, as the manual burden of tending to all of the steps involved in deploying to one or more target environments has been removed. Some organizations use DevOps practices to deploy hundreds of times a day, which would otherwise be nearly impossible. DevOps improves reliability by ensuring each step of the software delivery or infrastructure change process is monitored, and any automated tests successfully pass.

Instrument an application with telemetry

Application Insights is an extensible analytics service for application developers on multiple platforms that helps you understand the performance and usage of your live applications. With it, you can monitor your web application, collect custom telemetry, automatically detect performance anomalies, and use its powerful analytics tools to help you diagnose issues and understand what users actually do with your app. It works with web applications hosted on Azure, on-premises, or in another cloud provider. You can use it from web applications developed on multiple platforms, like .NET, Node.js, and J2EE. To get started, you just need to provision an Application Insights resource in Azure, and then install a small instrumentation package in your application. The things you can instrument are not limited just to the web application, but also any background components, and JavaScript within its web pages. You can also pull telemetry from host environments, such as performance counters, Docker logs, or Azure diagnostics.

Here is a comprehensive list of telemetry that can be collected by Application Insights.

From server web apps:

■ HTTP requests

■ Dependencies such as calls to SQL Databases; HTTP calls to external services; Azure Cosmos DB, table, blob storage, and queue

■ Exceptions and stack traces

■ Performance Counters, if you use Status Monitor, Azure monitoring, or the Application Insights collected writer

■ Custom events and metrics that you code

■ Trace logs if you configure the appropriate collector

From client web pages:

■ Page view counts

■ AJAX calls requests made from a running script

■ Page view load data

■ User and session counts

■ Authenticated user IDs

From other sources, if you configure them:

- Azure diagnostics
- Docker containers
- Import tables to Analytics
- OMS (Log Analytics)
- Logstash

The standard telemetry modules that run "out of the box" when using the Application Insights SDK send load, performance and usage metrics, exception reports, client information such as IP address, and calls to external services. If you install the SDK in development, this allows you to send your own telemetry, in addition to the standard modules. This custom telemetry can include any data you wish to send.

> **MORE INFO** **ABOUT APPLICATION INSIGHTS**
>
> For additional information about Application Insights see *https://docs.microsoft.com/azure/application-insights*.

> **MORE INFO** **SETTING UP APPLICATION INSIGHTS**
>
> For more information about setting up Application Insights on the portal and within your application see *https://docs.microsoft.com/azure/application-insights/app-insights-create-new-resource*.

> **MORE INFO** **COLLECT CUSTOM EVENTS AND METRICS IN APPLICATION INSIGHTS**
>
> A good resource for collecting custom event and metrics telemetry in Application Insights see *https://docs.microsoft.com/azure/application-insights/app-insights-api-custom-events-metrics*.

Discover application performance issues by using Application Insights

System performance depends on several factors. Each factor is typically measured through key performance indicators (KPIs), such as the number of database transactions per second or the volume of network requests your application can handle within a specified time frame. You can gather your application's KPIs through specific performance measures, or a combination of metrics.

Application Insights can help you quickly identify any application failures. It also tells you about any performance issues and exceptions. With the right configuration and tooling, Application Insights can also help you find and diagnose the root causes of slowdowns and failures.

When you open any Application Insights resource you see basic performance data on the overview blade. Clicking on any of the charts allows you to drill down into the related data to see more detail and related requests, as well as viewing different time ranges.

> **NOTE PERFORMANCE METRICS**
>
> Earlier in this chapter performance metrics were discussed for API Apps and Logic Apps - and these are also similar across other resource blades in the Azure Portal.

Application Insights offers a full-screen, interactive performance investigator through the Performance blade. The dashboard arranges a set of performance-related metrics that you can use to quickly explore possible performance bottlenecks, and adds additional insights, such as common properties of selected requests. The common properties are the users' location, performance bucket (in milliseconds), and cloud role of the resource. This information can help you find common variables that affect groups of users, such as response times being lengthier for users coming from certain countries or regions (Figure 4-117).

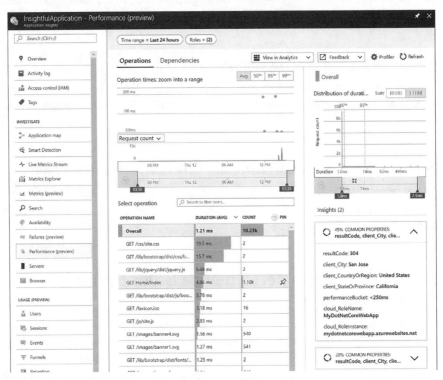

FIGURE 4-117 The Application Insights Performance blade

If your web application is built on ASP.NET or ASP.NET Core, you can turn on Application Insight's profiling tool to view detailed profiles of live requests. In addition to displaying 'hot paths' that are using the most response times, the Profiler shows which lines in the application code slowed down performance. You can view the profile request details to see trace information, showing the call stack through your application. This level of detail allows you to quickly pinpoint issues and address them faster than digging through logs alone. There is little overhead running the profiler because it executes for two minutes per hour, but should provide a satisfactory sample set of data.

To enable the Profiler, follow these steps:

1. From the Application Insights resource in Azure, select Performance from the left-hand menu.

2. Select Profiler Rules from the top of the Performance blade.

3. Select Add Linked Apps from the top of the Configure Application Insights Profiler blade.

4. Select the application you wish to link to see all its available slots. Click Add to link them to the current Application Insights resource.

5. After linking your desired apps, select Enable Profiler from the top of the Configure Application Insights Profiler blade. Note, linked applications require Basic or above service plans to enable the profiler (Figure 4-118).

FIGURE 4-118 The Application Insights Profiler actions to add linked apps and enable the Profiler

---

MORE INFO   **ABOUT APPLICATION INSIGHTS PROFILER**

For additional information about using the Application Insights Profiler, see this reference: *https://docs.microsoft.com/azure/application-insights/app-insights-profiler.*

MORE INFO   **MONITOR PERFORMANCE IN WEB APPLICATIONS**

For more information about using Application Insights to monitor performance in your web applications see *https://docs.microsoft.com/azure/application-insights/app-insights-web-monitor-performance.*

Deploy Visual Studio Team Services with continuous integration (CI) and continuous development (CD)

Visual Studio Team Services (VSTS) is a collection of hosted DevOps services for application developers, including Build and Release services, which help you manage continuous integration and delivery of your applications.

Continuous Integration (CI) is a practice by which the development team members integrate their work frequently, usually daily. An automated build verifies each integration, typically along with tests to detect integration errors quickly, when it's easier and less costly to fix. Output, or artifacts, generated by the CI systems are fed to the release pipelines to streamline and enable frequent deployments. The Build service in VSTS helps you set up and manage CI for your applications.

Continuous Delivery (CD) is a process where the full software delivery lifecycle is automated, including tests, and deployed to one or more test and production environments. Azure App Services supports deployment slots, into which you can deploy development, staging, and production builds from the CD process. Automated release pipelines consume the artifacts that the CI systems produce, and deploys them as new versions and fixes to existing systems. Monitoring and alerting systems run continually to drive visibility into the entire CD process. The Release service in VSTS helps you set up and manage CD for your applications.

Because a key component of the Build system is integrating code changes and automating builds, you must host your source code in a version control system. VSTS provides two different version control systems:

- Git
- Team Foundation Version Control

You can also host your source code in GitHub, Subversion, Bitbucket, or any other Git repository. The Build service can integrate with any one of these options.

VSTS build services provide preconfigured tasks to build many application types, such as .NET, Java, Node, Android, XCode, and C++. You can also run command line, PowerShell, or Shell scripts in your automation to support almost any type of application.

Azure App Services was mentioned earlier as a deployment target for the VSTS Release service. VSTS Release services can deploy to virtual machines, containers, on-premises and cloud platforms, or PaaS services. You can also publish your mobile applications to a store.

The following steps show one way to configure the CI/CD pipeline from the Azure portal (Figure 4-119):

1. Navigate to the portal accessed via *https://portal.azure.com*.
2. Select New on the command bar.
3. Select Web + Mobile, and then Web App.

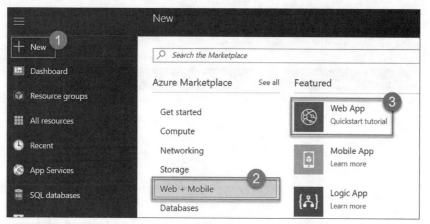

FIGURE 4-119 Completing the Response action form for the new condition's "If true" block in the Logic App Designer

4. Provide a unique name for your web app, and then click Create (Figure 4-120).

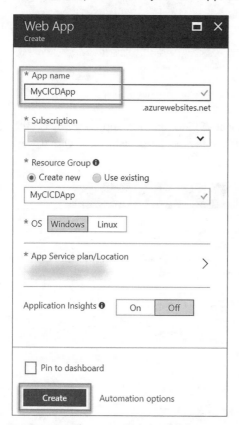

FIGURE 4-120 The create Web App blade

5. After the new web app is provisioned open it in Azure portal, and then select Continuous Delivery from the left-hand menu. Click Configure on the Continuous Delivery blade (Figure 4-121).

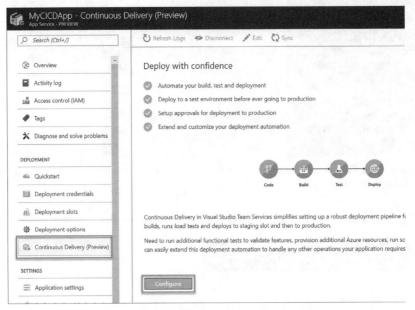

FIGURE 4-121 The Continuous Delivery blade on the provisioned web app

6. Select Choose repository, and then select VSTS for the code repository. Select the VSTS account, project, repository, and source code branch from which you wish to deploy. Click OK (Figure 4-122).

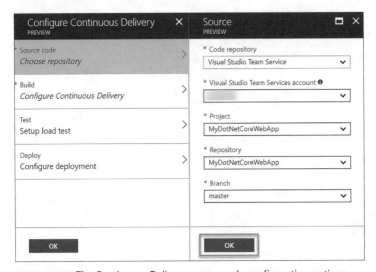

FIGURE 4-122 The Continuous Delivery source code configuration options

7. Select Configure Continuous Delivery, and then your web application framework. In our example, we selected ASP.NET Core. Click OK. Skip the other two steps for now, and then click OK to complete the configuration (Figure 4-123).

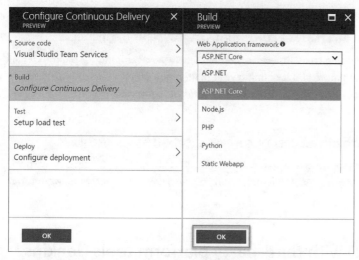

FIGURE 4-123 The Continuous Delivery build options

8. At this point, Azure Continuous Delivery configures and executes a build and deployment in VSTS. After the build completes, the deployment is automatically initiated. When you commit a change to the source code repository, the automated deployment appears in the Continuous Delivery application logs on your web app, as shown in Figure 4-124.

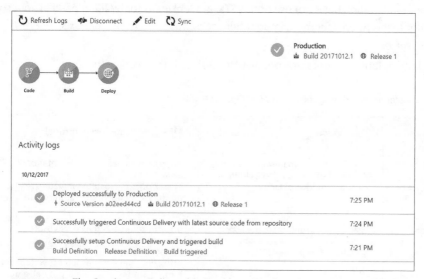

FIGURE 4-124 The Continuous Delivery blade with activity logs showing the initial build

Deploy CI/CD with third-party platform tools (Jenkins, GitHub, Chef, Puppet, TeamCity)

Azure allows you to continuously integrate and deploy with any of the leading DevOps tools, targeting any Azure service. Whether you are following your organization's established CI/CD procedures, or just getting started with DevOps, use the tools best-suited for your team.

If you are using VSTS to host your source code or as your CI service, you can use various build services, like Jenkins, through service hooks. In this way, you can use Jenkins for your continuous integration builds, or use both VSTS and Jenkins as for building parts of your solution. Refer to this tutorial for more information: *https://docs.microsoft.com/vsts/service-hooks/services/jenkins.*

In addition, Table 4-5 lists some popular DevOps tools that work with Azure.

TABLE 4-5 References for using third-party DevOps tools with Azure

Tool	Description	More Information and Tutorials
Chef	Use Chef to automate workloads on Azure, whether IaaS, PaaS, cloud or hybrid, Windows or Linux	https://www.chef.io/implementations/azure/ https://docs.microsoft.com/azure/virtual-machines/windows/chef-automation
Puppet	Use Puppet to automate the life-cycle of your entire Azure infra-structure	https://azuremarketplace.microsoft.com/marketplace/apps/PuppetLabs.PuppetEnterprise37 https://puppet.com/resources/whitepaper/getting-started-deploying-puppet-enter-prise-microsoft-azure

Tool	Description	More Information and Tutorials
Jenkins	The Jenkins and Azure teams have been collaborating on making tighter integrations between the two. Benefit from the extensive tooling as a result	https://docs.microsoft.com/azure/virtual-machines/linux/tutorial-jenkins-github-docker-cicd https://docs.microsoft.com/azure/jenkins/ https://docs.microsoft.com/azure/storage/common/storage-java-jenkins-continuous-integration-solution
TeamCity	Use TeamCity with Azure for a variety of DevOps processes, such as deploying Azure services or scaling out your build farm by having it automatically start agents on Azure when you need more power, and stop them, when they are no longer needed	https://confluence.jetbrains.com/display/TW/Microsoft+Azure+cloud https://blog.jetbrains.com/teamcity/2016/11/teamcity-dotnet-core/

Out of the box, Azure App Services integrates with source code repositories such as GitHub to enable a continuous deployment workflow. This is the simplest way to integrate a CD process without the need for installing and configuring additional tools and services. Follow these simple steps to enable continuous deployment from a GitHub repository:

1. Publish your application source code to GithHub.

2. Open your app's Menu blade in the Azure portal, and then select Deployment Options under Deployment in the left-hand menu.

3. In the Deployment option blade, select Choose Source, and then select GitHub from the list of sources.

4. Select Authorization, and then click the Authorize button to enter your GitHub credentials. When authorized, click OK.

5. In the Deployment Option blade, select your project and branch from which you wish to deploy your app, and click OK.

App Service creates an association with the selected repository, pulls in the files from the specified branch, and maintains a clone of your repository for your App Service app. Now, when you push a change to your repository, your app is automatically updated with the latest changes. More information about this process can be found at: *https://docs.microsoft.com/azure/app-service/app-service-continuous-deployment*.

Thought experiment

In this thought experiment, apply what you've learned about implementing App Services, Azure Functions, Azure Service Fabric, third-party PaaS, and DevOps to evaluate and determine a recommended set of features to use in a particular solution implementation.

You can find answers to this thought experiment in the next section. The following paragraphs describe the solution and the questions to answer.

You are designing a solution that issues certificates of insurance for end users. You are expecting insurance companies who you partner with to provide this service to their clients, your end user, through your solution. The following describes core components in the solution, and other requirements:

- Insurance companies can sign up with your service so that they can call your Policy Sync APIs and send insurance policy data using the X12 EDI standard. Their license with your API determines how much policy data they can upload to your service. This policy data is what supports certificate issuance to the end user owning the policy.

- Insurance companies can manage access to those policies through a Policy Management web application that allows them to create users who can later login and request certificates of insurance for their policy data.

- End users will, once invited by the insurance company, be able to login to the Certificate Issuance web application to request certificates of insurance on demand for their policies.

- When a certificate is requested, a workflow should be kicked off to generate a PDF from the policy data, save the PDF to a secure location from where it can be securely shared, and email a secure link to the PDF to a specified email address.

- While this is a new service, it is possible that many 100,000s of requests can be processed by a single insurance company per week so there is potential for large scale growth and the design must be ready to grow with demand.

- You are expecting to use a third-party Java-based executable component for PDF generation, alongside the other work, which will be based on ASP.NET Core.

- As a startup, you are looking for a solution that allows you to contain costs now, but grow into an architecture that can scale with your business growth.

Consider how you would answer the following questions for this solution:

1. How would you evaluate the core platform tools and hosting environment that you will use for the web apps and APIs? Consider these aspects:

   A. Cost containment early on with potential for growth.

   B. Manageability with a small team.

   C. Support for polyglot development and third-party application components.

2. How will you control the onboarding process to use your Policy Sync APIs and subsequent throttling of their use by license?

3. How will you handle the inbound EDI requests and store those for the partner?

4. How will you prepare to scale the requests for certificates of insurance based on the potential growth?

Thought experiment answers

This section contains the solution to the thought experiment.

1. Consider the following:

   - deploying the application to Web Apps on an App Service Plan that can scale as needed.

   - Consider if the main components of the application can be deployed as containers—in particular verifying that the Java component can be containerized. If so, standardizing around container deployments to Web Apps will keep things consistent and enable a future deployment to a container orchestration platform. If not, traditional Web App deployments for the ASP.NET Core applications will still reduce management overhead. The Java application may require a VM if it cannot be deployed to a Linux-based Web App due to underlying requirements.

   - Consider moving to a container orchestration platform, or Service Fabric cluster as the application needs to scale. Keep in mind the Service Fabric can support deployment of both ASP.NET Core applications alongside guest executables such as the Java application.

2. Consider using API Management for onboarding partners, setting up licensing, throttling access to the EDI process through licensing, and providing statistics on usage.

3. Consider using Logic App to handle X12 EDI transforms from API Management initiated calls. The Logic App can convert this payload to the target data format required for the application.

4. Look to scale out the requests for certificates of insurance by writing requests to a queue that triggers a Logic App to handle calls to generate PDFs and send emails through a workflow. Make sure the Java component is deployed to a tier that can scale independently given the potential for scale.

Chapter summary

- Azure App Services provide a simple PaaS solution for deploying, managing, and scaling web applications, APIs, API Apps, Logic Apps, and Mobile Apps.

- API Apps and API Management both provide ways to publish APIs for partner integration. API Management provides richer features for partner management, licensing, throttling, security, and related management tools.

- Logic Apps provide an easy way to create workflows, modern integrations, and even legacy integration with EDI formats.

- Azure Functions provide an easy way to trigger workloads that can scale based on consumption or a hosting plan. There are many integration points for triggering functions including queues, HTTP requests, and data triggers.

- Azure Service Fabric is a modern orchestration platform that can support native services that leverage unique features such as stateful services and actor patterns, in addition to guest and container processes.

- Azure supports several third-party PaaS platforms for containers and microservices including Cloud Foundry and OpenShift.

- You have many choices for DevOps and CI/CD workflows in Azure including Application Insights for diagnostics, monitoring and alerts; and VSTS, Jenkins, Chef, Puppet and more for CI/CD integration.

Index

T

X

About the authors

ZOINER TEJADA has more than 18 years of experience in the software industry as a software architect, CTO, and start-up CEO, with particular expertise in cloud computing, big data, analytics, and machine learning. He was among the first to receive a Microsoft Azure MVP ("Most Valuable Professional") designation and has since been awarded the MVP for six consecutive years, and most recently a dual MVP award for Azure and Data Platform. Additionally, he was recently recognized by Microsoft as a Microsoft Regional Director.

MICHELE LEROUX BUSTAMANTE is cofounder / CIO of Solliance, a Microsoft Regional Director and Azure MVP, has been awarded Azure Elite and Azure Insider status as well as the ASP.NET Insider designation. Michele is a respected technology executive / thought leader, who builds high performance teams and infrastructure. With over 20 years of experience Michele has held senior executive positions, assembled software development teams and implemented processes for all aspects of the software development lifecycle, and actively facilitated large-scale enterprise application deployments. Michele is a recognized expert in many fields including distributed systems architecture, cloud computing and identity and access management – the latter, an area with very few deep technical experts. Today, Michele specializes in delivering cloud-enabled solutions at scale, cloud migration, security, compliance, and micro-services platforms.

IKE ELLIS is a data architect who stays current on many database technologies. He specializes in the Microsoft Data Platform, including DocumentDB, Azure SQL Datawarehouse, and Azure Data Lake. He also loves visualizing data using Microsoft tools like Power BI, SQL Server Reporting Services, and mobile dashboarding. Ike is a current Microsoft MVP for the data platform team.